New Histories for Old

Edited by Ted Binnema and Susan Neylan

New Histories for Old:
Changing Perspectives on Canada's
Native Pasts

UBCPress · Vancouver · Toronto

16 15 14 13 12 11 10 09 08 07   5 4 3 2 1

Printed in Canada on ancient-forest-free paper (100% post-consumer recycled)
that is processed chlorine- and acid-free, with vegetable-based inks.

Library and Archives Canada Cataloguing in Publication

   New histories for old: changing perspectives on Canada's native pasts /
edited by Ted Binnema and Susan Neylan.

Includes bibliographical references and index.
ISBN 978-0-7748-1413-3

   1. Native peoples – Canada – History. 2. Indians of North America – British
Columbia – History. 3. Native peoples – Canada – Historiography. 4. Ray, Arthur J.,
1941- I. Binnema, Ted, 1963- II. Neylan, Susan, 1966-

E78.C2N485 2007   971.004'97   C2007-905385-8

Canadä

UBC Press gratefully acknowledges the financial support for our publishing
program of the Government of Canada through the Book Publishing Industry
Development Program (BPIDP), and of the Canada Council for the Arts, and
the British Columbia Arts Council.

This book has been published with the help of a grant from the Canadian
Federation for the Humanities and Social Sciences, through the Aid to Scholarly
Publications Programme, using funds provided by the Social Sciences and
Humanities Research Council of Canada.

The financial assistance of the Office of the Vice President Research, University
of Northern British Columbia, as well as the book preparation grant offered by the
Research Office, Wilfrid Laurier University, is also gratefully acknowledged.

UBC Press
The University of British Columbia
2029 West Mall
Vancouver, BC V6T 1Z2
604-822-5959 / Fax: 604-822-6083
www.ubcpress.ca

To Arthur J. Ray, friend, colleague, and mentor,
in whose honour all of these essays were written

Contents

Maps

Introduction

Ted Binnema and Susan Neylan

Interpretations and perceptions of history can have an immediate and "real world" impact when it comes to Canada's Aboriginal peoples. Whether on the pages of an academic monograph, in a report submitted to the Royal Commission on Aboriginal Peoples, or in the testimonies given during land claim litigation, interpretations of Native history have direct bearing on the present and future lives of Native peoples. Each generation of scholars has offered new histories for old – revisiting the past, revising our understanding of Native-newcomer interactions, and locating Native people in Canadian history.

This volume considers the influence of historical geographer, historian, and professor Arthur J. "Skip" Ray on the writing of Native history in Canada.[1] The original chapters in this collection explore and expand upon Ray's work by examining topics in some of his own fields of excellence. As several of Ray's senior colleagues have remarked, he has furthered our understanding of the relationships between Natives and newcomers and explained the code of conduct that arose from those sustained interactions, whether in the fur trade, at the treaty table, or within the foreign environment of the Canadian judicial system. All the central themes represented in the chapters in this collection are, in various degrees, ones well trodden by Ray himself: Aboriginal-newcomer interaction, Native struggles for land and resources under colonialism, "Indian" policy and treaties, mobility and migrations, disease and well-being, and questions about "doing" Native history.

The chapters appear in roughly chronological order. Selective and especially focused on western Canadian topics, they nonetheless reflect current research interests among some of Ray's colleagues and former students. We continue Ray's own focus not only geographically but also chronologically: the majority of chapters centre especially on the eighteenth and nineteenth centuries, when the commercial viability of the fur trade shifted from competition to monopoly and the fur trade waned in the face of the arrival of non-Aboriginal settlers. Only time and space constraints prevented the inclusion of chapters by others whom the editors first approached. And, frankly, the fact that no one initially declined the invitation to contribute to this collection speaks volumes about Skip's professional and personal influence on the careers of scholars working on Native history in this country. The present contributors reflect a healthy mix of new and well-established scholars and, like Ray himself, reflect the geographic and historical perspectives of interdisciplinary methodologies whereby Aboriginal perspectives and actions are highlighted alongside colonial voices.

After an introductory chapter by the editors, *New Histories for Old* begins with Jennifer S.H. Brown's examination of Aboriginal and non-Aboriginal conceptions of the central and western subarctic, which became the site for centuries of Native–non-Native interactions in western Canada during the fur trade. Next, the evolution of treaty relationships and Aboriginal interactions with colonialism are taken up in chapters by Victor Lytwyn, J.R. Miller, and Jody Decker. These are followed by five more tightly focused chapters that feature BC First Nations confronting the challenges posed by newcomers arriving and staying in their homelands (Dan Marshall, Keith Carlson, Paige Raibmon, Susan Neylan, and Robert Galois). Finally, the volume concludes with fellow geographer Cole Harris' overview of Ray's contributions to Native historiography in Canada.

New Histories for Old begins with a historiographical chapter by the editors, both former doctoral students of Arthur J. Ray. Research into the pasts of Aboriginal people in Canada can only be adequately understood in the context of trends in Canadian political and legal history. Scholars in the field of Aboriginal studies need to be aware that, regardless of the detachment and disinterest they achieve or aspire to achieve, their research has political and legal significance. To a greater degree than most fields of history, the results of research in Aboriginal history are likely to directly affect the lives of people today and in the future. So, our first chapter explores the significance of Skip Ray's research in Aboriginal history, beginning in the early 1970s, but it also explains how Ray (and scholarship more generally) was affected by the growing influence of Aboriginal political movements and Aboriginal claims in Canada and elsewhere.

Like Ray, Jennifer S.H. Brown established her career by effectively using the Hudson's Bay Company Archives (when they became publicly accessible in the 1970s) and by concentrating on the active role of Native peoples in the fur trade. For this collection, Brown examines perceptions of the Hudson Bay region before Rupert's Land was "invented" and how non-Native constructions of this region compared with those of the original inhabitants. The different ways of framing knowledge of the land and, later, possession of it that inform contemporary land claims have deep historic roots that are apparent in these early years of contact and trade between the *Omushkegowak*, or Swampy Cree, and the English and French newcomers. Her work shows how connections between the scholarly world and Native communities both inside and outside the context of litigation have enriched our understanding of Canada's past.

Brown's chapter is followed by one by Victor Lytwyn. Skip Ray and Victor Lytwyn provided historical and geographical evidence during the 1998 trial on Métis hunting rights, known as the *Regina* v. *Powley* case. Ray's findings provided key evidence for the Supreme Court of Canada's 2003 judgment in favour of the Métis, which ruled that the Métis at Sault Ste. Marie may be regarded as an Aboriginal community and possess the same hunting rights as other Native groups in the region. A version of Lytwyn's own research for *Powley* is presented here in "Echo of the Crane," wherein he traces the origins and termination of the Métis settlement at Sault Ste. Marie as well as the extinguishment of Aboriginal title among Ojibwa groups in the area (by 1850).

J.R. Miller, a well-known historian of Indian policy in Canada, co-authored *Bounty and Benevolence* with Skip Ray. In his contribution to this volume, Miller challenges the common perception that all treaties with First Nations in Canada have been imposed land cessions. In his chapter, Miller traces the historical diversity of "treaties" across Canada from the seventeenth century to the present, illustrating how they ranged from commercial and friendship compacts to territorial and property contracts and even to covenants of an ongoing relationship not only between Native and non-Native but also between these parties and their deities. Perceptive readers will recognize the many ways that Miller's research is influenced by, and builds upon, the work of Skip Ray.

A health care practitioner for years before becoming an academic, Jody Decker first crossed paths with Skip Ray when he served as the external examiner at her PhD defence. Decker is a geographer who shares Ray's interest in the history of disease among Aboriginal peoples. Her chapter explores the prairie borderlands' scare zone, which emerged through early twentieth-century outbreaks of smallpox, and how it affected Native and non-Native peoples in different ways. With efforts to contain the contagion through quarantine, under federal direction the provincial and territorial public health departments created inspections and restrictions that impinged on Aboriginal mobility. Decker's chapter illustrates the importance of pathogens in the creation of certain aspects of Indian policy in Canada.

Shifting the focus to the "west beyond the west," the next five chapters consider Aboriginal–Euro-Canadian encounters in British Columbia.[2] In "Mapping the New El Dorado," Dan Marshall, one of Ray's former graduate students, explores how the 1858 Fraser River gold rush reconceptualized space through naming and mapping practices. The ancient Aboriginal world, which linked people to place and spirituality to spaces along the river, was, in effect, appropriated then erased by the "California world" of the miner-invaders. While not all the place names survived the rush when the miners moved on, Marshall argues that the fact that many did "may be seen as both legitimizing the colonial presence along the Fraser River and the continued occupation of Native lands and culture."

Like Marshall, Keith Carlson, another of Ray's former doctoral students, has focused on British Columbia's Fraser River as a site of conflict over Aboriginal rights. Fishing rights were central to the social and economic welfare of all Coast Salish peoples living along the river. Their previous mode of resolving fishing disputes prior to the arrival of Europeans to the region involved the public bestowal and recognition of hereditary rights to particular locations along the river through potlatches. Instead of evoking the expected dichotomy used by other scholars to describe the Native battles for rights and resources in the colonial period, which pits tradition against assimilation, Carlson examines struggles over fishing sites in the lower Fraser Canyon for what they can reveal about the continuing value of "tradition" in Aboriginal adaptations to colonialism.

In her contribution, Paige Raibmon, a former student and now departmental colleague of Skip Ray, shows that many Aboriginal people in British Columbia were unable to secure their access to land and resources in the same ways as did the Salish and non-Natives. From the colonial perspective, land ownership meant permanent and continuous residence, and, through a policy of land pre-emption (something not available to First Nations people in British Columbia after 1865), non-Natives could gain title to Aboriginal land due to a narrow definition of occupancy. Sedentary lifestyles were encouraged for First Nations by missionaries and government officials alike. However, as Raibmon explains in her chapter in this volume, the tendency to restrict Aboriginal peoples to reserves, frequently on less arable pieces of land or where viable economic opportunities were limited, ironically propelled them into the capitalist marketplace, which often took them away from home. Drawing upon a variety of sources, including evocative Native testimony given before the McKenna-McBride Royal Commission, 1913-16, Raibmon illustrates the gap between indigenous and colonial understandings of mobile expressions of ownership and title to land and resources.

One of the themes emphasized in Ray's *Indians in the Fur Trade* is how centuries of close commercial ties to Europeans prompted Native groups to move and shift their territories. These migrations not only served Aboriginal needs in the fur trade but also allowed them to respond to changes to the balance of power among Native groups. Susan Neylan, another of Ray's former doctoral students, saw similar patterns in her own study of Protestant missionization on the Northwest Coast. In her chapter, Neylan explores the ways in which missions hastened a migration of Aboriginal peoples not to trading posts or seasonal work sites but, rather, to a whole new permanent village site. In 1887, the majority of Tsimshian residents from the mission town of Metlakatla on British Columbia's north coast left their traditional homelands for a new location on Annette Island in southern Alaska – New Metlakatla. Neylan's chapter examines discourses about the Tsimshian relocation as they were recorded in textual and oral sources.

As with Neylan, Robert Galois, one of Ray's fellow historical geographers at the University of British Columbia, centres his analysis on a single event in northern British Columbia in the 1880s that exemplifies Aboriginal people's struggle for self-determination and the free exercise of rights and customs within their territories. Early in 1888, in the Kitwancool valley on the Upper Skeena River, a man named Neatsqua was killed by another Gitxsan man, Kamalmuk (also known as Kitwancool Jim). Galois compares textual sources produced by the non-Native "settler" society in the region and by government officials who came to enforce British-Canadian presumptions about law and order. He insists that the incident itself and the differing interpretations of it must be viewed as part of the larger pattern of Native-newcomer tensions over land and resources.

The summary chapter in this volume is Cole Harris's piece on the contributions of Arthur Ray. Harris has been a colleague of Ray's for more than forty years, beginning as graduate students of Andrew Clark in the geography department of the University of Wisconsin, as collaborators on such projects as the *Historical Atlas of Canada*, and, until their retirements, as co-worker professors at the same institution (albeit in different departments), the University of British Columbia. In his chapter, Harris traces Ray's career as a historical geographer and historian of Native peoples from his early empirical impulses and originality in writing about the fur trade to his recent research projects. Throughout, Harris evaluates Ray's contributions to the field, notably in fur trade scholarship. Ray remained firmly rooted in these origins, even as he moved into the courtroom as an expert witness or engaged in a large comparative project about scholarly constructions of Native cultures and histories.

For over thirty years, Arthur J. Ray has occupied a leading position in scholarly attempts to reconstruct Canada's Native pasts. Indeed, the current trajectories of Ray's work continue to expand our understanding of Native pasts in Canada and elsewhere. Given the fact that Ray's work is destined to be influential for many more years, the editors and contributors hope that this volume allows scholars to better understand Ray's work over the past three decades, makes a contribution to various fields that have been of interest to Ray, and inspires other researchers, including those who have never met Skip Ray, to make inquiries in areas where our knowledge remains flawed and incomplete.

Notes

1 Always a popular undergraduate teacher, graduate advisor, and mentor and colleague to several contributors to this very volume, Ray was elected to the Royal Society of Canada in 2002 for his "outstanding contributions as a historian and historical geographer whose work reflects his broad interests in aboriginal-white relations, the fur trade, and the adaptive capacities of aboriginal peoples. He has also contributed to the understanding of disease and population decline, diet, and the impact of post-contact economic developments on the aboriginal-white relationships in Canada" (taken from the Royal Society of Canada citation). Ray was inducted as a Fellow of the Royal Society of Canada at Rideau Hall in Ottawa in December 2002. Throughout his career, Ray has received many awards, book prizes, and other honours, including, recently, a Canada Council National Killam Research Fellowship (2001-2), the Bora Laskin National Fellowship in Human Rights (2005), and a resident fellowship at the Woodrow Wilson International Center for Scholars in Washington, DC (2005-6).

2 "The west beyond the west" is Jean Barman's phrase, taken from her historical profile of the province. See Jean Barman, *The West beyond the West: A History of British Columbia*, rev. ed. (Toronto: University of Toronto Press, 2004 [1996]).

New Histories for Old

1

Arthur J. Ray and the Writing of Aboriginal History

Ted Binnema and Susan Neylan

In 1977, when Arthur J. (Skip) Ray presented a paper entitled "Fur Trade History as an Aspect of Native History" at the Western Canadian Studies Conference in Calgary, and when it was published the following year, his audience recognized the argument as revolutionary.[1] But by then scholars already knew Ray as part of a relatively small group of young scholars that was transforming perceptions of the history of the fur trade in North America and challenging the way people thought about Aboriginal history. In 1982, that article was included in the first edition of what became the most widely used collection of articles in undergraduate pre-Confederation Canadian history courses.[2] Ray's central argument was that "one important aspect of any new meaningful Indian history necessarily will be concerned with the involvement of the Indian peoples in the fur trade and with the impact of that participation upon their traditional cultures as well as those of the European intruders."[3] That argument quickly became so convincing, so common sense, even outside academia, that it soon became difficult to convince students that Ray had ever said anything new.[4]

Arthur J. Ray did not, of course, single-handedly change perceptions of Aboriginal people in Canada, but he emerged as a path-breaker for the "first wave" of academic Native history in the 1970s and 1980s, and he has remained a leader in the field ever since.[5] When Ray's career started, rapid and dramatic changes in public perceptions of Aboriginal peoples and of their roles in Western societies were well under way. Thus, Ray was thrust into a position in which his work became timely due to forces outside his control. Yet, the timeliness of his research and his empirical approach have ensured that he became not only a knowledgeable observer but also a participant in developments in Canada. As his career progressed, the applied nature of some of his research in the courtroom, along with his explorations of the applied research conducted by earlier generations of scholars interested in Aboriginal affairs, affected his research paths. In short, the work of Arthur J. Ray has both reflected and influenced the changing milieu within which he has lived and conducted his research.

In the late 1960s, when Skip Ray entered the doctoral program in geography at the University of Wisconsin, Madison, he was not intent on researching the historical geography of the fur trade in Rupert's Land. Born and raised in southern Wisconsin, he enrolled in the PhD program still open-minded about which direction his research might take him. His supervisor was the Canadian historical geographer, Andrew H. Clark (1911-75), who, according to another of his students, Cole Harris, was, more than anyone else, "the father of modern North American historical geography."[6] Descended from a Prince Edward Island family, Clark had been born on an Indian reserve (his father was a government surgeon) in Manitoba in 1911 and had studied at McMaster University and the University of Toronto, where he was mentored by the geographer Griffith Taylor and the economic historian Harold A. Innis. Then, following Innis' advice, he went to the University of California, Berkeley, in 1938 to complete a PhD under Carl Sauer. Although disposed towards researching Prince Edward Island, Clark took advantage of a two-year position at the University of Canterbury in New Zealand to complete a dissertation on New Zealand historical geography. The dissertation, published as a book in 1949, explored the invasion of New Zealand by Europeans and the animals and plants of Europe – an aspect of a global process now well known as "ecological imperialism."[7] But the term "ecological imperialism" carries a considerable assumption of determinism and inevitability, and Clark's scholarship, while emphasizing environmental change, always avoided either environmental determinism or cultural determinism – a tendency also evident in the work of some of his students, including Ray. Clark did turn, after completing his dissertation, to North American historical geography, and, by the time Ray became his student in the late 1960s, most of Clark's published work focused on European settler colonialism, particularly in the Maritime provinces of Canada.

In 1951, Clark took up a position in the geography department at the University of Wisconsin, Madison. From there, he supervised many historical geographers, including several Canadian graduate students who staffed geography departments in universities across Canada. Clark earned a reputation as a demanding and rigorous supervisor of graduate students. Students found him critical yet supportive. Over the years, his graduate seminars, in which students developed, researched, and defended original projects, launched many research careers and inspired many book-length studies.[8] Most of Clark's students pursued regional studies. In a sense, Ray's research topic was the most original among Clark's students because, rather than focusing on the colonizers, Ray examined the colonized. When it came time for Ray to decide on a dissertation topic, Clark suggested that he undertake a historical geography of the Métis of Red River.

Despite his mentor's suggestions and his own expectations, Ray's dissertation actually became a historical geography of the fur trade of the subarctic
regions of Rupert's Land, southeast of Hudson Bay. But he moved beyond
some of the preoccupations of scholars at the time. For example, geography
and anthropology were still dominated by culture-area approaches to understanding Native peoples and their history, whereas Ray focused on a boundary zone between such areas, Aboriginal movements across that boundary,
and the dynamic political-economic adaptations within various culture areas.
Ray's spatial and ecological analysis warrants categorizing the book as one
of the earliest efforts in Canadian environmental history – something that
scholars in the discipline of history were ill-prepared to undertake at the time.

Ray also approached fur trade history in a fresh way. The fur trade had
already figured prominently in Canadian historiography for many decades.
In fact, the preeminent scholar of the fur trade at the time was Andrew
Clark's friend and mentor, Harold A. Innis. Innis, well known for his elaboration of the famous "staples thesis," had written his major work on the
history of the fur trade in the 1920s. Innis argued that the fur trade was
central to the development of the country.[9] This emphasis on the significance of the fur trade in national and imperial expansion characterizes most
of the historical scholarship on the fur trade published before 1970, and it
is this Eurocentric scholarly tradition from which Ray departed.[10] Still, Ray
admired Innis' work at a time when many seemed ready to dismiss it. On
the fiftieth anniversary of the publication of *The Fur Trade in Canada*, the
University of Toronto Press issued a reprint with an introductory essay by
Arthur J. Ray. In that essay, Ray argues that Harold Innis' *The Fur Trade in
Canada* "remains essential reading for the study of Canada."[11] He explained
how, in his own time, Innis had also been breaking new ground in this field
– with an impact that, according to Ray, is seemingly overlooked by more
recent scholarship emphasizing "the deconstruction of metahistories of the
very type created by Innis."[12] In many ways, Ray's defence of Innis' work
can be seen as a general argument for the continued relevance of economically and geographically focused studies based on thorough and detailed
archival research – exactly the kind of studies Ray himself preferred. The
fact remains, however, that historians like Innis badly underestimated the
role that Aboriginal peoples played in fur trade history. And Innis assumed
that Aboriginal peoples must have expressed their economic motivations
much like Europeans, despite their very different lifestyles and worldviews.
As Bruce Trigger has written, to the extent that they did consider Aboriginal
peoples, historians like Innis depicted them as "economic stereotypes only
minimally disguised in feathers."[13]

Ray completed his dissertation in 1971, and the University of Toronto
Press published it as a book in 1974. It may seem almost conventional today, but, when it was published, its title, *Indians in the Fur Trade: Their Role*

as *Hunters, Trappers, and Middlemen in the Lands Southwest of Hudson Bay, 1670-1870*, signalled a dramatic departure from previous scholarly preoccupations.[14] The book showed very clearly that, unless the role of Indians as hunters, trappers, and intermediaries was considered, our understanding of the history of the fur trade would remain badly distorted. Indeed, as Ray himself recalls, when he first proposed looking at the Native side of the fur trade, Clark smiled and said he doubted it could be done. But only a handful of people, such as Harold Hickerson and Charles Bishop, knew the richness of the Hudson's Bay Company records, which the company had recently begun to make much more accessible to scholars.[15] The Public Archives of Canada (now the Library and Archives of Canada) had begun to acquire microfilmed copies of the Hudson's Bay Company's pre-1870 records during the 1950s, greatly facilitating the use of those records by North American scholars. The subsequent relocation of the entire archives from London, England, to Winnipeg in 1970 made the Hudson's Bay Company Archives an important gathering place for emerging scholars with interests in the history of the fur trade. Ray's dissertation, together with dissertations and theses by Jennifer S.H. Brown, Sylvia Van Kirk, John E. Foster, and John S. Milloy, was transforming the scholarship in Canadian Native history between 1971 and 1976; these people put the writing on the history of the fur trade in Rupert's Land on the leading edge of Aboriginal historiography.[16] This research altered the image of Aboriginal peoples from one of passive and historically unimportant participants in processes they could neither understand nor control to one of people who were willing, shrewd, sophisticated, and historically decisive partners in commercial and social relationships over which they exerted considerable influence. As Cole Harris points out in this volume, Ray's 1974 study "shifted studies of the fur trade towards Native people and the environment and, in so doing, created a framework that recontextualized the trade while exposing many understudied questions." Both Ray and those he influenced as colleagues or students not only took up these understudied questions to good effect but also placed Aboriginal peoples at the centre of the historical action. *Indians in the Fur Trade* went through several reprints and sold out three times before the University of Toronto Press reissued it in a second edition in 1998. When reflecting on the significance of its own centennial in publishing, the press listed Ray's work among the one hundred most important books it had published in the previous century.

Aboriginal peoples' economic behaviour was a focus of particular interest in the period in which Ray undertook his dissertation research. A lively debate emerged in North America after 1960, when the well-known historian of the Hudson's Bay Company (HBC), E.E. Rich, published an article that forced historians of the fur trade to confront what HBC traders had known long before Adam Smith proposed a market theory of economics and what anthropologists had been discussing for a number of years: that Indian trade behaviour appeared to contradict, in several fundamental respects, expected human economic behaviour. Neither Rich nor the formalists could explain these apparent contradictions.[17] The paradoxical economic behaviour of "primitive" peoples worldwide led to the emergence of a revisionist school of indigenous history known as the substantivists, or romantics. Essentially, substantivists explained the problem by arguing that Western and non-Western societies did not differ in degree, as the "formalist" historians such as Innis had assumed, but qualitatively. The roots of the substantivist school can be traced back to the Marxist economic historian of ancient economies, Karl Polanyi (1886-1964). Publishing his ideas in the 1940s and the 1950s, Polanyi argued that formal economic theory applies only to modern state economic systems, which (according to formalist and substantivist scholars) have divorced the economy from important social, political, and ideological constraints. Drawing on his own historical research as well as on anthropological literature, Polanyi suggested that non-Western human interactions needed to be studied in very different ways than Western human interactions because, in non-Western societies, humans sought merely to satisfy basic physical and social needs. In Polanyi's conception, economics, politics, and diplomacy in non-Western societies were so intertwined as to be inseparable.[18] Gone from his definition of economics was any suggestion – dominant in classical economic thought – that maximizing behaviour, unlimited wants, or the price mechanism of resource allocation naturally operated in human societies. George Dalton, a primary disciple of Polanyi, argued that "transactions of material goods in primitive society are expressions of social obligations which have neither mechanism nor meaning of their own apart from the social ties and social obligations they express."[19] Although Polanyi's thoughts were entirely consistent with Boasian anthropology, Polanyi and his followers did much to elaborate and popularize substantivism. Anthropologist Marshall Sahlins, Polanyi's colleague at Columbia University, introduced substantivist thought to students of Native history in North America during the 1960s. Sahlins argued that the genius of economics in primitive societies lay in the fact that primitive peoples learned to limit their wants. Thus, although they owned little, they attained "original affluence."[20] Polanyi's substantivism was applied to the fur trade in Abraham Rotstein's ahistorical PhD dissertation in political economy, completed at the University of Toronto in 1967, and in a subsequent article.[21] The substantivist approach has found its most extreme expression and most outspoken advocate in Calvin Martin.[22]

Ray, like many people in the late 1960s, was intrigued by the economic theories of the substantivists when he undertook his dissertation, but his research convinced him that the substantivists were mistaken. His rebuttal to the substantivists came in the years after he published *Indians in the Fur*

Trade, and especially in his second book, co-authored with Donald B. Freeman, *"Give Us Good Measure"* (1978).[23] In this work, Ray and Freeman argued that, although Aboriginal economic behaviour differed from European economic behaviour – with significant implications – Aboriginal peoples were driven by similar economic motives as were other peoples. For example, wealth acquisition was a common concern for Natives and non-Natives alike, but a key difference was the way in which wealth, status, and power were linked in different societies. Like the trading captains Ray described in *"Give Us Good Measure,"* most Aboriginal traders involved in economic exchange with Europeans redistributed acquired wealth in order to gain or reinforce status, but personal accumulation on its own was viewed as a highly antisocial activity. This did not mean that the Aboriginal trading captains who travelled annually to HBC posts were not concerned about the price of beaver pelts. They used competition between Europeans whenever they could to their best advantage and to garner the best quality goods for the pelts they exchanged. Thus Ray and scholars like him might be labelled rationalists in that they argue that historical Aboriginal behaviour is explicable today because, despite significant cultural differences, humans in all societies act according to rational assessments of their self-interests.[24]

Not surprisingly, soon after Ray completed his dissertation, he found himself at a Canadian university: he took up a position in the geography department at York University in Toronto. When he undertook his study of the role of Aboriginal peoples in the fur trade, he never dreamt that his work would have particular political, legal, or social relevance. Quite the contrary. The late 1960s witnessed urban race riots in many American cities. As Ray watched fellow graduate students embark on studies of the historical and social geography of American cities, he easily understood the relevance of their studies, but his own work seemed unrelated to the major issues of the day. That changed very quickly. In fact, although Ray's study turned the scholarship on Aboriginal history towards an entirely new path, changes in Canada's relationship with its Aboriginal peoples changed even more dramatically between the time Ray began his research and published his findings. Those changes guaranteed that such research and expertise would be relevant outside academia for some time to come.

Two major developments, their significance magnified by international developments, altered the state of Aboriginal affairs dramatically in the late 1960s and early 1970s. On 25 June 1969, exactly one year after it was elected, Pierre Trudeau's Liberal government introduced its *Statement of the Government of Canada on Indian Policy, 1969,* better known as the "White Paper."[25] Reminiscent of the United States' policy of termination, which had been abandoned by 1969, the Canadian government's White Paper proposed to eliminate all legal and constitutional distinctions relating to Indians. This meant abolishing the Indian Act and shutting down the Department of

Indian Affairs within about five years. Indian reserves, held in trust by the government since before Confederation, were to pass to Indian ownership. With regard to Aboriginal land claims, the policy paper suggested that they were "so general and undefined that it is not realistic to think of them as specific claims capable of remedy except through a policy and program that will end injustice to Indians as members of the Canadian community."[26] Perhaps the most significant legacy of the White Paper is the political organizations and activism that it encouraged. Coinciding with events such as the Indian occupation of Alcatraz, which began in November of 1969, reactions to the White Paper propelled Aboriginal issues to the front pages of Canada's newspapers. Within two years, in the face of very vocal and adamant opposition on the part of Aboriginal leaders and groups, the government formally withdrew the paper. In the 1970s, Aboriginal peoples were displaying the kind of sophistication that Ray argued they had shown during the fur trade period.

The second pivotal event was the Canadian Supreme Court's January 1973 decision in *Calder* v. *Attorney-General of British Columbia*, which arose from a demand for rights and recognition put forward by the Nisga'a of British Columbia's north coast. Although a split decision (3:3, with one abstention), half of the judges decided there was such a thing as Aboriginal title in Canadian common law, and they made it clear that Aboriginal peoples might still be able to make legal claims based on that title. Bracketed by the Trail of Broken Treaties and the occupation of the offices of the Bureau of Indian Affairs in Washington in October and November 1972 as well as the siege at Wounded Knee in South Dakota in the spring of 1973, and occurring against the backdrop of an increasingly aggressive American Indian Movement (AIM) in the United States, the *Calder* decision induced the government of Pierre Trudeau to develop a land claims policy that acknowledged Aboriginal title.[27] In August 1973, Jean Chrétien, the minister of Indian affairs, introduced the new land claims policy. Nineteen seventy-four, the year *Indians in the Fur Trade* was published, was marked by many Aboriginal protests in Canada, the most prominent being the five-week occupation of Anicinabe Park in Kenora, Ontario, and the "Native Caravan" in September, which culminated in the occupation of a government building and the storming of Parliament on 30 September 1974. In the short span of about five years before Ray's *Indians in the Fur Trade* was published, the significance of government Indian policy and, indeed, of Aboriginal grievances in Canada generally, had been transformed; in turn, academic interest in Native history was stimulated by court cases like *Calder* and those that followed.

In the early 1970s, the failed attempt by the Liberal government to abolish Indian status, the establishment of a land claims process and Aboriginal rights litigation, the emergence of vocal and assertive Aboriginal leaders and organizations, and growing public awareness of and sympathy for

Aboriginal peoples drew many historians into the field of Aboriginal history. Academics soon learned that doing Native history had real consequences for the lives of Aboriginal people. Modern Aboriginal land and rights claims drew upon academic research and/or hired academics as expert witnesses, bringing Canadian scholars into a process that, in the United States, had already been under way for two decades. In the fifteen years after the White Paper, at least five graduate students completed dissertations or theses on the history of Indian policy in Canada.[28] The claims process certainly drew Arthur J. Ray into new areas of research.[29] Curiously, however, Arthur Ray is one of the few historians who has researched both fur trade history and Indian policy history. Ray's *Indians in the Fur Trade* argues that Aboriginal peoples were not only reactive but also creative and innovative participants in the trade. His subsequent work similarly argues that Aboriginal peoples continued to be resourceful and innovative throughout their postcontact histories.[30]

Furthermore, some of Ray's work suggests that the fur trade left a legacy that influenced Aboriginal-government relations long after it had ended. During the 1980s, much of his research examined periods during which the significance of the fur trade waned in the broader economy but continued to be central to Native economies. For example, in two important essays Ray suggests that an understanding of the paternalistic relationship that existed between the HBC and Aboriginal people is important for understanding later Native perspectives on welfare.[31] He focused on these very issues, and specifically on the decline of the old company paternalism during the fur trade of the late nineteenth and twentieth centuries in his 1990 book *The Fur Trade in the Industrial Age* (another sequel of sorts to his first monograph).[32]

However, in general and until recently, historical scholarship on Aboriginal-newcomer relations during the fur trade contrasted sharply with the literature on Native-government relations after the fur trade. Perhaps because fur trade history and Indian policy history were distinct and separate fields of history, historians have concluded that Native-newcomer relations changed suddenly and dramatically when the fur trade ended and governments began to devise and implement Indian policies. Almost inevitably, then, as J.R. Miller argues in *Skyscrapers Hide the Heavens*, the only general history of Indian-government relations in Canada holds that, whenever and wherever the economic partnerships and military alliances waned in significance, relationships between Aboriginal peoples and newcomers quickly changed from cooperative to coercive.[33] But Miller is among those who have expressed dissatisfaction with the image of Aboriginal peoples as supine victims of Indian policy. Shortly after he published his first edition of *Skyscrapers Hide the Heavens*, he decried the fact that "discussions of nineteenth-century assimilative policies have persisted in an older tendency to treat the Indians as objects rather than agents, victims rather than creators of their history."[34]

Miller explicitly suggests that historians of Canadian Indian policy should draw inspiration from the fur trade historiography pioneered by scholars like Arthur J. Ray and Robin Fisher during the 1970s in order to better understand relations in the subsequent periods of history. Miller then goes on to argue that Aboriginal resistance had rendered many Canadian Indian policies ineffective.[35] Miller was not the only historian who began to examine the historical significance of Indian resistance, or, more correctly, "creative opposition," to government coercion. During the 1990s, Douglas Cole and Ira Chaikin and Tina Loo argued that, although there were laws that outlawed the potlatch among the Indians of the west coast, Indian interactions (running the full gamut of resistance, ignorance, and adaptation) with these laws helped ensure that they were rarely enforced.[36] In this way, the work of historians like Miller, Cole, and Loo has changed our perceptions of how Indian policy was developed and administered. Several of Ray's students have since examined the history of Indian policy in similar ways. Hence, historians of Aboriginal-state relations in Canada now assume that Aboriginal resistance to policies they opposed significantly undermined the effectiveness of those policies and that an understanding of this resistance is crucial for an understanding of how government officials implemented policy.

In *Bounty and Benevolence: A History of the Saskatchewan Treaties*, Arthur Ray, J.R. Miller, and Frank Tough argue that Aboriginal understandings of the numbered treaties of the Canadian Prairies were heavily influenced by the context of the practices of the fur trade.[37] Ray's contribution to the volume was strongly influenced by his involvement in the Ermineskin and Samson Cree case (*Buffalo et al.* v. *Regina*, 2005). His testimony at this court case led him to revisit the political dimension of the fur trade not in terms of formalist/substantivist academic debate but, rather, in terms of the implications it had for settling patterns of relations between the Crown and First Nations, especially with respect to treaty-making and interpretation.[38] The co-authored publication that came to include Ray's interpretation had its origins in a research report commissioned by the Office of the Treaty Commissioner in Saskatchewan and had been intended as a contribution to a process seeking to facilitate greater understanding of treaty rights and to foster discussion between government agencies and First Nations in matters of child welfare, education, health, justice, and resource use.[39]

Although the work was originally intended to encompass both oral and textual sources on treaties, time constraints necessitated a splitting of the two types of sources into separate projects. Thus, the study conducted by Ray, Miller, and Tough was derived exclusively from documentary, primarily non-Native, sources. Despite the uncritical government perspectives endemic to these sources, Ray and his colleagues argued that "First Nations played a more active role in initiating and shaping treaties than academic scholarship has acknowledged in the present" and that "less praise is due the federal government and Canadians at large for the making of the treaties."[40] They argued that the creation of treaties in Saskatchewan, and across the entire area north and west of the Great Lakes, should be understood within a larger historical continuum of different phases of the Western fur trade, earlier colonial diplomatic traditions, and the active role of Native negotiators bent on ensuring the Crown's "bounty and benevolence" for their independence and continued survival.

Ultimately, this study illuminates the fact that, if one privileges only governmental viewpoints, one's perspectives on the treaty process will be both incomplete and inaccurate. When written accounts are read against the grain for Native perspectives (and, indeed, some Native leaders' speeches and oral testimonies were captured in the treaty commissioners' reports), as the authors did, it becomes clear that "the implementation of the treaties was fraught with difficulties for First Nations communities." [41] In this way the book makes a significant contribution to our understanding of Native-newcomer relations and treaty history in Canada.

In 1981, Ray went to the history department at the University of British Columbia, a move that put him in the province in which Aboriginal land claims were most active. Soon he was researching on behalf of Native claimants in British Columbia and elsewhere. With acknowledged expertise in the fields of Native economic history and cultural ecology, Ray participated as an expert witness in several landmark cases, including *Horseman* (1990), *Delgamuukw* (1991), and *Powley* (2003). Ray's empirical style is based on thorough research in archival sources, and his economic focus helps explain his affinity for Innis; however, in many ways it also explains why he has ended up providing expert evidence in the courts. His non-Marxist materialist emphasis meant that his research was particularly relevant to those making claims to land and hunting and fishing rights. It is also probably true that Ray's research related to litigation reinforced his commitment to detailed research, an empirical approach, and an economic focus. Ray's work rarely explicitly addresses theory, gender, religion and spirituality, or other themes that have become increasingly prominent in the field. Never a theoretician, Ray has been little influenced by the postmodern turn, and his experience in the courts may partially explain why this is true even in the present. While theory generalizes historical experience, in the courtroom it is the particularities that come under the microscope.[42]

Ray's encounters with the Canadian legal system changed him as a scholar. History in the courtroom, as he immediately discovered, is profoundly different from how historians usually practise their craft and defend their interpretations. Ray noted the negative impact of the confrontational environment of the courtroom not only upon the conceptualizations of Native peoples but also upon one's ability to *do good history* in such a context.

"The expert witnesses, who often are academics, find themselves in the unusual circumstances of having to do ethnohistory in an adversarial environment," he explains, "where their personal credibility and that of their report are sharply challenged."[43]

In the mid-1980s, after a relatively pleasant first experience without cross-examination in the *Horseman* case (concerning the treaty hunting rights of a Bert Horseman, a Cree man who lived in Alberta), Ray agreed to a request by a group of fifty-one hereditary chiefs in British Columbia to research the history of early European-Native contacts, notably between the Gitxsan and Wet'suwet'en people and HBC officers and other company employees (who comprised the first group of Europeans to maintain sustained direct contact). His account highlighted the records of William Brown, the HBC chief trader who, in 1822, established Fort Kilmaurs on Babine Lake, a primary source that nearly all of the subsequent ethnographic studies of the region had overlooked. Brown's writings proved to be a rich source of information on Native social structures, land tenure systems, and local economies and trading networks. The information Ray highlighted was based on Brown's work and complemented Gitxsan and Wet'suwe'ten oral records regarding how their "ancestors had exercised their title in the claims area" and responded to economic changes brought by the fur trade.[44]

After a version of his report was submitted by the chiefs as evidence during *Delgamuukw* v. *Regina*, Ray was asked to appear in the courtroom as an expert witness on their behalf. The encounter proved to be an arduous one:

> I faced four days of stressful cross-examination by two teams of lawyers who represented the province and the federal government. They not only challenged the evidence I presented to the court, but put my scholarly publication record on trial too. This experience, and my subsequent involvement in other treaty and Métis rights cases, sparked my interest in the history of cultural/historical research oriented to claims and other litigation, as well as the presentation of this evidence in court and in other quasi-judicial settings.[45]

In the courtroom, with its oppositional approach to presenting and arguing the merits of historical evidence, there is frequently little understanding of, or appreciation for, the historian's craft. Lawyers seeking to make their case may take documents out of their historical contexts and ignore the role of the scholar as interpreter, not merely collector, of such written evidence.[46] Clinging to outmoded models of Native history, the courts have a tendency to essentialize Aboriginal cultures or portray First Nations according to simplistic and often negative stereotypes. Ray's experiences of Native history in the courtroom prompted him to write a popular history of Canada's Aboriginal Peoples – *I Have Lived Here Since the World Began* – wherein Native economies and societies are highlighted as the complex and dynamic entities they have been in the post-Columbian context.[47]

During *Delgamuukw,* Ray was especially frustrated by the Crown's portrayal of the Gitxsan and Wet'suwet'en as violence-prone peoples living under lawless circumstances (something he vehemently disputed from the stand, almost to the point of anger). Sadly, this Eurocentric perspective was shared by the judge himself, Chief Justice Alan McEachern, who, in his 1991 reasons for judgment against the hereditary chiefs' claims, characterized life in their territories with the nineteenth-century Hobbesian descriptor: "nasty, brutish, and short."[48] In the end, both the British Columbia Court of Appeal (1992-93) and the Supreme Court of Canada (1997) overturned his decision. In fact, the latter went further, stating that, in the future, the Canadian judicial system must accommodate Aboriginal oral evidence on par with documentary sources and must take seriously the constitutional recognition of Aboriginal title where it has not been extinguished.

A year before the Supreme Court overruled McEachern's judgment, the nationwide Royal Commission on Aboriginal Peoples issued its report (1996), highlighting the utility of historical study and education about Native history as central to achieving social justice and reconciliation for First Nations in Canada.[49] The commissioners observed that "questions of voice, research, evidence, and the way history is used in the litigation process" have emerged as issues of direct concern to Native historiography and in the lives of contemporary First Nations.[50] While some scholars have warned of the dangers of "advocacy history," Ray and his colleagues, who have acted as expert witnesses in such cases at *Delgamuukw* and *Powley,* effectively demonstrate how history research has the potential to function as a mechanism for acknowledging and addressing the wrongs done to First Nations in this country over the last five hundred years or more.[51]

Aggravating as they may be, ultimately, close engagement with constructions of history in the courtroom can be stimulating to the individual scholar. Ray's work in *Powley* – the first Métis rights case to make it to the Supreme Court of Canada and whose decision is already having a major impact in legal and political circles today – brought him full circle back to hunting rights in the context of the fur trade and Métis history (the area Clark had once encouraged him to pursue and to which he had only briefly alluded to in *Indians in the Fur Trade).*[52] Ray felt that "the *Powley* decision and subsequent emergence of Métis communities across the country is forcing us to re-think Métis history, which has had a prairie-centric focus."[53] In claims work, scholars talk with at least two other constituents (Aboriginal and legal), creating a greater potential for revisionist interpretations than is produced by insular academic discourses alone. Canadian Native historiography as a whole, therefore, has come to incorporate different issues and questions and to pursue diverse avenues of inquiry because of the community concerns with which claims research has to contend. We might call this simply a "reality-check" effect of indigenous postcolonial challenges to scholarly knowledge production systems. Claims research is innovative in that one or both parties engaged in the case not only force the academics acting as expert witnesses to re-examine historical scholarship but also help determine the direction of their research inquiries (e.g., many claimants' ancestors had not been the focus of scholarly work prior to filing claims), making the courts sometimes the *first* place to weigh new scholarship.

Most recently, Ray has shifted away from the fur trade and, inspired by his experiences as an expert witness in a number of high-profile Native land and resource rights court cases, has turned his scholarly gaze towards the history of those who, like him, have been both academics and expert witnesses.[54] In this research he has been inquiring into the relationship between people's political and legal involvements and their academic and scholarly lives. In a large comparative research project, he is seeking to better understand how academics construct evidence in the courtroom and how pervasive their analytical models are with regard to knowledge about indigenous societies, economies, and concepts of territory, treaties, resources, and land rights in four countries (Canada, the United States, Australia, and New Zealand).[55] He found that scholars' involvement in Native claims, particularly in the United States after the creation of the Indian Claims Commission in 1946, was more significant than he had realized. Ray's work shows a deep and mature concern for and understanding of the construction of knowledge about Native history. His research has put him in some ironic positions. Ray, who has devoted most of his research career to studying Aboriginal peoples, now has begun to study those who study Aboriginal peoples. And many anthropologists accustomed to conducting interviews with Aboriginal people have found themselves speaking into microphones, they themselves being the subject of scholarly study, they themselves providing the oral evidence that will be analyzed by others. Many of Ray's discoveries and arguments have yet to be reported, but what he has already published has shed new light upon how past scholars in Canada, the United States, Australia, and New Zealand have tried to conduct their research when they have had to wear the hats of dispassionate researchers and expert witnesses, on how academia has influenced the courts, and on how the courts have influenced trends in academia. Thus, Ray is studying a phenomenon that has been clearly evident in his own life and work.

Arthur J. Ray began presenting his research on Aboriginal history just as, in Canada, Aboriginal issues were thrust into the limelight. While he observed with interest the rapidly growing influence of Aboriginal peoples during the early 1970s, he must have been surprised to learn how relevant his research had become. By the 1980s, Ray had become not only an interested observer but also a participant in the processes by which Aboriginal peoples were asserting their claims. Although even his earliest research was relevant to Aboriginal claims, Ray began to focus specifically on issues related to litigation. Eventually, that experience led him to explore the process by which the academy and the courts have influenced one another over the years. In this way, Ray was not only influenced by historical trends but also influenced them. No students of Aboriginal history today, certainly not any of Arthur J. Ray's students, can escape the reality that research into Aboriginal issues, even the most dispassionate research into ancient Aboriginal history, has direct implications for people who are alive today and whose lives have not yet begun.

Notes

1 Donald B. Smith, personal communication, 20 October 2006. The article was published as A.J. Ray, "Fur Trade History as an Aspect of Native History," in *One Century Later*, ed. D. Smith and I. Getty, 7-19 (Vancouver: UBC Press, 1978).
2 The reprinted article can be found as Arthur J. Ray, "Fur Trade History as an Aspect of Native History," in *Readings in Canadian History: Pre-Confederation*, ed. R.D. Francis and D.B. Smith, 149-60 (Toronto: Holt, Rinehart and Winston, 1982). It was also reprinted in the 2nd (1986), 3rd (1990), 4th (1994), 5th (1998), and 6th (2002) editions of the book.
3 Ray, "Fur Trade History," 7.
4 Indeed, the scholarship on the fur trade and on Aboriginal peoples has changed significantly since 1978, and so it is not surprising that Ray's article was dropped for a newer article in the most recent edition of that collection. After 1982, "First Nations" had replaced "Indian" so quickly that, by the 1990s, students found Ray's use of "Indian" jarring. Under these circumstances, it is even more difficult to convince students that Arthur J. Ray is among the most important people to present, defend, and establish scholarly arguments that they now see as given.
5 Kerry Abel identified Ray, along with the likes of Robin Fisher and Sylvia Van Kirk, as authors of path-breaking books on the first wave of Native historiography in Canada. See Kerry Abel, "Tangled, Lost, and Bitter? Current Directions in the Writing of Native History in Canada," *Acadiensis* 26 (1996): 92.
6 R. Cole Harris, "Andrew Hill Clark, 1911-1975: An Obituary," *Journal of Historical Geography* 2, 1 (1976): 16.
7 Andrew Hill Clark, *The Invasion of New Zealand by People, Plants and Animals* (New Brunswick, NJ: Rutgers University Press, 1949).
8 Cole Harris, personal communication with Theodore Binnema, 23 September 2005.
9 Harold A. Innis, *The Fur Trade in Canada* (Toronto: University of Toronto Press, 1930). See, especially, pp. 118 and 386-92.
10 Readers can also turn to E.E. Rich, *The History of the Hudson's Bay Company, 1670-1870* (London: Hudson's Bay Record Society, 1958-59); and Arthur S. Morton, *A History of the Canadian West to 1870-71* (London: T. Nelson, 1939).
11 Arthur J. Ray, "Introduction," in Harold A. Innis, *The Fur Trade in Canada* (Toronto: University of Toronto Press, 1999), xix.
12 Ibid., v.
13 Bruce G. Trigger, *Natives and Newcomers: Canada's "Heroic Age" Reconsidered* (Montreal and Kingston: McGill-Queen's University Press, 1985), 183-84.
14 Arthur J. Ray, *Indians in the Fur Trade: Their Role as Hunters, Trappers, and Middlemen in the Lands Southwest of Hudson Bay 1660-1870* (Toronto: University of Toronto Press 1974).
15 Previously, only Arthur S. Morton and official historians for the company had had direct access to these documents. A.J. Ray, personal communication with S. Neylan, 3 December 2005, Washington, DC.

16 John S. Milloy, *The Plains Cree: Trade, Diplomacy and War 1790 to 1870* (Winnipeg: University of Manitoba Press, 1988) (derived from a master's thesis completed at Carleton University in 1972); John E. Foster, "The Country-Born in the Red River Settlement: 1820-1850" (PhD diss., University of Alberta, 1973); Sylvia Van Kirk, *"Many Tender Ties": Women in Fur-Trade Society, 1670-1870* (Winnipeg: Watson and Dwyer, 1980) (based on her doctoral dissertation completed at the University of London in 1975); Jennifer S.H. Brown, *Strangers in Blood: Fur Trade Company Families in Indian Country* (Vancouver: UBC Press, 1980) (based on a doctoral dissertation completed at the University of Chicago in 1976). In the year Ray completed his dissertation, James Walker published his well-known assessment of the state of historical writing on Native history in Canada: James W. St. G. Walker, "The Indian in Canadian Historical Writing," Canadian Historical Association, *Historical Papers* (1971): 21-51. For a discussion of the historical literature of the early 1970s, see Sylvia Van Kirk, "Fur Trade Social History: Some Recent Trends," in *Old Trails and New Directions: Papers of the Third North American Fur Trade Conference*, ed. Carol Judd and Arthur J. Ray, 160-73 (Toronto: University of Toronto Press, 1980).

17 E.E. Rich, "Trade Habits and Economic Motivation among the Indians of North America," *Canadian Journal of Economics and Political Science* 26 (1960): 35-53. Rich's article did no more than present the apparent contradictions. An interesting but unsuccessful attempt to deal with them from within the paradigm of classical economics is found in John McManus, "An Economic Analysis of Indian Behavior in the North American Fur Trade," *Journal of Economic History* 32 (1972): 36-53.

18 Karl Polanyi, *The Great Transformation* (New York: Farrar and Rinehart, 1944); Karl Polanyi, Conrad M. Arensberg, and Harry W. Pearson, eds., *Trade and Market in the Early Empires* (Glencoe, IL: Free Press, 1957). For a fine study of the influence of Polanyi, see S.C. Humphreys, "History, Economics, and Anthropology: The Work of Karl Polanyi," *History and Theory* 8 (1969): 165-212.

19 George Dalton, "Economic Theory and Primitive Society," *American Anthropologist* 63 (1961): 21.

20 See Marshall D. Sahlins, *Tribesmen* (Englewood Cliffs, NJ: Prentice Hall, 1966), and his *Stone Age Economics* (Chicago: Aldine-Atherton Press, 1972), esp. chap. 1, "The Original Affluent Society." The use of the term "original affluence" is significant. It not only underscores the evolutionary assumptions that underlie the idea but also betrays the romantic notions with which Marxists and other substantivists imbue non-state societies.

21 Abraham Rotstein, "Fur Trade and Empire: An Institutional Analysis" (PhD diss., University of Toronto, 1967); and Abraham Rotstein, "Trade and Politics: An Institutional Approach," *Western Canadian Journal of Anthropology* 3 (1972): 1-28.

22 See Calvin Martin, *Keepers of the Game: Indian-Animal Relationships and the Fur Trade* (Berkeley: University of California Press, 1978); his contributions to *The American Indian and the Problem of History* (New York: Oxford University Press, 1987); and his *In the Spirit of the Earth: Rethinking History and Time* (Baltimore: Johns Hopkins University Press, 1992). In this last book, Martin argues that Western societies are so different from band societies that it would be impossible to write the history of a band society. A different but equally extreme view has been presented by Huron philosopher-historian Georges E. Sioui in *For an Amerindian Autohistory: An Essay in the Foundations of a Social Ethic*, trans. Sheila Fischman (Montreal/Kingston: McGill-Queen's University Press, 1992).

23 Arthur J. Ray and Donald B. Freeman, *"Give Us Good Measure": An Economic Analysis of Relations Between the Indians and the Hudson's Bay Company before 1763* (Toronto: University of Toronto Press, 1978). See also Arthur J. Ray, "Indians as Consumers in the Eighteenth Century," in *Old Trails and New Directions*, 255-71 (Toronto: University of Toronto Press, 1980); and Arthur J. Ray, "Competition and Conservation in the Early Subarctic Fur Trade," *Ethnohistory* 25 (1978): 347-57.

24 For an explicit presentation of the rationalist perspective, see Bruce G. Trigger, "Early Native North American Responses to European Contact: Romantic versus Rationalistic Interpretations," *Journal of American History* 77 (1991): 1195-215. This article disputes the conclusions of Christopher L. Miller and George R. Hamell, "A New Perspective on Indian-White

Contact: Cultural Symbols and Colonial Trade," *Journal of American History* 73, 2 (1986): 311-28; and George R. Hamell, "Strawberries, Floating Islands, and Rabbit Captains: Mythical Realities and European Contact in the Northeast during the Sixteenth and Seventeenth Centuries," *Journal of Canadian Studies* 21, 4 (1986-87): 72-94.

25 *Statement of the Government of Canada on Indian Policy, 1969* (presented to the First Session of the Twenty-Eighth Parliament by the Honourable Jean Chrétien, Minister of Indian Affairs and Northern Development) (Ottawa: Queen's Printer, 1969).

26 Ibid., 11.

· 27 This atmosphere also influenced how academics approached their subject matter. Ray recalls the tensions in the air when he presented "The Fur Trade as an Aspect of Native History" at the Western Canadian Studies Conference in 1977 due to the presence of AIM (A.J. Ray, personal communication to S. Neylan, 3 December 2005, Washington, DC). That paper was subsequently published as "The Fur Trade as an Aspect of Native History," in *One Century Later: Western Canadian Reserve Indians since Treaty 7*, ed. Ian A.L. Getty and Donald B. Smith, 7-19 (Vancouver: UBC Press, 1978).

28 J.D. Leighton, "The Development of Federal Indian Policy in Canada, 1840-1890" (PhD diss., University of Western Ontario, 1975); Donald B. Smith, "The Mississaugas, Peter Jones, and the White Man" (PhD diss., University of Toronto, 1975); J.S. Milloy, "The Era of Civilization: British Policy for the Indian of Canada, 1830-1860" (D.Phil thesis, Oxford University, 1978); R.J. Surtees, "Indian Land Cessions in Ontario, 1763-1862: The Evolution of a System" (PhD diss., Carleton University, 1982); Anthony Hall, "The Red Man's Burden: Land, Law, and the Lord in the Indian Affairs of Upper Canada, 1791-1858" (PhD diss., University of Toronto, 1984). Like Ray, Robert Surtees had already been drawn to Aboriginal history before the White Paper was introduced. See R.J. Surtees, "Indian Reserve Policy in Upper Canada, 1830-1845" (MA thesis, Carleton University, 1966).

29 Arthur J. Ray, "Native History on Trial: Confessions of an Expert Witness," *Canadian Historical Review* 84 (2003): 253-73.

30 Arthur J. Ray, *I Have Lived Here since the World Began: An Illustrated History of Canada's Native People*, rev. ed. (Toronto: Lester Publishing and Key Porter Books, 2005 [1996]).

31 Arthur J. Ray, "Periodic Shortages, Native Welfare and the Hudson's Bay Company, 1670-1930, in *The Subarctic Fur Trade: Native Social and Economic Adaptations*, ed. S. Krech, 1-20 (Vancouver: UBC Press, 1984), and "The Decline of Paternalism in the Hudson's Bay Company Fur Trade, 1870-1945," in *Merchant Credit and Labour Strategies in Historical Perspective*, ed. Rosemary Ommer, 188-202 (Fredericton: Acadiensis Press, 1990).

32 Arthur J. Ray, *The Fur Trade in the Industrial Age* (Toronto: University of Toronto Press, 1990).

33 J.R. Miller, *Skyscrapers Hide the Heavens: A History of Indian-White Relations in Canada*, 3rd ed. (Toronto: University of Toronto Press, 2000).

34 J.R. Miller, "Owen Glendower, Hotspur, and Canadian Indian Policy," *Ethnohistory* 37 (1990): 386.

35 J.R. Miller, "Owen Glendower," 387. The work by Robin Fisher is *Contact and Conflict: Indian-European Relations in British Columbia, 1774-1890* (Vancouver: UBC Press, 1977).

36 Douglas Cole and Ira Chaikin, *An Iron Hand upon the People: The Law against the Potlatch on the Northwest Coast* (Vancouver: Douglas and McIntyre, 1990); Tina Loo, "Dan Cramner's Potlatch: Law as Coercion, Symbol, and Rhetoric in British Columbia, 1884-1951," *Canadian Historical Review* 73, 2 (1992): 125-65. See also J.R. Miller, *Shingwauk's Vision: A History of Native Residential Schools* (Toronto: University of Toronto Press, 1996).

37 Arthur J. Ray, Jim Miller, and Frank J. Tough, *Bounty and Benevolence: A History of Saskatchewan Treaties* (Montreal/Kingston: McGill-Queen's University Press, 2000).

38 The chapters Ray contributed to *Bounty and Benevolence* were based on the report he had submitted for the Cree during *Buffalo et al.* v. *Regina* (2005), again demonstrating the growing connection between Aboriginal claims litigation and academic research.

39 Judge David M. Arnot, Treaty Commissioner for Saskatchewan, "Foreword," in Ray, Miller, and Tough, *Bounty and Benevolence*, ix.

40 Ray, Miller, and Tough, *Bounty and Benevolence*, xvii.

41 Ibid., 204.

42 Nancy Shoemaker observed that the generalizing commonplace to theoretical frameworks also tends to downplay commonalities and emphasize difference, something equally true in the adversarial context of the courtroom. See Nancy Shoemaker, ed., *Clearing a Path: Theorizing the Past in Native American Studies* (New York: Routledge, 2002), x.

43 Arthur J. Ray, "Creating the Image of the Savage in Defence of the Crown: The Ethnohistorian in Court," *Native Studies Review* 6, 2 (1990): 13. The first scholarly publication that clearly exhibits how Ray's contract work changed the direction of his research is A.J. Ray, "Fur Trade History and the Gitksan-Wet'suwet'en Comprehensive Claim: Men of Property and the Exercise of Title," in *Aboriginal Resource Use in Canada: Historical and Legal Aspects*, ed. Kerry Abel and Jean Friesen, 301-16 (Winnipeg: University of Manitoba Press, 1991).

44 Ibid., 14.

45 Arthur J. Ray, "Native History on Trial," 254.

46 Ray, "Ethohistorian in Court," 25.

47 Ray, *I Have Lived Here since the World Began.*

48 Alan McEachern, Supreme Court of British Columbia, no. 0843, Smithers Registry, 8 March 1991, p. 13. Ray addressed this issue in "Creating the Image of the Savage in Defense of the Crown: The Ethnohistorian in Court," Special Issue, *Native Studies Review* 6, 2 (1993): 13-28.

49 Royal Commission Report on Aboriginal Peoples, 1996, is available online at http://www.ainc-inac.gc.ca/ch/rcap/index_e.html.

50 Ray, "Confessions of an Expert Witness," 255.

51 Kerry Abel laments that scholars whose interpretations unequivocally argue for recognition of Aboriginal rights have lost "an opportunity to participate more fully in the public debate they are trying to influence" by not following through as fully "activist-historians." See Abel, "Tangled, Lost, and Bitter?" 92. Ray himself decried the tendency to see scholarly expert witnesses merely as "hired guns, jackals, and whores." See Ray, "Confessions of an Expert Witness," 269. Carlson, Jetté, and Matsui identified courtroom history as having the greatest impact on the writing of Aboriginal history in the 1990s. See Keith Thor Carlson, Melinda Marie Jetté, and Kenichi Matsui, "An Annotated Bibliography of Major Writings in Aboriginal History (1990-2000)," *Canadian Historical Review* 82, 1 (2001): 122.

52 For example, Ray recounted some of his findings regarding Métis movements between Turtle Mountain and Red River at the annual meeting of the American Society for Ethnohistory, Williamsburg, Virginia, 3 November 2006.

53 A.J. Ray, personal communication with S. Neylan, 3 December 2005, Washington, DC.

54 The earliest evidence of this interest is found in A.J. Ray, "The Historical Geographer and the Gitksan and Wet'suwet'en Comprehensive Claim: The Role of the Expert Witness," in *Indigenous Land Rights in Commonwealth Countries: Dispossession, Negotiation and Community Action*, ed. Garth Cant, John Overton, and Eric Pawson, 81-87 (Christchurch, NZ: Dept. of Geography, University of Canterbury and the Ngai Tahu Maori Trust Board for the Commonwealth Geographical Bureau, 1993).

55 For example, his current project is entitled "'History Wars and Human Rights: Aboriginal Rights Claims in the United States, Canada, Australia, and New Zealand."

2

Rupert's Land, *Nituskeenan*, Our Land: Cree and English Naming and Claiming around the Dirty Sea
Jennifer S.H. Brown

Rupert's Land, or the Hudson's Bay Company Territories as it is sometimes called, is not widely known, even in its Canadian homeland. Most Americans have never heard of it, even though the Hudson Bay watershed, which eventually defined it, reached into four present US states and was much larger than any of the thirteen British American colonies. In Great Britain, it is even less known. Prince Rupert, Hudson's Bay Company (HBC) founder and nephew of King Charles I, remains famous in the United Kingdom as leader of the royalist forces in Cromwell's time and as a naval commander against the Dutch after the Restoration. But historians with whom I talked at the University of Oxford while visiting in 2002 were unfamiliar with his namesake territory in North America and his role in founding the HBC.

When the HBC was chartered in 1670, Rupert's Land became the English term for the entire region, approximately the northern third of North America. It existed as a rather curious kind of British colony for two centuries, until 1870, longer than Canada (founded 1867) has existed as a country. But it is almost invisible in most North American histories, and even in histories of European colonization.[1] Its obscurity is doubtless due in part to its northern, largely subarctic, location; its relatively small, dispersed populations; its distance from major North American settlements and theatres of war; and the fact that its name faded from the scene when it was annexed to Canada in 1870. Another factor may be that much of its history was stored for a long time in scholarly boxes packed away in certain rather specialized fields of study. There is the Canadian fur trade box built by Harold Innis (1930) and his followers, tracing the expansion of the trade westward from the St. Lawrence and Great Lakes and beyond, from New France to the rise of the North West Company; and the HBC history box, framed by such scholars as William Schooling (1920) and Douglas MacKay (1936) and fitted out in great detail by E.E. Rich (1958), thirty-two Hudson's Bay Record Society documentary volumes, and much other work besides. Somehow, the rich contents of these boxes did not get displayed on the larger historical stage; their interest and scope remained limited, and Rupert's Land remained in the shadows.

Just over three decades ago, however, Arthur J. Ray published a book that opened those boxes and explored their baggage in new ways. *Indians in the Fur Trade* (1974) was a seminal work for the history of Rupert's Land and its peoples. Along with its sequel, *"Give Us Good Measure"* (1978), by A.J. Ray and Donald Freeman, it laid out new paths for fur trade history.[2] These books still relied on the documents conventional to the older works but mined them by asking new questions, directing attention towards the dynamic interactions of Aboriginal people with the fur trade. They provided interpretive frames in which researchers began to inquire about and take seriously, at long last, the multiple and evolving perspectives of the Native people whom the European traders and explorers met. Since the 1970s, these and many other studies have generated new ways to look at Rupert's Land and at the terrain beneath that label, bringing fresh approaches to an old subject.

This chapter explores early English constructions of the Hudson Bay region before Rupert's Land was invented and compares them to some Aboriginal perspectives on its geography and places, and on the newcomers themselves as expressed through naming. It then looks at concepts of land and landscape as viewed by Aboriginal people and, as conceived of and claimed by the founders of the HBC in 1670 and in the two decades immediately following. As the HBC struggled to become established in the midst of intense English-French conflicts over Rupert's Land, its various gestures of possession and naming met Aboriginal ways of thinking and naming that reveal fundamentally different frames of reference still enduring in language and thought.

What's in a Name? People and Places in Cree and English

The lands and waters of Hudson Bay had been "discovered" many times before the HBC received its royal charter in 1670. After the Ice Age glaciers retreated, Aboriginal people spread northward as the landscape, vegetation, and animal populations recovered. The earliest occupants of the Hudson Bay Lowlands have been dated to about 4000 years ago.[3] To judge by the later predominance of the Cree language across the region, they were probably ancestral to the Cree, and their lifestyles would have been similar. They were river and shore people, never far from fresh water and its resources. For countless generations, they harvested the fish, furred animals, migratory birds in spring and fall, and larger game, notably the woodland caribou herds that migrated across their lands and rivers in the spring and fall.[4]

The Hudson Bay Lowland Cree whose ancestors met the first Europeans on the shores of Hudson Bay describe themselves as *Omushkegowak*, people

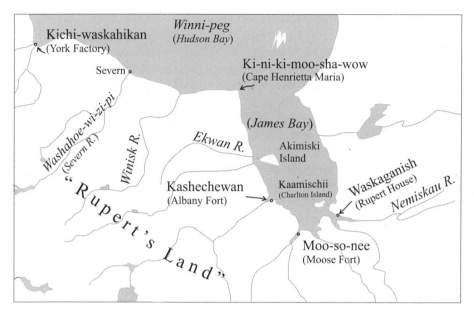

Map 2.1   Hudson Bay and James Bay, featuring Cree place names (with English interpolations in parentheses).
Source: Prepared by Ted Binnema and Jennifer S.H. Brown.

of the muskeg (singular, *Omushkego*). Such localized descriptors evoking place and environment are typical of Aboriginal people's ways of naming themselves in their own languages; see also, for example, the local Native names that HBC men recorded in the 1700s. "Cree" is an outsiders' label that spread into general use in the nineteenth century, as observers became aware of the linguistic unity of the region.[5]

The Omushkegowak travelled principally on inland waterways and the old beach ridges along the Hudson Bay coast – and on the muskeg when it was frozen. From their perspective, Hudson Bay itself was unattractive and dangerous. The Cree term for Hudson and James bays is *Winni-peg*, the sea of dirty (salt) water (see Map 2.1). This distinguishing characteristic is explained by an old legend. As Omushkego (Cree) storyteller Louis Bird relates, long ago, the Giant Skunk, *Mishi Shiikaak*, was threatening and terrorizing the other animals. They combined to kill him and enlisted Wolverine to hold his bum so they would not be sprayed during the attack. But after the job was done, Wolverine had to let go and was hit by the smell. He was not allowed to wash in fresh water because he would pollute it; he had to make a great dash all the way to the sea (Hudson Bay), where he plunged in to clean himself off. The sea has been dirty ever since.[6]

Not only is the water undrinkable, but the coastal shallows are tidal, extend great distances, and become very rough in storms. Aboriginal people in birch canoes avoided the open water. For example, Omushkego travellers used inland waterways to get from the Winisk River on Hudson Bay to the mouth of the Ekwan River on James Bay rather than venture onto the bay around Cape Henrietta Maria. Louis Bird translates Ekwan as "the preferable way to go" (Map 2.2). Given their caution about *Winni-peg*, they would have found the first European sailors who tried to navigate this inland sea memorable for their bravery or rashness as well as for their strange activities and sounds and the appearance of the ships themselves. The noise and flashing of the guns, the cries of the crews hoisting the sails ("Heave ho! Heave ho!"), the ropes and anchors, the hardtack or ship's biscuit that the sailors ate, are all subjects of remark in the stories told by Louis Bird.[7] These first impressions made by the newcomers are epitomized by the term that James Bay Cree speakers still use for "white men": *wemistikosiwak*, the literal meaning of which refers to people with wooden boats.[8]

The old stories offer insights into how these big wooden boats attracted attention in earliest times. European ships sometimes got stranded, driven ashore by rough seas and high tide. Louis Bird tells a story of how some Omushkego people made their first contact with newcomers. A ship became grounded on Akimiski Island in James Bay, and when the people cautiously approached, the sailors clearly were asking for help to haul the ship back to the water. They all prepared a channel and rollers and refloated the ship when a high tide came with the next full moon, and the people received some of their first European goods in thanks for their help. This memorable occurrence may well date back to the 1600s, although it is impossible to link it with a specific ship or time – which in any case is not the point of the Omushkego narrative. The story has been retold over three hundred or more years to explain what a first meeting with these men in a strange wooden vessel was like, how some of the first new goods arrived, and also how some Omushkegowak found ways to deal peacefully with strangers in ways that expressed their own values (caution, circumspection, and finding means to set up a reciprocal relationship).[9]

"James his Baye": Early Imprints on Omushkego Spaces and English Maps

In the early 1600s, in and around James Bay, the wooden-boat sailing men were in fact English. And just as the Omushkegowak were observing and naming the new arrivals, so the first English explorers and mapmakers began naming *Winni-peg* and the Aboriginal lands and waters around it in accord with their own values and priorities. The first two English expeditions to winter in James Bay left traces not only on the land (and probably in Omushkego memories) but also on maps. Although Henry Hudson and Thomas James failed in their goals to find a Northwest Passage around North America to Asia, their travels permanently imprinted their respective

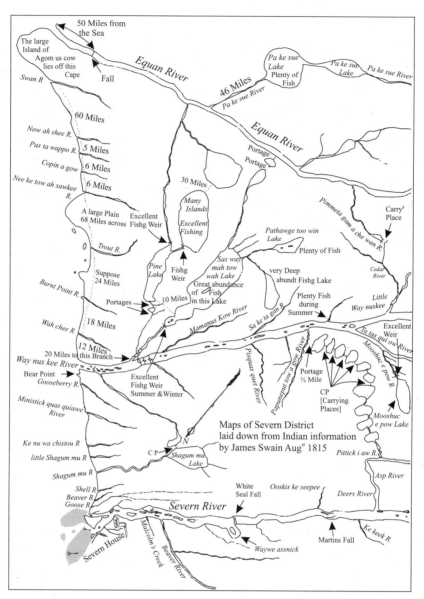

Map 2.2   Map of the Severn River Region of Hudson Bay, originally drawn by James Swain in 1815. The inland waterway details and notes on portages ("CP" and "carrying place") and fish resources indicate how readily Cree people travelled among the rivers and lakes, avoiding the storms and tides of Hudson Bay, the "Dirty Sea."

Source: Redrawn by Ted Binnema, with transcriptions by Anne Lindsay, Jennifer S.H. Brown, and Ted Binnema. The original map is in HBCA G.1/34.

surnames, originally in possessive form (Hudson's Bay, James his Baye) on maps of northern North America.[10]

The tragic fate of Henry Hudson and some of his crew, set adrift on James Bay after a mutiny on his ship, is well known in English histories, as is his meeting with a lone Cree man in the spring of 1611. Although more famous than Thomas James, Hudson left a slim legacy of English place names in Hudson Bay and James Bay compared to that of James, who wintered on Charlton Island in James Bay twenty years later. James never met or saw an Aboriginal person during that year, although his expedition and its tracks must have been observed; but his nominal traces on maps are numerous. Over a dozen place names that he assigned in honour of royalty, expedition sponsors, and his home area of Bristol and south Wales made it onto his and other charts of the region, some for a time and others permanently.

The names that James chose, like those of other European explorers, sometimes expressed nostalgia for home but often had a strong colonizing and appropriative tenor. They contrast strikingly with indigenous names, which typically encode key local features that serve as essential visual cues for travellers. On 20 August 1631, James named the whole southwestern Hudson Bay coastal region rather vaguely as "the new Principality of South Wales," or, on his map, "New South Wales," a territorial creation that complemented fellow Welshman Thomas Button's 1612-13 designation of the upper west coast as "New Wales."[11] These names were eventually subsumed under "Rupert's Land." Then on 26 August, coasting along western Hudson Bay, James reached the mouth of a large river whose spreading estuary reminded him of home; he named it the New Severn after the river that flows through Bristol, England. The Omushkego name for it is *Washahoe-wi-zi-pi*, "big bay river." Both James and the Omushkegowak were impressed by its size near its mouth; James' name evoked the river that flowed through his home city, while the Cree name points to the distinguishing feature of the river itself.

James' next major landfall was the cape that marks the entrance to western James Bay. He named it after royalty – the queen of King Charles I. On 3 September 1631, he wrote, "we knew we were at a Cape Land, and named it Cape Henrietta Maria, by her Majesties name, who had before named our Ship."[12] The Omushkego name again offers contrast: *Ki-ni-ki-moo-sha-wow* signifies "barren or treeless headland" and provides a concrete image of the place. Cree speakers retain that name when speaking their own language, although in English they use the English name. As with many of these toponyms, English-speakers (Aboriginal or not) need to make an effort to learn the persisting Native names, which are not translations but distinct terms that are functional for Aboriginal life and travel and expressive of connections with places.[13]

Continuing south, "in a most miserable distresse, in this so unknowne a place," James then came upon a large island, which he christened after another patron: "my Lord Westons Iland."[14] This was Akimiski Island, whose Cree name has endured despite a series of English renamings from James onwards. It means "the land across," so named because it is a large presence when viewed from the mainland across a channel. It is a traditional destination for hunting caribou and waterfowl.[15]

From Akimiski, James continued on to what became his wintering place for 1631-32, Charlton Island. Its English name derives from the small habitation that James and his men built for their shelter and named Charles Town, after King Charles I. In eastern Cree, its name, like Akimiski, reflects a view from the mainland and is probably the same word: *Kaamischii*, or roughly, "island across the sea." But in this instance, the English name won the contest for recognition, probably because the HBC later used the island as a depot for many years, whereas Akimiski remained a seasonal Cree hunting domain.[16]

The names left on maps in the wake of Thomas James' voyage of 1631-32 were more than honorifics and evocations of home. They arose from a literate sea captain's deliberate choices on particular occasions, recorded in a ship's log and in memoirs with a view to making history. Paul Carter, in his studies of Australian exploration, expresses the point well: "By the act of place-naming, space is transformed symbolically into a place, that is, a space with a history. And, by the same token, the namer inscribes his passage permanently on the world, making a metaphorical word-place which others may one day inhabit and by which, in the meantime, he asserts his own place in history."[17] It is safe to say that James, intent on making history and never meeting a local resident, never imagined that these places already had names. Likewise, Omushkego people learned only much later that the strangers in wooden boats had imposed foreign monikers on their places and on maps, tending to erase local descriptive names that had meaning and practical value for them as well as being embedded in stories and long community associations.[18]

Nituskeenan and Rupert's Land: Whose Land?

As noted, Omushkego place names tend to be concrete and specific, focused on such features as rivers, capes, and islands; there was never any call for naming (or defining) broad territorial entities such as "New South Wales." Similarly with "Rupert's Land": there is no ready way to translate that name or concept into Cree. Louis Bird has made interesting comments on this subject. Growing up on Hudson Bay, he had never heard the name "Rupert's Land" until some years ago when talking with a young surveyor about the history of the region. When we talked about how to express the concept of this huge watershed in Cree, he suggested, after some consideration, two terms. One refers to the land sloping down, *ka-i-shi-chi-wa-ki-si-pi-ya*, and the other evokes lands where the waters run down, *shik-ka-shi-muk*.[19] But Cree people did not name large geographical entities if names were not useful or meaningful to travellers or others on the ground. Northern Aboriginal people were also not in the early-modern European business of filing claims and counter-claims to large territories they scarcely knew or naming lands as possessed by or in honour of an individual.

The question of possession presents not only historical issues but also some fundamental translation problems when we move from English to Cree. Cree and other Algonquian languages have two varieties of "we" and "our," inclusive and exclusive, depending on to whom one is talking. Keith Goulet, a Cree from Cumberland House, Saskatchewan, has compared Cree ways of speaking about land to European usages. He cites the term *kituskeenuw*, "our land," as "one of the most important concepts in the Cree Nehinuw language." It is inclusive in the sense that it covers the lakes and rivers on the land that a community occupies and over which its people claim some shared authority. But it is also inclusive grammatically: a speaker using this form of "our," the prefix *ki-*, is including all the persons he or she is addressing. It would be the term used by a Cree speaking to other Cree people using and occupying that land. Cree usage is different, however, if one is speaking to outsiders; here, the exclusive "our," with the prefix *ni-*, is correct: *nituskeenan*. Cree speakers would have used this term in speaking of land to, say, explorers and fur traders; their reference group would have included only their own people.[20] It is doubtful that the Europeans they met had any grasp of these grammatical nuances or of the understandings that could be lost in translation.

These possessive markers, whether inclusive or exclusive, do not define a bounded or enclosed space or outright ownership in European terms; rather, they allude to the lands and waters that people know and use, radiating out from their core settlements and camping spots. The Cree of "Cumberland House" (an HBC name that arrived in 1774), for example, have long called their core settlement near that spot *Kaministigo-minuhigoskak*, or Spruce Island. It was their major traditional summer gathering place, and *kituskeenuw* in that context would be the familiar lands and wintering grounds that they used in that area. Goulet also contrasts the non-possessive root form *uskee* (land) in these words with another term, *uskeegan*, "land that has been divided up and parceled off." *Uskeegan*, a term much needed once the newcomers settled in, refers to any land that has been surveyed or fenced, made private, by the drawing of lines on maps or on the ground. The suffix, *-gan*, denotes artificiality, or something that is substituted, as opposed to what is real or genuine. A parallel example is *ogimagan* (substitute or artificial leader), which is the standard word for a treaty or Indian Affairs chief, as opposed to *ogimaw*, a real chief.[21]

In light of these insights, was Rupert's Land the first *nituskeegan* in north-western North America, representing the first European effort in the region to create a bounded proprietary entity? Yes, in the sense that it was a colonial construct, a territory called into being along with the HBC through a royal fiat of 1670. But no, in the sense that, as of 1670, it was not clearly bounded or "parceled off" by lines on maps or on the ground, or in the HBC royal charter itself: that process really began with the Canadian surveyors and treaty commissioners of the 1870s. In modern times, mapmakers have no trouble defining it: they simply trace the heights of land around the Hudson Bay watershed. The authors and signers of the charter, however, not only lacked knowledge of the North American continental interior, they even lacked the term and concept of "watershed," a word that, according to the *Oxford English Dictionary*, did not enter the language until 1803. Accordingly, their text struggled with defining this new territory.

Conferred by King Charles II, the HBC charter of 2 May 1670 named its prime grantee as "Our Deare and entirely Beloved Cousin Prince Rupert Count Palatyne of the Rhyne Duke of Bavaria and Cumberland &c." Prince Rupert and his fellow "Adventurers" received rights to "the sole Trade and Commerce of all those Seas Streightes Bayes Rivers Lakes Creekes and Soundes ... that lye within the entrance of the Streightes commonly called Hudsons Streightes together with all the Landes Countryes and Territoryes upon the Coastes and Confynes of the Seas Streightes Bayes Lakes Rivers Creekes and Soundes aforesaid which are not now actually possessed by any of our Subjectes or by the Subjectes of any other Christian Prince or State." The charter further declared "that the said Land bee from henceforth reckoned and reputed as one of our Plantacions or Colonyes in America called *Ruperts Land*."[22] But it had, at the time, no words to express where the borders of this land might lie.

Germaine Warkentin has described Rupert's Land as "a concept as much as a place," a "great unimagined space" with "vague immense boundaries."[23] Her description seems apt; in fact, the charter's broad allusion to the lands along the coasts and confines of Hudson Bay and connecting waterways could be compared in its fluidity to the open-ended Cree concept of land described by Keith Goulet above. The attitudes underpinning the charter, however, were significantly different. The text also named Prince Rupert and his seventeen fellow "Adventurers" (investors) "the true and absolute Lordes and Proprietors of the same Territory lymittes and places aforesaid,"[24] however defined. And Rupert's Land, at the end of its existence in the 1870s, did become defined by borders and lines on maps; the surveyors who arrived with its annexation to Canada in 1870 converted vast portions of the watershed to *nituskeegan*. At that time, as for wooden ships and treaty chiefs, the Cree found they needed a new form of an old word to express a foreign concept.

Crosses and Habitations: Gestures of Possession

Both before and after 1670, the English left certain kinds of markers to mark their arrival and presence in local settings around Hudson Bay, as in other parts of the world where they claimed possession. Patricia Seed has highlighted the English habit of making de facto claims by building houses and fences; their small settlements declared possession by deeds rather than words, with much less public ceremony than was practised by their French and Spanish rivals. The English and French both erected crosses or plaques, but the English did so with little fanfare, and usually with no indigenous audience to witness their claim, whereas the French from Jacques Cartier on placed great value on the presence of indigenous audiences and appearances of assent.[25]

English installations of crosses are attested from the expeditions of Thomas Button, Luke Foxe, and Thomas James in search of the Northwest Passage, although none are mentioned in surviving records of the Henry Hudson voyage. In 1612-13, Button led an expedition to seek the Passage and also to try to learn the fate of Hudson. He wintered at the mouth of the Nelson River, which he named after his ship's master who died there. Button's journal has been lost, but when Captain Luke Foxe visited the site in August 1631, he found a cross that Button had evidently erected as a sign of possession. Foxe recorded: "I caused the Crosse which we found to be newly raised, and this inscription of lead nailed thereon: 'I suppose this Crosse was first erected by Sir Thomas Button, 1613. It was again raised by Luke Foxe, Captain of the Charles, in the right and possession of my dread Soveraigne Charles the first, King of Great Brittaine, France and Ireland, Defender of the Faith, the 15 of August, 1631.'"[26]

Captain Thomas James, whose renaming practices were noted above, expressed claims to the land through building and naming his winter settlement of "Charles Town," on Charlton Island, in 1631. But he also used crosses for two other more explicit gestures. On 24 June 1632, before leaving Charlton Island, he made a cross from "a very high tree" and fastened to it pictures of King Charles I and Queen Henrietta Maria, "drawne to the life and doubly wrapped in lead," and the arms of the king and of the city of Bristol, along with a shilling and sixpence. He and his men then "raised it on the top of the bare Hill where we had buried our dead fellows [three men who had died during the winter]; formally by this ceremony, taking possession of these Territories to his Majesties use." Then, heading out of James Bay, they landed at Cape Henrietta Maria on 22 July. Here, too, a cross was fitted out with the arms of the king and the city of Bristol and erected "upon the most eminent place";[27] the weary expedition then limped home to Bristol. In none of these instances did local people show themselves to observe or express their views, although Foxe and James sensed the likely proximity of the "Salvages." As Foxe wrote, "It cannot be thought also but that we were seene by them, although they were not seene by any of us ... and although they might see us, whether they durst come or no, I know not, having, as I suppose, never seene ship in their lives before."[28]

In 1633, Thomas James published a vivid account of his arduous voyage, entitled, in part, *The Strange and Dangerous Voyage of Captaine Thomas James, in his Intended Discovery of the Northwest Passage into the South Sea wherein the Miseries Indured, Both Going, Wintering, Returning ... are Related.* This dramatic narrative of his hardships and the failures of James and his rival seeker, Luke Foxe, to find the Northwest Passage discouraged further Hudson Bay expeditions for almost another four decades.

A Little House on the Rupert River: HBC Beginnings

In 1668, a new phase of English enterprise began around the "dirty sea." In the summer of that year, the men who were to found the Hudson's Bay Company sent two ships to trade in James Bay, each carrying one of the French instigators of the enterprise. A storm forced the *Eaglet*, with Pierre Radisson aboard, to turn back, but the *Nonsuch*, with Zachariah Gillam as captain and carrying Médard Chouart, Sieur Des Groseilliers, landed at the mouth of the Rupert River. The men built a house to winter in, which they called Charles Fort after their king. Radisson later wrote that they built "upon the ruines of a House which had been built there above 60 yeares before by the English";[29] these were almost surely the remains of Henry Hudson's wintering house of 1610-11. The word of the new arrivals spread quickly, for in the spring of 1669 they had a highly successful trade with about three hundred Cree people and sailed home with a rich supply of furs.

In the fall of 1670, equipped with their new HBC charter, the traders returned to Charles Fort, which served as their base in southeastern James Bay until the French destroyed it in 1693. In 1776, the company rebuilt on the site, starting with what was described as a "log tent." The new post, called Rupert House, thereafter became one of the more important and long-lived fur trade settlements on James Bay. In current usage, the settlement is known as Waskaganish and the name is translated as "little house."[30] Cree speakers also apply this name to the Rupert River. It is a simplified version of the Cree term *Waskahiganish* and may possibly date from Henry Hudson's time or from the building of Charles Fort in 1668; the use of the name was probably reinforced by the appearance of the log tent in 1776. The translation has been simplified as the Cree would not have had the European concept of "house."

Brian Craik observes that *waska* means "confined to a certain area," while *higan* signifies an instrument or means of doing something and *-ish* is a diminutive: hence, in sum, the term signifies a means of enclosing or confining a small space with walls. He adds, "I believe that this word was created when the Crees first saw that the European houses, unlike their own, allowed for people to move around more and had spaces devoted to different tasks that were quite separated from one another."[31] The Cree name, more descriptive and far less pretentious than the royal names invoked by the HBC, seems to grasp key features of the carpentered world of the English: their squared, enclosed, rigid structures, with parts walled off from one another and from outsiders. Compared to the round and flexible forms of Cree dwellings and their open interiors, such buildings were as novel to the local residents as were the timbered ships that brought their creators.

The Cree of the Rupert River area maintained long oral traditions, reinforced by place names, about their early contacts with the English. But "first contacts" repeated themselves as new strangers on both sides met each other and reflected on the event. The old stories might receive various interpretations, even in one HBC instance, from the same person. Andrew Graham was a prolific writer and observer who wrote at two different times about a Cree story he heard about first contacts around the Rupert River. In 1775, he wrote simply that the Cree in that area "were the first people who saw Europeans in the Bay and we have heard them relate the arrival of the first Ships as deliver'd to them by the tradition of their ancestors."[32] Francis and Morantz read this statement as referring to the building of Charles Fort in 1668.[33] Graham, however, later rewrote and elaborated on various of his "Observations." In 1791, he changed this sentence, declaring that these Cree "were the first people who saw and traded with Europeans in Hudson's Bay; and they relate the arrival and wintering of the unfortunate Captain Henry Hudson, as handed down to them by the tradition of their ancestors."[34] Hudson and his men, as noted, did leave a house on the landscape at Rupert River. They met no Native people during their sojourn (although they probably were observed), except for one Cree who traded a few goods in the spring of 1611, and certainly the Cree had no occasion to learn or remember Hudson's name. But in 1791, Graham was interpolating material into his narrative (and possibly he had heard something about the old house remains). He may have thought to enhance interest by projecting into his text a name known to the English but not to the Cree. The injection of "Hudson" also served as an implicit reminder that the English had frequented and claimed Hudson Bay for nearly two centuries.

Such reminders were not much needed in 1791. But one century earlier, they had assumed tremendous importance for the English and for the HBC. A look at English and French naming and claiming in the 1670s and 1680s reveals the disjunctions between the two contending European powers and the much deeper and largely unarticulated disjunctions between European and Cree values and understandings about land and possessions, about Rupert's Land and *nituskeenan*. Rupert's Land presented serious problems of definition for both the English and for their French rivals because its edges and most of its interior were unmapped, unmarked, and ambiguous. No boundary markers informed the Canadian French explorers and traders when they were entering Rupert's Land or the English when they were leaving it. Nor could mapmakers give much help; as HBC governor John Nixon commented in the 1670s, "our patent is verry darke in that it is not bounded with any line of latitude or longitude."[35] European names that got printed on published maps, crosses, plaques, and European structures or settlements, however modest they were (the HBC *waskahiganish* impressed the Cree as small even if it was novel), therefore assumed grand importance as means of claiming dominion.

A Great House, Moose River, and Strong Current: The Second Decade

After Charles Fort, the HBC made three other major efforts to settle in the Bay in the 1670s. Its founding stories somewhat amplify the picture of HBC-Cree relations, or lack thereof, in the company's first decade. HBC settlement at and around Port Nelson (the name derived from Thomas Button's ship captain) did not stabilize at the site of what became York Factory for some time. But a first effort was made in September 1670, when Governor Charles Bayly and several men landed near the mouth of the Nelson River. Meeting no local people, they spent a night "in an Indian Tent, they found there ... and the next day the said Governor Baily ... took possession of Port Nelson and all the Lands and Territoryes thereof, for his Ma[jest]ie, and in tocken thereof nayld up the King's Armes in Brasse on a small Tree there, and afterwards returned on board againe." Almost immediately, his ship was driven out of the river by a storm. Finding it impossible to return, the HBC men decided to sail to Rupert House. The company made no further real effort to settle there until the fall of 1682, by which time interlopers from New England, and Radisson and Des Groseilliers (now on the French side), were also settling in; seven different short-lived posts were built in the vicinity in the next five years.[36]

In 1684, on the north side of the Hayes River, just south of the mouth of the Nelson River, the HBC established the post that became York Fort, named after James, Duke of York, governor of the company from 1683 (following the death of Prince Rupert) to 1685, when he succeeded to the throne on the death of King Charles II. Its growing size and prominence compared to other more transitory posts is expressed in its Cree name, *Kihci-waskahikan*, or great house, a contrast to *Waskahiganish*, the little house at Rupert River.[37]

Two other posts of eventual significance date to this decade. Charles Bayly, the HBC's first overseas governor, oversaw the beginning of trade on Moose River, where a small house was built in the summer of 1673. That summer, according to E.E. Rich, "A treaty was made with the Indians, giving the English trading rights and possession of the soil."[38] Moose Fort (later "Factory") was the only major HBC post to retain a Cree name, derived from the name of the river.

At the new post, Governor Bayly met people he called "Shechittawams," who had come fifty leagues to trade. In July 1674, he travelled up the coast and briefly visited their home river, variously spelled Schettawam, Chichewan, or Chechechewan, renderings of the Cree name *kisechiwun*, "strong current."[39] Here he "treated with the King, and his Son made them a Promise to come with a Ship and trade with them the next Year"; in turn, the Indians promised "Store of Beaver, and bring the *Upland* Indians down." Details are scant, but the company had a building there by 1679.[40] The company renamed the post Albany Fort in 1683, in honour of the HBC governor's secondary title – James, Duke of York and Albany – the latter being an old name for the region of Scotland north of the firths of Clyde and Forth. John Nixon, who, in 1680, succeeded Bayly as governor in the Bay, worked to cultivate trade there, although he was frustrated at being stationed at the company's depot on Charlton Island in James Bay, isolated from the mainland and river-travelling Cree. His report of 1782 recorded his visit to "Chechecheawan" in the summer of 1681 and how he "stopped 4000 skins that was a going away, for want of goods to purchase them, and for want of victuals to mentaine them till the goods came, which I prevented in good time." Logistical problems were endemic: while he was at Chechewan, "there came doune ane ould Indian, that never sawe yeuropians before, the discreetest salvage that ever I heard. Which promised me to come doun this summer [1682] with ane hundered Cannow's to trade, but oh my grief that I am not there to encourage him, and to treate him. For want thereof, and men and goods in the factorie."[41] The company struggled to maintain a presence there, as at Charles Fort and Moose Fort, but in 1686, the French under the Chevalier de Troyes captured Charles Fort, Moose Fort, and Albany, and the most severe period of competition was under way.[42]

Leagues of Friendship and Tallies of Wood

The English-French contest, both diplomatic and military, over Hudson Bay was intense from the early 1680s until the Treaty of Utrecht, in 1713, asserted English dominion over the Bay. Verbal claims and counter-claims intensified as forts were attacked and prisoners taken. Both sides embellished and enlarged upon their previous acts of possession in this adversarial correspondence, and, in doing so, they helpfully generated documents that richly reveal their values and assumptions about such acts and their significance. For example, James Hayes, deputy governor of the HBC, responded to French claims in January 1683 with a letter addressed to King Charles II. He stated that the king's subjects, unlike the French, "have for above 100 yeares last past Discovered and frequented the said Bay & the Rivers Islands & Territorys thereabouts and from time to time in the reignes of severall of your Royall Predecessors have taken possession of severall places there."[43] He then declared that Captain Zachary Gillam of the *Nonsuch*, on the 1668 expedition to Rupert River, having "met with the Native Indians & having made a league of Friendship wth. the Capt. of the said River & firmely purchased both the river it selfe & the Lands there aboute, he gave it the name of Rupert River ... and built [Charles] Fort, & tooke possession of the said River & all the Land & Territory there aboute in the name of your Majesty."[44] This account tells us very little about Gillam's actual proceedings and certainly does not convey Cree perspectives on the event. But it does suggest an effort to build ties with real people – unlike the earlier raisings of crosses by Button, Foxe, and James. We have no clue about Gillam's "purchase price," but here, as in the following two centuries elsewhere in North America, the English newcomers gave implied recognition to Indian land entitlement through their efforts to extinguish it.

The instructions given to Captain Gillam have not survived, but those given by the HBC in the 1680s do outline the steps its traders were to take to secure the company's proprietary rights as it established various other posts in the Bay. In May 1680, the London Committee instructed Governor John Nixon to forestall French incursions by taking possession of Port Nelson and New Severn (later the approximate locations of York Factory and Fort Severn) and also of any other rivers and harbours on either side of the Bay that were likely to serve the "designs of our Enemies." In all places where Nixon settled, he was to "contrive to make compact wth. the Captns. or chiefs of the respective Rivers & places, whereby it might be understood by them that you had purchased both the lands & rivers of them, or at least the only freedome of trade [an ambiguous phrasing]." Further, he was to "cause them to do some act wch. by the Religion or Custome of their Country should be thought most sacred & obliging to them for the confirmation of such Agreements." Similar instructions were given to those in charge of establishing posts in 1682 and 1683.[45] The records do not tell us what acts the Cree considered "most sacred & obliging." But the London Committee, for its part, made an interesting choice, devising a secular ritual borrowed from a method sometimes used to make binding contracts in England. A postscript to the instructions of May 1680 spelled out in more detail what John Nixon was to do with all the Indians he met to "ascertain to us all liberty of trade & commerce and a league of friendship & peaceable cohabitation":

So wee have caused Iron marks to be made of the figure of the Union Flagg, wth. wch. wee would have you to burn [brand] Tallys of wood wth. such ceremony as they shall understand to be obligatory & sacred, The manner whereof wee must leave to your prudence as you shall find the modes & humours of the people you deal with, But when the Impression is made, you are to write upon the Tally the name of the Nation or person wth.

whom the Contract is made and the date thereof, and then deliver one part of the Stick to them, and reserve the other. This wee suppose may be sutable to the capacities of those barbarous people, and may much conduce to our quiet & commerce, and secure us from foreign or domestick pretenders.[46]

When the English compiled and recited their discoveries and acts of possession on the Bay, the French replied with claims going back to the time of Cartier and Champlain. For example, an edict of King Francis I in 1540 authorized the Sieur de Roberval "to take possession of all the Lands which the said King had caused to bee Discovered [by Verrazzano and Cartier] ... in which Comission the Bay on the North of Canada Since called Hudson is included." After citing other royal edicts, "The French Answere to the English Title to Hudson's Bay" (1687) asserted that, in 1661, Indians from the Bay "came expressly to Quebeck to confirme that they would Continue to live under the Dominion of the French and to desire a Missionary." In 1663, a Monsr. Couture and five men went to James Bay "pursuant to the Desire of the Indians"; he "Caused a New Crosse to bee affixed on the Lands at the Bottome of the Bay, and the Kings Armes Ingraven upon Copper fixed betweene two peeces of Lead at the Bottome of a Greate Tree." Further, when the French gathered "all the Nations for above 100 Leagues round" at Sault Ste. Marie in 1671, and M. de St-Lusson erected a cross and the king's arms, the lands of which he took possession were said to include all those to the north "and of the Bay of Hudson."[47]

In 1671-72, Father Albanel, a Jesuit priest, and Paul Denis, Sieur de St-Simon travelled down the Nemiskau, or Fish River (adjacent to or sometimes confused with the Rupert River), to "where the savages doe ordinarily assemble to Sell their Furrs." St-Simon noted the unimposing appearance of Charles Fort; as no HBC expedition came that year, its two houses, built of upright logs and thatched roofs, were unoccupied, lacked windows and doors, and were in disrepair. Exploring along the Bay, the Frenchmen found a Cree encampment. There, they "planted a Crosse and left the Kings Armes upon a Tree by Consent of Capt. Kias Kow cheife of all the Savages which Inhabite the North Sea & Hudson's Bay," a grand claim indeed as no Cree leader would have claimed such vast authority.[48]

The English in turn rebutted the French claims over such vast regions and noted that the French had scarcely or never visited most of the Hudson Bay area. The naming of places was among the issues raised. The English rightly pointed out that, even on French maps of the Bay, the English place names introduced by Button, James, and others predominated.[49] Although each party could point to the slender presence of the other, the English observed that no French claimants had ever settled in the Bay until Pierre Radisson, on their behalf, preempted the HBC post at Port Nelson in 1682.

Established Rights and a Pipe of Tobacco

In May 1687, Thomas Pinfold, a judge writing on behalf of the HBC, went a step further in its defence than had previous protagonists. He argued that the English, having priority in claiming possession, did not have to settle everywhere to secure their dominion: "The English possessing the Bay and Streights, it's not necessary that a particular factory bee settled in every River and Creeke in order to give a Title to the whole, noe more then the possessing of every particular Spott of Ground in Virginia or New England ... is requisite to give his Ma[jes]tie. a Title to the said plantation, for it's Sufficient to exclude any other Prince by possessing any One part." As for "How farr the rightfull Occupant of any river and Shore in an infidel Country may Clayme the District and Lymitts of such possession," Pinfold wrote, "The Rightfull Occupant of a River or Shore hath right soe far into the countrey until they meete with the confines of some other Prince."[50]

Pinfold's statement of claim went beyond the language used by the HBC men of the 1670s and 1680s, invoking, as a given, the right of Christians and their princes to claim an "infidel Country." This took the argument into a domain familiar to the French, the concept of terra nullius, or territory considered "unoccupied" because its people were migratory and not subject to a Christian ruler.[51] This line of thinking raises a question about what standing the HBC agreements with Aboriginal people – tallies of wood and the like – actually had in English (or French) legal and political discourse of the time. The HBC London Committee and its men in the Bay seemed to take them seriously. Committee instructions, as seen above, firmly directed HBC traders to carry out acts of purchase, and the early HBC governors, Charles Bayly and John Nixon, knew that their success relied on building and legitimizing their relationships with Aboriginal trading partners. But Pinfold implicitly dismissed the existence of an Aboriginal land right (and, hence, of any need for purchase): "infidels" lacked such a right.

In the same year, 1687, Richard Graham, Viscount Preston, a privy councillor and envoy extraordinary to the Court of France during the 1680s, went further, granting no validity to any agreement (French, in this instance) made with Aboriginal people or to rights claimed on that basis. Not only were the Natives unreliable, but their acts were, in any case, ineffectual in the face of established claims: "All that are acquainted with the nature of the Indians well know their wandring and variable Dispositions and it is easy to produce on his [French] Ma[jes]ties. part Submissions & Capitulations of those People. Which doe very much Effect the French Intrest & pretentions in those parts but it is enough to say that noe action or Resolution of those Savages can Alter an Established right."[52]

In 1699, Pierre Radisson, back in England again and lending support to the HBC in its arguments with the French, was also critical of the import of agreements with Aboriginal people, but without invoking established right.

In a rather cynical vein, he wrote of the "Savages" that, "as to their Acknowledging the Sovereignty they have no More than a propriety for [desire to possess?] the presents they have need of [and] would give themselves up this day to God if they had Knowledge of him and tomorrow they would give themselves to the Devil for a pipe of Tobacco and they would even deliver up their Inheritance for the like things. And they received at each place where the English have been Settled theire presents for takeing Possession whosoever hath known those Savage Nations doth understand the Same things."[53] This is a different line of argument from that of Pinfold or Preston. Radisson did not say that Natives lacked rights; rather, he suggested that they did not acknowledge (or understand?) the Europeans' acts of taking territorial possession and that they simply chose to gain the best material return that they could on these occasions. But he overlooked or chose to ignore, in this passage, the Native understandings about reciprocities that could be inferred from his words. The Cree, in accepting "presents," were establishing a relationship in their terms. If they did not acknowledge European notions of dominion over territory, their acceptance of gifts would still express, from their perspective, a giving of permission for the HBC traders to settle, build a post, and share resources. Further, Radisson's remark about "a pipe of tobacco" sidestepped the meanings that the smoking of the pipe probably had in such meetings. We cannot be certain about its significance for the Cree at the various HBC posts in the late 1600, but forty-four years after Radisson's comment, James Isham at York Fort wrote at length about the importance of the pipe, or calumet, ceremony in conducting trade at York Fort.[54] Pipe smoking at ceremonial gatherings usually had both spiritual and social significance, establishing or reaffirming mutual bonds of trust and responsibility, even if not as elaborated as in Isham's descriptions at York.

The verbal contests between the English and French in the late 1600s generated documents that articulated ways of thinking on both sides as the parties were obliged to defend their positions and explain their actions and assumptions. Unsurprisingly for this early period, the English, at least, did not have a fully developed or consistent position or consensus on issues of land rights and claims. The HBC, working from a common-law or common-sense perspective, took the view that some act of purchase or treaty was called for: hence, for example, its introduction of tallies of wood that could be used to certify a kind of contract. For their part, judges and diplomats invoked the right of Christian princes to appropriate infidel lands without consent, on the basis of formal gestures of possession. And then there was Radisson, who, independent from the rest, seemed to dismiss such agreements on two counts. First, he said, the "Savage Nations" did not acknowledge European sovereignty (whether because they resisted it or could not even fathom the concept). Second, and perhaps jaundiced by a life of fur trade bargaining, Radisson asserted that Aboriginal people simply used occasions of "takeing Possession" to take what presents they could get. In both these instances, treaties would be amiable but meaningless instruments, if for different reasons.

Contestations and Conversations Continued

The early agreements made between the HBC and the Aboriginal people around Hudson Bay ultimately did not gain standing as binding treaties that either recognized or extinguished Aboriginal land titles. Yet, in acknowledging an Aboriginal interest that required attention, they did begin to present that potentiality during the heated debates of the late 1600s over claims to Rupert's Land. The adversarial exchanges between the English and French read remarkably like harbingers of modern court cases over treaty issues and land claims, except that the contesting parties were both European and Aboriginal voices were absent. Also, of course, those who spoke for the plaintiffs and defendants of the 1600s did not yet include witnesses who were "expert" in the sense of providing the court "with knowledge that lies beyond the realm of ordinary judgment and experience ... to serve the court rather than act as an advocate for one of the litigants."[55] But they were steeped in developing contesting arguments about what constituted land title and possession, French versus English.

The Canadian numbered treaties that were negotiated from the 1870s onward papered most of Rupert's Land with formal documents in the name of Queen Victoria. But they left new legacies of ambiguity and contested understandings. Some old themes soon resurfaced, for example, in the legal disputes of the 1880s between the Canadian federal government and the Province of Ontario over the *St. Catherine's Milling* case and the issue of whether Aboriginal treaties constituted real cessions of land (implying recognition of a prior Aboriginal title) or gestures of friendship to keep the peace.[56] As A.J. Ray has noted, seventeenth-century English ideas about indigenous societies' lack of political organization and lack of legitimate claims to land have continued to influence contemporary legal and scholarly thinking.[57]

What has changed profoundly, however, is the extent to which Aboriginal voices are speaking and being heard. The *Delgamuukw* case, tried and lost in British Columbia in 1991 and then won in the Supreme Court of Canada in 1997, is the best known, setting precedents across the country and giving new weight to oral history testimonies. Many other cases on land and resource issues are ongoing. On 22 May 2003, seven James Bay Mushkegowuk Cree First Nations filed a lawsuit in the Ontario Superior Court of Justice "to find Canada accountable for promises made in 1869 and 1870 when Rupert's Land ... was transferred to Canada."[58] Their claim makes a number of valid points going back to the seventeenth century. First, in the HBC charter of 1670, Rupert's Land was "very vaguely described ... but did purport to include the Mushkegowuk Territory." Second, the charter "created no political or legal or governmental rights" over the Mushkegowuk nations (true enough, as indeed it did not mention indigenous peoples). Third, "at some point prior in time to 1867, the King or Queen of Great Britain claimed sovereignty over the lands and people of Mushkegowuk Territory," the people being "unaware at the time (whatever time it was) that such a claim was being made." The statement of claim points out: "The Plaintiffs are still unaware of when, how and on what basis that claim of sovereignty was made."[59]

Almost three centuries after the Treaty of Utrecht, 1713, conferred the Hudson Bay region on England, and almost three decades after A.J. Ray published *Indians in the Fur Trade* (1974), the Mushkegowuk and other Aboriginal people of the old colony of Rupert's Land are playing their part in the political and legal discourse of Canada and also in the writing and making of both their own and Canadian history. Skip Ray has been an important figure in getting the historical profession to listen and attend to those voices in fur trade history; as he has listened, Ray has taken a strong supporting role in making them heard in the courts as well as in history – a role he recently reviewed in his essay, "Native History on Trial: Confessions of an Expert Witness."[60]

The Aboriginal people, of course, have been there all along, speaking their languages, living in and using places that they named for their own purposes, observing and making choices about their relations with European newcomers, and developing vocabularies, concepts, and methods for dealing with the strangers and assimilating them into their own worlds. The HBC governors and London directors did not control or rule over Aboriginal peoples, despite the English statements of claim to their homelands and despite popular histories such as Peter C. Newman's, which refer endlessly to the HBC as "empire." Native peoples largely maintained their autonomy and self-governance throughout the history of Rupert's Land, quietly and without high visibility. As Keith Goulet put it, the land remained *kituskeenuw*, our land (*nituskeenan* to outsiders), even as the surveyors and treaty commissioners moved north and west laying out the lines and boundaries that imposed a new artificial landform, *uskeegan*. Louis Bird and others may express these ideas in different dialects of Cree or in other Aboriginal languages, but the concepts are there even if the words vary.

For all historians, the most fortunate aspect of the work and discourse of Louis Bird, Keith Goulet, and growing numbers of other Aboriginal thinkers is not only the fact that they are being heard but also the relatively new development that some real conversations are taking place between Aboriginal and non-Aboriginal scholars, students, and others who care about achieving the highest possible standards of mutual understanding and knowledge. A.J. Ray ends his essay on expert witnesses with a kind of charter for everyone working in these fields. We could wish the English and French protagonists of the seventeenth century had read and followed it; but it applies equally today for us all, whether in the courts or not: "In the face of all these challenges, it is clear that historical experts have to be guided by the highest ethical and professional standards to maintain their integrity and avoid becoming merely advocates who do 'courtroom history.'"[61]

Notes

1 Lynn Hunt et al.'s *The Making of the West: Peoples and Cultures*, vol. 1, *To 1740* (Boston: Bedford/St. Martin's, 2001), provides one of many examples: a map captioned "European Trade Patterns, c. 1740" (map 18, p. 648) demarcates a stretch around eastern and southern Hudson Bay and James Bay as a part of British North America, but the entire blank area westward from present-day Manitoba is anachronistically labelled "Canada."

2 Arthur J. Ray, *Indians in the Fur Trade: Their Role as Trappers, Hunters, and Middlemen in the Lands Southwest of Hudson Bay, 1660-1870*, was reprinted with a new introduction in 1998.

3 Victor Lytwyn, *Muskekowuck Athinuwick: Original People of the Great Swampy Land* (Winnipeg: University of Manitoba Press, 2002), 39, citing Kenneth Lister on radiocarbon dates from the Shamattawa River.

4 Ibid., 82-85.

5 Ibid., 12-15, lists the old local names. The term "Cree" is an abbreviated form of *kiristinon*, which the French recorded in the 1600s as the name of a little-known Algonquian group south of James Bay; the French broadened that term to include all Cree speakers (Pentland, "Synonymy [of Cree]," in *Handbook of North American Indians*, vol. 6, *Subarctic* [Washington, DC: Smithsonian Institution, 1981], 227).

6 Louis Bird, *Telling Our Stories: Omushkego Legends and Histories from Hudson Bay* (Peterborough, ON: Broadview Press, 2005), chap. 2.

7 Ibid., chaps. 5, 6. On Cree words and place names, see the Glossary of Cree Terms at the beginning of this book.

8 This etymology from linguist Douglas Ellis is cited by John S. Long, "Treaty No. 9 and Fur Trade Company Families: Northeastern Ontario's Halfbreeds, Indians, Petitioners and Metis," in *The New Peoples: Being and Becoming Métis in North America*, ed. Jacqueline Peterson and Jennifer S.H. Brown (Winnipeg: University of Manitoba Press, 1985), 162n62.

9 Bird, *Telling Our Stories*, chap. 5. The old Omushkego stories implicitly teach and reinforce values and worldview rather than laying them out prescriptively. The ship story does not answer outsiders' historical questions about who and when. Louis Bird noted in telling the story that, with hindsight, we know the newcomers were Europeans. But the Omushkegowak had no way of identifying their language or home country; the impression made by the strangers in association with their wooden vessels here and elsewhere could be epitomized in the new ethnonym, *wemistikosiwak*.

10 In 1625, English mapmaker Henry Briggs was the first to place the name "Hudson's Bay" on a map: see Derek Hayes, *Historical Atlas of the Arctic* (Vancouver: Douglas and McIntyre, 2003), 27, caption. "James his Baye" appeared on Thomas James' map of 1632. See Wayne K.D. Davies, *Writing Geographical Exploration: James and the Northwest Passage, 1631-33* (Calgary: University of Calgary Press, 2003), fig. 5.1.

11 Davies, *Writing Geographical Exploration*, 197, 202-3. On his map James converted Button's New Wales to "New North Wales" and inscribed it on the region northwest of present-day York Factory, Manitoba.

12 James in Miller Christy, ed., *The Voyages of Captain Luke Foxe of Hull, and Captain Thomas James of Bristol, in Search of a North-West Passage in 1631-32* (London: Hakluyt Society, 1894), 88-89:490.

13 Paul Carter, in *The Road to Botany Bay: An Exploration of Landscape and History* (Chicago: University of Chicago Press, 1989), 327, comments with reference to Australia on the

disjunctions between English and Aboriginal place names, and on the larger consequence of English linguistic dominance: "From the beginning of white occupation, the Aborigines were made to speak a language which was not theirs ... Consequently by a deadly irony, it is the attempt of the Aborigines to speak English which consigns them to historical silence."

14 Christy, *The Voyages*, 493.

15 Bird, *Telling Our Stories*, chapter 6.

16 On the Cree name for Charlton Island, thanks to Kreg Ettenger, e-mail communication, 24 January 2005. Lytwyn, *Muskekowuck Athinuwick*, 97, 153.

17 Carter, *The Road to Botany Bay*, xxiv.

18 This sort of disjunction is vividly evoked by the Dene in the book *Dehcho*: *"Mom, We've Been Discovered!"* (Yellowknife, NWT: Dene Cultural Institute, 1989) – *Dehcho* ("Great River") being the river that got renamed after Alexander Mackenzie "discovered" it in 1789.

19 Bird, personal communication, 28 September 2003.

20 Keith Goulet, "The Cumberland Cree Nehinuw Concept of Land," 3, 12, 18, paper presented at Indigenous Knowledge Systems Conference, Saskatoon, Saskatchewan, May 2004. Goulet, e-mail communication, 18 April 2006. This text follows his transcriptions of the Cree terms. Thanks also to David Pentland, e-mail communication, 17 November 2006, who has made the same points and included examples of this distinction from other Algonquian languages.

21 Goulet, "Cumberland Cree Nehinuw Concept," 17, 12.

22 E.E. Rich, ed., *Minutes of the Hudson's Bay Company, 1671-1674* (London: Champlain Society for the Hudson's Bay Record Society, 1942), 5:131-32.

23 Germaine Warkentin, ed., *Canadian Exploration Literature: An Anthology* (Toronto: Oxford University Press, 1993), xii.

24 E.E. Rich, ed., *Minutes of the Hudson's Bay Company, 1671-1674* (London, UK: Champlain Society for the Hudson's Bay Record Society, 1942), 5:139.

25 Patricia Seed, *Ceremonies of Possession in Europe's Conquest of the New World* (Cambridge: Cambridge University Press, 1998), chaps. 1, 2. On French concerns with Aboriginal responses and consent to ceremonial erecting of crosses, see the record of Jacques Cartier's meeting with Iroquoian leader Donnacona in 1534, in Ramsay Cook, ed., *The Voyages of Jacques Cartier* (Toronto: University of Toronto Press, 1993), 26-27, and the vivid accounts in the *Jesuit Relations* and elsewhere of the 1671 ceremony to claim the lands beyond Sault Ste. Marie.

26 Christy, *The Voyages*, 348.

27 Ibid., 559, 571.

28 Ibid., 336.

29 Grace Lee Nute, *Caesars of the Wilderness: Médard Chouart, Sieur des Groseilliers and Pierre Esprit Radisson, 1618-1710* (St. Paul: Minnesota Historical Society Press, 1978), 349.

30 Daniel Francis and Toby Morantz, *Partners in Furs: A History of the Fur Trade in Eastern James Bay, 1600-1870* (Montreal and Kingston: McGill-Queen's University Press, 1983), 22-24, 30; Richard Preston, *Cree Narrative: Expressing the Personal Meaning of Events*, 2nd ed. (Montreal and Kingston: McGill-Queen's University Press, 2002), 21.

31 Brian Craik, e-mail communication, 3 February 2005.

32 "Observations," 1775, E.E. Rich and A.M. Johnson, eds., *Copy-book of Letters Outward &c: Begins 29th May, 1680, ends 5 July, 1687* (Toronto: Champlain Society for the Hudson's Bay Record Society, 1948), 315.

33 Francis and Morantz, *Partners*, 33.

34 Glyndwr Williams, ed., *Andrew Graham's Observations on Hudson's Bay, 1767-1791* (London: Hudson's Bay Record Society, 1969), 204.

35 Quoted in Rich and Johnson, *Copy-book*, xxv.

36 Rich and Johnson, *Copy-book*, 363-64.

37 E.E. Rich, *History of the Hudson's Bay Company, 1670-1870* (London: Hudson's Bay Record Society, 1958), 1:105, 165; Flora Beardy and Robert Coutts, eds., *Voices from Hudson Bay: Cree Stories from York Factory* (Montreal and Kingston: McGill-Queen's University Press, 1996), xi.

38 Rich, ed., *Minutes ... 1671-1674*, 211. We lack the treaty's text and specific terms, if any.

39 Ibid.; Richard Faries, ed., *A Dictionary of the Cree Language* (Toronto: General Synod of the Church of England in Canada, 1938), 51. The Cree name survives in Kashechewan, the name of the modern community across the river from Fort Albany.

40 Rich and Johnson, *Copy-book*, 345-46.

41 Rich, *Minutes ... 1679-1684*, 281.

42 Rich and Johnson, *Copy-book*, 346-47.

43 The reference to "above 100 yeares last past" alludes to the voyages of Martin Frobisher to Baffin Island in the 1570s as well as to the visits of Hudson, Thomas Button, and others. On 19 July 1577, Frobisher and forty of his men climbed a high hill near the mouth of what became Frobisher Bay, "on the top whereof our men made a Columne or Crosse of stones heaped up togither in good sorte, and solempnely sounded a Trumpet, and said certaine prayers ... and honoured the place by the name of Mount Warwicke" after a noble patron. Some Inuit watched from a distance but did not participate (Robert McGhee, *The Arctic Voyages of Martin Frobisher* [Montreal and Kingston: McGill-Queen's University Press, 2001], 68, 31).

44 Rich and Johnson, *Copy-book*, 69-70.

45 Ibid., 6, 7, 9, 36, 79.

46 Ibid., 12-13. The London Committee minutes of 24 May 73 (Rich, ed., *Minutes ... 1679-1684*, 73) include a drawing of these "marks" showing the crosses of England and Scotland superposed (the focal motif of the "Union Flagg"); an order for iron stamps bearing these marks was placed on that day. From the 1400s to the 1600s in England, tallies of wood were used to record debts or payments, or as receipts. Notches marking the transactions were inscribed on a stick or rod, which was then split lengthwise, with each party retaining one half (*Oxford English Dictionary*). Presumably the tallies bearing the brand marks were to be split in a similar way. No record appears to survive either of the implementing of this procedure or of Cree responses to it.

47 Rich and Johnson, *Copy-book*, 275-78.

48 Nute, *Caesars*, 149; Rich and Johnson, *Copy-book*, 288.

49 Rich and Johnson, *Copy-book*, 297-99, 281.

50 Ibid., 257.

51 Cf. Olive P. Dickason, "Concepts of Sovereignty at the Time of First Contacts," in *The Law of Nations and the New World*, ed. L.C. Green and O.P. Dickason, 141-295 (Edmonton: University of Alberta Press, 1989).

52 Rich and Johnson, *Copy-book*, 292. In his *History of the Hudson's Bay Company* (*History*, 1:63), Rich misleadingly attributed this statement to the HBC.

53 Nute, *Caesars*, 348. E.E. Rich (*History*, 1:63) abbreviated this quotation, reducing intelligibility and providing no context. Thanks to Germaine Warkentin for directing me to the entire document ("The Narative of Mr Peter Espritt Radisson in Refferance to the Answar of the Commrs of France to the Right and Title of the Hudson Bay Company," probably written in 1699, and published in Appendix 12 in Nute, *Caesars*).

54 Rich and Johnson, *Copy-book*, 82-85.

55 A.J. Ray, "Native History on Trial: Confessions of an Expert Witness," *Canadian Historical Review* 84, 2 (2003): 254.

56 Olive P. Dickason, *Canada's First Nations: A History of Founding Peoples from Earliest Times* (Don Mills, ON: Oxford University Press, 2002), 323-26.

57 Ray, "Native History on Trial," 261-62.

58 Mushkegowuk Council, *Press Kit: Rupert's Land Protection Pledge Lawsuit* (Moose Factory, ON: Mushkegowuk Council, 2003). The press kit cites the ruling that, when Rupert's Land was transferred to Canada, it became "the duty of the [Canadian] government to make adequate provisions for the protection of the Indian tribes whose interests and well-being are involved in the transfer" (10).

59 Mushkegowuk Council, *Press Kit*, 6.

60 Ray, "Native History on Trial," 253-73.

61 Ibid., 273.

3

Echo of the Crane: Tracing Anishnawbek and Métis Title to Bawating (Sault Ste. Marie)

Victor P. Lytwyn

Canada's constitution recognizes the Métis as a people with Aboriginal rights, but the federal and provincial governments have been slow to accept any territorial or resource-harvesting rights that belong to them. A recent Supreme Court decision in the case known as *R. v. Powley* affirmed that the Métis of Sault Ste. Marie have constitutionally protected hunting rights. In the spring of 1998, Professor Arthur J. (Skip) Ray and I provided historical and geographical evidence relating to that case in a Sault Ste. Marie courtroom. That court case was won at the trial level and appealed all the way to the Supreme Court of Canada, which, in 2003, decided in favour of the Métis. As historical geographers, we were able to show that the relationship between the Métis and the land was critical to their existence as a distinct community. Professor Ray's evidence, in particular, was recognized as central to the finding that the Métis at Sault Ste. Marie constitute an Aboriginal community possessing the same hunting rights as neighbouring Anishnawbek First Nations. In that case, the government of Ontario argued strenuously against accepting that a Métis community even existed at Sault Ste. Marie. While the courts have spurred governments into negotiating resource-harvesting agreements with Métis leaders in Ontario, the issue of territorial rights remains untested. The Métis land base at Sault Ste. Marie has long disappeared, but the reasons for its demise have not been examined. This chapter reviews the origin and termination of the Métis settlement at Sault Ste. Marie.

Shortly after the arrival of Europeans, the fur trade in the Great Lakes region produced distinct communities of people from unions of men employed by fur companies and Aboriginal women. These communities usually developed in proximity to trading posts located at strategic places, such as portages and river mouths. Early English writers commonly described the people as "half-breeds" to denote their mixed ancestry. French terms such as "bois brulé" also conveyed this meaning, and the term "Métis" was employed mainly west of the Great Lakes but is currently used in many parts of North America.[1] One of the largest Métis communities was located at Sault Ste. Marie, along both sides of the narrows between Lake Superior and Lake Huron. The Anishnawbek, or original people, lived in close proximity to the Métis and shared their lands and resources with their mixed relatives.

Anishnawbek Origins at Sault Ste. Marie

The water of Lake Superior rushed into Lake Huron through a long cascade of rapids, known in the Anishnawbek language as *pawitiik*, or *Bawating*.[2] Anishnawbek oral tradition spoke of the origin of the rapids, an early French visitor explained: "The Indians tell a tale about this rapid. They say that it was once a beaver-dam, but one of their gods, called Michapoux, crushed it in as he crossed over it."[3] Bawating was one of the stopping places in their ancient westward migration. The *Otchichack,* or crane clan, was the first group of people to settle at the rapids and, along with the people of the catfish clan, occupied the area before the time of European contact.[4] A French census in 1736 enumerated thirty warriors at the rapids, organized into two "divisions" that possessed the crane and catfish "devices," or totemic symbols, of their clans.[5] Samuel de Champlain's 1632 map, based on Aboriginal information, depicted seven lodges on the north side of the rapids. When French fur traders and missionaries arrived in the region in 1642, they called the people "Saulteurs," after the rapids, and the Jesuit mission gave the place its French name of Sault Ste. Marie. English writers preferred the name Chippewa, or Ojibwa, to describe the people, and the latter term is commonly used in Canadian literature.

The rapids that constricted the waterway between Lake Superior and Lake Huron also provided a strategic geographical advantage to the Sault Ste. Marie Ojibwa. The Jesuits reported that they acted like gatekeepers, whose permission was needed in order to pass between the lakes.[6] The abundant fishery at the rapids provided sustenance from spring until fall and supported a seasonal village. The fishery attracted neighbouring nations to visit the rapids and fostered social, political, and commercial exchanges. The bounty of the waters allowed large gatherings of people unique to the upper Great Lakes region. Jesuit missionaries Charles Raymbault and Isaac Jogues, the first Europeans to visit and write about Sault Ste. Marie in the fall of 1642, described a gathering of about two thousand people.[7] This large gathering had assembled for the fall whitefish run and included people from distant nations. In 1664, Jesuit missionary Claude Allouez noted that Sault Ste. Marie was "the resort of twelve or fifteen distinct nations – coming, some from the North, others from the South, and still others from the West; and they all betake themselves either to the best parts of the shore for fishing, or to the Islands, which are scattered in great numbers all over the

Lake. These peoples' motive in repairing hither is partly to obtain food by fishing, and partly to transact their petty trading with one another."[8] Jesuit missionary Claude Dablon described the Sault Ste. Marie area in 1671 and noted: "This convenience of having fish in such quantities that one has only to go and draw them out of the water, attracts the surrounding Nations to the spot during the Summer. These people, being wanderers, without fields and without corn, and living for the most part only by fishing." Dablon explained that the nations who lived at the rapids during the fishing season were "borrowers" and that the real owners of the land had allowed them to use their fishery. However, they had allowed three other nations more permanent territorial rights at the rapids. Dablon noted that they had "made a cession of the rights of their native Country; and so these live here permanently, except the time when they are out hunting."[9]

For a brief period between about 1650 and 1662, Sault Ste. Marie appears to have been unoccupied because of hostile raids launched by warriors from the *Haudenashone*, or Five Nations Iroquois Confederacy. Supported by the English in colonial New York, the Five Nations destroyed Huron villages south of Georgian Bay and caused the temporary dislocation of some Anishnawbek nations who lived around Lake Huron. Jesuit missionaries reported that some had fled northward to James Bay and westward to Lake Nipigon.[10] Western James Bay Cree oral traditions include stories of Five Nations warriors raiding as far north as the Albany River.[11] The long-distance raids into the northern regions by Five Nations warriors, however, could not be sustained for long. The nations around the Great Lakes forged their own military confederacy and began to strike back at the Five Nations. One of their most celebrated victories took place in 1662 near Sault Ste. Marie, on a point of land along the southern shore of Lake Superior known as Iroquois Point. The Jesuits reported that they fought with muskets, bow and arrows, and hatchets, scoring a decisive victory with very few Iroquois warriors escaping.[12] This particular battle was preserved in Ojibwa oral tradition and was recorded by many French and English writers. For example, Nicolas Perrot, a French fur trader active in the upper Great Lakes region in the early eighteenth century, recorded the details of the battle in which the Ojibwa and their allies surprised the Iroquois and killed all but a few scouts (who were away at the time).[13]

The long period of war between Aboriginal nations drew to a close in the final decade of the seventeenth century. In 1701, a peace treaty was concluded at Montreal between the Five Nations and the Ojibwa and other allied nations from the Great Lakes region. Ouabangué, a chief who signed the treaty document with a crane, the mark of his totem, represented the "Sauteurs." Although conflicts sometimes flared after 1701, the Montreal Treaty was maintained through diplomacy.[14]

French Territorial Claims

French and Anishnawbek concepts of land ownership differed widely. Dablon's explanation that the Ojibwa at Sault Ste. Marie had made a "cession of their rights" to three other nations likely involved an agreement to share the land and resources. French and other European people viewed land cessions as permanent land alienations with rights of exclusive occupation. The Ojibwa welcomed the French into their country and allowed them to occupy small parcels for mission stations and trading posts, but not with a view to giving away or selling their land. However, the French sought to protect their colonial interests in North America against other European nations by proclaiming territory around their posts as property of the king. The Sieur St. Lusson did this at Sault Ste. Marie in 1671. He planted a cedar stake in the ground ornamented with the royal arms of France and asked a large gathering of nations to be placed under the King's protection.[15] St. Lusson also declared: "We take possession of the said place of St. Mary of the Falls as well as of Lakes Huron and Superior, the Island of Caientolon [Manitoulin] and of all other Countries, rivers, lakes and tributaries.[16] The local Ojibwa did not take French ceremonial acts of taking possession of territory seriously. William Eccles explained: "The sovereignty that the French claimed over this territory was for British and Anglo-American political consumption only. They never dared even.hint that they regarded the Indian nations as, in any way, subjects of the French Crown. Moreover, some of those nations made it plain to the French that they were on their lands only on sufferance. French sovereignty in the Indians' country never extended farther than the range of their muskets."[17] Charles Cleland was more animated in his rejection of French territorial claims at Sault Ste. Marie. He observed: "It is certain that the Ojibwe had a much different understanding of what transpired on that date than their French counterparts. Just before the French left the Sault, they tucked a folded copy of their proclamation of usurpation behind the iron coat of arms. As soon as they were gone, the local Ojibwe removed the document and burned it, fearing the paper contained a spell that would cause their deaths."[18]

After 1671, the French continued to engage in land transactions without the consent or full understanding of the Sault Ste. Marie Ojibwa. In 1750, the French colonial governor in Quebec granted a large tract of land around Sault Ste. Marie to two military officers, Captain Louis de Bonne and Chevalier de Repentigny. A year later, French King Louis XV confirmed the grant. Like the St. Lusson proclamation in 1670, it is unlikely that the Ojibwa understood their land to have been given away by a French king to two strangers (Captain Bonne never visited Sault Ste. Marie, and Repentigny left the area in 1759). The Ojibwa gave him four strings of wampum when he took possession of the fort, which the governor believed to be a token of their agreement to give up the land. However, Theresa Schenck concluded that the Ojibwa "regarded the wampum as a seal upon their agreement to share, not dispose of, land."[19]

British Occupation and Anishnawbek Resistance

When the French military capitulated to the British in 1760, the Anishnawbek were quick to point out that the Conquest did not apply to them. Ojibwa Chief Minewehweh greeted the British at Michilimackinac and gave the following speech:[20]

> Although you have conquered the French, you have not yet conquered us! We are not your slaves. These lakes, these woods, and mountains, were left to us by our ancestors. They are our inheritance; and we will part with them to none. Your nation supposes that we, like the white people, cannot live without bread – and pork – and beef! But you ought to know, that He, the Great Spirit and Master of Life, has provided food for us, in these spacious lakes, and on these woody mountains.[21]

Minwehweh's speech, recorded by British fur trader Alexander Henry, presaged conflicts between the Anishnawbek and the British over land ownership. In fact, Henry had already purchased some land at Sault Ste. Marie. In partnership with Major Robert Rogers, commander of the incoming British military forces and Jean Baptiste Cadotte, a resident French trader, Henry obtained a deed for a tract of land on both sides of the river at Sault Ste. Marie. The deed was signed at Detroit on 23 December 1760, in exchange for "Fifty Blankets, twenty pair of leggins [sic], Twenty pounds of vermilion, Ten Barrels Rum, Ten thousand Wampum [beads], for [four] Barrels powder, and three hundred pounds of shot and Ball."[22] Almost one hundred years later, Cadotte's grandson William Warren recounted an oral tradition concerning the land grant from the chiefs and warriors to Cadotte.[23] Theresa Schenck has examined other Cadotte family oral traditions concerning the deed and concluded that Cadotte was unaware that Rogers and Henry were included. She explained that the Ojibwa gave Cadotte and others permission to use the land but not to alienate their title to it.[24] In any event, the British government officially prohibited these kinds of land deeds.[25] The land-jobbing taking place at Detroit and elsewhere in the Great Lakes region would soon give rise to widespread resistance by Aboriginal people and a change in British policy regarding protection of their territories.[26]

On 10 February 1763, Britain and France officially ended their war by signing the Treaty of Paris. News of the peace agreement spread quickly to North America. On 20 April 1763, George Croghan reported that the Ojibwa and allied nations around Detroit were angry after hearing that the treaty had given their country to the English.[27] Croghan explained: "I understand the Indians in them parts, seem uneasy in their Minds, since they heard so much of North America is Ceded to Great Britain; and the Indian nations this way seem somewhat Dissatisfied since they heard it, and Says, the French had no Right to give away their Country; as, they Say, they were never Conquered by any Nation."[28] Within months, Aboriginal warriors rallied to the side of chiefs who sought to drive the British from their lands. Popularized by historians as "Pontiac's Conspiracy," after the Ottawa war chief who led the attacks in the Detroit area, it was a movement that quickly spread to all parts of the Great Lakes region. An accidental fire destroyed the small fort at Sault Ste. Marie in December 1762, and Fort Michilimackinac fell on 2 June 1763. Soon after, the warriors controlled the entire upper Great Lakes region. Detroit was under siege, and heavily armed canoe brigades along the lakes and rivers blockaded the British military. However, the weather conspired against the armed uprising of Pontiac and other war chiefs. They could not keep their warriors in the field during the cold winter months, and so, by late fall in 1763, the siege was lifted and peace talks replaced armed resistance to the British occupation.

In England, the Pontiac uprising signalled the need to negotiate a peace treaty with the Aboriginal nations of the Great Lakes region. British officials were spurred on to prepare a proclamation, signed by King George III on 7 October 1763, that set the stage for peace negotiations. The Royal Proclamation recognized that Aboriginal nations owned their hunting grounds and pledged British protection against any encroachment. It also set out formal procedures for purchasing land, which could only be done by appointees of the Crown and Aboriginal chiefs in public meetings. British officials quickly communicated the proclamation to colonial administrators and instructed them to use the document to negotiate peace. Sir William Johnson was chosen as the King's representative, and he sent runners to summon the chiefs to Niagara in the summer of 1764 for the peace conference. During July 1764, thousands of people from the Great Lakes region converged on the "crooked place" to negotiate with Johnson. The delegates included a party from Sault Ste. Marie, and on 31 July 1764 a peace treaty was made. The treaty was memorialized on a large wampum belt that was entrusted to the people of Sault Ste. Marie and Michilimackinac.[29]

The Niagara Peace Treaty did not immediately lead to significant changes for the Ojibwa at Sault Ste. Marie. The British continued fur trade practices that had been developed by the French, and many French traders remained in the business as partners with British suppliers and merchants. Jean Baptiste Cadotte was one of many French traders who continued to work in the upper Great Lakes region. When British traveller Jonathan Carver visited Sault Ste. Marie in 1767, he found Cadotte in possession of the rebuilt fort. Carver explained, "Mons. Cadot, a French Canadian, who being proprietor of the soil, is still permitted to keep possession of it."[30] Carver's map showed the location of the fort on the south shore of the river.

A Boundary Line Imposed

Not long after the British had settled in at Sault Ste. Marie, the drums of war sounded again. This time, British colonials rebelled against home country rule in the American Revolutionary War. Although warfare did not physically manifest itself at Sault Ste. Marie, the 1783 treaty of peace between the United States and Britain had a lasting impact. Article 2 of the treaty described an international boundary line that bisected the Great Lakes, running through the middle of Lake Huron and then through the "water communication" and into Lake Superior.[31] The Ojibwa were not consulted on the boundary or informed of its effect on their territory. In fact, the British assured them that the treaty with the Americans had no effect on them. A visible proof at Sault Ste. Marie was the British military and fur trade companies that continued to operate on the south side of the river for over a decade after the treaty. Inevitably, and after years of protracted negotiations between British and American diplomats, an agreement was finally made with respect to the boundary line. That agreement, made on 19 November 1794, and known as the Jay Treaty after American negotiator John Jay, settled the boundary line and other outstanding issues. Article 3 of the Jay Treaty was intended to ensure that Aboriginal people would continue to have the right to cross the boundary line freely for trade.[32] Ojibwa leaders insisted that the boundary line was ineffective since they had not been consulted and had not agreed to the line running through their territories. William Warren explained, "They could not be made to understand or acknowledge the right which Great Britain and the United States assumed, in dividing between them the lands which had been left to them by their ancestors, and of which they held actual possession."[33]

British traders continued to work within American territory after the Jay Treaty, and some sought to secure titles to land. For example, on 15 September 1794, four Ojibwa chiefs from Sault Ste. Marie placed their totemic marks on a parchment deed involving a narrow strip of land on the south side of the river. The purchaser was fur trader Jean Baptiste Nolin, who paid four kegs of rum and sixteen pounds of tobacco.[34] Six Nations chief Joseph Brant reported that land jobbers were swarming at Detroit, buying land from Aboriginal people and expecting that American general Anthony Wayne would confirm their deeds. Brant explained: "There is a swarm of Land Jobbers at Detroit, I mean the Kings subjects buying lands from the Lake Indians, giving them rum which made those Indians continually drunk and not doing any Business with them, many of those Land Jobbers are now gone with the Indians to Wayne with their Deeds to get them confirmed by him and a great many other old Deeds besides the new ones are also sent as I was told."[35] One of the "old deeds" may have been Nolin's deed to land at Sault Ste. Marie. General Wayne had been instructed to negotiate a treaty with the chiefs of the Aboriginal nations at Fort Greenville. Coming on the heels of Wayne's victory at the Battle of Fallen Timbers, many historians have viewed the 1795 Greenville Treaty as a humiliating defeat for Aboriginal people. However, General Wayne was instructed to deal only with the chiefs who were the "true owners" of land to be purchased by the United States.[36] The recognition of Aboriginal ownership of land and the necessity to purchase title was a major development in American policy. General Wayne also dealt a severe blow to the wishes of land speculators who had obtained land deeds from various chiefs. Colonel England at Detroit reported, "all the land speculators in purchases from the Indians have been severely disappointed by the Treaty, and their purchases of course set aside."[37]

American Indian Policy and Land Purchases

The 1795 Greenville Treaty in the United States laid the framework for future land purchases by the government. Year after year, American treaty commissioners were sent out to Aboriginal nations to purchase land. In 1818, the US military sent Alexander Macomb on a tour of the upper Great Lakes. He reported that he found a site at Sault Ste. Marie suitable for a fort, which would "have an excellent effect both as it regards our Indian relations & the revenue laws."[38] In 1820, the US government made plans to "extinguish the Indian title to the soil" at Sault Ste. Marie (Michigan) and elsewhere in the Lake Superior area.[39] On 16 June 1820, the "Chippeway tribe of Indians" at Sault Ste. Marie, Michigan Territory, made a treaty with Governor Lewis Cass on behalf of the US government. That treaty involved the cession of a tract of land measuring 4,134.98 hectares in and adjacent to the rapids for "a quantity of goods." The description of the treaty clearly indicated that the area included part of the St. Mary's River up to the boundary line with the British Province of Upper Canada, which was defined as the middle of the river. However, the treaty also protected the rights of the Ojibwa to the fishery in the river. Article 3 of the treaty stated: "The United States will secure to the Indians a perpetual right of fishing at the falls of St. Mary's, and also a place of encampment upon the tract hereby ceded."[40]

On 28 March 1836, some of the Sault Ste. Marie Ojibwa chiefs travelled to Washington, DC, and agreed to a treaty with Henry Schoolcraft on behalf of the United States. That treaty involved a vast territory south of Lake Huron and Lake Michigan in exchange for temporary land reserves and annuities. Like the 1820 treaty, it included the area covered by the waters of the Great Lakes and connecting waterways to the middle thread, or boundary, with Upper Canada. It also confirmed the fishery right that had been included in the earlier treaty.[41] The 1836 treaty also included a specific provision for the "half-breeds" who lived in the area ceded to the United States. The treaty stipulated that $150,000 was to be appropriated as a fund for the "half-breeds," and individual payments were to be decided in consultation with the chiefs.[42] The inclusion of "half-breeds," also known as Métis, in reserves or annuities became a common article in US treaties.[43] For example, the 1847 Fond du Lac Treaty recognized Métis in the same terms as the Ojibwa. Article 4 stipulated, "The half or mixed bloods of the Chippewas residing with them shall be considered Chippewa Indians, and shall, as such, be allowed to participate in all annuities."[44]

British Indian Policy and Land Purchases

The British colonial government in Upper Canada also embarked upon a series of treaties designed to purchase territory from Aboriginal peoples. The Jay Treaty set 1 June 1796 as the date that British posts had to be removed from the American side of the boundary line. The British chose St. Joseph Island, located about forty kilometres southeast of Sault Ste. Marie, for the site of its new fort. Following the rules established by the 1763 Royal Proclamation, the British negotiated a treaty with the local Ojibwa leaders to obtain title to the island. On 30 June 1798, the "Principal Chiefs and Warriors and people of the Chippawa Nation of Indians" signed an agreement to surrender the island in return for goods valued at 1,200 pounds Quebec currency.[45] The North West Company chose a site on the north bank of the river, close to the rapids. The relocation of the trading post necessitated an agreement with the Ojibwa leaders. William Warren explained, "The Indians could not, or would not, understand the necessity of this movement, as they claimed the country as their own, and felt as though they had a right to locate their traders wherever they pleased."[46] On 10 August 1798, the North West Company negotiated an agreement with the "Chiefs and Old Men of the Chipeway Tribe" for a tract of land measuring 25,899.88 hectares for five pounds currency and other "goods and valuable considerations."[47] One year later (1799), rival fur traders, Phyn Inglis and Company, complained to the duke of Portland, claiming that the deed was based on a fraudulent purchase. They stated that the North West Company had "given the poor people a roll of Tobacco and some spirits for their rights." They also explained that it was necessary for all traders to have storehouses at Sault Ste. Marie and that it would be unfair to give one company a grant of land that would give it a monopoly in the trade.[48] The duke of Portland agreed with Phyn Inglis and Company and replied, "It must be very much for the benefit of the Fur Trade, that about four or five Leagues or perhaps the whole of the Land along the Straight in question should be forever retained in the hands of the Crown."[49] In 1802, the North West Company renewed its application for a Crown grant of land at Sault Ste. Marie. Other rival fur companies protested immediately, claiming that "none of His Majesty's Subjects have a right to assume exclusive privileges, or to make exclusive appropriations to themselves of either Land or Water, without Legal sanction or Title."[50] The British government refused to grant land to any company and, by the terms of the Royal Proclamation, the territory remained in the ownership of the Ojibwa.

The Emergence of the Métis Nation

By the end of the eighteenth century, both American and British governments recognized the emergence of the Métis as a distinct group of people at Sault Ste. Marie and elsewhere in the Great Lakes region. When Alexander Mackenzie visited the area in the 1780s, he found only a small village on the south shore of the river. It comprised about thirty Ojibwa families and ten or twelve mixed families of Canadian traders who had married Ojibwa women.[51] Jacqueline Peterson observed, "These people were neither adjunct relative-members of tribal villages nor the standard bearers of European civilization in the wilderness. Increasingly, they stood apart or, more precisely, in between."[52] Edward B. Borron, who was appointed by the government of Ontario in 1891 to investigate Métis claims, provided the following description of their way of life:

> They lived in log houses and when not employed by the Hon. [Honourable] Hudson Bay company or others – as voyageurs, boatmen, couriers and labourers – would eke out a subsistence by hunting and fishing or in various other ways. In early spring they and their families made considerable quantities of maple sugar. During the summer small patches of potatoes and corn were cultivated, and hay cut and made on the marshes, for their cattle, if they had any, in winter. In "the fall" when white-fish and trout sought the shallow water to spawn – they would go to well known points on lakes Huron and Superior and if provided with a sufficient number of nets would generally catch and salt down an ample supply of fish for their own use during the winter. In the winter season – cutting and hauling cordwood for their own use or for sale, and catching rabbits were the principal occupations.[53]

By 1826, the Métis community on the north bank had grown to about eighty houses that stretched along the river for about two miles.[54] The geographical pattern of the Métis settlement at Sault Ste. Marie was similar to that of other French and Métis settlements in the Great Lakes region. The river was the lifeblood of the community. Homes were built with access to the river as the first priority. The settlement stretched along the river, with fields stretching in long thin strips behind. R.C. Harris described the riverside settlements along the St. Lawrence River as "a ribbon of settlement in a wilderness of trees, rock, and water."[55] The same could be said of the settlement along the St. Mary's River. Joseph Boissineault, whose grandfather had originally settled at Sault Ste. Marie around 1816, recalled the close-knit community that developed along the river. He noted in particular the annual New Year's celebration involving the entire community.[56]

"My Blood Runs through Their Veins": Ojibwa Incorporation of the Métis

As noted above, the American government recognized the Métis in treaties with Aboriginal nations and provided money or land as compensation for land that was purchased. Until about 1830, the British colonial government treated Métis like other Aboriginal people in the Great Lakes region. They shared in the annual distribution of presents that were given to Aboriginal people as tokens of the British Crown's alliance and friendship. When the British changed their policy and stopped giving presents to Métis, Ojibwa leaders voiced their disapproval. In 1830, Chief Shingwaukonse of Sault Ste. Marie met with James Givins, chief superintendent of the Indian Department, and pleaded with him to restore the presents to the Métis.[57] He explained that the Métis had met in council and decided to place themselves under his control so that he could plead their case. Chief Shingwaukonse noted that the Métis were poor and "live[d] like Indians." Givins replied that he would present their case to the governor but added that his personal feeling was that the Métis would not be treated like "full-blooded Indians."[58]

In the summer of 1839, Chief Shingwaukonse attended the annual distribution of presents at Manitowaning (on Manitoulin Island) and spoke to Colonel Samuel P. Jarvis, then chief superintendent, about treating the Métis the same as Indians. Shingwaukonse said: "Give to the half breeds of my band the same presents that we get. They live with us & we love them as ourselves." Later that summer, at Sault Ste. Marie, Shingwaukonse spoke again to Jarvis on the Métis issue. He said, "Those whom you now see are all of my Blood – which is precious to me ... The young men who now surround you, although half breeds belong to me, – my Blood runs through their veins, and they have one and all given themselves up to me, and now form part of my tribe." Jarvis replied that he was unable to make a decision without consulting the governor general but promised an answer the next year.[59] The following winter, the Métis issue was presented in a petition to the governor general by twenty "half-breeds" residing in Penetanguishene.[60] Jarvis advised the governor general that the Métis at Penetanguishene, Sault Ste. Marie, and elsewhere should not be discriminated against with regard to the issue of Indian presents. He explained that the decision to withhold presents from the Métis had been made to discourage intermarriage between Indians and whites. Jarvis argued that such intermarriages were beneficial to Indian women and constituted a step forward in the "civilization" of Indians.[61] An internal Indian Department memorandum supported Jarvis and added, "It ought also to be remembered that but very few of the resident Indians in the old settled parts of the Province who receive assistance from the government are of pure Indian race."[62]

"A Nuisance to Missionary Labours"

Chief Shingwaukonse was disappointed to find that no answer from the government was forthcoming at the 1840 distribution of presents at Manitowaning. Thomas G. Anderson, who was in charge of the distribution that year, wrote: "Shin-gwa-konce from St. Mary's came down here with part of his Tribe to enquire whether the *halfbreeds* would be cloathed as mentioned last year but I could not enlighten his understanding on the subject."[63] Government policy towards the Métis was also influenced by Protestant missionary activities at Sault Ste. Marie. An Anglican mission was founded in 1831 to convert the Ojibwa, but friction soon arose between the missionaries and the Métis, who were mainly Roman Catholic. Abel Bingham, a Baptist missionary at Sault Ste. Marie, Michigan, came into conflict with a Roman Catholic priest in 1834. The priest threatened to burn a Bible that Bingham had given to a Métis named Cadotte, calling it "the word of the devil."[64] Indian Superintendent Thomas G. Anderson, who visited the Canadian side of Sault Ste. Marie, recalled that incident a year later. In Anderson's version of the story, the Roman Catholic priest "actually burnt an English Bible." Anderson also noted that he had previously received a letter from "a half breed named John Bell," who claimed Protestant missionary William McMurray was "doing no good here with his religion, only sending the Indians to hell and forever rot." While Bell was said to have recanted his words when confronted by Anderson, it is clear that tension between Catholic and Protestant ideology was present at Sault Ste. Marie. Anderson, on his part, clearly sided with the Protestant missionaries.[65] He advised the people at Sault Ste. Marie that the Catholics had no right to build a mission without the government's permission.[66] Lieutenant-Governor John Colborne also sided with Anderson and the Protestant missionaries when he proposed in 1835 that the rapids be reserved exclusively for the Anglican Church and that the Métis be removed from their settlement.[67]

The government's pro-Anglican position regarding settlement at Sault Ste. Marie was consistent with the prevailing sentiment in Upper Canada at the time. The rapid spread of the Orange Lodge in the nineteenth century brought with it anti-Catholic attitudes that influenced government policy. Historian Arthur Lower argued that the Orange Order was "one of the largest and most powerful of political forces and pressure groups," completing "the great Trinity of Protestant Upper Canadian [or Ontarian] hates: hatred of the 'Yankees,' hatred of the French, hatred of the Pope of Rome."[68] Other scholars have presented more moderate views of the Orange Order, but there is general consensus that Orangemen wielded significant political influence in Upper Canada in the nineteenth century. Hereward Senior noted the link between Orangeism and political office and influence in Ontario: "Orangemen felt the need for political influence if only to secure title deeds to their lands and the remuneration or prestige which went with holding public office."[69] Senior also noted that Orangemen made up almost half of the militia in Upper Canada in the 1830s.[70]

As part of the government's plan to support the Anglican mission, Anderson was instructed to remove the Métis from Sault Ste. Marie. Anderson reported that a few Métis had "authority from commanding officers to occupy three acres in front [without mentioning the depth of their lots] until required by Government." He also reported: "These people are very poor and live almost entirely on fish without any prospect of ever doing better for themselves, or their families." Accordingly, he met in council with the Métis leaders and suggested that the government purchase their properties. When they claimed a total value of £1800, Anderson refused to negotiate and made a final offer to relocate them to St. Joseph Island. The Métis flatly rejected that proposal, and Anderson left the meeting with a harsh warning that they would come to regret their decision. He advised the government that "the Canadians and other squatters be induced to leave their locations."[71]

Anderson favoured evicting the Métis "squatters" and replacing them with Ojibwa whose village was located about sixteen kilometres east at Garden River. This recommendation was guided by the fact that the Métis were associated with the Roman Catholic Church and indications that the Ojibwa were more amenable to Protestant missionaries. However, the Ojibwa had long preferred the Garden River area for their village. In 1842, John Strachan, Anglican bishop of Toronto, visited Garden River and explained: "They live chiefly at this place Sault Ste. Marie on account of the Fish, but they go to Garden River in the Spring to plant corn, potatoes, pumpkins & pease."[72] Despite the wishes of the Métis to remain at Sault Ste. Marie, Indian Superintendent Anderson attempted to recruit Charles Oakes Ermatinger to help evict them. He confided to a friend that he had asked Ermatinger to "use his influence with his tribe to execute the extinguishments of the land ... with a view to dispossess a number of squatters who are a nuisance to missionary labours."[73]

Discovery of Mineral Wealth and Plans by the Government of Upper Canada to Extinguish Aboriginal Title

The discovery of minerals in the area around Lake Huron and Lake Superior in the 1840s spurred on the government's plans to get rid of the nuisance Métis and extinguish Aboriginal title in the region. The government had powerful supporters in the business world. Sir George Simpson, governor of the Hudson's Bay Company,[74] displayed his negative view of the Métis in a letter to a colleague in 1846. Simpson confided: "Until mining operations be entered upon a large scale it [Sault Ste. Marie] is not likely to be occupied by any other than the wretched half-caste population by whom the neighbourhood is at present infested." William Mactavish, HBC chief factor at Sault Ste. Marie, held a similar view of the Métis, writing that the settlement consisted of "a few miserable hovels inhabited by Half breeds who vegitate [sic] on whitefish."[75]

In 1844, Thomas Parke, surveyor general of Upper Canada, wrote to Indian Agent John W. Keating and asked for information on the "position & extent of the settlements, the probable number of persons resident in that quarter, the occupations as Fishermen or otherwise pursued, the state of agriculture & products of the lands, the description of soil & timber & the general character of the adjacent country. The advantages likely to arise from surveying farm lots, and the price per acre at which it is probable land might be sold; or any other information."[76] Keating decided to work instead for the Montreal Mining Company, but the government received a report from Lieutenant Harper, commander of the HMS *Experiment*, who visited Sault Ste. Marie in September 1845. Harper's report pointed out that the Aboriginal title to the land had not been purchased or otherwise extinguished and recommended that the government take action so that the Métis could obtain title deeds. Harper wrote:

> Secondly not one individual on the British side (with the sole exception of the Hudson's Bay Company) own one foot of soil or land – their Houses are built and their little gardens planted under the fear that they may be ordered off at any moment and lose all. No title deeds can be got as the Indians here claim the land, and the Government I am told has not yet admitted their claim to it. The present occupants therefore have no interest in the soil, nor any inducement to cultivate or improve an acre of it, although they say it is much better land than on the American side, and would produce much more. Were it possible Sir, to give these poor people a personal and paramount interest in the land they occupy, and a chance of obtaining more, I feel that it would be of vast benefit to that vicinity, and fix (what I believe to be) a loyal population on our frontier.[77]

Thomas G. Anderson provided supplementary information about the Sault Ste. Marie area. He argued that the land belonged to the Ojibwa who lived on both sides of the river. He also explained that some Métis claimed the land by virtue of promises made by British military officers and the fact that some had lived there for thirty years. Anderson recommended that title deeds be given to the Métis after the Aboriginal title was purchased from the Ojibwa. He wrote:

The poor Canadian and half breed settlers, who are not very numerous may be termed squatters as many of them located themselves without other authority than a permission from the natives who, notwithstanding the Territory is said to be theirs cannot sell or give a title to any but the British Government; others of them applied for and received from different Commanding officers at Saint Joseph's and Drummond Island a permit to occupy a certain parcel of land, by which permission they felt themselves thus far secure. They considered & in fact it was promised them, that when the Government should extinguish the Indian title they would have a preemption right and their claim be confirmed by the Government. But notwithstanding this and tho some have been in possession for more than thirty years I would venture to say there is not one of them who has ten acres under cultivation and in my opinion it would be folly to attempt farming at the Sault St. Marie, as neither the soil nor the climate would warrant a dependence on crops of any description. In this opinion I am borne out by the fact that the Americans who are well known to be an enterprising & industrious people do not farm there to any extent.

With regard to the HBC, Anderson noted that its claim was based on permission from the Ojibwa to occupy the land and an assurance from the government that its claim would be ratified after the land was purchased.[78]

On 10 October 1845, an Order in Council was passed recommending that appropriate measures be taken for extending the authority of the government over the part of the province bordering the north shore of Lake Huron. The order also explained: "Should it appear that none of the Indians in that quarter can be regarded as descendants of the original tribes who inhabited the Country in question, and do not possess authority to cede their title to the Crown, that your Excellency may instruct the Commissioner of Crown Lands to survey a Town Plot and Park Lots at the Sault Ste. Marie, giving to the occupants a title to such lots as by the survey they may appear to be possessed of."[79]

In 1846, Alexander Vidal was appointed to survey a townsite at Sault Ste. Marie. Upon his arrival, Vidal met with Chief Shingwaukonse and Chief Nabenagoching,[80] who claimed the land. Vidal reported that, according to the chiefs, "The government have never purchased the land from them, and [they] expressed their indignation at my having been sent to survey it, and more particularly at the Government having licensed parties to explore the mineral region on the North Shore of Lake Superior without consulting with them or in any way acquainting them with their intentions regarding it." The chiefs allowed Vidal to make his survey only after he agreed to make their claim to the land known to the government.[81]

Vidal hired local Métis to work as axe men and cooks for his survey party. The names of the workers indicate that a number of Métis were engaged.

These included Michel Sarette, Pierre Crepeuil, Peter Bell, John Bell, Trott, M. Biron, Sayers, Whalen, M. Cadotte, Larose, Charles Cadotte, and Alexis Thibo. On 1 May 1846, Vidal completed his survey and compiled a list of thirty-three Métis households with information on their property and length of occupancy. Lists prepared at a later date by Joseph Wilson and John Driver, two non-Métis settlers, identified thirty-four additional heads of households.[82] The discrepancy may have been due to the land claim definition used by Vidal. There were obviously many other Métis whom Vidal ignored because he felt they did not legitimately occupy the land. Some Métis may have been travelling on fur trade business, an occupation common to many of the men in the settlement.

In 1847, the governor general received a petition from chiefs Shingwaukonse, Nebenagoching, Puhyahbetahway, and Kabeosa, complaining about miners encroaching on their land. The miners told them they had purchased the land from government, a claim the chiefs found preposterous. They reminded the governor general that they had been promised the land would never be sold without it first having been purchased from them. The petition stated that the chiefs would be "happy to make over by Indian treaty or in any other way that may be required, the tract of land above mentioned on the promise of such compensation as may be agreed upon."[83] In 1848, Thomas G. Anderson recommended that the government purchase the land and noted the strong claims of the Ojibwa to the territory around Lake Huron and Lake Superior. He wrote:

> There does not appear a doubt but what the present race are the proprietors of the vast mineral beds and unceded forests from Grand Bature near Mississaging River on Lake Huron to the Boundary Line at Pigeon River on Lake Superior through which region numerous Locations have been granted. Their claim it appears continued unmolested from time immemorial to the present day. They do not admit that it can be owned by any power under pretext of the right of conquest because the French were admitted into their country on terms of friendship as traders and when the English waged war against the French the Indians at the instance of the Commander of the British Forces became their allies and have acted in the capacity in all subsequent wars in which the English have been engaged in this country to the present time.[84]

Thomas G. Anderson and Alexander Vidal were jointly appointed by an order of the Executive Council of the Province of Canada on 4 August 1849 to investigate the willingness of the Ojibwa to enter into a treaty with the British Crown. Vidal and Anderson met with several Ojibwa leaders at various locations along the shores of Lake Huron and Lake Superior. The Métis made several representations, but Vidal and Anderson declined to listen to them. At Fort William, Jesuit missionary Nicolas Frémiot reported that the Métis had been purposely excluded from a meeting that had been organized by HBC chief trader John Mackenzie. Frémiot confided to his superiors, "The meeting began with a roll call from the list prepared the evening before by Mr. Mackenzie. The half-breeds were passed by in silence, for they have not the right to speak at such gatherings. Is this wise? Do some people fear that they, better informed than the Indians themselves, might be in a better position to defend their rights?"[85] Vidal's report to the government revealed his personal view that the Métis should not be excluded from the proposed treaty:

> Another subject which may involve a difficulty is that of determining how far the Half breeds are to be regarded as having a claim to share in the remuneration awarded to the Indians, and (as they can scarcely be altogether excluded without injustice to some) where and how the distinction should be made between them: – many of them are so closely connected with some of the bands, and being generally better informed exercise such an influence over them, that it may be found scarcely possible to make a separation, especially as a great number have already been recognized as Indians, as to have presents issued to them by the Government at the annual distribution at Manitowaning.[86]

While Vidal and Anderson were optimistic about the success of a treaty to extinguish Aboriginal title, the Ojibwa and Métis felt the government had betrayed them. Together with several non-Aboriginal supporters, an armed party took forcible possession of a mining camp at Mica Bay on Lake Superior. The mine was taken without bloodshed, and the miners were safely evacuated. In response, the government sent a detachment of soldiers to Sault Ste. Marie, but before its arrival the leaders of the Mica Bay incident voluntarily gave up and travelled to Toronto to stand trial. The trial did not proceed, however, as Chief Justice John Beverly Robinson ruled against the charges on procedural grounds.[87] At Sault Ste. Marie, reports spread of further acts against the miners. William Mactavish advised Sir George Simpson: "the latest news is that 2,000 Red River half breeds are to be down in spring to act as allies of Shingwaukonse , having sent him a wampum belt with a message to that effect this autumn."[88]

The Mica Bay incident accelerated the government's plan to extinguish Aboriginal title. On 11 January 1850, William Benjamin Robinson, brother of the chief justice, was appointed to act as treaty commissioner to obtain a surrender of Aboriginal title to the land along the north shores of Lake Huron and Lake Superior. On 16 April 1850, the Executive Council instructed

Robinson on the amount of money that had been approved for the purchase. The instructions provided Robinson with little room for negotiation.[89] Robinson made a preliminary trip to Sault Ste. Marie in May and laid the groundwork for the treaty. On 25 August 1850, Robinson returned to obtain the land surrender. He met the Ojibwa chiefs in council on 5 September and described the government's offer: $16,000 and an annuity forever of $1,000. Robinson also promised that they would be able to make "reasonable reservations for their own use for farming" and "would still have the free use of all the territory ceded to Her Majesty."[90] Chief Shingwaukonse and Chief Nebenagoching (Joseph Sayer), representing the Lake Huron Ojibwa, rejected the offer and demanded more money and a guarantee of a larger reserve territory. Robinson was able to convince the Lake Superior chiefs to accept the initial offer, but Shingwaukonse continued to oppose the deal. Robinson repeated his promise that they would have the "same privileges as ever of hunting and fishing over the whole territory," but he threatened that they would receive nothing if they refused to sign the treaty. Chief Shingwaukonse made one last demand on 9 September. He asked for a guarantee of annuities and one hundred acres of land for each of the Métis. Robinson replied that he "had nothing to do with any body but the Indians," but they could do what they pleased with their treaty money and reserves.[91] A.W. Buchanan, post manager for the HBC at Sault Ste. Marie, reported: "Jos. Sayer [also known as Nebenagoching] and Shingwaak declined the offers made, and caused a delay of two or three days, but at last, seeing that there was a large majority against them, and that they were likely to be set aside altogether, gave in and signed the paper."[92] The schedule of reserves attached to the treaty described a reserve for Chief Shingwaukonse and his band at Garden River and Chief Nebenagoching at Batchewana, including Whitefish Island near the rapids at Sault Ste. Marie, which was used as a fishing station. No mention was made of the land occupied by the Métis.[93]

Robinson, however, did make a verbal promise to the Métis about their lands. That promise was explained in a letter, dated 24 September 1850, to Colonel Bruce, superintendent general of Indian affairs. Robinson confided that he had advised the Métis to send a petition to the government and that he had "little doubt that the Government would do them justice."[94] Robinson was given several petitions to forward to the governor general, including one endorsed by Shingwaukonse and Nebenagoching, explaining:

> Certain lands at the Sault de Ste. Marie, whereon several parties had settled and cultivated, several of them for upwards of forty years by and with consent of ourselves and people, and with scarce one exception all have married Indian women, and by them have families, with these exceptions the whole of the inhabitants of the Sault are what are termed half-breeds, very many of them the children of the sisters and daughters of your memorialists,

thus having an inheritance in the country equal to our own, and bound to it by as strong and heartfelt ties as we ourselves.[95]

The Ojibwa chiefs followed Robinson's advice by sharing the treaty money with the Métis. The treaty paylists indicate that Chief Shingwaukonse and Chief Nebenagoching distributed treaty money to a number of Métis families who lived at Sault Ste. Marie.[96] The land issue, however, was far more complicated. In 1851, John Rolph, commissioner of Crown lands, rejected the Métis petitions for title to their land. He recommended instead that they purchase their own land like other people in the province at the normal rate of one shilling per acre. An Order in Council also rejected free grants of land to the Métis at Sault Ste. Marie.[97]

It is evident that many Métis were unable or unwilling to purchase their own land. They had limited access to currency in the 1850s. Their economy was based on a barter system, involving the exchange of furs, fish, game, maple sugar, and other natural products for goods in kind. Even those who were employed as labourers for the HBC received payment mainly in the form of goods purchased at the company store. Some may have found the idea of purchasing land they considered to be their own repugnant. Others decided to move to the nearby reserves to be with their Ojibwa relatives. The "Indian annuity lists" compiled in the 1850s indicate that some Métis opted to identify as Indians and live on reserves. The lists for the Garden River and Batchewana bands included eighty-four people who can be identified as Métis.

Ten years after the signing of the treaty, the human geography of Sault Ste. Marie had changed dramatically. The straight lines and rectangular blocks of Alexander Vidal's surveyed town plot had replaced the irregular-shaped field of the original Métis river lots. The titles to the new Sault Ste. Marie were mainly in the hands of newcomers from the southern and eastern parts of the province. Of the 542 lots sold by the government, the Métis, who had claimed the land in 1846, obtained only fifty-seven (or about 10 percent).[98] The pattern of land dispossession is shown in Map 3.1. It is evident that some government officials and HBC officers who were involved in the 1850 Treaty were interested in land speculation at Sault Ste. Marie. For example, Treaty Commissioner Robinson sold a lot in 1854 and received fifty pounds (about $200), while HBC post manager Wemyss Simpson was involved in numerous land transactions.[99] Joseph Wilson, Crown land agent, was allowed to purchase twenty-six lots despite the fact that government policy was not to allow its agents to engage in such transactions.[100] The HBC obtained title to 108 lots, about double the number for the entire Métis population. The "Honourable Company" never intended to use the land for its business, and it sold most of the lots in a three-year period, from 1899 to 1902, netting almost $80,000.[101] James Morrison calculated that

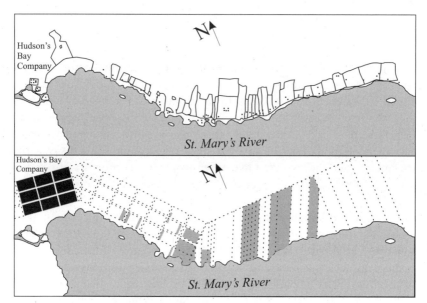

Map 3.1   Sault Ste. Marie settlement in 1846 (top) and ca. 1866 (bottom).
Source: Prepared by Ted Binnema.

Métis were involved in only eighteen of 114 property transactions between the years 1858 and 1871. He concluded, "Only a half dozen métis still owned property in Sault Ste. Marie by 1900, by which time their holdings had been reduced to [the] size of a municipal lot."[102] The 1861 census for the town of Sault Ste. Marie listed one hundred names, representing about twenty-eight households, of which only Stephen Jollineau, Louis Miraux (Miron), and Xavier Biron remained from the 1846 Vidal census. The new landowners were predominantly of British origin and Protestant religion. By 1875, the most visible sign of Protestant pride, an Orange Lodge, had been built in the centre of the once predominantly Roman Catholic Métis settlement.[103]

Conclusion

Sault Ste. Marie is a central place in Ojibwa tradition and spirituality. The Ojibwa did not claim to own the land, as Europeans did, but were willing to share it. Europeans exploited their generosity to gain possession of the land and to claim ownership of it. The French, British, and, later, American and Canadian governments also exploited their relationship with the Ojibwa in arranging treaties to extinguish Aboriginal title to the land. In the late eighteenth century, the Métis emerged as another distinct community at Sault Ste. Marie. The American government recognized the Métis as Aboriginal people; so, too, did the British colonial government in Canada. But after

1830 they were treated as squatters and were seen as a nuisance to missionary and government affairs. The Ojibwa leaders considered the Métis as their brethren, with the same attachment to the land. This conflicted with the government's plan to establish a town at Sault Ste. Marie peopled with citizens loyal to the British flag and church. Treaty Commissioner William B. Robinson offered verbal assurances to the Métis that the government would confirm them as owners of their land, but they were forced to purchase their own property. This they would not or could not do, and, within a decade, the Métis settlement at Sault Ste. Marie had been transformed into a town that reflected the image of Upper Canadian society.

Notes

1 "Métis" is currently accepted as a proper designation for the people of the Great Lakes region and will be used in this chapter.

2 Ives Goddard, "Synonymy of Southeastern Ojibwa," in *Handbook of North American Indians*, vol. 15, *Northeast* (Washington, DC: Smithsonian Institution, 1978), 79.

3 "Of the Saulteur Indians and the Places where they Live" (memoir attributed to Antoine Denis Raudot, 1710), in *The Indians of the Western Great Lakes, 1615-1760*, ed. Vernon Kinietz (Ann Arbor: University of Michigan Press, 1972), 371.

4 William Warren, *History of the Ojibway People* (St. Paul: Minnesota Historical Society Press, 1984 [1852]), 78-79, 88.

5 E.B. O'Callghan, ed., *Documents Relative to the Colonial History of the State of New York* (Albany: Weed, Parsons and Company, 1855), 9:1,054.

6 Reuben G. Thwaites, ed., *The Jesuit Relations and Allied Documents* (Cleveland: The Burrows Brothers, 1896-1901), 33:149. See also, William J. Newbigging, "The History of the French-Ottawa Alliance" (PhD diss., University of Toronto, 1995).

7 Thwaites, *Jesuit Relations*, 23:223-25.

8 Ibid., 50:267.

9 Ibid., 54:129-131.

10 Ibid., 45:219.

11 Victor P. Lytwyn, *Muskekowuck Athinuwick: Original People of the Great Swampy Land* (Winnipeg: University of Manitoba Press, 2002), 76-77.

12 Thwaites, *Jesuit Relations*, 48:75.

13 Nicolas Perrot, *Mémoire sur les moeurs, coustumes et religion des sauvages de l'Amérique septentrionale; publié pour la première fois par le R.P. J. Tailhan, de la Compagnie de Jésus* (Paris, 1864), trans. and ed. Emma H. Blair, *The Indian Tribes of the Upper Mississippi Valley and Region of the Great Lakes* (Lincoln: University of Nebraska Press, 1996, [1911]), 179-81. William Warren gave a similar account of the battle in his book of Ojibway history published in 1885. Like Perrot, Warren noted that this was the last military incursion by the Iroquois into the Lake Superior area (Warren, *History of the Ojibway People*, 147-48). Charles Kawbawgam, who was born at Sault Ste. Marie, related the oral tradition to Homer Kidder, who recorded it in the period 1893-95. Kawbawgam said that the heads were cut off the slain Iroquois warriors and placed along the beach in a line that stretched half a mile (*Ojibwa Narratives of Charles and Charlotte Kawbawgam and Jacques LePique, 1893-1895*, ed. Arthur P. Bourgeois [based on notes by Homer H. Kidder] [Detroit: Wayne State University Press, 1994], 114-15).

14 Gilles Havard, *The Great Peace of Montreal of 1701: French-Native Diplomacy in the Seventeenth Century*, trans. Phillyis Aronoff and Howard Scott (Montreal and Kingston: McGill-Queen's University Press, 2001); and Victor P. Lytwyn, "A Dish with One Spoon: The Shared Hunting Grounds Agreement in the Great Lakes and St. Lawrence Valley Region," in *Papers of the Twenty-Eighth Algonquian Conference*, ed. David H. Pentland, 210-27 (Winnipeg: University of Manitoba Press, 1997).

15 Perrot, *Mémoire sur les moeurs*, 222-25.

16 O'Callaghan, *Documents*, 9:803-4.

17 William J. Eccles, "French Imperial Policy for the Great Lakes," in *The Sixty Years' War for the Great Lakes, 1754-1814*, ed. David Curtis Skaggs and Larry L. Nelson (East Lansing: Michigan State University Press, 2001), 29.

18 Charles Cleland, *The Place of the Pike (Gnoozhekaaning): A History of the Bay Mills Indian Community* (Ann Arbor: University of Michigan Press, 2001), 11.

19 Theresa Schenck, "Who Owns Sault Ste. Marie?" *Michigan Historical Review* 28, 1 (2002): 118. In 1827, descendants of Repentigny filed a land claim in the District Court of the United States for the District of Michigan. The United States Supreme Court ultimately rejected that claim.

20 The published account employed the name "Minavavana," but that was evidently a transcription error for "Minwehweh," an Ojibwa war chief of the Michilimackinac area. See Greg Curnoe, *Deeds/Nations*, Ontario Archaeological Society, Occasional Publication No. 4 (London: Coach House Printing, 1996), 70-71.

21 Alexander Henry (the elder), *Travels and Adventures in Canada and the Indian Territories between the Years 1760 and 1766*, ed. James Bain (Boston: Little, Brown, 1921), 44.

22 Copy of a Deed of Land at Sault Ste. Marie, Archives of Ontario [hereafter AO], RG 1 A-I-1, no. 18, MS 626/6, pp. 412-16.

23 Warren, *History of the Ojibway People*, 221.

24 Schenck, "Who Owns Sault Ste. Marie?" 118.

25 Victor P. Lytwyn and Dean M. Jacobs, "'For Good Will and Affection': The Detroit Indian Deeds and British Land Policy, 1760-1827," *Ontario History* 92, 1 (2000): 9-30.

26 In 1843, the government of Upper Canada received a petition from William Henry, son of Alexander Henry, requesting that his title to land at Sault Ste. Marie be confirmed. He relied on the deed his father had obtained from the Chippewa on 23 December 1760. The Committee of the Executive Council ruled against the petition based in part on the long passage of time (Library and Archives Canada [hereafter LAC], RG 1, E8, pp. 2,166-7, 2,174-5, 2,182). In 1842, the claim was presented to the United States, requesting compensation for land in American territory granted by the deed. That claim was also rejected. In 1849, Alexander Vidal investigated the Henry land deed and found that the chiefs at Sault Ste. Marie had no knowledge of it. Vidal noted, "The oldest men among them [does not] remember any mention ever having been made by their Fathers or old men of any such thing, although they have often conversed together on all subjects connected with, or affecting, the Indian interests. They are strongly and decidedly averse to any recognition of the claim" (letter dated 11 December 1849, from Vidal to the Commissioner of Crown Lands, LAC, RG 10, vol. 123, p. 6,618).

27 The Ojibwa were allied with the Odawa and Potàwatomi, forming a military and political confederacy known as the Three Fires Confederacy. A larger alliance included other nations around the Great Lakes and was called the Lakes, or Western, Confederacy.

28 "Letter from George Croghan to Col. Bouquet," *The Papers of Col. Henry Bouquet*, ed. Sylvester K. Stevens (Harrisburgh, PA: The Pennsylvania Historical and Museum Commission, 1940), 158-59.

29 Minutes of a Council at Niagara, Niagara Council, LAC, RG 10, vol. 7, pp. 159-61.

30 Jonathan Carver, *Travels throughout North America in the Years 1766, 1767, 1768* (London: J. Walter, 1778), 141.

31 Articles of the Definitive Treaty of Peace concluded at Paris, between His Britannic Majesty and the United States of America on the 3rd of September, copy in *Michigan Pioneer and Historical Collections* 24 (1895): 8-11.

32 Printed copy of the Treaty of Amity, Commerce, and Navigation, between His Britannick Majesty and the United States of America, Public Record Office, London, FO/95/512, pp. 328-44d.

33 Warren, *History of the Ojibway People*, 293.

34 Deed between Quesgoistacamequescame, Whettounessa, Mestesaquis, Bouanieche and Jean Bpte. Nolin, for lands on south west side of Sault Ste. Marie. Register of Deeds, Wayne County (Detroit, Michigan), Liber 1, p. 143.

35 Copy of a letter from Capt. Brant, Grand River, to Lt. Col. Butler, LAC, RG 8, C-series, vol. 248, pp. 211-12.

36 Copy of a letter dated 8 April 1795, from Thomas Pickering to Anthony Wayne, Glenn Black Laboratory, Great Lakes Ethnohistorical Collection, Indiana University, Ottawa, Ottawa Binder, 1795, n.p.

37 E.A. Cruikshank, ed., *The Simcoe Papers,* vol. 4, *1795-1796* (Toronto: Ontario Historical Society, 1926), 91-92.

38 Clarence Edwin Carter, ed., *The Territorial Papers of the United States: The Territory of Michigan, 1829-1837* (Washington: Government Printing Office, 1942), 10:781.

39 Ibid., 11:4-6.

40 Charles J. Kappler, ed., *Indian Affairs: Laws and Treaties* (Washington: Government Printing Office, 1904), 2:188.

41 Ibid., 2:451.

42 Ibid., 2:452.

43 The inclusion of "half-breeds" in US treaties had been made as early as 1818 in the treaty with the Miami Nation. A similar clause was included in the 1821 treaty with Ottawa, Chippewa, and Potawatomi nations at Chicago (ibid., 2:171-74, 199).

44 Ibid., 2:199.

45 Deed of sale for St. Joseph Island, LAC, RG 10, vol. 1,841, n.p.

46 Warren, *History of the Ojibway People*, 293.

47 Indenture, or deed to land at Sault Ste. Marie, AO, Russell Papers, MS 75/4, n.p. The North West Company also secured a deed for a tract of land at the mouth of the Kaministikwia River, where it built Fort William. See Victor P. Lytwyn, "The Anishinabeg and the Fur Trade," in *Thunder Bay: From Rivalry to Unity*, ed. Thorold J. Tronrud and A. Ernest Epp, 16-37 (Thunder Bay: The Thunder Bay Historical Museum, 1995).

48 LAC, RG 8, C-series, vol. 363, pp. 6-7.

49 Ibid., 35.

50 Ibid., 11-13.

51 Alexander Mackenzie, *Voyages from Montreal on the River St. Laurence through the Continent of North America to the Frozen and Pacific Oceans in the Years 1789 and 1793* (London: Cadell and Davies, 1801), 45-46.

52 Jacqueline Peterson, "Many Roads to Red River: Métis Genesis in the Great Lakes Region, 1680-1815," in *The New Peoples: Being and Becoming Métis in North America*, ed. Jacqueline Peterson and Jennifer S.H. Brown (Winnipeg: University of Manitoba Press, 1985), 41.

53 AO, Irving Papers, F 1,027-1-2, MS 1,780, n.p.

54 Thomas L. McKenney, *Sketches of a Tour to the Lakes, of the character and customs of the Chippeway Indians, and of incidents connected with the Treaty of Fond du Lac* (Minneapolis: Ross and Haines, 1972, [1827]), 158.

55 Richard Colebrook Harris, *The Seigneurial System in Early Canada: A Geographical Study*, rev. ed. (Montreal and Kingston: McGill-Queen's University Press, 1984 [1966]), 194-95.

56 James Bassingthwaite, "Joseph Boissineault and Emory Boissineault," *Sault Ste. Marie Historical Society Papers and Records* 1 (1920-21): 63-67.

57 It is interesting to note that Shingwaukonse told Givins he was a "Half-breed." For more on Shingwaukonse and his Métis identity, see Janet Chute, *The Legacy of Shingwaukonse: A Century of Native Leadership* (Toronto: University of Toronto Press, 1998), 24-25.

58 "Second Speech of Chinguakons and Reply [of James Givins]," 1830, typescript copy in the James Givins Papers, Metropolitan Toronto Reference Library, S 20, file 1, n.p.

59 "Speech of the Chief Shinguack delivered at Sault Ste. Marie, August 10th 1839 [and reply of S.P. Jarvis]," Metro Toronto Reference Library, Jarvis Papers, B 57, pp. 384-95.

60 LAC, RG 10, vol. 72, pp. 67,089-90.

61 Ibid., 67,103-7.

62 Ibid., 67,110-11.

63 LAC, RG 10, vol. 124, pp. 69, 712-68, 713.

64 Abel Bingham Papers, "Journal Continued, Second Book (at Sault Ste. Marie), 1832-1836," box 1, file 1-7, Clarke Historical Library, Central Michigan University, n.p.

65 Anderson's son, Gustavus, was an Anglican missionary who worked at Sault Ste. Marie in 1848.
66 AO, Strachan Papers, vol. 1, n.p.
67 Chute, *The Legacy of Shingwaukonse,* 62.
68 Arthur R.M. Lower, *Colony to Nation: A History of Canada* (Toronto: Longmans, Green and Company, 1946), 186.
69 Hereward Senior, *Orangeism: The Canadian Phase* (Toronto: McGraw-Hill Ryerson Limited, 1972), 12.
70 Ibid., 31.
71 AO, Strachan Papers, vol. 1, n.p.
72 Ibid., p. 3.
73 LAC, RG 10, vol. 124, pp. 69,765-69, 69,767.
74 Simpson was also a director and shareholder of the Montreal Mining Company, which had an interest in mines on the north shores of Lake Huron and Lake Superior.
75 AO, MU 1,391, box 7, item 7, photocopy of Sault Ste. Marie Letterbook, William Mactavish, 1848-49, pp. 36-37 (originals in the Gerald F. Welburn Collection, Victoria, BC).
76 AO, RG 1, A-I-2, vol. 32, p. 412.
77 LAC, RG 10, vol. 151, pp. 87,759-60.
78 Ibid., 87,755-59.
79 LAC, RG 1, E8, pp. 6,439-40, 6,442-3, 6,454.
80 Nebenagoching, also known as Joseph Sayer, was a hereditary chief of the Sault Ste. Marie Anishnawbek. He was also a Métis on his mother's side and lived a "Métis lifestyle near his Métis relations at the British Sault, engaging in the fur trade, exploring for minerals, and planting near his wooden house" (Chute, *Legacy of Shingwaukonse,* 30).
81 AO, RG 1, A-1-6, vol. 25, pp. 21,675-77.
82 AO, Irving Papers, F 1,027-1-2, MS 1,780, n.p.
83 LAC, RG 10, vol. 123, pp. 6,192-98.
84 Ibid., vol. 534, n.p.
85 "Report of Father Frémiot to his Superior in New York, 18 October 1849," in *Thunder Bay District, 1821-1892: A Collection of Documents,* ed. Elizabeth Arthur (Toronto: University of Toronto Press, 1973), 14.
86 "Report of Commissioners A. Vidal & T. Anderson on a visit to Indians, North Shores of Lakes Huron & Superior for purpose of investigating their claims bordering those Lakes, 5 December 1849," typescript copy in AO.
87 Rhonda Telford, "Aboriginal Resistance in the Mid-Nineteenth Century: The Anishinabe, Their Allies, and the Closing of the Mining Operations at Mica Bay and Michipicoten Island," in *Blockades and Resistance: Studies in Actions of Peace and the Temagami Blockades of 1988-1989,* ed. Bruce W. Hodgins, Ute Lishke, and David T. McNab (Waterloo: Wilfrid Laurier University Press, 2003), 79.
88 Hudson's Bay Company Archives (Winnipeg), D.5/26, p. 693.
89 LAC, RG 10, vol. 266, pp. 163, 163-64, 166.
90 AO, MU 5,906, F44, p. 16.
91 Ibid., 19-23. Robinson's flat refusal to deal with the Métis in the treaty may have been influenced by his support for the Anglican Church and disdain for Roman Catholics. While none of Robinson's writings on the treaty reflect such a position, there is evidence from other sources. For example, twenty-eight years after the treaty, an Ojibwa chief from Lake Nipigon told a visiting missionary that his father, Muhnedooshans, had been told by Robinson not to "join the French religion" (Edward F. Wilson [Rev.], *Missionary Work among the Ojebway Indians* [London: Society for Promoting Christian Knowledge, 1886], 202).
92 Hudson's Bay Company Archives, D.5/28, pp. 589-90.
93 LAC, RG 10, vol. 1844, n.p.
94 Ibid., vol. 191, p. 111,706.
95 LAC, RG 1, L3, vol. 182B, petitions E, bundle 6, no. 21, n.p.
96 AO, Irving Papers, MU 1,465, 26/31/3, n.p.
97 LAC, RG 1, L3, vol. 182B, petitions E, bundle 6, no. 21, n.p.; Order in Council, 20 February 1852, LAC, RG 1, E8, pp. 23,501-32.

 98 AO, RG 1-63, vol. 77-N, pp. 1-58.
 99 AO, RG 1, C-IV, MS 658-466, p. 10; and GSU, 1686160, vol. 29, n.p.
100 LAC, RG1, E8, pp. 39,999-40,001, 40,017.
101 AO, GSU, 1686160, vol. 29, n.p.
102 James Morrison, "The Robinson Treaties," unpublished report prepared for the Royal Commission on Aboriginal Peoples (1995), 201.
103 Cecil J. Houston and William J. Smyth, *The Sash Canada Wore: A Historical Geography of the Orange Order in Canada* (Toronto: University of Toronto Press, 1980), 42.

4

Compact, Contract, Covenant: The Evolution of Indian Treaty-Making

J.R. Miller·

The history of treaty-making between First Nations and Europeans in Canada has had a lengthy history and many phases. The earliest agreements, usually informal and generally unrecorded in a lasting form that Europeans would recognize, were compacts governing commercial relations between European traders and indigenous suppliers of fur. Alongside these commercial pacts, treaties of peace and friendship emerged in the late seventeenth and eighteenth centuries as the dominant form of treaty-making in northeastern North America. Like commercial agreements, these procedures for making and maintaining diplomatic and military associations largely followed Aboriginal practices. In the latter decades of the eighteenth century and throughout the first part of the nineteenth, land-related treaties emerged as the most frequent form of treaty-making between First Nations and Europeans in Canada. Very often these territorial agreements resembled, at least superficially, simple contracts for straightforward transactions. Perhaps because later record keeping has proven better and more enduring, it is clear that, in the latter part of the nineteenth century, land-related treaties shifted in character. From the 1870s onward, the agreements by which Europeans obtained access to First Nations territory took the form of a covenant, a three-sided agreement to which the deity was a party. Through the twentieth century, especially in its latter decades, First Nations have insisted on the covenant nature of treaty-making as the norm, while for a long time the government of Canada emphasized that land-related treaties were contractual in nature. In all the discussion, the original form of treaty as commercial compact tended to get lost. If, as the Supreme Court of Canada decreed in 1985, treaties between First Nations and the Crown were sui generis, unique, it might be because, historically, they had taken so many forms.

In sorting out the complex and shifting history of treaty-making in Canada, no scholar has been of greater assistance than Arthur J. Ray. As Ray has noted, First Nations objectives in making treaty and the nature of treaties are important issues: "For Canada's First Nations it is a crucial question that has a bearing on the pursuit of treaty rights issues" that have become so important since the refashioning of the Constitution in 1982. With characteristic modesty, Ray has suggested that he contributed to the discussion about the nature of treaties by proposing an alternative to the interpretation "that the accords should be seen primarily as peace agreements through which Aboriginal nations agreed to share their lands with newcomers." His alternative interpretation stressed the economic aspects of treaty-making: "I closed *Indians in the Fur Trade* with the observation that the Aboriginal people of the prairie West sought to adapt through treaty negotiations to the radical economic developments that were taking place in western Canada in the late nineteenth century. In other words, I emphasized the economic dimension."[1]

In spite of Ray's modest statement, his contributions to scholarly understanding of First Nations treaties with Europeans throughout Canadian history extend far beyond his emphasizing the economic aspect of treaty-making. This is not to say that Ray's emphasis was not important and badly needed. Prior to publication of his work, treaty-making had been but dimly understood. For a long time the prevailing view seemed to be that of the federal government: treaties were simple contracts for land that in some cases – the numbered treaties, for example – were also distinguished by the inclusion of provident and far-sighted provisions to encourage agricultural development and schooling by a wise and benevolent government in Ottawa. While that perspective, celebrated most notably in George Stanley's 1936 *The Birth of Western Canada*,[2] was starting to be questioned in the late 1970s and early 1980s,[3] it had not been dislodged by the time Ray began to publish his work on Indians in the fur trade.

The second major contribution to treaty studies made by Arthur Ray's scholarship was its explanation of trade protocol and, later, how that protocol informed treaty talks in nineteenth-century western Canada. More so than in *Indians in the Fur Trade*, in *"Give Us Good Measure"*, his quantitative history written with Donald Freeman, Ray laid out the elaborate ceremonialism with which the trade was conducted, particularly at York Factory.[4] Quoting contemporary observer Andrew Graham, Ray and Freeman explained that, when a trading party got about three kilometres from a Hudson's Bay Company (HBC) post, they halted out of sight while their trading captains organized their approach. They "soon after appear in sight of the Fort, to the number of between ten and twenty in a line abreast of each other. If there is but one captain his station is in the centre, but if more they are in the wings also; and their canoes are distinguished from the rest by a small St. George or Union Jack, hoisted on a stick placed in the stern of the vessel."[5] When they got closer to the fort, a group of would-be traders would join other parties to form a flotilla of canoes. The approaching Natives saluted the post by firing "several fowling-pieces," while the HBC post master, having already given the order to hoist "the Great Flag" at the fort, returned the compliment with his twelve pounders. These opening salutations and honours were merely the prelude to more elaborate ceremonialism.

Once the Aboriginal traders had landed and the women had set up camp, the trading captains and their immediate subordinates engaged in a lengthy ceremony with HBC personnel. The man in charge of the post, on learning the leaders of the Natives had arrived, had his trader introduce them formally: "Chairs are placed in the room, and pipes with smoking materials produced on the table. The [Indian] captains place themselves on each side [of] the Governor, but not a word proceeds from either party, until everyone has recruited his spirits with a full pipe."[6] Then, and only then, the leaders of the two parties would make speeches of welcome. The spokesman for the visiting Aboriginal people would begin by explaining how many there were in the party, what had transpired with other traders who were not accompanying them this year, and general news since last the parties had met to trade. He likely would also make a call for fair and generous treatment in trade, and he would always ask how things had been with his English partners since they met last. For his part, the post factor would welcome them and assure them of his good will and generosity.

The factor would conclude his presentation by providing gifts to his Aboriginal trading partners. The presents usually consisted of clothing, food, smoking materials, and alcohol. The items of clothing were especially significant for the development of a treaty-making tradition in Canada:

> A coarse cloth coat, either red or blue, lined with baize with regimental cuffs and collar. The waistcoat and breeches are of baize; the suit ornamented with broad and narrow orris lace of different colours: a white or checked shirt; a pair of stockings tied below the knee with worsted garters; a pair of English shoes. The hat is laced and ornamented with feathers of different colours. A worsted sash tied round the crown, and end hanging out on each side down to the shoulders. A silk handkerchief is tucked by the corner into the loops behind; with these decorations it is put on the captain's head and completes his dress. The lieutenant is also presented with an inferior suit.[7]

The factor would also present his gifts of food, tobacco, and liquor, and escort the Natives from the trading post to their encampment in a formal procession.[8] At the Aboriginal encampment, the other half of the reciprocal ceremonial welcome and exchange occurred. The factor and perhaps an officer or two would be invited into the carefully prepared lodge and seated in the place of honour. The Aboriginal trading captain would then make a speech and cause gifts to be distributed to his visitors.

After a period of a day or more during which the Natives indulged in liquor, songs, and dance in their encampment, both sides were prepared to move on to the main event: trading furs. However, before the truly commercial part of the visit got under way, more ceremony was required. The Natives came back to the trading post to smoke the calumet, or ceremonial pipe, with the Europeans and to complete trade preliminaries. An observer at York Factory reported:

> As the ceremony of smoking the calumet is necessary to establish confidence, it is conducted with the greatest solemnity, and every person belonging to that gang is admitted on the occasion. The Captain walks in with his calumet in his hand covered with a case, then comes the lieutenant and the wives of the captains with the present, and afterwards all the other men with the women and their little ones. The Governor is genteely dressed after the Indian fashion, and receives them with cordiality and good humour. The captain covers the table with a new beaver coat, and on it lays the calumet or pipe; he will also sometimes present the Governor with a clean beaver toggy or banian to keep him warm in the winter. The Puc'ca'tin'ash'a'win [gift of furs prepared in advance] is also presented. Then the Governor sits down in an arm-chair, the captain and the chief men on either hand on chairs; the others sit round on the floor; the women and children are placed behind, and a profound silence ensues.[9]

The solemn smoking of the pipe then occurred, with the factor first lighting the pipe. The ceremonial smoking was followed by another exchange of speeches, quite lengthy this time, and the HBC man's distribution of food to the Natives.[10] On this occasion, the Aboriginal traders might also renew their calls for fair and generous treatment in trade with phrases such as "pity us" and "give us good measure," followed by an examination of the measures used in trading to satisfy themselves as to their "goodness." In some cases, as Arthur Ray pointed out more recently, the HBC representative would make gifts of medicines to those of his visitors who had responsibility for curing: "The captains and several others are doctors, and are taken singly with their wives into a room where they are given a red leather trunk with a few simple medicines such as the powders of sulphur, bark, liquorice, camphorated spirit, white ointment, and basilicon [ointment of 'sovereign' virtues], with a bit of diachylon plaster [an ointment made of vegetable juices]."[11]

As Ray and others have noted, the significance of these and other trade-related events that are known thanks to the richness of HBC records and researchers' efforts is great. In the ceremonies of welcome, speech making, gift-giving, and reassurance, the newcomers were adjusting to the Natives and their ways. These ceremonies and exchanges were part of Aboriginal protocol that governed interactions, including trade relations, between First Nations. In other words, the European newcomers had to accommodate

Aboriginal values, observances, and practices in order to establish their sincerity and bona fides as trading partners. What was being created by these ceremonial observances was a commercial relationship that was enduring. They did not signal a one-time trade transaction. Further supporting this interpretation of HBC trade protocol was one further Aboriginal practice that Ray underlined. A First Nations trading captain who was content with how he and his party had been treated would leave his pipe at the post to be used the next year; if he was unhappy, he would take the pipe with him. The actions, respectively, signified maintaining or rupturing the commercial partnership.[12] The pipe was laden with symbolic significance. More generally, the entire protocol surrounding fur trade activity demonstrated European adjustment to Aboriginal ways.

Arthur Ray's scholarship on the fur trade also contributed one other important point relevant to the story of treaty-making: he outlined how HBC practice recognized First Nations occupancy and control of territory in Rupert's Land. Even though the Royal Charter of 1670, which authorized the "Gentlemen Adventurers" to monopolize trade in all the lands drained by Hudson Bay and James Bay, also purported to confer on the HBC freehold ownership of the lands, the company, in practice, behaved as though it had no foreordained territorial rights. Just as Cornelius Jaenen has explained that French claims and pretensions to ownership of Aboriginal lands in New France were a formality intended for European, rather than Aboriginal, ears,[13] so Ray demonstrated that the HBC recognized the necessity of securing First Nations permission to operate in their lands. The distinction is parallel to one of Walter Bagehot's insights about the British system of government. In *The English Constitution* (1867), Bagehot distinguished between two "two parts" of the Constitution: "First, those which excite and preserve the reverence of the population – the *dignified* parts, if I may so call them; and next, the *efficient* parts – those by which it, in fact, works and rules."[14] The same point was expressed, acidly as usual, by Goldwin Smith, who observed of the monarch and governor general that: "Religious Canada prays each Sunday that they may govern well, on the understanding that heaven will never be so unconstitutional as to grant her prayer."[15] The distinction was between the formality of the strict letter of theory and the reality of practice on the ground.

Arthur Ray explained very clearly that this distinction applied to the HBC and the title to Rupert's Land that the company derived from its charter. He pointed out how, in 1680, the directors of the HBC instructed their representative in James Bay as follows:

There is another thing, if it may be done, that wee judge would be much for the interest & safety of the Company. That is, In the several places *where you are or shall settle,* you contrive to make compact with the Captns, or chiefs of the respective Rivers & places whereby it might be understood by them that you had purchased both the lands & rivers of them, and that they had transferred the absolute própriety to you, *or at least the only freedome* of trade, And that you should cause them to do some act wch. By the Religion or Custome of their Country should be thought most sacred & obliging to them for the confirmation of such Agreements ...

As wee have above directed you to endeavour to make such Contracts wth. The Indians in all places where you settle as may in future times ascertain to us *all liberty of trade & commerce and a league of friendship & peaceable cohabitation,* So wee have caused Iron marks to be made of the figure of the Union Flagg wth. wch. wee would have you burn Tallys of wood wth. Such ceremony as they shall understand to be obligatory & sacred. The manner whereof wee must leave to your prudence as you shall find the mode & humours of the people you deal with, But when the Impression is made, you are to write upon the Tally the name of the Nation or person wth. Whom the Contract is made and the date thereof, and then deliver one part of the Stick to them, and reserve the other. This wee suppose may be sutable to the capacities of those barbarous people, and may much conduce to our quiet & commerce, and secure us from foreign or domestic pretenders.[16]

Ray's insight into the practical nature of HBC practice is the key element in demonstrating that the fur trade yielded the earliest form of First Nations treaties. Agreements of the sort that the directors instructed their man in James Bay to secure were, in effect, commercial compacts and, as such, a form of treaty. The record of the French fur trade of the seventeenth and eighteenth centuries also yields examples of Europeans entering into agreements with First Nations to further their exploration and fur commerce. The famous pact between Champlain and the Huron in the early years of the seventeenth century, whereby the French secured permission to operate in Huron country and the Huron received French help against their Iroquois enemies is only one of many.[17] The relationship between trade and peaceful relations was well expressed by an eighteenth-century Iroquois orator, who said, "Trade and Peace we take to be one thing."[18] Ray and Freeman made the same point for the western trade: "Exchange between North American Indian groups was a political as well as an economic activity. Indians would not trade with groups with whom they were not formally at peace. Therefore, prior to the commencement of trade, ceremonies were held to conclude or renew alliances."[19] In Aboriginal society, trade relations were impossible outside a friendly relationship established and renewed according to First Nations protocols. There is even some evidence from the later period of ententes that were, in effect, fur trade compacts. According to Canon Edward Ahenakew, in the nineteenth century Chief Thunderchild noted that the HBC "gave one boat load of goods for the use of the Saskatchewan River" to Natives at Fort Carlton.[20] Hugh Dempsey documented the use of pre-trade ritual – including welcoming ceremonies, gift-giving, smoking of the pipe, and speeches – at Rocky Mountain House down to the 1850s.[21]

Arthur Ray further contributed to scholarly understanding of the treaty-making process by linking HBC practices to events of the latter part of the nineteenth century:

> The First Nations of western Canada forged their relations with Europeans in the crucible of the fur trade. Successful long-term commercial intercourse required the development of institutions and practices that accommodated the sharply different diplomatic, economic, political, and social traditions of the two parties. When First Nations treaty-making with Canada began in the nineteenth century, Aboriginal people carried over into negotiating practices and strategies many long-established fur trading customs that they incorporated into the treaties.[22]

Such practices as welcoming formalities, speeches, exchanges of gifts, smoking of the pipe, and assurances of good will figured as prominently in the making of the numbered treaties, for example, as they had in the earlier commercial exchange. Moreover, First Nations formed their opinions and expectations of nineteenth-century European or Euro-Canadian emissaries in accordance with earlier fur trade exchanges. Both because the agreements forged in the fur trade, especially the HBC trade, bore the characteristics of commercial compacts and because they bequeathed a tradition that manifested itself in the numbered treaties of the late nineteenth century and early twentieth century, these fur trade arrangements deserve to be recorded as the first phase of treaty-making in Canadian history.

Two other forms of treaty-making soon emerged. The first, which developed contemporaneously with the commercial relationships of New France, was the treaty of peace and friendship. Administrators, most notably the governor in New France, had constructed an elaborate system of alliances on the base of France's extensive fur trade networks during the seventeenth century. On occasion, in the case of the Huron Confederacy for example, the combined commercial-military alliance did not survive. With the Huron, repeated Iroquois attacks on Huronia, about which French forces were not able to do much, resulted in the dispersal of the Huron. In most other cases, however, the alliances that France forged with nations such as the Montagnais, Algonkin, and a large variety of "western Indians" proved to be enduring and effective. As was the case with the HBC's commercial dealings with northern and western Indians, the French style of treaty diplomacy featured essentially Aboriginal practices such as gift-giving, elaborate ritual, speeches, and ceremony. Onontio, as the governor of New France was known, was expected to strike an imposing figure and make both grand gestures and elaborate gifts to renew the alliances that were established. The giving of presents was especially important for both material and symbolic reasons. Presents sustained First Nations allies who might have been hard pressed by poor hunting or harrying attacks by their enemies. But, equally important, presents represented a renewal of alliance and another token of good will and intentions. In the diplomatic parlance of the seventeenth and eighteenth centuries, presents "dried the tears" of allies who had suffered losses, "opened the throats" of people so they could speak, and "opened the ears" of partners so that they would hear what was said. The speeches, gifts, and other rituals that were held regularly when French and forest diplomats met were a mechanism for renewing the alliance.

The British south of the lower Great Lakes and St. Lawrence learned to practise diplomacy as the First Nations did as well. Indeed, from the Thirteen Colonies, and more particularly from New York, came one of the most remarkable artefacts of the era of treaties of peace and friendship: the Covenant Chain. In the late seventeenth century, England began to fashion an extended system of alliances with the Five Nations of the Iroquois. (Early in the eighteenth century, the Tuscarora would move north into Iroquoia, and the Iroquois Confederacy would become the League of the Six Nations.) In time, an extensive structure evolved that paralleled the French alliance with the western Indian nations. By the late 1600s, the Covenant Chain linked the English, with greater or lesser effectiveness depending on the exigencies of the moment, to a vast range of First Nations. In this system, the governor of New York, known as Corlaer to the Natives, functioned as the counterpart of Onontio in New France. Indeed, Aboriginal diplomats frequently used "Onontio" or "Corlaer" as shorthand references for their links to the French or the English.[23]

Over time, the English developed methods of reaching arrangements with their First Nations allies that were very similar to those employed by the French. They, too, used elaborate ritual, speech making, gifts, and other ceremonies to maintain their links to their allies. Most remarkable, perhaps, was the way in which British diplomats learned and employed the elaborate rituals of the Iroquois, including the condoling and requickening ceremonies. When an Iroquois chief died, there were lengthy ceremonies to mourn his passing (the condoling ceremony) as well as rituals to recognize publicly the man who would succeed the deceased in office (the requickening ceremony). Another example of European adaptation to Aboriginal ways in the diplomatic field involves the use of wampum to record important actions. Wampum, belts made of shells or beads of different colours arranged in patterns, were for the First Nations of northeastern North America both a mnemonic, or memory-assisting, instrument and a way of recording events.

So, a First Nations diplomat – and in time European diplomats, too – would deliver a section of his speech and then lay a belt of wampum before the people to whom he was making his oral proposal. In an important conference diplomats might eventually present a dozen or more belts of wampum. Equally important was the use of wampum to record the results of conferences designed to secure peace or alliance. The principal terms of the deal would be commemorated graphically in a wampum belt. One of the most famous of these instruments was the *gus wenta*, or the two-row wampum, which the Five Nations of the Iroquois fashioned with the Dutch in the seventeenth century. The two-row wampum contained symbols that represented the two parties in separate water craft that travelled side by side. The meaning, Iroquois maintain even today, is that the two parties agreed to work together in partnership but to respect each other's difference and not to attempt to interfere with each other. Iroquois also insist that the British inherited the Dutch role after they took control of New Netherlands in 1664.

These complex treaty-making systems came to a meeting of sorts in 1701. In that year, the French and a variety of First Nations, the Iroquois prominent among them, fashioned the Great Peace of Montreal, while the Iroquois also concluded a separate arrangement with the English at Albany. The motives of the various parties were complex but complementary.[24] The Iroquois, who were weakened by disease and population loss after some seven decades of off-again-on-again warfare with the French and their allies, wanted to relieve the pressure and replenish their ranks by an exchange of prisoners. The Five Nations were also anxious about the persistent worrying of their western flank by New France's Aboriginal allies. The French were similarly wearied by long periods of devastating guerilla warfare and sought peace for the respite and stability it would provide. The English hoped, by treaty-making, to maintain their ties with the Five Nations and spare themselves attacks by the Aboriginal allies of the French.

The complex treaty talks of 1700-1 revealed Native-newcomer treaty-making at a very sophisticated level. The Great Peace of Montreal, called "great" partly because over three dozen First Nations from a region stretching from the Maritimes to the edge of the Prairies signed it, established peace among the Iroquois, the French, and the allies of the French; promised a return of prisoners; and guaranteed the Iroquois the right to remain neutral in any hostilities between France and England. The last clause was enormously beneficial to both New France and the Five Nations, for both had been gravely weakened by the attrition of prolonged warfare.[25] If those terms understandably worried the English, who saw their Covenant Chain allies removed to a neutral category by the Peace of Montreal, further diplomatic action by the Iroquois in the same year attempted to reassure them. By a treaty often referred to as the Albany Deed, the Five Nations renewed their friendship with Corlaer and his people, while simultaneously purporting to convey hunting grounds north of the Great Lakes to English protection. While interpretations of the significance of this arrangement differ,[26] it clearly provided some reassurance to the English allies of the Iroquois, while simultaneously leaving untrammeled the Five Nations' right to stand neutral in a European imperial rivalry that seemed certain to play itself out in the interior of North America before very long. In any event, the Iroquois would choose their own course of action – neutrality or alliance with a European power – as their interests dictated whenever conflict broke out. That had always been the case with First Nations approaches to diplomacy and alliance in wartime; it would continue to be so during the war-torn eighteenth century in eastern North America.

Although the Great Peace of Montreal of 1701 and the Albany Deed were important instances of the genre of treaty-making known as the treaty of peace and friendship, they were by no means the only examples. European-First Nations diplomacy figured prominently in the succession of imperial clashes that culminated in the Seven Years' War (or the French and Indian War, as it is more commonly known in the United States) as well as the War of the American Revolution and, ultimately, the War of 1812. A particularly important and revealing theatre of the wars of imperial rivalry of the period to 1760 was the Atlantic. Acadia, the French colony in peninsular Nova Scotia, along with the St. Lawrence River Valley colony of Canada, constituted what the French called New France. If Canada stood for access to the fur trade and its attendant system of Indian alliances, Acadia represented the entrée to the Atlantic fishery and to strategically important sites. France would develop the latter in the early 1720s, after the 1713 Treaty of Utrecht forced it to concede "Acadia with its ancient limits" to Great Britain, by building the massive fortress of Louisbourg on Cape Breton. Acadia had one other strategic asset so far as the French were concerned: the Mi'kmaq.

The Mi'kmaq, an Algonkian people who dominated Nova Scotia, Prince Edward Island, and northern New Brunswick, were drawn to the French for both negative and positive reasons. As Cornelius Jaenen has well explained, the French presence in Acadia after 1604 did not threaten Mi'kmaq territorial interests because the settlers who would evolve into the Acadians settled in areas largely unused by the Mi'kmaq – farming land reclaimed from the waters by dyking and draining. To this compatibility of location and land usage was added the fact that French representatives from the earliest days of contact with the Mi'kmaq wove bonds of friendship and affinity between the two peoples. The most important of those links was religion: from the early conversion of Chief Membertou and his entire family in 1610, French Roman Catholic missionaries worked among the Mi'kmaq, ministering both to Acadians and Natives. Over time, the process of intermarriage and acculturation developed close ties between the two communities. This experience of the seventeenth century stood in dramatic contrast to events of the first half of the eighteenth. Following the Treaty of Utrecht, Britain moved to make good its claim to Nova Scotia, as it preferred to call what had been "Acadia" to the French, by settlement and military presence. Unfortunately for British-Mi'kmaq relations, the territorial compatibility that had figured so prominently in Acadian dealings with the Mi'kmaq did not exist in the portions of the colony where British and British-sponsored settlers chose to locate. Unlike the French, the British presence brought to the surface a strong territorial incompatibility between the indigenous people and the new European power in the region.

Religion played an important role in the growing friction between the British and the Mi'kmaq. His Britannic Majesty, as head of a militantly Protestant country, took a dim view of Roman Catholicism in his new Atlantic colony and among an Aboriginal people who for so long had had close relations with His Most Catholic Majesty, the king of France. For their part, the Mi'kmaq had close ties to Roman Catholic missionaries from France and, according to at least one authority, even believed that they had entered into a *concordat*, a treaty-like agreement between the Vatican and their nation, as a result of the conversion of Membertou in 1610.[27] During the first half of the eighteenth century, and most especially after about 1720, the governor of New France regularly employed Catholic missionaries as emissaries in Acadia to influence the Mi'kmaq in ways that assisted French strategic designs of maintaining a presence in Nova Scotia. Such complications explain why the British had such difficulty making their hold on Nova Scotia good between the Treaty of Utrecht and the end of the Seven Years' War as well as why British forces found it necessary to expel the Acadians in 1755. One measure of the greater difficulty the British had in the region compared to the French is that, over the century and a half that the French associated with the Mi'kmaq, France made precisely one formal treaty with the First Nation, whereas the British entered into no fewer than thirty-two treaties with them between 1720 and 1786.[28] The unusual treaty history of Canada's maritime region illustrates that treaty arrangements, which could be founded on factors such as trade and religion, took many forms and that a propensity to make treaty by itself did not guarantee stability in a country's treaty regime.

In contrast to the impermanence and ineffectiveness of its treaty system in eighteenth-century Nova Scotia, Britain's next foray in Native policy would have a profound and long-lasting impact. The Royal Proclamation of October 1763, which Britain issued to provide institutions of government and law for territories newly acquired in the Seven Years' War, contained extremely important provisions concerning First Nations lands. Although the Proclamation, which was a unilateral Crown document, is often described as the "Indians' Magna Carta" and is said to bestow many territorial blessings on First Nations, it was written as though the royal author assumed the territories all belonged to the Crown. When the Proclamation turned to the First Nations and their territorial rights, it described them as "the several Nations or Tribes of Indians with whom We are connected, and who live under our Protection," and said that they "should not be molested or disturbed in the Possession of such Parts of Our Dominions and Territories as, not having been ceded to or purchased by Us, are reserved to them, or any of them, as their Hunting Grounds." In other words, the Proclamation said that the Crown reserved from its dominions land for First Nation allies and associates as their grounds for hunting and maintaining themselves. Be that limited recognition as it may, it then went on to lay out a regime that was to govern those lands "reserved to them ... as their Hunting Grounds." First, it forbade settlement in the interior beyond the height of land and regulated commercial penetration of the region by requiring traders to get licences from the governor before going beyond the mountains. The purpose of these clauses was to hold back and control non-Native entry into the interior so as to placate the First Nations and prevent clashes between them and intruding colonists intent on making Aboriginal "Hunting Grounds" into settlers' fields. The fact that Pontiac's War, a rising of interior First Nations against the newly victorious British, was raging when the Proclamation was issued underlined the need to control non-Native access to lands beyond the mountain ranges west of the Thirteen Colonies.

The Proclamation continued with important clauses concerning interior Indian territories. It reserved "for the use of the said Indians, all the Land and Territories not included within the Limits of Our said Three new Governments, or within the Limits of the Territory granted to the Hudson's Bay Company," and the King did "hereby strictly forbid, on Pain of our Displeasure, all our loving Subjects from making any Purchases or Settlements whatever, or taking Possession of any of the Lands above reserved, without our especial leave and Licence for that Purpose first obtained." The objective of forbidding settlement or purchase of First Nations lands was to put an end to "great Frauds and Abuses [that] have been committed in purchasing Lands of the Indians, to the great Prejudice of our Interests, and to the great Dissatisfaction of the said Indians." Or, as American historian Francis Jennings was later to put it, the Proclamation aimed to put a stop to the "deed game," the dubious practice by which pioneers or land speculators – the distinction between the two categories was often a fine one in settler societies – obtained a transfer deed from a Native by fraud or employment of alcohol. When the colonists acted on the dubious deed, trouble ensued between the First Nations and incoming settlers.

The Proclamation's alternative to the "deed game" was a policy for acquiring First Nations land that would give the document its long-lasting influence:

In order, therefore, to prevent such Irregularities for the future, and to the end that the Indians may be convinced of our Justice and determined Resolution to remove all reasonable Causes of Discontent, We do, with the Advice of our Privy Council strictly enjoin and require, that no private Person do presume to make any purchase from the said Indians of any Lands reserved to the said Indians, within those parts of our Colonies where We have thought proper to allow Settlement: but that, if at any Time any of the said Indians should be inclined to dispose of the said Lands, the same shall be Purchased only for Us, in our Name, at some public Meeting or Assembly of the said Indians, to be held for that Purpose by the Governor or Commander in Chief of our Colony respectively within which they shall lie.

Analogous rules were laid down for acquiring First Nations lands in colonies where there already was a colonial government. In other words, in both the lands beyond settlement that were reserved for First Nations and within settled colonies the Proclamation held that the only way Aboriginal lands could be obtained lawfully was by a representative of the Crown, not a private citizen or company, and only through a public process that would help to avoid fraudulent dealings. As the Proclamation also said, these restrictions on acquiring lands were motivated in large part by Britain's desire that "the Indians may be convinced of our Justice and determined Resolution to remove all reasonable Causes of Discontent."

Although these terms of the Royal Proclamation of 1763 were important in their own right, they paled in significance with the implications and legacy of the document. For one thing, according to one Aboriginal law specialist, British officials in 1764 took actions that converted the Proclamation from a unilateral Crown document into a treaty. According to John Borrows, in 1764 William Johnson, Britain's superintendent of the northern Indians, called together some two thousand First Nations representatives from districts stretching from Nova Scotia to the Mississippi, explained the contents of the Royal Proclamation, and procured their agreement to them.[29] The implication of the events, according to Borrows' interpretation, is that, through the Niagara conference of 1764, the Royal Proclamation became a treaty protected by Section 35 of Canada's 1982 Constitution Act. Although documentary sources such as the published Johnson Papers, *New York Colonial Documents*, and government-compiled collection of treaties do not explicitly support his argument, there is evidence that Johnson explained the Royal Proclamation's territorial guarantees to Iroquois groups early in 1764.[30] If he did this with relatively small groups of Iroquois in January 1764, it is reasonable to infer he did the same thing with much larger numbers of First Nations at Niagara that summer. Borrows also points out that First Nations oral traditions and wampum do provide evidence for his view of the Proclamation.[31] If this interpretation is upheld, the Proclamation will itself be a key development in the Canadian treaty-making tradition.

Whether or not the courts treat the Proclamation as a treaty, there is no doubt that, since the late eighteenth century, it has profoundly influenced treaty-making. Although the requirements of the Proclamation were not followed scrupulously in every case, from 1764 until Confederation treaties were made by the Crown with a variety of First Nations in central British North America to gain access to First Nations lands. For the first half-century after 1763, the acquisitions were motivated by a desire to obtain lands on which to settle allies of the British and then immigrants to British territory. The former motive was exemplified by the acquisition of lands immediately north of Lake Erie and Lake Ontario for Mohawk allies defeated in the War of the American Revolution. The latter reason, the need to provide access to lands for immigrants, became especially compelling after the creation of Upper Canada as a separate political unit in 1791. In this first fifty years of Proclamation-style treaty-making, the documents that resulted provided for a straightforward transfer of territory in return for a one-time payment, often in goods. So, for example, Treaty No. 8 in 1797 provided access to 3,450 acres of land north and east of Burlington Bay. A group of Mississauga (Ojibwa) negotiated the pact with William Claus, superintendent of Indian Affairs "on behalf of the Crown," in return for "seventy-five pounds two shillings and sixpence Quebec Currency in value in goods estimated according to the Montreal price." A certificate attached to the government version of the treaty listed blankets, several types of cloth, and butcher knives and brass kettles to the specified value as having been conveyed to the First Nations signatories.[32]

The land-related treaties of this fifty-year period following the Royal Proclamation are the agreements that bear the closest resemblance to simple contracts in Canadian history. At least as explained in the government's version of them, they exchanged a specific tract of land, usually a relatively small piece, from the First Nation in return for a one-time payment. The treaties usually were negotiated, as the example (above) was, by an official who clearly represented the Crown. There were, however, exceptions. One was the so-called Selkirk Treaty of 1817, negotiated in the Red River area by a representative of Lord Selkirk, the landlord who had acquired a large tract of land from the HBC and established a struggling colony on it in the second decade of the nineteenth century. The origins of this agreement were anything but exemplary of Proclamation policy, which, in any event, was not intended to apply to Rupert's Land. The background of the Selkirk Treaty was a violent clash between mixed-blood forces and colonists at Seven Oaks in 1816. Only then was Selkirk, who had acquired lands from the HBC in

1811 and started his colony in 1812, moved to have an arrangement with local Saulteaux (Western Ojibwa) negotiated. Also instructive was the fact that Selkirk's text labelled the agreement "This Indenture," an indenture being a legal agreement or contract that bears a seal. The treaty or indenture conveyed 3.2 kilometres on either side of the Red and Assiniboine rivers to Selkirk on "the express condition that the said Earl, his heirs and successors, or their agents, shall annually pay to the Chiefs and warriors of the Chippewa or Saulteaux Nation, the present or quit rent consisting of one hundred pounds weight of good and merchantable tobacco."[33]

The Selkirk Treaty, whether or not it was part of a treaty-making tradition founded upon the Royal Proclamation of 1763, stands at a transitional point in the history of such agreements in Canada. Between 1763 and the War of 1812, the agreements that had been made covered small areas, provided for one-time compensation to the Aboriginal signatories, and resembled simple contracts. By means of such agreements, the Crown had dealt with First Nations territorial rights in a large portion of Upper Canada, now southern Ontario, in preparation for settlement by allies and immigrants. In retrospect, Selkirk was a harbinger of change that was on its way in British practice in Upper Canada. What the Selkirk Treaty unknowingly foreshadowed was a shift in the type of compensation provided by the Crown, a change that introduced an element to treaty-making that was both a novelty and a throwback. The change that was introduced by the British in 1818 was the use of annuities, annual payments to the First Nations in compensation for land rights obtained by treaty. From that time onward, the Crown used annuities mainly for reasons of economy. In another surge of treaty-making in preparation for immigration and settlement after the War of 1812, Britain moved to reduce its financial obligations by using annuities. The theory was that, once settlement commenced and colonists paid fees for the lands, income from this source would fund the annual payments to the First Nations. The annuity system would thereby reduce Britain's outlay.

However, annual payments to First Nations would be reminiscent of earlier transactions with allies, transactions that were still carried out down to 1858 in central British North America. Annuities resembled the annual presents that first the French and later the English had used to cement their alliances with First Nations. They "wiped the rust from the chain of friendship," "dried the tears" of bereaved partners, and "opened the ears and throats" for friendly dialogue. Moreover, to First Nations, the giving of presents, like the annual exchange of gifts at fur-trading posts, symbolized the renewal of a partnership, whether commercial or diplomatic and military. Introducing annuities into treaty-making linked land treaties in the nineteenth century to the commercial compacts and diplomacy of an earlier era. The action also complicated the view of Upper Canadian treaties as simple contracts and paved the way for a more complex form of treaty-making.

Before that complicated type of treaty emerged, however, the making of land treaties continued and evolved in Upper Canada. Between 1783 and the War of 1812, the Crown dealt with First Nations territorial rights in a band covering the "front" (river-front and lake-front). The depth back from the water that was embraced in these treaties was usually moderate, but in the regions at the east end of Lake Erie and along the river in the eastern part of the province the land treated for stretched noticeably further inland.[34] These were the treaties in which the compensation for First Nations took the form of one-time payments. Between 1818 and the 1830s, the Crown dealt with a broader band of territory to the north in a series of treaties in which the compensation was annuities. For example, Upper Canadian Treaty No. 27 between the Crown and Mississauga dealt with a large tract in eastern Upper Canada that stretched to the Ottawa River, and it guaranteed the First Nation signatories "the yearly sum of six hundred and forty-two pounds ten shillings, Province Currency, in goods at the Montreal price to be well and truly paid yearly and every year by His Majesty, His Heirs and successors, to the said Mississaugua [sic] Nation inhabiting and claiming the said tract."[35] For the Upper Canadian treaties, a culmination occurred in 1850 with what are known as the Robinson Treaties.

The Robinson Huron and Robinson Superior treaties, named for the Great Lakes to which they were adjacent, advanced treaty-making in the pre-Confederation era. Geographically, they extended the Crown's claim to lands stretching well up into the Canadian Shield, where the attractions of mining had begun to draw non-Natives. They also advanced treaty-making practice by dealing with much larger tracts than had hitherto been the case in Upper Canada. The Robinson Treaties also broke new ground by specifying that provision of reserves was a Crown obligation flowing from the treaties. Prior to this time, reserves had existed as a result of missionary or Indian Department initiative, but they were not associated with treaties or Crown treaty obligations. From the time of Robinson onward, treaties and reserves normally went together. Finally, the Robinson Treaties reintroduced an element that had been present in some of the eighteenth-century Nova Scotia treaties: Crown recognition of the First Nations' continuing right to hunt and fish. As Commissioner Robinson explained to his superiors, this concession was not altruistic: by acknowledging "the right of hunting and fishing over the ceded territory, they cannot say that the Government takes from their usual means of subsistence and therefore have no claims for support, which they no doubt would have preferred, had this not been done."[36] Commissioner Robinson gave the Ojibwa who signed the 1850 treaties the choice of a lump sum payment or a small upfront sum and annuities; they chose the latter. The Robinson Treaties combined elements that would form the template of later treaties in the West: they dealt with large territories, they established reserves for the First Nations, they included annuities, and they recognized a continuing Aboriginal right to hunt and fish.

By the time of Confederation, the Upper Canada treaty-making tradition had evolved into a sophisticated protocol that conformed in many respects to the requirements of the Royal Proclamation. That the Proclamation was not always followed was demonstrated in the background to both the Selkirk and Robinson treaties. In both instances, Native resistance had brought on overtures to make treaties. However, treaty-making in Upper Canada did involve the Crown and First Nations in public negotiations concerning territory. During the first fifty years after the Proclamation, the use of one-time payments had made the agreements resemble simple contracts for territory, although practice after the War of 1812 shifted to the use of annuities, which would prove to be the harbinger of a different style of treaty-making. Another exception to the general use of annual payments for compensation was to be found in colonial British Columbia. When Governor James Douglas responded in the 1850s to the pressure of encroaching settlement on Vancouver Island, he entered treaty talks with a variety of groups; this led, by 1854, to the conclusion of fourteen treaties for small parcels of land on the Island. In the talks, Douglas explained, he offered the First Nations leaders the choice of one-time compensation or annuities. The Natives chose a single payment upfront, making BC treaties unconventional in their compensation clauses as well as in the amount of territory they covered. Elsewhere in British North America, however, annuities were the norm, as were provision of reserves, large tracts, and guarantees of hunting and fishing.

The numbered treaties that were concluded in the West between 1871 and 1877 introduced a third category of treaty: the covenant. Of course, the official record, the government's version of the treaties that was published in 1880, continued to portray the agreements that covered the region from the Lake of the Woods to the foothills of the Rockies as simple contracts transferring territory from First Nations to the Crown. For example, Treaty 1, the Stone Fort Treaty in Manitoba, had the "Chippewa and Swampy Cree Tribes of Indians ... cede, release, surrender, and yield up to Her Majesty the Queen, and her successors for ever, all the lands included within the following limits, that is to say," in return for reserves, a signing payment, schools, and annuities of fifteen dollars paid in goods. Later, after the First Nations had successfully argued that there were other "outside promises" that did not turn up in the printed version of the treaty, Treaty 1 also increased annuities, made four rather than two headmen eligible for annual stipends, and provided livestock and equipment for the pursuit of agriculture.[37] The view of treaties between the Crown and First Nations as contracts for territory would prevail on the government side of transactions through the later negotiation of the northern numbered treaties between 1899 and 1921. The same interpretation informed the federal government's approach to dealing with claims arising from the treaties throughout the twentieth century.

Western First Nations in particular insisted upon a different view of the nature of their treaties. Rather than a contract involving two parties – Crown and First Nations – Indian communities see the treaties as three-cornered agreements to which the deity is a party. A covenant is an agreement between humans, in which the deity participates and provides oversight. For Christians, for example, establishing a sacred relationship in marriage is generally described as a covenant because God is witness and participant in the solemn pact. In a similar fashion, First Nations argue that the western numbered treaties are covenants. One of the terms that Plains Cree use to describe treaties is *itîyimikosiwiyêcikêwina*, which means "arrangements ordained or inspired by our Father [Creator]."[38] Saskatchewan Saulteaux elder Danny Musqua told interviewers, "We made a covenant with Her Majesty's government, and a covenant is not just a relationship between people, it's a relationship between three parties, you [the Crown] and me [First Nations] and the Creator."[39] A contract between two or more parties is specific and relies on the precise letter of its terms; a covenant among two or more humans and the deity creates a special, solemn relationship in which the partnership is more important than its specific terms.

First Nations point to several forms of evidence to sustain their argument that the numbered treaties of the 1870s were covenants rather than contracts. In particular, with the exception of Treaty 4, the making of these seven treaties was preceded by observance of First Nations ceremonies and forms. (Apparently, First Nations negotiators at Fort Qu'Appelle in 1874 did not include Commissioner Alexander Morris in ceremonies – an omission on which Morris pointedly commented[40] – because they were angered by the transfer of Rupert's Land to Canada without their having been consulted or paid.) Morris described a typical instance of First Nations ceremonialism at Fort Carlton in August 1876:

On my arrival, the Union Jack was hoisted, and the Indians at once began to assemble, beating drums, discharging fire-arms, singing and dancing. In about half an hour they were ready to advance and meet me. This they did in a semicircle, having men on horseback galloping in circles, shouting, singing and discharging fire-arms.

They then performed the dance of the "pipe stem," the stem was elevated to the north, south, west and east, a ceremonial dance was then performed by the Chiefs and head men, the Indian men and women shouting the while.

They then slowly advanced, the horsemen again preceding them on their approach to my tent. I advanced to meet them, accompanied by Messrs [W.J.] Christie and [James] McKay [fellow commissioners], when the pipe was presented to us and stroked by our hands.

After the stroking had been completed, the Indians sat down in front of the council tent, satisfied that in accordance with their custom we had accepted the friendship of the Cree nation.[41]

The significance of the ceremonies was far greater than the commissioner apparently realized. While joining in friendship was certainly part of the ritual's meaning, there was far more to it than that. The use of the pipe invoked the Great Spirit as a participant at the talks that were to follow and bound everyone who smoked the pipe to tell only the truth. Moreover, any agreement produced by such solemn talks was sacred and could not be violated without grave ills befalling the violator. On the more positive side, according to two researchers who conducted many interviews in Saskatchewan, the ceremonies had an inclusive effect: "The treaties, through the spiritual ceremonies conducted during the negotiations, expanded the First Nations sovereign circle, bringing in and embracing the British Crown within their sovereign circle."[42] Inclusion in any sort of family relationship with Aboriginal peoples was a potent development. The attribution or creation of kin relationships, as in the language used in the Covenant Chain of the seventeenth and eighteenth centuries, was a prelude to conducting business of any kind, commercial or diplomatic, in North American Aboriginal societies. By embracing the Queen's treaty commissioner through ceremonies, the western First Nations were establishing kinship with the Crown and, through the Crown, with the Queen's people. Little wonder that when Governor General Lord Lorne, the husband of a daughter of Queen Victoria, visited the Prairies in 1881, Kakishiway, a chief who had signed Treaty 4 in 1874, greeted him with, "I am glad to see you my Brother in Law" as both of them had a family relationship to the Queen.[43] The chief's link was through the treaties, while Lorne's was by marriage.

A second type of evidence supporting the interpretation of the western treaties as covenants came from the mouths and the actions of the Queen's treaty commissioners. First Nations would have been impressed by the presence and participation of Christian missionaries as interpreters or witnesses at the talks. There were Christian ministers or priests in attendance at the negotiation of treaties 4, 5, 6, and 7. Moreover, the treaty commissioner's insistence on suspending talks so that the Christians could observe the Sabbath properly testified to their adherence to spiritual practices and values.[44] The Queen's commissioners frequently involved the deity in their arguments, and for a variety of purposes. For example, at Treaty 4 talks, Commissioner Alexander Morris used a reference to the "Great Spirit" to counter Saulteaux arguments that the HBC had stolen their territory from them when it took the money Canada paid for the HBC lands: "Who made the earth, the grass, the stone, and the wood? The Great Spirit. He made them for all his children to use, and it is not stealing to use the gift of the Great Spirit."[45] At other times, the occasion of a reference to the deity was more positive. When summing up the Treaty 6 talks at Fort Carlton in 1876, Commissioner Morris noted: "What we have done has been done before the Great Spirit and in the face of the people."[46] At times, a treaty commissioner's language would have sounded as though the Queen's representative was explicitly accepting the First Nations understanding of treaty as covenant and kin relationship. For example, at Blackfoot Crossing in 1877, Commissioner David Laird said: "The Great Spirit has made all things – the sun, the moon, and the stars, the earth, the forests, and the swift running rivers. It is by the Great Spirit that the Queen rules over this great country and other great countries. The Great Spirit has made the white man and the red man brothers, and we should take each other by the hand. The Great Mother loves all her children, white man and red man alike; she wishes to them all good."[47] If western First Nations saw the numbered treaties as covenants involving the Great Spirit, the Crown, and themselves, and if they believed that the Queen's white-skinned children understood them the same way, it is hardly surprising.

For western First Nations leaders who invoked the Creator with their rituals, it would not have been difficult to conclude that the Queen's commissioners were acting in the same spirit. Their words and their actions both seemed to involve their god in the proceedings. In this way, treaty commissioners in the nineteenth-century West embraced the protocol that Aboriginal people had developed and that, earlier, the HBC had adopted. Other aspects of the customary rites were the Crown's provision of treaty uniforms ("suits of clothing") to chiefs and headmen, much as HBC post masters had issued clothing along with food to trading captains who brought furs to the HBC forts. All these practices illustrated the continuity of Aboriginal and HBC practices, a system of protocol that invoked and involved the deity through the ritual smoking of the pipe. Given this pattern of western treaty-making, it is not surprising that First Nations regard the agreements they made with the Queen's commissioners in the 1870s as covenants, establishing a sacred and permanent relationship between themselves and the Crown.

In the twentieth century, First Nations were to experience a great disillusionment with the way that the Queen's Canadian government interpreted and applied treaties. Indeed, the disappointment did not have to wait for the twentieth century. Once the treaties were concluded (by 1877) and the buffalo economy – the foundation of Plains culture and the source of Plains strength – collapsed (by 1879), Canada began to take a narrow, legalistic, and parsimonious approach to treaty-making and treaty implementation. As early as the 1880s, western First Nations leaders were complaining that the Crown's representatives had used "'sweet promises' ... to get their country from them" and then ignored the Crown's obligations to them.[48] Another manifestation of the federal government's attitude was its refusal to act on petitions from a variety of First Nations in regions north of the seven numbered treaties to make treaties with them. Ottawa's attitude was that it was not interested in making further treaties, which would entail financial obligations to First Nations, unless and until the lands on which they resided became desirable in the eyes of non-Native economic interests that sought to develop them. Accordingly, numerous petitions for treaty were ignored, but when oil was discovered at Norman Wells in 1920, the wheels were set in motion to make Treaty 11, which covered the region in 1921.[49] After the early 1920s, the federal government declined to make any further treaties. For the time being there were no southerners coveting the untreatied lands of the North and British Columbia, and, in any event, by 1920 Ottawa and its Department of Indian Affairs had entered a phase of pursuing coercive and controlling policies towards First Nations that would not lift until the middle of the century.

When treaty-making did resume, with the James Bay and Northern Quebec Agreement in 1975, it was only because better organized and highly assertive First Nations political organizations, specifically the James Bay Cree, went to court to secure a temporary injunction to halt the massive James Bay hydroelectric power development. That contretemps and the 1973 Supreme Court of Canada decision on Aboriginal title in *Calder*, the Nisga'a case, led the federal government to develop a comprehensive claims settlement process to deal with Aboriginal title claims in regions where there were no effective treaties. As the Department of Indian Affairs website notes, the Comprehensive Claims Branch's purpose is "to negotiate modern treaties which will provide a clear, certain and long-lasting definition of rights to lands and resources for all Canadians." Comprehensive claims settlements were joined in the 1990s by individually negotiated agreements such as the Nunavut pact and the Nisga'a treaty to round out Canada's modern treaty-making processes. In the twenty-first century, Canada and First Nations must negotiate treaties concerning access to territory for Atlantic Canada, parts of northern Quebec, most of British Columbia, and portions of the Far North.

Through those times in the twentieth century when treaties were being made, and certainly since the resumption of treaty-making in the 1970s, the federal government's view of treaties as contracts whose contents are recorded in the government's version has been prominent. As Cumming and Mickenberg pointed out in their 1970 *Native Rights in Canada*, the courts had often found that Aboriginal treaties were akin to contracts in law. As late as 1969, Pierre Trudeau, initially no friend of treaty or Aboriginal rights, in the aftermath of the uproar over his government's White Paper said that, while his government "won't recognize aboriginal rights[,] We will recognize treaty rights. We will recognize forms of contract which have been made with the Indian people by the Crown."[50] The implications of the government's attitude became clear in the 1980s in the context of comprehensive claim resolution discussions. As a review of the comprehensive claims process put it, "progress has, in the past, been blocked by the fundamental difference between the aims of each party. The federal government has sought to extinguish rights and to achieve a once-and-for-all settlement of historical claims. The aboriginal peoples, on the other hand, have sought to affirm their aboriginal rights and to guarantee their unique place in Canadian society for generations to come."[51] The federal position, which only slowly and grudgingly gave way by century's end to a policy that sought "certainty" rather than explicit extinguishment, was consistent with a view of treaties as contracts. The stand of the First Nations who opposed the extinguishment doctrine was the product of a view of treaty that emphasized treaties as the formalization of a relationship that was regularly renewed and might, if necessary, be modified in detail.

These twentieth-century differences in interpreting treaty are a reminder that, in the more than three hundred years that Europeans and Aboriginal peoples have been making agreements in Canada, there have been several different views regarding what constitutes a treaty. In their earliest forms, which emerged in the commercial forum in which European fur trader and Aboriginal fur supplier met, treaties were commercial compacts. They arose from traders' common-sense recognition that, whatever rights royal charters or licences might purport to bestow on them, in Indian Country the practical thing to do was to secure permission from the occupants, on whom they relied heavily in any event, to establish themselves and carry on commerce. Making these commercial compacts drew the Europeans into the First Nations system of values and protocol as they learned to carry out the ceremonies of welcome, gift exchange, and pipe smoking that governed Aboriginal peoples' relations with one another. Later, in the century after the Royal Proclamation of 1763 produced land-related treaties, the ensuing agreements often appeared to resemble contracts. At least according to the government versions of the ententes that have survived, a straightforward swap of land and title for compensation occurred. In the first half-century after 1763, the Crown's reliance on one-time payments strengthened that impression. By the time the Canadian state was established, this view of treaty as contract was firmly established in the minds of Canadian politicians.

As the numbered treaties of the West have shown, however, there was another, in many ways richer, view of treaty that vied with the contract interpretation for prominence. This was the conception of treaties that were ostensibly about access to territory as covenants. As treaty-related ceremonies suggest and oral history evidence confirms, western First Nations saw the agreements that they made between 1871 and 1877 as establishing relationships under the oversight of the Creator, relationships that were intended to be renewed annually, last forever, and be modified as circumstances required. As the number and power of First Nations declined and non-Native Canada became correspondingly dominant, that interpretation of treaties was pushed back into the shadows. In an era when First Nations were viewed as "a vanishing race" that was "melting like snow before the sun," and when the government of Canada pursued aggressive policies to control and refashion them through the Indian Act and its attendant programs, an exclusive emphasis on treaties as contracts and an insistence that the government text was the valid version were championed by the government and usually acquiesced to by the courts.

As attitudes and power relationships between First Nations and non-Natives began to shift in the late years of the twentieth century, perceptions of treaty were modified, too. Thanks both to the revelations of oral history research and the efforts of a new generation of researchers, including in particular Arthur J. Ray, a more complex understanding of treaties as having taken a variety of forms has emerged. Compacts, contracts, and covenants have at different times and in different quarters been seen as the single authentic form of treaty. In British Columbia in the 1990s, when a stalled treaty-making process left uncertainty about ownership that deterred investment in resource industries, pragmatic resource-company executives and First Nations quietly negotiated local agreements to pave the way for investment and job creation on First Nations lands.[52] In a sense, the approach that fur traders had used in the earliest decades after contact to ensure peaceful and assured access to Aboriginal territory and resources emerged again in the Pacific province in the 1990s. Given such historical ironies, one looks forward eagerly to see what a postmodern age such as the twenty-first century holds for Canadians' understanding of treaties.

Acknowledgments

The research on which this chapter is based was funded by a Standard Research Grant of the Social Sciences and Humanities Research Council of Canada. The chapter has also benefited from the research assistance of Rebecca Brain.

Notes

1 Arthur J. Ray, *Indians in the Fur Trade: Their Role as Trappers, Hunters, and Middlemen in the Lands Southwest of Hudson Bay, 1660-1870*, rev. ed. (Toronto: University of Toronto Press 1998 [1974]), xxiv. The introduction to the revised edition provides valuable insights into Ray's intellectual development and his views on many topics, including treaties, of importance in Native-newcomer history.
2 G.F.G. Stanley, *The Birth of Western Canada: A History of the Riel Rebellions*, rev. ed. (Toronto: University of Toronto Press, 1961 [1936]).
3 John L. Taylor, "Canada's North-West Indian Policy in the 1870s: Traditional Premises and Necessary Innovations" (1978), and John L. Tobias, "Canada's Subjugation of the Plains Cree, 1879-1885" (1983), in *Sweet Promises: A Reader on Indian-White Relations in Canada*, ed. J.R. Miller, 207-40 (Toronto: University of Toronto Press, 1991).
4 Arthur J. Ray and Donald Freeman, *"Give Us Good Measure": An Economic Analysis of Relations between the Indians and the Hudson's Bay Company before 1763* (Toronto: University of Toronto Press, 1978), esp. 55-59.

5 Ibid., 55.

6 Ibid., 56.

7 Ibid.

8 Ibid.

9 Ibid., 57

10 Ibid.

11 Ibid., 59. See also Arthur J. Ray, Jim Miller, and Frank Tough, *Bounty and Benevolence: A History of Saskatchewan Treaties* (Montreal and Kingston: McGill-Queen's University Press, 2000), 8. Professor Ray drafted the chapter on Aboriginal-Hudson's Bay Company relations in *Bounty and Benevolence*.

12 "Each leader leaves his grand calumet at the Fort he trades at unless he is affronted, and not designed to return next summer, which is sometimes the case." Andrew Graham in Ray and Freeman, *"Give Us Good Measure"*, 70.

13 Cornelius J. Jaenen, "French Sovereignty and Native Nationhood during the French Regime," in Miller, *Sweet Promises*, 19-42.

14 Walter Bagehot, *The English Constitution,* with an introduction by R.H.S. Crossman (London: C.A. Watts, 1964 [1867]), 61.

15 Goldwin Smith, *Canada and the Canadian Question* (Toronto: Hunter, Rose, 1891), 147.

16 E.E. Rich and A.M Johnson, eds., *Copy-book of Letters Outward &c: Begins 29th May, 1680, ends 5 July, 1687* (Toronto: Champlain Society for the Hudson's Bay Record Society, 1948), 4-13, emphasis added. For a second example, see *Copy-book,* 36.

17 On these early pacts and their relationship to the fur trade, see E.E. Rich, *The Fur Trade and the Northwest to 1857* (Toronto: McClelland and Stewart, 1967), 9-14.

18 Gilles Havard, *The Great Peace of Montreal of 1701: French-Native Diplomacy in the Seventeenth Century,* trans. Phyllis Aronoff and Howard Scott (Montreal and Kingston: McGill-Queen's University Press, 2001 [1992]), 16.

19 Ray and Freeman, *"Give Us Good Measure,"* 22.

20 Edward Ahenakew, *Voices of the Plains Cree,* ed. Ruth M. Buck (Toronto: McClelland and Stewart 1973), 72-73.

21 Hugh A. Dempsey, "Western Plains Trade Ceremonies," *Western Canadian Journal of Anthropology* 3, 1 (1972): 29-33, esp. 31-32.

22 Ray, Miller, and Tough, *Bounty and Benevolence,* 3. See also J.E. Foster, "Indian-White Relations in the Prairie West during the Fur Trade Period: A Compact?" in *The Spirit of the Alberta Indian Treaties,* ed. Richard Price (Edmonton: Pica Pica Press 1987 [1979]), 184. It should be noted that Foster's article refers to a general Aboriginal-European compact – similar to the compact between French Canada and English Canada that George Stanley champions in an article entitled "Act or Pact? Another Look at Confederation," Canadian Historical Association, *Report of the Annual Meeting 1956,* 1-25 – rather than to commercial compacts in the fur trade.

23 The literature on the English alliance system, including the Covenant Chain, is vast. The best approach is via the works of Francis Jennings: *The Invasion of America: Indians, Colonialism, and the Cant of Conquest* (Chapel Hill: University of North Carolina Press, 1975); *The Ambiguous Iroquois Empire: The Covenant Chain Confederation of Indian Tribes with the English Colonies from Its Beginnings to the Lancaster Treaty of 1744* (New York: W.W. Norton, 1984); and *Empire of Fortune: Crowns, Colonies and Tribes in the Seven Years War in America* (New York: W.W. Norton, 1988).

24 José António Brandão, *"Your fyre shall burn no more": Iroquois Policy toward New France and Its Native Allies to 1701* (Lincoln and London: University of Nebraska Press, 1997); J.A. Brandão and William A. Starna, "The Treaties of 1701: A Triumph of Iroquois Diplomacy," *Ethnohistory* 43, 2 (1996): 209-44; Havard, *Great Peace.*

25 A facsimile of the original 1701 treaty in French is found in Havard, *Great Peace,* 112-18 (an English translation is found in app. 3, 210-15, and a photograph of a wampum that some believe commemorates the 1701 Peace is found on page 124 [LAC reference number C-38948]).

26 Starna and Brandão regard it as part of a "triumph of Iroquois diplomacy" in 1701; Havard sees it as a French victory. The clash of interpretations derives, as is often the case, in large

part from the different sources upon which the respective historians relied. Starna and Brandão used both British and French documents extensively, while Havard's account is based on a wider range of French sources than Starna and Brandao employed.

27 James Youngblood Sákéj Henderson, *The Mi'kmaw Concordat* (Halifax: Fernwood, 1997). Authorities on Rome's relations with Canada, including with First Nations in the early period, hold that whatever relations existed between the Mi'kmaq and Roman Catholic clergy, the Vatican would not have considered their arrangement a *concordat*. Rome had no need of a *concordat* with the Mi'kmaq, and Rome in the early seventeenth century would not have considered the Mi'kmaq a society with a form of government with which it could have formal relations. Private correspondence with Luca Codignola, University of Genoa, 20 September 1999; and Roberto Perin, York University, 29 June 1999.

28 David L. Schmidt and B.A. Balcom, "The Règlement of 1739: A Note on Micmac Law and Literacy," *Acadiensis* 23, 1 (1993): 110.

29 John Borrows, "Wampum at Niagara: The Royal Proclamation, Canadian Legal History, and Self-Government," in *Aboriginal and Treaty Rights in Canada: Essays on Law, Equity, and Respect for Difference*, ed. Michael Asch (Vancouver: UBC Press, 1997), 155-72 and 256-67.

30 James Sullivan, ed., *The Papers of Sir William Johnson* (Albany: University of the State of New York 1921-65), 11: 30-31, 34.

31 For a more equivocal portrait of wampum and the Niagara commitments, see Paul Williams, "The Chain" (LL.M. thesis, Osgoode Hall, York University, 1982), chap. 4, "The Ojibways, the Covenant Chain and the Treaty of Niagara of 1764," 72-94. I am indebted to Professor Brian Slattery of Osgoode Hall, who kindly made a copy of this chapter available to me.

32 Canada, *Indian Treaties and Surrenders*, vol. 1, *Treaties 1-138* (Ottawa: Queen's Printer. 1891), 22-23.

33 Alexander Morris, *The Treaties of Canada with the Indians* (Saskatoon: Fifth House, 1991 [1880]), 299. The Selkirk Treaty is 299-300; the transfer of land from HBC to Selkirk is 300-1.

34 See Map 6.3 in Robert J. Surtees, "Land Cessions, 1763-1830," in Edward S. Rogers and Donald B. Smith, eds., *Aboriginal Ontario: Historical Perspectives on the First Nations* (Toronto: Dundurn, 1994), 103. Many of the later Upper Canadian treaties are depicted in Map 6.4, ibid., 114.

35 *Indian Treaties and Surrenders*, vol. 1, 62-63.

36 Morris, *Treaties*, 19

37 Ibid., 314-16. The inclusion of the "outside promises" is found on pp. 338-42. See also Ray, Miller, and Tough, *Bounty and Benevolence*, 81-85.

38 Harold Cardinal and Walter Hildebrandt, *Treaty Elders of Saskatchewan: Our Dream Is That Our Peoples Will One Day Be Clearly Recognized as Nations* (Calgary: University of Calgary Press, 2000), 53.

39 Ibid., 32.

40 Morris, *Treaties*, 97. Alexander Morris: "I held out my hand but you did not do as your nation [the Saulteaux] did at the [North West] Angle [last year]. When I arrived there the Chief and his men came and gave me the pipe of peace and paid me every honor."

41 Ibid., 182-83.

42 Cardinal and Hildebrandt, *Treaty Elders*, 41. For an elder's understanding of the binding nature of the pipe ceremony at Treaty 6 talks, see *The Counselling Speeches of Jim Kâ-Nîpitêhtêw*, ed. and trans. Freda Aheanakew and H.C. Wolfart (Winnipeg: University of Manitoba Press 1998), 109-13.

43 Notes of Lord Lorne's meetings with chiefs, 1881, LAC, RG 10, Records of the Department of Indian Affairs, vol. 3768, file 33,642.

44 For example, at Qu'Appelle in 1874. See Morris, *Treaties*, 86.

45 Ibid., 102.

46 Ibid., 221.

47 Ibid., 267.

48 J.A. Macrae to E. Dewdney, 25 August 1884, LAC, RG 10, vol. 3697, file 15,423.

49 For instances of government's rejecting First Nations requests for treaty, see the following: for Treaty 8, Ray, Miller, and Tough, *Bounty and Benevolence*, 148-55; and René Fumoleau,

As Long As This Land Shall Last: A History of Treaty 8 and Treaty 11, 1870-1939 (Toronto: McClelland and Stewart, 1975), 36-37. For Treaty 9, see John S. Long, *Treaty No. 9: The Indian Petitions, 1889-1927* (Cobalt, ON: Highway Book Shop, 1978), 2ff. For Treaty 10, see Ray, Miller, and Tough, *Bounty and Benevolence*, 170-73. And for Treaty 11, see Fumoleau, *As Long*, 134-49, 158, and 199-200.

50 P.A. Cumming and N.H. Mickenberg, *Native Rights in Canada*, 2nd ed. (Toronto: Indian-Eskimo Association, 1972 [1970]), 56-57. The Trudeau quotation is from an 8 August 1969 speech delivered in Vancouver.

51 [Murray Coolican], *Living Treaties: Lasting Agreements: Report of the Task Force to Review Comprehensive Claims Policy* (the Coolican Report) (Ottawa: Indian Affairs and Northern Development, 1985), 30.

52 I am indebted to my colleague Keith Carlson, who drew this point to my attention.

5
Smallpox along the Frontier of the Plains Borderlands at the Turn of the Twentieth Century
Jody Decker

In 1818, the 49th parallel between Lake of the Woods and the Rocky Mountains became the world's longest continuous international borderline, but it was not until 1874 that the approximately 1,287-kilometre line was surveyed. Even then, only 388 stone cairns, or earth mounds, defined the limits of sovereignty.[1] That span of line along the western interior had few natural boundaries and was, in effect, little more than a political construct and a geometric demarcation. Then, around 1895, Canadian government officials grew concerned about reports that smallpox was spreading into Canada from the United States. Along the western interior border, the federal government instituted "frontier inspections" to contain the outbreaks. By 1900, when the epidemic had peaked, those who attempted to cross the border had to answer sets of questions about where they had come from and whether they had been vaccinated or had recently been in contact with a sick person. These inspections altered the once porous border between the two countries. The borderline became a permeable shield and the zones adjacent to it, I suggest, a widened borderlands "scare zone" of multiple meanings, where cultural practices, border politics, and border enforcement intersected.

Thomas King, in *One Good Story, That One* (1993), illustrates this notion of porosity. He tells of a Native mother, born on the Canadian side of the border on an Alberta reserve, the father on the American side, taking her son to visit his sister in the United States, who is challenged at the border. She is asked by several border guards to state her citizenship, and in every case she replies, "Blackfoot." Asked *which side* she comes from, American or Canadian, she replies, "Blackfoot side." When asked by reporters how it felt to be an Indian without a country, she replies that she has a nice home on the reserve.[2]

For King's contemporary fictional Blackfoot woman, the border was more than a set of questions and a demarcation point. The legal boundary line created a cultural borderland for the Blackfoot woman. Her collective identities and the borderless plains over which her people had roamed, once porous, were severed by the political line. King created the Blackfoot woman's border experience to help us understand cultural identities and the meaning of "Native."[3] Her border experience demonstrates how identities are shifting and multiple in ways that are framed not only by national identity but also by other identities, such as ethnicity, class, and gender.

King's Blackfoot woman also helps us understand the often confusing concepts of a border, a boundary, and a borderland.[4] In this chapter, I use the term "border" to mean a political line of demarcation and the term "boundary" to refer to a socially constructed dividing line and perceptual filter between spatial groups that is embedded in daily discourse and action. The term "borderland" has largely replaced the more evocative term "frontier," which is usually used in reference to an east/west line of settlement. Unlike boundaries, borderlands are amorphous zones of varying width on either side of borders or boundaries. They change over time and space in response to local and non-local influences.[5] A borderland can have both material and metaphorical characteristics and is typically a conceptual tool for examining how difference and conflict are lived out. As well as being spaces of violence and conflict and hatred, borderlands are also mixing zones in which people share feelings, beliefs, and values; they are often characterized by a tendency to foster cooperation, innovation, and hybridity. Residents in borderlands tend to have more in common with each other than they do with the members of their respective dominant cultures.[6] Boundaries and borderlands influence and affect each other and may overlap, as this chapter shows, with regard to matters dealing with infectious disease.

Infectious diseases permeate borders and boundaries. For an infectious disease such as smallpox, the border can be both a political line and a sanctuary line, in that public health systems and quarantines aim to protect geographically defined populations. Increased levels of trade, mobility and migration, rising numbers of susceptible populations, lax surveillance methods, and misconceptions about communicable processes are open doors to infectious diseases that, as opportunists, do not respect imaginary political borders or socially ascribed boundaries. Susan Craddock employed border theory in her recent work on disease epidemics in San Francisco in the nineteenth century, in which she pointed out how the Chinese community was pathologized to keep it in its place. She argued in her study that infectious diseases, unlike people, could not be contained by political lines, and their permeation through space destabilized boundaries and created what she termed "border anxiety."[7] A similar situation evolved in the western interior, as this chapter shows, but vulnerability within the borderlands' "scare zone," as I term it, was played out differently between Native and non-Native groups as well as between reserve and non-reserve groups.

I was born and raised in the "scare" zone. When I first read Ray's (1974) seminal work *Indians in the Fur Trade,* the geography that I lived took on a whole new world of meaning, sparking my geographic sensibilities and launching a career in medical geography. The transitional parkland belt, or bio-geographical zone he identified in that study as being pivotal to the human geography of the western interior, was my homeland.

I knew the woodland and grasslands on either side of this zone less intimately than the parkland belt, but I was very aware that these three separate ecological zones delimited different Native groups. Ray described their historic tribal territories, the seasonal exploitation cycles of people and animals in and out of the parkland belt, and the reasons for demographic shifts that led to tribal migrations before 1870, when the process of territorially confining them on reserves began. His thesis was simple yet eloquent: the diffusion of infectious diseases, which was partly responsible for some of the shifts, was intimately tied to parkland seasonal exploitation cycles by different Native groups.

This study takes place within a vastly more structured geography in the interior, when territories became bounded political and administrative units, when survey lines and rail lines sliced through the interior with no regard to Native homelands, when time had led to the evolution of new infectious diseases that were brought to the interior by non-Native migrants. It is to this human and physical geography at the turn of the twentieth century that I now turn.

Setting the Stage

The overwhelming majority of Canadians live in a borderland shared with the United States. Yet northern borderlands have received far less attention than have the southern Mexican borderlands, despite their potential for consideration of borders and borderlands, and national and regional identities.[8] Francis Kaye contends that the borderlands of the prairie/plains region of the western interior are a region in which blending and contrasts "are most precise simply because two cultures, two nations, meet face to face on territory differentiated only by that political abstraction, the border."[9] Diseases and their impact in the western interior and northwest have been documented, but such studies have not focused on the effects of infectious disease on Native groups as played out in the borderlands of the plains/prairie region. Here, the borderlands interactions are particularly interesting because of the many Native people who inhabit the region and the physical landscape that offers few obstacles to those who might move across the border.[10]

The large-scale scientific expeditions from 1857 to 1860, sent to assess the western interior lands for settlement and potential resource use, helped spread knowledge of the physical and human geography of the southern boundary regions of the present-day provinces of Manitoba, Saskatchewan, and Alberta. Three geomorphic prairie levels were identified, which framed a topographic change from flatland near the eastern section, through to undulating terrain that included Turtle Mountain near the Manitoba-Assiniboia border, to a third prairie steppe peaking in the Cypress Hills of the southwestern districts of Assiniboia and Alberta (Map 5.1). These levels consisted of varying ecological zones exploited by different Native groups. Two natural regions of the plains were identified that would determine settlement patterns and resource usage: the more southern semi-arid grassland region straddling the border, deemed unsuitable for sustained agriculture, which became known as Palliser's Triangle, and the fertile or parkland belt to the north of Palliser's Triangle, which was championed for agriculture. With Confederation in 1867 and the sale of Rupert's Land to Canada two years later, a fundamental shift in economic activities, from furs to agricultural colonization, took place in the interior. Between 1871 and 1877, with the collapse of the buffalo-hunting economies (the staff of life for many plains Native peoples) and rapid white immigration into the interior, treaty-making between the Canadian government and starving Native peoples took place on the Prairies. Land was formally surrendered and reserve lands were surveyed. Aboriginal people became wards of the state, covered by a federal legal and administrative framework laid down in 1876 and known as the Indian Act. Despite a growing medical bureaucracy in the late nineteenth century, which included a board of health established in 1877 and a medical superintendent position created for the Province of Manitoba and the North-West Territories, health on reserves deteriorated. One lesson the Department of Indian Affairs had learned from previous smallpox outbreaks was that they were "expensive to control, dangerous to business, and preventable through vaccination."[11] Thus, in 1877, Dr. D.W.J. Hagarty, the first medical superintendent, was given the immediate task of vaccinating as many treaty Natives as possible. This practice, which usually took place when annuities were distributed in the spring, continued into the twentieth century.

Railways carried the settlers west. The St. Paul, Minneapolis, and Manitoba Railway (later the Great Northern Railway), which entered North Dakota near Grand Forks, was the first to reach Winnipeg in 1878, connecting that nodal city with St. Paul and Chicago. It was the main entrance to Manitoba until the completion of the Canadian Pacific Railway (CPR), and it solidified Winnipeg as the gateway to a vast hinterland.[12] During the last decades of the nineteenth century, it was also a major conduit for immigrants from

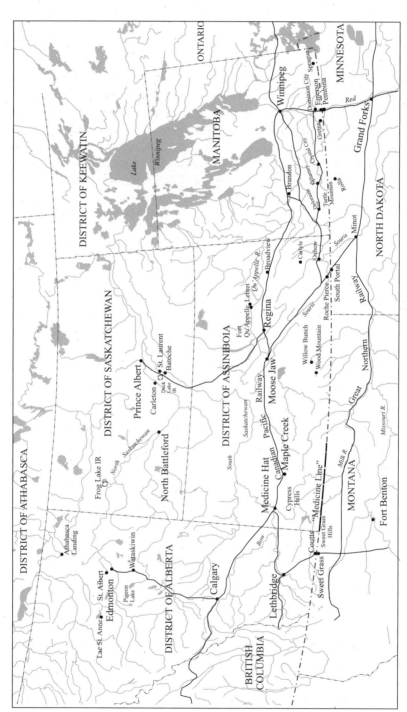

Map 5.1 The western interior, ca. 1900

the United States, who unwittingly brought smallpox with them over the border. The disease spread easily along the network of branch lines north and south of the main CPR lines. Winnipeg and southern Manitoba were settled first by homesteaders, with westward expansion occurring along proposed rail routes. By 1885, the CPR had crossed through the southern semi-arid grasslands and over the mountains to the Pacific coast. The rail had passed on or near many reserves in districts allocated for the Plains Cree bands (Treaty 4) and Blackfoot bands (Treaty 7) further to the west. By the turn of the twentieth century, those bands had been forced by the government to yield up large portions of their reserves to land-hungry immigrants.[13] Some rail lines also ran through or along established Métis buffalo-hunting trails and robe-trading routes south and west of Winnipeg.

The Métis, a new population of mixed Native and European ancestry that was created by the fur trade and that grew rapidly in the Red River area during the nineteenth century were not included in the Indian Act and had been unable to solve land issues with the government. Twice in the last quarter of the nineteenth century, they took up arms to force recognition of their needs as a distinct society but were defeated both times. Demoralized, they became the "forgotten people," most of whom were not covered under the Indian Act and thus were not eligible for any special health and social service benefits, such as vaccinations during the turn-of-the-century small-pox outbreak. They dispersed from their Red River homeland to the fringes of the dominant society, some migrating southwest to Dakota territory and westward to Montana to join kindred peoples, and others travelling north-west to the Qu'Appelle Valley, Prince Albert, and Edmonton regions. Arthur J. Ray summarized the situation at the end of the nineteenth century:

> In the end, the failure of government agricultural-training programs, the loss of reserve lands, and the dispossession of most Métis made many descendants of the Plains nation and the Métis – two of the most powerful nineteenth-century Native groups – into paupers who scratched out a miserable existence on the edges of a land their ancestors had dominated and roamed over freely.[14]

For northern plains Native groups – the Blackfoot, Cree, Assiniboine, Ojibwa, and Métis – who rapidly became the minority in the nineteenth century in western Canada, and who maintained ethnic ties on either side of an abstract legal line, the boundary was as much a homeland as it was a vague and undetermined place. Such a place was the one-hundred-mile stretch of the Montana-Saskatchewan borderlands along the 49th parallel, designated as "the Medicine Line" in Canada and the "Highline" in northern Montana (Map 5.1). In her recent book, *The Medicine Line,* Beth La Dow eloquently describes this borderland:

The border was medicine, it had power. It was also a "road" or "way." While a line is a mapmaker's abstraction, an inert barrier, a road is a path of something living. For whites, the line was a frontier in the European sense, a way of establishing the law, where one declared and fortified one's political identity. For natives, by contrast, the line was an instrument of camouflage, a stay against the erosion of life that had begun decades earlier.[15]

The spiritual, neutral Medicine Line along the Saskatchewan-Montana border, which held so much mystical sway for the Cree and Blackfoot, in particular, was also a concept understood by Native groups along the entire prairie border. It played a crucial role in the human geography of the plains/prairie region during the last quarter of the nineteenth century. Movements across this porous borderland by Native groups, for various reasons, established a pattern of behaviour that lingered until the time of the smallpox outbreaks at the turn of the twentieth century.[16] These movements were particularly evident around the 1870s, when a subsistence crisis arose in Medicine Line country due to the disappearance of the buffalo. It affected the Plains Cree in particular and, despite government attempts to restrict them, set the stage for cross-border movements by Native groups searching for food.[17] Whisky trading, which precipitated the Cypress Hills Massacre of 1873, led to Prime Minister John A. Macdonald forming the North-West Mounted Police (NWMP) and sending them west the following year to engage in law enforcement duties and to protect Native peoples. The NWMP played a major role during the smallpox epidemic in attempting to enforce quarantines and to curtail the cross-border traffic. In 1877, the ultimate borderlands strategist, as La Dow called Chief Sitting Bull, brought his starving and hunted group of Sioux across the Medicine Line into the Canadian sanctuary after the battle of the Little Bighorn. They lived just north of the Medicine Line, criss-crossing it to hunt, until they were deported in 1881. They felt safer north of the line under the protection of the Great Mother than south of the line under the US cavalry and sheriffs.

To the south of the Medicine Line, in Montana, groups of Métis had emigrated, partly in response to failed political aspirations and partly in response to labour relocations due to the buffalo-robe trade. These Métis were largely *hivernants*, or winterers, who took advantage of hunting buffalo on the plains in the winter months when the pelts were thickest. Several of these *hivernenent* camps straddled the border from the Turtle Hills in Manitoba to the Cypress Hills in Medicine Line country.[18] For the Métis, several of whom had intermarried with Aboriginal people, a vague ethnic boundary and an imaginary political border led to cross-border migrations well into the twentieth century.

The last half of the nineteenth century in the western interior was indeed dynamic, with Rupert's Land being bought and annexed to Canada, Natives groups being either placed on reserves or dispersed and their lands being surveyed for immigrant settlers, and railroads being built. The geographic and cultural transformation of the Prairies was dramatic. Even Palliser's Triangle, part of Medicine Line country and deemed unsuitable for agriculture, was settled by 1900. The Medicine Line, which was once considered a place of refuge for Natives, was about to be challenged by a microbe.

"Smallpox Has Eyes"

A microbe that kills its host, the person it makes sick, risks killing itself. To stay alive, microbes use ingenious ways to spread their weaponry. Some, like malaria or the plague, hitchhike on arthropods such as fleas or mosquitoes. Still others pass their germ from the mother to a foetus, while one of the more common microbes, influenza, will induce its host to cough the germs into the air. Air droplets from coughing or sneezing, along with direct, person-to-person contact are the primary ways the highly contagious virus, *Variola major*, or smallpox, enters the body. Humans are the only known host. The disease broadcasts its germs through forming a rash, which progresses to raised pustules, which, if they converge on the body, form a putrid, vile-smelling, oozing mass. After two weeks, scabs start to form, which, in about a month, are replaced with scars. A person is infectious until the last scab falls off. Unfortunately for humans, the virus is robust and, in certain conditions, can live outside the human host for days, on clothes, blankets, or even dust. With an average incubation period of twelve days, an infectious period often characterized by intense headaches, backaches, and general malaise, frightening disfiguration from skin lesions, a probability, albeit low, of blindness, and fatality rates of 20 percent and higher in unvaccinated individuals, it is little wonder the virus has been dreaded throughout history.[19]

Edward Jenner ameliorated the impact of the virus in 1796 when he discovered the process of vaccination by observing that milkmaids exposed to cowpox did not contract smallpox. The vaccine against smallpox, made from this different but related live virus, was known as *vaccinia*. Another procedure, called inoculation (or variolation), had been used for centuries in other parts of the world before Europeans discovered it in the eighteenth century. Inoculation was performed by deliberately implanting the live *variola* into the skin (or, as was common in Asia, inhaling the ground scab material into the nose) to produce immunity. The procedure had a low case fatality rate; the risk was in having an actual case of smallpox, which did not occur if one was vaccinated.

Microbes are living entities that evolve and change. A new form of smallpox appeared throughout the world in the 1890s, a much less virulent form named *Variola minor*, which was associated with case fatality rates of 1 percent or less.[20] Its hallmark signs were that it spread slowly and that morbidity (sickness) rates tended to be higher than mortality (death) rates. To the untrained eye, the disease resembled chicken pox, a common childhood disease, which meant that it was difficult to trace its occurrence. Because it produced a milder illness than did *Variola major*, it allowed infected hosts to remain ambulant during the course of their disease, and this resulted in more close contacts. In response to this scourge, containment measures such as quarantine (restricted movement on infected individuals) and cordon sanitaire (restricted movement of infected communities) were put in place; however, in general, health officials did not take surveillance, isolation of cases, and vaccination of contacts as seriously for *Variola minor* as they did for *Variola major*.

It was *Variola minor* that struck the plains in 1900. It first appeared in Pensacola, Florida, in 1896 and subsequently spread throughout the United States and Canada. Between 1900 and 1905, the case fatality rates in the United States from *Variola minor* ranged from 0.3 percent to 1.8 percent, with the number of reported cases peaking at around 62,000 in 1902.[21]

Just as microbes evolved, so did concepts of contagion and public health policy. Cultural practices come heavily into play here. Most plains Natives in the eighteenth century believed that smallpox had eyes and could see who was afraid of it, so they would gather around the ill person, smoke from the same pipes, and use the same blankets. Their "grand remedy" – the sweltering hot sweat bath, followed by the cold plunge into an icy river – led to even more deaths. By the nineteenth century, Native understanding of contagion had grown, as we see from the Cree, who knew that by rubbing the smallpox exudate on door handles and window frames, and by leaving unburied corpses close to the doors of European traders, they could convey the infection into the fort. Variolation had been available since the first part of the eighteenth century and was not replaced by vaccinations, or what the Natives called the Europeans' "grand medicine," until after 1800.[22] Such a treatment was concerned with individuals, not communities. Native worldviews included a medical/healing complex that was intricately tied to ceremonial life, community-wide responses to illness, applications of herbs and roots, and spiritual interventions.

During the last quarter of the nineteenth century, when Natives were being placed on reserves, these culturally appropriate responses to illness (the use of a healer and dances) were suppressed by the government as the new science of bacteriology and the medicalization of reserves gained ground. Lux argues that the shift in understanding from diseases being caused by specific germs rather than from miasmas or the wrath of a god also led to a shift in mainstream perceptions of Native peoples: rather than being seen as a waning race they were now seen as a race capable of spreading disease to non-Natives. Around the turn of the twentieth century, vaccination programs and quarantines for Natives were ostensibly carried out to prevent the spread of smallpox to non-Natives. As Dr. Peter Bryce, the medical officer for the Department of the Interior at the time, pointed out, the vaccination program was critical because there were so many railway construction workers in the West who posed a smallpox threat to Native peoples.[23] The federal government bore quarantine and vaccine costs for Native peoples (who were wards of the state) and the costs for quarantine inspection sites frequented by immigrants; however, for other people, the costs of quarantines were the responsibility of the provinces and municipalities. Despite the difficulties of quarantine enforcement (a task usually assigned to the NWMP) and debates over its efficacy, it proved to be an effective tool for medical officers and, as Lux argues, a rationale for the segregation of Native peoples.

A Few Words on the Data

This chapter draws heavily, but not totally, on the records of the Department of National Health and Welfare (RG29) between 1815 and 1986. These are kept in the Library and Archives of Canada and contain a wide variety of records, ranging from administrative files, to personal case files, to medical files and reports. Within this record group, there are around forty files entitled "Smallpox–Frontier Inspections."[24] The documents consist of correspondence from the inspectors; the NWMP; physicians; Dr. James Patterson, director general of public health for the Territories; and his federal counterpart, Frederick Montizambert, director general of public health in Ottawa. The inspectors were required to file monthly reports. Telegrams reporting current outbreaks and requests for supplies such as vaccines and monies abound. Many letters focus on political aspects of the outbreaks. Several letters, for example, are from rail operators claiming their business was being interrupted by inspection practices and regulations. Others discuss the behaviour of some of the inspectors. In all, it is a large, diverse group of documents, and it permits me to cross-check data with other sources, such as records of the Royal Canadian Mounted Police (RG18).

Patches of Pox to 1902

J.R. Stratton, secretary of the Province of Ontario, wrote to Sidney Fisher, minister of agriculture, in the spring of 1900, declaring that eight thousand cases of smallpox had occurred in the United States in the last three months and that it would be prudent to watch larger ports of entry like Detroit and Thunder Bay. Fisher replied directly that he had already appointed special medical inspectors to work with local health officials at ports to repel "the present threatening invasion of smallpox from the United States."[25] In the Atlantic Maritimes, smallpox had been epidemic during the winter of 1900, and concerns from coastal towns had been raised about how fishing boats from the United States should be handled. Similar reports were coming from west of the Rocky Mountains, with requests to have inspectors placed at boundary points and to have boats examined. In the western interior, inspectors were stopping all trains. Mail from the United States, Japan, and China was being fumigated.[26] Vaccine was ushered across Canada, but only for the use of frontier arrivals from the United States, not for the general populace, as one doctor in southern Manitoba was reminded by Montizambert, the director general of public health.[27]

Despite raising the shield to repel the invasion, the border proved to be porous. The disease had been prevalent in the United States since about 1895, said a provincial health officer in Manitoba who had been to a "sanitary convention" in St. Paul, Minnesota. While there, he learned smallpox had come from Cuba and "was brought to the US by refugees from the island before the [Spanish-American] war, and then when American soldiers came back, they also spread the infection."[28]

The frontier inspection documents reveal several different processes contributing to the outbreaks and spread of smallpox in the western interior. The immediate source of the 1900 outbreaks of smallpox in Canadian communities was the northern states.[29] Men from lumber camps in Minnesota who came to work on the Ontario and Rainy River Railway brought smallpox with them, which subsequently spread along the rail line. Other lumbermen from Minnesota and North Dakota, along with job seekers as far away as the Maritimes, who were hired as harvest hands during the summer and fall, also carried smallpox. Two land seekers, who escaped inspection at the border, became so ill from smallpox that they crawled into a farmer's wooden granary to die. (They survived, but the farmer whose granary and hay had to be burnt sent off a bill for damages to the government for $150 – which was refused.) "Wandering Crees" who were once deported but slipped back over the Montana-Assiniboia border; Natives who entered Canada via the Sweet Grass Hills (south of Lethbridge near the Montana-Alberta borderline) without reporting to customs; and "roving half-breeds," especially those around the Turtle Mountain Indian Reserve on the Manitoba-North Dakota borderline, which contained both American and Canadian First Nations, were cited as sources of smallpox throughout the frontier inspection documents. Various visitors who passed inspection at rail stations, railway workers and employees, telegraph construction workers, and miners at Roche Pierce near the border also harboured the virus at one time or another. Immigrants from infected districts, who daily, in large numbers, passed rail inspections during the season of immigration, were also carriers. For many people, as Dr. George DeVeber wrote from Lethbridge in the spring of 1901, the borderline was an imaginary one, and people came and went "over the bald headed prairie roads" as they wished, knowingly and unknowingly releasing the virus north of the boundary line.[30]

The alarm was raised about the porosity of the borderline in the spring of 1900, when a Mrs. Dye from Minnesota entered Manitoba through a rail inspection station at Emerson. Three days later, in Winnipeg, she died from smallpox. She would never know that her family in Minnesota had also succumbed to the disease. Dr. Henderson, the border inspector at Emerson, was questioned by his superiors in Ottawa as to the efficacy of his inspection; but Mrs. Dye had likely presented to the inspector in a prodromal state, perhaps not feeling well but with no visible signs of a rash.[31] A few months later, another local outbreak was reported further west at Maple Creek in "Medicine Line" country, where twelve cases had erupted. The disease was "eruptive in nature, and great difficulty is being experienced in properly diagnosing it."[32] *Variola minor* was a new disease to most doctors. A doctor from Westaskiwin, a town near Edmonton, went so far as to declare that the outbreaks in his region that appeared in February 1901 were certainly not smallpox and that the misdiagnosis was an "evil and injustice to the people of this community."[33] Another doctor from that region, however, sent a letter to Montizambert a few days later with drawings of the rash and a statement that smallpox was brought into the area from an infected man travelling from Pigeon Lake.[34] How could you track and contain a disease that was at worst undetectable in the latency period and at best not easily diagnosed?

Very little can be gleaned from the documents about the outbreaks of smallpox that occurred in the first few months of 1901 in the western interior towns of Medicine Hat, Edmonton, or Maple Creek, but the documentation of an outbreak in Lethbridge in February reveals how the disease spread to the interior. Smallpox in Lethbridge was said to originate in Coutts, where the only railway station along that region of the borderline was located. In February alone, over five hundred settlers, mostly Mormons, crossed through its gates. One man, a visitor from California, who concealed his disease at the Coutts station, was traced by authorities through a trail of infectives and was subsequently fined. He did not know that his action would have consequences as far north as Edmonton and as far east as Maple Creek.[35] By April, the disease had also permeated the Frog Lake Reserve near North Battleford and found susceptibles amongst a group of Métis east of Edmonton and, later that summer, at Lac St. Anne.

In May, a botched quarantine effort near South Portal, a North Dakota borderline town, was said to be the cause of a localized outbreak there. Further to the east, an outbreak in the North Dakota border town of Rollo prompted Montizambert to order the NWMP to patrol the region around Killarney, Manitoba, "for the purpose of directing and restricting the ingress of passengers to the points controlled by you or your guards."[36] In the borderline town of Crystal City, Manitoba, Dr. Riddell wrote to Montizambert that an outbreak in the Turtle Mountain Reserve showed no sign of waning, and he added that "the sources of danger are from the roving half-breed bands & from emigrants from the infected districts. This being a port of entry nearly all the emigrants come here."[37] The fear that smallpox from this region would be carried north by the "Indians and half-breeds" who passed through the Indian reserve at Swan Lake was voiced by residents around that region through Dr. Wood to Montizambert.[38]

As the winter drew to a close, outbreaks waned, and this prompted officials to ease up on quarantines and to withdraw the police and inspectors along parts of the frontier inspection line. Vaccinations, now compulsory for rail crews moving back and forth across the land and all workers in lumber camps in Minnesota, would surely stop the outbreaks.[39]

To the south of the borderline, however, smallpox was reportedly raging in numerous reservations across several states.[40] Predictably, a few cases slipped over the borderline, and localized outbreaks were reported inland (around Broadview and Carlyle in southeastern Assiniboia in the early fall). Later in the fall, a rail worker en route from Moose Jaw to Regina was found to have smallpox, but this was obviously contained as only a few other cases were reported from those two towns that year. Another patch of outbreaks was reported in various southwestern Manitoba towns and a subdivision of Winnipeg; threshing gangs from North Dakota were cited as a source for some of these outbreaks. Another outbreak was reported in October 1901 at Athabasca Landing, north of Edmonton. Fifteen of seventeen Métis, who had moved there from Edmonton a few months earlier to escape quarantine, had smallpox. They had been on their way back to Edmonton to exchange ducks and chickens for flour, bacon, and tea. After seeing the tell-tale scabs on the children, the doctor requarantined them, with the promise of food.[41] All too often, such instances of quarantine noncompliance occurred.

Quarantine was contested and unwelcomed for several reasons. Various debates about the efficacy of the practice were put forth. Notices posted on doors of houses evoked public statements of shame. Because of sheer numbers, business dealings, informal communications, and ever-growing transportation networks, cordon sanitaire of entire urban communities was not an option, except in the case of Natives being contained on reserves, ostensibly to protect them from settlers.[42] Then there were the costs of quarantine. The usual quarantine period, according to the ordinance first established in 1898, was eight weeks after the rash first appeared – the time it took for the skin to be clear of scabs.[43] Breaking quarantine could elicit a fine of $100. Natives, already poverty-stricken, were worried about how they would feed themselves and make a living if they could not hunt and sell their goods during the required two-month containment period. From an NWMP perspective, lack of compulsory vaccination among Métis, who were "nearly all destitutes" and had to be fed when they were quarantined, was costly for the government.[44] Other costs included vaccines and quarantine inspectors and doctors. Quarantine doctors cost the federal government $100 per month plus living and travelling expenses and were required to submit monthly reports.

Miners, lumbermen, and railway workers did not welcome quarantine inspectors in their camps for fear that they would close them. Late in the fall of 1901, most miners were placed in strict quarantine at Roche Pierce and further west in Lethbridge.[45] Railway operators took every opportunity to inform Ottawa that undue delays at border crossings, mandatory proof of vaccination for every passenger, and the quarantining and disinfecting of the infected cars at the railway's expense was detrimental to business. In the absence of a satisfactory vaccination certificate, all baggage and household effects coming into Canada from any infected district were to be disinfected and fumigated. As Montizambert reminded one railway manager who questioned the rights of inspectors to eject passengers who refused to be vaccinated before crossing the frontier, "The power of holding unvaccinated persons and preventing their entry into the country, at least until the expiry of the period of incubation of smallpox, is distinctly given to our maritime quarantine officers in the Regulations and it has always been assumed that frontier quarantine officers have similar powers."[46]

Patches of Pox, 1902 and Beyond
On 24 January 1902, the headline of the *Winnipeg Free Press* read "HONEY-COMBED WITH SMALLPOX – Alarming state of Affairs in Winnipegosis District – Indians and Halfbreeds Suffer the Worst – Ten Percent of the Cases Considered Severe – Precautionary Measures Taken to Prevent Further Spread of the Infection."[47] The article that followed quoted the provincial health officer as saying that he learned from attending a conference in Minnesota that smallpox cases there had jumped from 357 in 1899 to 8,500 in 1901. It was no surprise that Dr. Mitchell, the inspector for the Moose Jaw region, found a case of smallpox on the train at the borderline town of South Portal, North Dakota, in January of 1902. He removed the infected man from the train, locked its doors, and left it on the American side of the border with twenty passengers still inside. A telegraph from Montizambert to Dr. Mitchell gave explicit directions that the train was to remain in quarantine for twenty-one days and to be disinfected. Further, all the people were to be vaccinated, with "expenses to be borne by the railway company."[48] The frustration of the rail company officials in this situation can only be imagined.

In February 1902, in the town of Lebret, north of South Portal, one of the worst outbreaks of smallpox to be seen by Dr. James Patterson, director general of public health for the Territories, was "in full bloom." Twenty-five French Métis, all unvaccinated, living in six houses within 3.2 kilometres of each other, were very ill with smallpox, and could not fend for themselves. Those who were mildly afflicted had secretly visited friends on a nearby reserve, and some children had attended a day-school, which was, unfortunately, located beside a large industrial school in nearby Fort Qu'Appelle.[49] Patterson's fears of a widening spread of smallpox materialized. It was not long before dozens of cases were quarantined in the Fort Qu'Appelle Post Office. By mid-March, an NWMP memo reported fifty-nine cases around Qu'Appelle, twelve under observation, and sixteen houses in quarantine.[50] There were no cases observed at nearby Piapot Reserve, but, as Inspector J.O. Wilson warned, "It is quite impossible to tell where the disease will make its appearance next, as the half-breeds have all been mixed in and outside the boundaries of the reserves."[51] Outbreaks were reported from this region until April.

Meanwhile, in southern Manitoba at Emerson, Dr. Henderson reported to Montizambert that numerous Americans were migrating north; happily, most of them were vaccinated. The epidemic persisted, he posited, because the disease was mild and not being reported. Such was the case of a woman who became afflicted after being in contact with a man from the lumber camps located near Sprague, a Manitoba border town. She admitted to dreading quarantine and, as she was feeling reasonably well, unwisely did not report her disease. In a highly contagious state, and without her house and its contents being disinfected, she went about her business, spreading smallpox to unwitting souls with whom she came in contact.[52] A week later, Henderson was reporting an additional outbreak of smallpox among lumbermen from Minnesota, whom he had quarantined at the border town of Dominion City. From yet another nearby border town, Waskada, the inspector reported smallpox among Scandinavian immigrants who were "next to impossible to properly quarantine."[53]

Outbreaks of smallpox south of the border seemed endless, and the effects were being felt beyond the borderline into the western interior. In Assiniboia and elsewhere in the North-West Territories, reports of outbreaks in the winter and spring of 1902 reached the Public Health Director's Office in Ottawa. One cluster had developed in May and June around Prince Albert and Fort Carlton. Forty cases were reported from the Métis settlements at Batoche, Duck Lake, and St. Laurent in the same region. A second outbreak took place around Prince Albert, bringing the total number of cases there to 212, with almost 600 people quarantined and 430 receiving rations.[54] In his May report for that area, Patterson recounted that a well-to-do white family with nine children had refused vaccination, and when he revisited the family four days later, all nine children were sick in bed with smallpox. Despite also reporting that there were many cases of Métis with smallpox in the northwest region, he added that the majority of cases in southern Manitoba were whites, not Natives.[55] The members of one white family in the borderlands town of Oxbow, Assiniboia, were stricken with what they thought was chicken pox, and they had put up an NWMP constable overnight. It was not long afterward that the constable became sick, saw a doctor, and was told, too late, that his illness was smallpox. Over the next month, reports from Oxbow indicated that there were seven very severe cases of smallpox.[56] Obviously, it cannot be argued that only Aboriginal people spread the disease.

An additional cluster of smallpox had developed in the summer of 1902 near Fort Qu'Appelle at the town of Rocanville in both its railway camps and residences. In the nearby rail town of Moosomin, a railway worker was the source of an outbreak.[57] In the Fort Qu'Appelle region, which included File Hills and Lebret, where the disease had broken out earlier in the winter and had abated by July, Patterson reported that, out of 112 cases, there had been only six deaths.[58] His figures suggest that the case fatality rate (an indicator of a disease's deadliness) of around 5 percent for this region was higher than the expected 1 percent for *Variola minor*.

Further west that summer, in Medicine Hat, an outbreak occurred from a case known to have come from the German settlement of Josephberg, sixty-four kilometres to the south. The case had erupted in a house of "half-breeds" and was traced to a man who had been travelling all summer with his family south of the Medicine Line in Montana.[59] Near Lethbridge, an outbreak occurred in a telegraph construction gang and was traced to a man who had buried a dead Native he had found out on the prairie two weeks earlier. In the same regional cluster south of Lethbridge, the NWMP had been placed on high alert because a group of American Indians had entered Canada via the Sweet Grass Hills and had not reported to Customs. Six of the eight had smallpox. These Indians were members of a band of "Wandering Crees," who, having fled Canada earlier, had now returned in an infected state.[60]

During the winter – traditionally the season when smallpox flourished – disquiet blanketed the interior. Montizambert was inundated with requests to rehire quarantine inspectors, even in regions where there had been none before, and even for freight as well as passenger trains. The Emerson inspector had warned Montizambert that

the disease is now more liable to be introduced into the Province by emigrants from the States, who are now commencing to rush into this country, quite a number of them complain very much of the Canadian emigration at the boundary, had they been warned of it they would provide themselves with certificates, and those not already vaccinated could have it attended before leaving home.[61]

In a related letter, Dr. Henderson wrote from Emerson in March 1903 that "it is very difficult to keep posted about infected districts as the Public Press keeps silent about smallpox during the emigration season."[62] Inspection stations were re-established at the border towns of Gretna and Emerson; however, due to a marked decline in the number of smallpox cases in the United States, by May the Province of Manitoba was attempting to curtail inspections at all frontier points along its border. By July, with very few cases reported in the United States, the Territories also considered stopping frontier inspections, even though they suspected that, due to economic consequences, many towns were not reporting outbreaks.

Late in 1903 there had been rumours of the return of smallpox south of the line, and an outbreak along the CPR line had resulted in a few cases erupting in Sprague, Manitoba, in the fall, but no other significant outbreaks emerged. From the government's dollar-and-cents viewpoint, ongoing inspections were unnecessary, and most of them were suspended as of August 1903. One North Dakota citizen, however, did not agree with the federal government's decision and wrote a letter to the local physician, who subsequently sent it on to the director general of public health. This citizen complained that the lack of inspections signalled imminent danger for him: "Now I live on Section 3, 1, 18, and just across the border in Dakota there is a large number of cases of small-pox, and we are in danger of infection. There is no restriction of traffic. Would you kindly have some precautions taken at once."[63] It is not clear how the federal government responded to this specific request, but, according to the report of the director general of public health, frontier quarantine inspections were maintained at Morden and Crystal City in Manitoba due to outbreaks of the disease in North Dakota. They were withdrawn completely along the frontier borderlines as of July 1904.

Occasional outbreaks in the United States and Canada continued in the years to follow. One outbreak in the interior in 1907 led to an unorthodox procedure. A man died whose head was "swollen three times normal size, his tongue also swollen the same, blue marks all over the body, small pimples on skin, wife and the children sick, blue marks and swelling on body, reddish pimples on skin, no vaccination marks."[64] Fluids from the body were injected into guinea pigs. Because the guinea pigs survived the injected matter, it was assumed that the man had not died from smallpox but from German measles. The other sixteen members of the family were no doubt greatly relieved. This "much-feared" disease, as Montizambert had once called it, was embedded in the psyche of both Natives and non-Natives.

The Scare Zone

Table 5.1 provides a summary of yearly smallpox events referred to in this chapter, either as outbreaks or as reported diffusion routes in the interior.

For 1901, there were clusters of outbreaks, primarily involving Natives in the Edmonton region, the Métis around Turtle Mountain, and major rail crossing points along the border. For 1902, a major cluster of outbreaks occurred around the Métis settlements in the Batoche region, Native reserves near the main rail line in Assiniboia, and further north around Prince Albert. Clusters in these districts could be expected as Natives were concentrated in settlements and reserves throughout the region. Major borderline towns such as Emerson in the Province of Manitoba, North Portal in the District of Assiniboia and South Portal across the borderline in North Dakota, and Coutts further west in the District of Alberta, were the primary border-crossing sites for both immigrants and smallpox. Many of the outbreaks were concentrated along the Manitoba borderline, where settlement had been first established and population densities were high enough to sustain the disease. The subsequent spread into the interior was usually linear, along rail lines and routes used by waged labourers, and in patches, where Native reserves, Métis settlements, and mining and lumber camps were located. Conflicting vaccination policies, lack of quarantine compliance, difficulties with differential diagnosis of the disease, and circumvention of inspection stations (by Native groups in particular) were major contributing factors to the spread of the disease and the occurrence of outbreaks. Denial of and silence about having the disease, underestimation of the transmission capabilities of the virus, unwarranted faith in inspectors, and self-interested parties such as the railroads and the press also determined the diffusion patterns of the disease and contributed to the emergence of a risk-society along the borderline.

The political borderline became a site of contestation between public health officials, rail companies, and citizens of both countries travelling across the border. Delays at inspection points due to shortages of doctors (who were put in charge of two different entry points), uncooperative passengers, uncertainty on the part of quarantine officers regarding what to do with infected individuals, and the time-consuming process of disinfecting all goods and fumigating the mail increased "border anxiety." The boundary area around the borderline, where local spatial groups engaged in daily practical tasks of transferring goods and people, became a heightened zone of activity related to smallpox inspection endeavours. It became more than an inconvenience to everyday living: it was an irritant that saw risk-taking and avoidance behaviour played out in various degrees. In this zone, fear of the disease produced a greater problem than the disease itself warranted, and a borderlands scare zone was created due to both real and perceived threats of smallpox. The traditional borderlands of the Medicine Line were no longer a safety net for Natives but, rather, a safety hazard: those who travelled to visit relatives south of the borderline ran the risk of contacting smallpox and carrying it back across the border to friends and relatives. For them, the

Table 5.1

Summary of smallpox events in the western interior, 1901 and 1902

Date reported	Outbreak locations	Primary groups affected
1901		
February 19	Maple Creek/Edmonton	"adults"
February	Coutts	unknown
April 26	St. Albert/Morinville	"cases"; woman and child
April 26	Edmonton to Witfords	"cases of half-breeds"
April 30	Turtle Mountain Reserve	"roving half-breeds"
April 30	Lethbridge-Coutts region	settlers
July 23	Lac St. Anne, Devil's Lake	"Indians"
August 31	Beaver Lake, Carlyle, Broadview	cases
October 1	Turtle Mountain area	"half-breeds"
October 6	Regina, Moose Jaw	unknown
October 15	Regina from Moose Jaw	harvesters
October	Lower Fort Garry (Wpg)	threshing gang
October	Deloraine, Hartney, Brandon	unknown
October (near end)	Athabasca Landing	"half-breeds"
November 15	Edmonton/Strathcona	large number of cases
November 15	Lethbridge	miners
December 4	Winnipeg from Toledo	two women
December 9	Morinville	cases
December 15	Roche Pierce from Hartney	miners
1902		
January 23	Moose Jaw from Minot	CPR worker
January 24	Winnepegosis district	"Indians & half-breeds"
February 18	Lebret from File Hills	"half-breeds"
February 19	"all over the dominion"	
March 12	Qu'Appelle, File Hills area	112 cases
March 17	Qu'Appelle district	116 cases
April	Pembina & Winnipeg	"frequent new cases"
April 30	Winkler from Dakota	"white fellow"
May	Moosomin region	miles of quarantine camps
May 2	Prince Albert	40 cases "mostly half-breeds"
May 19	Oxbow	7 cases; NWMP officer
May 26	Waskada, Souris district	Scandinavian immigrants
May 31	Emerson from Sprague	lumber camps; a woman
June 4	Dominion City from Minnesota	lumber men from camps
June 11	Bressaylor near Battleford	unknown
June 17	Moosomin	rail worker
June 23	St. Laurent, Carleton, Wingard district	"nearly all half-breeds"
July 29	Lethbridge	13 cases
July 29	Duck Lake & Prince Albert	160 cases of "usual class"
August 21	Vegreville/Beaver Lake	two "half-breeds"
September 10	Medicine Hat; Prince Albert from Josephburg Settlement from Montana	"half-breed father"; 212 cases
October 27	Boundary Creek/Coutts	Indians
November 10	Lethbridge area	telegraph construction gang
November 20	Lethbridge from Montana	"wandering Crees"

borderlands remained a porous region, one that signified a continuation of their past, not a sharp break in their identity.

In the spring of 1901, Montizambert received a letter from Robert Thornton, who was stationed in the Manitoba border town of Deloraine. In it, he outlined what he believed were three "danger sources for the territory": Turtle Mountain Indian Reserve, which, according to him, contained Indians from the United States; Métis passing through or near the reserve; and road travel to and from Dakota, which offered exposure to the south.[65] Turtle Mountain, per se, spanned the borderline, but the reserve was located in Canada just south of Deloraine. The reserve's inhabitants were a small band of around forty Dakota Sioux, who had come from the United States in the 1860s and settled in this mountain area to hunt. A group of "stragglers" were also present with them on this reserve. The outbreaks of smallpox in the region had led to economic hardships and forced many of the reserve's younger people to return to the United States. Others gradually moved to the Oak Lake Reserve further north on the Souris River, where they had close ties with related Dakota bands.[66] The movement of these Natives (particularly of the stragglers with no fixed home) between reserves or across the border for visitation or economic purposes, placed them at a high risk of acquiring and/or spreading smallpox.

In her recent book, *The Line That Separates*, Sheila McManus argues that two of Canada's nationalist goals were to "attract the right kind of white immigrants to settle the West, and prove that Canada could use its superior spaces, services, and political system to lure top-quality immigrants away from the United States."[67] Scandinavians were very favoured, for instance, as they had already proven themselves in the United States. Despite the fact that some immigrant groups, such as the Scandinavians and whites, contracted smallpox, it was the Métis who could not seem to shake the disease or gain the confidence of others. References throughout the inspection papers describe them as a highly mobile group. As E.M. Wood, secretary to the Provincial Board of Health in Winnipeg, reported:

> There is a lot of alarm amongst our citizens over the outbreak of small-pox, which the breeds at Rock Lake have. As they are travelling back and forth now, our people are afraid ... The half-breed population are a class that are continually on the move. They move from one place to another and visit each others' houses regularly, and without the slightest apprehension of contracting the disease or infecting others.[68]

Similar sentiments were less well articulated: "Half Breed are diggin snake Root and Picking Berry and come a cross to sell them we think that the government should keep the Quarantine yet."[69] In one instance, a Native group's lack of adherence to quarantine measures resulted in their houses being burned and their clothes disinfected. This was to stand as an example to others.[70] Shortly after Patterson started his new job as director general of public health for the Territories, he called for universal vaccination of all peoples; but he doubted the efficacy of burning houses. As he wrote:

> I believe successful vaccination of every one to be the only practical way of stamping out the epidemic ... the only way to disinfect these houses is to burn them and their contents. The epidemic is too widespread to think of doing this.[71]

General vaccination of the populace was not mandatory in Canada, and, as the Métis were not wards of the state as were the First Nations, they could not be forced to accept vaccinations, despite calls from Patterson and the NWMP for that to happen. In a letter from Acting Deputy Minister of the Interior T.G. Rothwell to Montizambert, the minister stated that the matter of vaccinating "half-breeds," who were not wards of the state, was not one with which his department should interfere.[72] Many Métis did accept vaccination, however, as was reported by Sergeant Bird at the Duck Lake Reserve and by Patterson with regard to the St. Laurent settlement in June 1902.[73] Once again, the Métis fell between administrative cracks – and not just as "forgotten people" but often as neglected people. Impoverished as they may have been, reserve Indians may have been protected by their status, while the freedom of the Métis furthered their risk of infection. For them, the borderline, once imaginary, had, in the smallpox scare zone, become a visible reality.

Final Thoughts

For most of the nineteenth century, the power of the international boundary line remained limited in the lives of different groups of peoples. Visas and travel documents were not required until after 1914, border controls were few and tended to be local rather than national issues. It was the federal government that initiated the process of redefining rules at the borderline by implementing frontier inspections. Authority at the borderline fell into the hands of provincial public health departments that were under federal direction. The logistical capacity of the various governments to contain the disease along the border was challenged by the mobility of Natives, trade traffic, the circulation of seasonal workers involved in resource extraction, and immigration at rail crossings.

In an attempt to reduce transborder health risks, inspection officers reported outbreaks and probable cases of smallpox to each other along the borderline. Their efforts were undermined by people who remained silent about their disease and, especially, their children's disease for fear of being quarantined; by people who used darkness and seldom-used crossing points as a way of penetrating the border shield; by railway companies who complained bitterly about the untimely and confusing inspection process mandated by the federal government; by the press, which, at times, suppressed publication of outbreaks when it thought that to do otherwise would be disadvantageous for business or emigration; by smaller communities that felt that the economic fall-out from an outbreak would be worse than the consequences of reporting it; by sentiments such as the one expressed by a Canadian public health official, who felt that, due to lax public health measures in the United States, Canada was being used as a "dumping ground";[74] and by Montizambert, who, in 1903, suggested that the waning incidence of the disease was because "more intelligent and satisfactory measures are being adopted and carried out by the American Health Authorities."[75] Canadian inspectors made repeated trips across the border to monitor health on reservations and to talk with American health officials. Despite a few charged comments, efforts at containing the disease did not overtly affect international relations; however, heightened anxieties did affect interpersonal relations. Fellow citizens accused each other of starting an outbreak. The Métis, who ignored the existence of the borderline and the precautionary measures against smallpox that came with it, were often implicated in outbreaks. For them, as for the Blackfoot woman in King's story, there was no right or wrong side as what was being referred to was a borderland of shared feelings, values, and social characteristics – a region of blended communities in which they lived and died.

We may also look to the disease itself to see how transborder health risks were played out along borders. The fear of smallpox had long been embedded in the psyche of both Natives and non-Natives because *Variola major* epidemics had spread from points in the United States north into the interior, and their impact had been devastating for Native groups.[76] *Variola minor*, however, was not the killer *Variola major* had been. There is not enough information from this data to compute morbidity and mortality rates among Native and non-Native groups, but anecdotal accounts suggest that mortality in the 1900 epidemic was small.

Interestingly, both Natives and non-Natives were vulnerable to this new form of smallpox, but it was the perceived risk behaviour of Native groups, the mobile Métis, in particular, which was most often cited as the cause for the spread of smallpox. The Métis moved from place to place, in and around Native reserves and across the borderline, to sell wood and hay to make a living and to visit their relatives. White seasonal labourers were also mobile but were not negatively labelled as disease carriers. Why this was so is not clear, except that the non-white Métis tended to move with their entire families and seasonal labourers did not. Perhaps the discourse that developed around the disease intensified after the disease penetrated the borderline shield. Perhaps some Native groups appeared complacent because biological explanations for the outbreaks were foreign to them. Perhaps other vulnerable groups, such as migrant workers and immigrants, made economic concerns their priority and were thus willing to take certain risks. Perhaps, in the grinding face of poverty, the risk of contracting smallpox was acceptable for some. Or perhaps this series of outbreaks was just one in a litany of wake-up calls regarding infectious diseases that shook the confidence of politicians, the public at large, and public health workers. Clearly, cultural practices and behaviours influenced and shaped disease patterns during this smallpox epidemic. Disease is a human invention. Micro-organisms such as viruses and bacteria exist in nature but disease, as such, does not; what does exist are cultural practices. In looking at a time of rapid cultural transformation in the interior, during which the introduction of a new infectious disease led to the instigation of new rules and regulations along the boundary, border theory gives us the flexibility to navigate how and why difference and indifference were played out. The borderland I write of in this chapter ceased to exist when the rules and reasons for protecting the boundary no longer gave it meaning. Arguably, a borderland scare zone was created most recently along sections of the Canadian-American border with the introduction of another new infectious disease – SARS.

Notes

1 The long process of the demarcation and definition of the boundaries between the United States and Canada has been detailed in C. Ian Jackson, ed., *Letters from the 49th Parallel, 1857-1873: Selected Correspondence of Joseph Harris and Samuel Anderson* (Toronto: The Champlain Society, 2000), xi-cvi.
2 Thomas King, *One Good Story, That One* (Toronto: HarperPerennial, 1993), 136, 139.
3 In this chapter, the term "Native" includes First Nations, Métis, and Inuit. The term "Indian" is used when the historical context requires it.
4 According to Daniel Drache, a border has four elements. It is a security moat; a regulatory wall consisting of domestic rules and norms for health, transportation, and the environment; a commercial gate to facilitate transnational flows of goods, services, and people; and a citizenship checkpoint for immigration and refugees. See Daniel Drache, *Borders Matter: Homeland Security and the Search for North America* (Black Point, NS: Fernwood, 2004), 2-3. In the last decade, the study of borders has re-emerged as a strong and interdisciplinary theme, and this has led to a conflation of the term "border" with the terms "boundary" and "frontier." David Newman discusses the disparate meanings and emerging themes of boundaries and boundary phenomena in "Boundaries," in *A Companion to Political Geography*, ed. John A. Agnew, Katharyne Mitchell, and Gearóid Ó Tuathail, 123-37 (Malden, MA: Blackwell Publishing, 2002). Another important review of boundary studies and the convergence of political geography and social theory is found in David Newman and Anssi Paasi, "Fences and Neighbours in the Postmodern World: Boundary Narratives in Political Geography," *Progress in Human Geography* 22, 2 (1998): 186-207.
5 Barbara J. Morehouse, "Theoretical Approaches to Border Spaces and Identities," in *Challenged Borderlands: Transcending Political and Cultural Boundaries*, ed. Vera Pavlakovich-Kochi, Barbara J. Morehouse, and Doris Wastl-Walter (Burlington, VT: Ashgate Publishing Company, 2004), 33.
6 Lauren McKinsey and Victor Konrad, *Borderlands Reflections: The United States and Canada*, Borderlands Monograph Series No. 1 (Orono, ME: University of Maine Press, 1989), 4.

7 Susan Craddock, *City of Plagues: Disease, Poverty, and Deviance in San Francisco* (Minneapolis: University of Minnesota Press, 2000).

8 John M. Findlay and Ken S. Coates, eds., *Parallel Destinies: Canadian-American Relations West of the Rockies* (Seattle/Montreal: University of Washington Press/McGill-Queen's University Press, 2002), 6.

9 Francis Kaye, quoted in Victor Konrad, "Borders and Borderlands in the Geography of Canada-United States Relations," in *North America without Borders? Integrating Canada, the United States, and Mexico,* ed. Stephen J. Randall, Herman Konrad, and Sheldon Silverman (Calgary: University of Calgary Press, 1992), 202.

10 Recent works that have looked at the impact of the border on Aboriginal peoples include: John Lutz, "Work, Sex, and Death on the Great Thoroughfare: Annual Migrations of 'Canadian Indians' to the American Pacific Northwest," in Findlay and Coates, *Parallel Destinies,* 80-103.

11 Maureen Lux, *Medicine That Walks: Disease, Medicine, and Canadian Plains Native People, 1880-1940* (Toronto: University of Toronto Press, 2001), 139.

12 John Warkentin and Richard Ruggles, *Historical Atlas of Manitoba: A Selection of Facsimile Maps, Plans and Sketches from 1612-1969* (Winnipeg: Manitoba Historical Society, 1970), 390.

13 Arthur J. Ray, *I Have Lived Here since the World Began: An Illustrated History of Canada's Native People* (Toronto: Lester Publishing and Key Porter Books, 1996), 259-62.

14 Ibid., 267. For a cartographic story of the dispersal of the Métis, see D.N. Sprague, Barry Kaye, and D. Wayne Moodie, "Dispersal of the Manitoba Métis and the Northwest Rebellion, 1870-1885," in *Historical Atlas of Canada II: The Land Transformed, 1800-1891,* ed. R. Louis Gentilcore (Toronto: University of Toronto Press, 1993), plate 35. As the fur trade era of two centuries wound down on the plains, settlement proceeded unrelentingly. When Manitoba became a province in 1870, fur traders, Métis, and the few other settlers in the Red River colony (present-day Winnipeg) numbered around 12,000. By 1886, rapid immigration to the province led to a total population of 109,000, with the Métis becoming a minority. Settlement within the North-West Territories and Assiniboia District was also experiencing rapid growth. By 1914, combined with Manitoba, the population in the northwest had jumped from 300,000 in 1889 to 1.8 million. See Donald Kerr and Deryck W. Holdsworth, *Historical Atlas of Canada III: Addressing the Twentieth Century, 1891-1961* (Toronto: University of Toronto Press, 1990), plate 17.

15 Beth La Dow, *The Medicine Line: Life and Death on a North American Borderland* (New York: Routledge, 2002), 41. As La Dow points out, the concept of a medicine line was not limited to western Native groups. The term was used by the Mohawk and may have originated in the east and spread west as the boundary line was laid down.

16 Wallace Stegner lived in this region with his family from 1914 to 1920, and his classic and powerful work, *Wolf Willow,* is the quintessential explanation of what a medicine line means to Natives and non-Natives, Americans and Canadians. He maintained that rum- and gun-running, created largely by the Medicine Line, along centuries old north-south trails, led to a tradition of "border-jumping" that was still very much a part of his childhood in the twentieth century: Wallace Stegner, *Wolf Willow: A History, A Story, and a Memory of the Last Plains Frontier* (New York: Penguin Books, 2000), 97. The cross-border mobility of the Blackfoot, fuelled largely by the whisky trade, has been detailed by Sheila McManus: *The Line Which Separates: Race, Gender, and the Making of the Alberta-Montana Borderlands* (Edmonton: University of Alberta Press, 2005), 76-82. She argues that the border drastically reduced the mobility of Aboriginal women, in particular.

17 Michel Hogue, "Disputing the Medicine Line: The Plains Cree and the Canadian-American Border, 1876-1885," *Montana: the Magazine of Western History* 52 (2002): 2-17.

18 Gerhard Ens, "Dispossession or Adaptation? Migration and Persistence of the Red River Metis, 1835-1890," in *The Prairie West. Historical Readings,* ed. R. Douglas Francis and Howard Palmer, 2nd ed., 136-61 (Edmonton: Pica Pica Press, 1992).

19 A case fatality (or mortality) rate is the number of people who die from a disease divided by the number of people diagnosed as having that disease within a given time period. High

case fatality rates indicate that the agent causing the disease is virulent. See Stanley Plotkin and Walter Orenstein, eds. *Vaccines*, 3rd ed. (Philadelphia: W.B. Saunders Company, 1999).

20 One of the classic and extensive references for smallpox is F. Fenner, D.A. Henderson, I. Arita, Z. Ježek, and I.D. Ladnyi, *Smallpox and Its Eradication* (Geneva: World Health Organization, History of International Public Health No. 6, 1988), 38.

21 Ibid., 330. The initial study on the origin and diffusion of the 1896 outbreak was written by C.V. Chapin, "Changes in the Type of Contagious Disease as Shown by the History of Smallpox in the United States, 1895-1912," *Journal of Infectious Diseases* 13 (1913): 171-96.

22 For the shift from variolation to vaccination in western Canada in the eighteenth and nineteenth centuries, see P. Hackett, "Averting Disaster: The Hudson's Bay Company and Smallpox in Western Canada during the Late Eighteenth and Early Nineteenth Centuries," *Bulletin of the History of Medicine* 78 (2004): 575-609. On vaccination after the fur trade era in the late nineteenth century, see Lux, *Medicine That Walks*, 138-88. For a discussion on disease concepts, see Jody F. Decker "Country Distempers: Deciphering Disease and Illness in Rupert's Land before 1870," in *Reading Beyond Words: Documenting Native History*, ed. Jennifer Brown and Elizabeth Vibert, 156-81 (Peterborough, ON: Broadview Press, 1996).

23 Natives did incorporate European medicine into their healing complex, but while some ceremonies and dances and therapeutics changed with the times, others such as the Sun and Thirst dances have gained in popularity. Medicine and healing in Plains cultures after 1880 is detailed in Chapters 2 and 4 of Lux, *Medicine That Walks*, 182-84.

24 National Health and Welfare, "Smallpox–Frontier Inspections" [hereafter SFI], Library and Archives Canada [hereafter LAC], RG 29, file 937022, vol. 9, pts. 1-4; National Health and Welfare, "Small Pox–Manitoba, BC & NWT" [hereafter SMBN], LAC, RG 29, vol. 10, pts. 5-36; LAC, RG 29, file 937023, vol. 16, pts. 1-4; and LAC, RG 29, vol. 17, pts. 2-9.

25 Letter from Sydney Fisher, Minister of Agriculture, to J.R. Stratton, Secretary of the Province of Ontario, 17 May 1901; and letter from J.R. Stratton to Sydney Fisher, 23 May 1901: LAC, RG 29, SFI, vol. 16, pt. 35.

26 Letter from P.J. Veniot to J. McDougland, Commissioner of Customs, 2 May 1900, LAC, SFI, RG 29, vol. 16, pt. 35.

27 Letter from Dr. C.T. Sharpe at Morden, Manitoba, to Montizambert, 26 April 1901, LAC, SFI, RG 29, vol. 14, pt. 29.

28 *Winnipeg Free Press*, 24 January 1902, LAC, SFI, RG 29, vol. 13, pt. 20.

29 The Dawson Road from Thunder Bay to Winnipeg was Canada's first east-west route and was largely abandoned in 1873. The rail from St. Paul to Winnipeg, completed in 1878, was the main entrance to the province until the CPR "bridge road" between Fort Francis and Winnipeg, which replaced the Dawson Road, began operations in 1886. To the south, there were several routes that traversed the Manitoba-North Dakota-Minnesota border, such as cart trails, Native trails, rivers, and numerous railroads. Major entry points from which the rail ran north to Winnipeg, roughly parallel to "the great highway" (as the Red River was called), included rail stations at Emerson, Pembina, and further west at Gretna. By 1900, a well-integrated rail system was completed for southern Manitoba. But westward, on the plains towards the Fertile Belt, only a few main lines were in operation. See Warkentin and Ruggles, *Historical Atlas of Manitoba*, 175, 180, 333, 412.

30 30 April 1901, LAC, SFI, RG 29, vol. 10, pt. 30.

31 Unsigned letter, 24 May 1900, LAC, SFI, RG 29, vol. 16, pt. 36.

32 Letter from Peterson to R.G. Brett, MD, 23 January 1901, LAC, SFI, RG 29, vol. 10, pt, 31.

33 Letter to Deputy Commissioner, Department of Agriculture, Regina, Assiniboia, from Dr. H.C.R. Walker, 18 February 1901, Wetaskiwin, Alberta, LAC, SFI, RG 29, vol. 14, pt. 29. Dr. Walker's letter elicited an eight-page rebuttal from a Dr. Macdonald in the Department of Agriculture, outlining the symptoms of smallpox and citing numerous references.

34 Letter to Montizambert from Dr. Sharpe, Edmonton, 24 February 1901, LAC, SFI, RG 29, vol. 14, pt. 29.

35 Letter from E. Wood to Deputy Commissioner of Agriculture, 24 February 1901, LAC, SFI, RG 29, vol. 13, pt. 29.

36 Letter from Montizambert to Dr. J.T. Whyte, Killarney, Manitoba, 21 May 1901, LAC, SFI, RG 29, vol. 14, pt. 29.

37 30 April 1901, LAC, SFI, RG 29, vol. 14, pt. 30.
38 Letter from Dr. Wood to Montizambert, Winnipeg, 29 May 1901, LAC, SFI, RG 29, vol. 14, pt. 27.
39 *St. Paul Dispatch* newspaper clipping, 1 July 1901, LAC, SFI, RG 29, vol. 14, pt. 26.
40 Telegram from H. Phair to F. Montizambert, 31 July 1901, LAC, SFI, RG 29, vol. 14, pt. 26.
41 Letter from James Patterson to Montizambert, Regina, 5 November 1901, LAC, SFI, RG 29, vol. 10, pt. 23.
42 Lux, *Medicine That Walks*, 182.
43 Memo from Montizambert, n.d., LAC, SFI, RG 29, vol. 10, pt. 10.
44 Memo from Sgt. Bird at Duck Lake and Corp. St. Dennis at Batoche, 15 June 1902, LAC, SFI, RG 29, vol. 10, pt. 12.
45 Letter from R.M. Mitchell at Weyburn, Assiniboia, to Montizambert, 15 December 1901, and letter from Patterson to Montizambert, Winnipeg, 15 November 1901, LAC, SFI, RG 29, vol. 10, pt. 21.
46 Letter from Montizambert to P.L. Naismith, Manager, the Alberta Railway & Coal Co. of Lethbridge, 23 May 1901, LAC, SFI, RG 29, vol. 14, pt. 29.
47 24 January 1902, LAC, SFI, RG 29, vol. 13, pt. 20.
48 Telegraph from Montizambert to Dr. Mitchell, Ottawa, 17 January 1902, LAC, SFI, RG 29, vol. 10, pt. 18.
49 Letter from Dr. James Patterson to Fred Montizambert, Winnipeg, 25 February 1902, LAC, SFI, RG 29, vol. 10, pt. 17.
50 Letter from Sgt. W.B. Higinbotham to the Commanding Officer, NWMP, Regina District, Ft. Qu'Appelle, 17 March 1902, LAC, SFI, RG 29, vol. 10, pt. 15.
51 Letter from Wilson to O/C Regina District, 2 March 1902, LAC, SFI, RG 29, vol. 10, pt. 16.
52 Letter dated 31 May 1902, Emerson, LAC, SFI, RG 29, vol. 10, pt. 14.
53 Letter from Dr. R.B. Thompson to Montizambert, Waskada, 26 May 1902, LAC, SFI, RG 29, vol. 10, pt. 14.
54 Letter from Patterson to Montizambert, Winnipeg, 10 September 1902, LAC, SFI, RG 29, vol. 10, pt. 9.
55 Letter from Patterson to Montizambert, Winnipeg, 2 May 1902, LAC, SFI, RG 29, vol. 10, pt. 14.
56 Letter from Patterson to Montizambert, Winnipeg, 29 June 1902, LAC, SFI, RG 29, vol. 10, pt. 12.
57 NWMP memo from Constable Lowe, 15 June 1902, LAC, SFI, RG 29, vol. 10, pt. 12.
58 Letter from Patterson to Montizambert, Winnipeg, 29 June 1902, LAC, SFI, RG 29, vol. 10, pt. 12.
59 Letter from Patterson to Montizambert, Winnipeg, 10 September 1902, LAC, SFI, RG 29, vol. 10, pt. 9.
60 Letter from Director of Public Health to William Oliver, Mayor of Lethbridge, Alberta, Ottawa, 20 November 1902, LAC, SFI, RG 29, vol. 10, pt. 8.
61 Letter from Montizambert to Deputy Minister of the Interior, based on notes from Inspector at Emerson, 4 March 1903, LAC, SFI, RG 29, vol. 16, pt. 2.
62 Letter from Henderson to Montizambert, Emerson, 4 March 1903, LAC, SFI, RG 29, vol. 16, pt. 2.
63 Letter from a man in Killarney, quoted by Dr. Henderson to Montizambert, 6 January 1904, LAC, SMBN, RG 29, vol. 17, pt. 5.
64 Letter to the Officer Commanding RNWMP, Calgary, to R.R. Tucker, 1 December 1907, LAC, SMBN, RG 29, vol. 17, pt. 8, 937023.
65 Letter from Robert. L. Thornton to Montizambert, 26 April 1901, LAC, SFI, RG 29, vol. 14, pt. 29.
66 Peter Douglas Elias, *The Dakota of the Canadian Northwest: Lessons for Survival* (Regina: Canadian Plains Research Center, University of Regina, 2002), 31 and 131-46.
67 McManus, *The Line Which Separates*, 124.
68 Letter from E.M. Wood, secretary of the Provincial Board of Health in Winnipeg, to Montizambert, 6 May 1904, LAC, SMBN, RG 29, vol. 17, pt. 6.
69 Letter from Watts to Dr. Riddell in Crystal City, 25 July 1904, LAC, SMBN, RG 29, vol. 17, pt. 6. Black snake root is native to Canada and the United States. The herb is harvested in

the fall after the fruits have ripened. It is used to ease the pain of childbirth and menstrual cramps; because it was used by Aboriginal people, it received the name "Squaw Root." It is also used in the treatment of rheumatic pains, neuritis, rheumatoid-arthritis, and osteoarthritis.

70 Letter from Sgt. D. Laird, Indian Commissioner, to Montizambert, 25 April 1901, LAC, RG 29, vol. 14, pt. 29.
71 Letter from Patterson to Montizambert, Edmonton, 1901, LAC, RG 29, vol. 14, pt. 30.
72 Letter from T.G. Rothwell, Acting Deputy Minister of the Interior, to Montizambert, 28 February 1902, LAC, SMBN, RG 29, vol. 10, pt. 17
73 Letter from Patterson to Montizambert, Winnipeg, 29 July 1902, LAC, SMBN, RG 29, vol. 10, pt. 11.
74 Letter from Dr. Patterson to Montizambert, 19 February 1902, LAC, SFI, RG 29, vol. 10, pt. 17.
75 Letter from Montizambert to E.M. Wood, Secretary, Provincial Board of Health, Winnipeg, 25 April 1903, LAC, SFI, RG 29, vol. 14, pt. 29.
76 Jody F. Decker, "Depopulation of the Northern Plains Natives," *Social Science and Medicine* 33, 4 (1991): 381-93.

6
Mapping the New El Dorado: The Fraser River Gold Rush and the Appropriation of Native Space
Daniel Marshall

> You can not ascend the mountains, towards the mining towns
> or pass from one mining camp to another, without noticing
> the contrast in the scenes around you to anything you ever saw
> before ... Men met in groups packing their provisions; then a train
> of Indians ... Anon you met throngs of Chinamen packing up the
> river; they pass and greet you in broken English with, "how do
> you do John," ... Next comes the Negro, with a polite "good
> morning sar," or Chileano, Mexican or Kanaka, each with a
> heavy load.
>
> – *Victoria Gazette* (1858)[1]

In describing the Fraser River gold rush of 1858, most academics have been content to offer the image of as many as thirty thousand miners descending upon New Caledonia, all of them "Old Californians" of primarily Anglo-American origin. Certainly, one of the principal cultural forces that existed during this time was that of the California mining world, in addition to the fur trade and British worlds represented by the Hudson's Bay Company (HBC) and their Native allies and the neighbouring colony of Vancouver Island, respectively. These three worlds together represented the dominant political, economic, and social influences that defined the cataclysmic year of 1858, although to the exclusion of racial and ethnic minorities that had also joined the rush north. One of the most permanent indications of this racial and ethnic diversity can still be found today in the place names that continue to exist along the banks of the Fraser River – names such as China Bar, Kanaka Bar, or Nicaragua Bar – yet names that are but a mere residue of the flood tide of the California mining frontier that receded as quickly as it had risen to encompass British Columbia.[2] These gold-rush place names that existed in 1858-59, far greater in number then, are evidence of the multi-ethnic and racial composition of the BC rush and, more particularly, evidence of the ethnic and racial segregation embedded in the very geography of this waterway. California mining culture appropriated the Native cultural landscape of the Fraser and brought with it the ethnic and racial tensions that marked the California goldfields. Evidence of both of these processes was present in the myriad gold-rush bar names stretching from south of Fort Hope to just north of Lillooet.

When I was a doctoral candidate at the University of British Columbia, it was Arthur J. Ray who first made me aware of the critical importance of geography for interpreting historical questions. While a significant portion of Ray's work examined the fur trade as "the most pervasive force influencing the economic and political development of Western Canada," in the case of the Pacific province it was the California mining frontier that turned the fur trade world upside down and led to the creation of the Crown Colony of British Columbia.[3] Nevertheless, the spatial dimensions of contact as found throughout Ray's scholarship (and exemplified by gold-rush place names) informs my analysis of the ethnic and racial segregation embedded in the geography of the Fraser River.

These landmark names are explored as the spatial-discursive forms that the gold-mining culture used to stake out its presence in the Fraser River corridor. This geographical naming is a process that Paul Carter defines as "transforming space into place, the intentional world of the texts."[4] It is within this theoretical context that the historical significance of gold-rush bar place names will be established. In addition, the existence of such place names today may be seen as legitimizing both the colonial presence along the Fraser River and the continued occupation of Native lands and culture.

Prior to the gold rush, Native peoples had inhabited the lands of the Fraser River corridor for millennia, and the gravel bars and bench lands renamed by the California mining frontier occurred where ancient place names had long existed. To the non-Native miner, a stream, river, or lake represented the practical power of water that would assist in washing the landscape in the pursuit of gold. A canyon wall or sheer rock cliff was considered an impediment to developing the mines. But to the First Nations of the region, the natural watercourses and pools were home to spiritual beings, while the boulders, mountains, and rock spires were markers steeped in the oral history of these peoples. Writing of the Coast Salish peoples known as the Stó:lō (who inhabit the lower Fraser River), historian Keith Carlson points to the larger spiritual significance of the Native world that these miners entered: "The Rocks and other objects [known as transformer sites] bear witness to the unique and longstanding relationship between the Stó:lō and the land and resources of Stó:lō territory." Carlson continues: "the Stó:lō walk simultaneously through both spiritual and physical realms of this landscape, connected to the Creator through the land itself ... transformer sites are akin to Catholic stations of the cross, each a unique and integral feature of a larger narrative, each physically embodying the Creator's existence, actions and relationship to mankind."[5] Sonny McHalsie, a Stó:lō cultural advisor, states that these stl'áleqem sites (locations inhabited by spiritual beings known as stl'áleqem) "are both sacred and immovable, and stl'áleqem themselves are essential to Stó:lō well-being."[6] It was into this seemingly permanent and sacred world of long-standing that tens of thousands of goldseekers rushed, bringing not only their picks, pans, and shovels but also transplanting large-scale water companies from California that drained lakes and diverted streams, while early road builders levelled many of the natural rock monoliths that held the history of countless generations. This rapid despoiling of the Native world was not limited to the rapacious designs of Anglo-Americans, but, in this one instance, all goldseekers of varying race and ethnicity pursued a common goal in the single-minded pursuit of gold.

Many witnesses to the actual events of 1858 recorded the extent of ethnic and racial diversity. Landing at Victoria, James Bell wrote that "every country of the world seemed to be presented."[7] Touring Yale in June 1858, Dr. Carl Friesach, a professor of mathematics and later chief of the Observatory of Austria, believed that "[i]t would be difficult to find in one place a greater mixture of different nationalities. Americans were in the majority – California, especially had sent a large contingent. Then followed the Germans, French, and the Chinese. Next come Italians, Spaniards, Poles, etc. The feminine population consisted of only six."[8] Governor James Douglas was undoubtedly relieved to see such a cosmopolitan mix: "There is no congeniality of feeling among the emigrants," he initially concluded, "and provided there be no generally felt grievance to unite them in one common cause there will, in my opinion, always be a great majority of the population ready to support the government."[9]

If there was little rapport found among emigrants, it can be safely assumed that such a representative sample of Californian society also embraced the racial and ethnic animosities for which California was famous. Like the Fraser River region, California represented all the nations of the world. J.S. Holliday's well-known work, *The World Rushed In*, aptly describes the similar cultural geography of California while recalling the splendid diversity of gold-rush place names of the past. "California's dynamic intermingling," he stated, "was colorfully reflected in the names of mining camps and towns: German Bar, Iowa Hill, Irish Creek, Cape Cod Bar, Tennessee Creek, Chinese Camp, Georgia Slide, Dutch Flat, French Corral, Michigan Bluffs, Illinois Town, Nigger Hill, Washington, Boston, Bunker Hill, Italian Bar, Dixie Valley, Vermont Bar and Kanaka Bar."[10] Compare to this list the brief tallying of BC bar names provided by Alfred Waddington to the *Victoria Gazette* on 15 September 1858. Waddington's reconnaissance of the goldfields examined a twenty-three-kilometre stretch of claims that ran from below Fort Hope to Fort Yale. At the commencement of his trip, he related: "I now started in my canoe [Sept. 7th] at 8 in the morning ... and visited every bar in succession up to Fort Yale as follows: Fifty-Four Forty Bar, Union, Deadwood, Express, American, Puget Sound, Victoria, Yankee Doodle, Eagle, Alfred, Sacramento, Texas, Emory's, Rocky, Hill's, Casey, and Fort Yale."[11] One can see by this list that many of the Fraser River names are not only as colourful as are their Californian equivalents but also reflect ethnicity. Yet they also give the impression of an American-dominated gold rush, and this is not completely accurate.[12] There were, in fact, at least a hundred different gold-rush bar names along the full extent of the Fraser in 1858 and 1859; although only a few have found a permanent place in the toponymy of the Fraser River landscape, many of the original names were neither American nor British in origin (see Appendix A at the end of this chapter).

If the events of 1858 are followed more closely, it becomes apparent that there were two distinct periods in the initial year of the gold rush. There were also two distinct regions, both dictated by the natural flow of the Fraser and defined by the peculiar geography found above Fort Yale: two regions, two times, and two distinctly different human geographies.

Initial cartography of the Fraser River reflected the difficult terrain that early explorations encountered. In 1808, upon descending the watercourse of Hell's Gate and the approach to Black Canyon, Simon Fraser declared, "It is so wild that I cannot find words to describe our situation at times. We had to pass where no human being should venture."[13] David Thompson's map of this region recorded that three separate portage sites were required before navigation would again be possible above Fort Yale.[14] All subsequent maps pinpointed Fort Yale as the head of navigation for the Fraser due to the impassable nature of the falls above, particularly once the river swelled during late spring and summer. The falls between Spuzzum and Yale also seemed to have acted as a natural dividing line for rival Native groups. A.C. Anderson, the HBC's acknowledged authority on the geography of the region, claimed that "a ceaseless feud ... prevail[ed] between the Couteau [Nlaka'pamux] and the lower Indians [Stó:lō], who differ from each other in many respects."[15] Natives along the upper Fraser River and Thompson River were much more hostile than the Stó:lō towards the Americans (or "Boston Men," as they were known) who had attempted early intrusions into their country.[16] When, as a consequence of unique geography and the potential enmity of the Nlaka'pamux, the gold rush commenced in spring of 1858, the vast majority of miners were prevented from prospecting further than the Fort Yale vicinity. Most remained within a short twenty-three-kilometre stretch of waterway below the falls. Prior to this, the earliest non-Native goldseekers on the Fraser, mainly from neighbouring Washington and Oregon territories, had worked their placer claims before the spring thaw and consequent rise of the river.[17]

Individuals such as James Moore, one of the first miners from California, confirmed that any reconnaissance above Yale was essentially impossible until the retreat of summer flood conditions in late fall.[18] Once news of Hill's Bar and other lucrative claims had reached the outside world via newspaper reports printed in Pacific Northwest locales and reprinted by San Francisco editors, large numbers of California miners flooded into British Columbia just as the Fraser deluged its banks.[19] Then commenced a waiting game by those all too impatient to enter the Upper Country in order to stake out the unclaimed stretches of river, the richest diggings along the lower Fraser already having been claimed. By July, as many as six thousand sojourned in Victoria ready to embark at a moment's notice once the river had fallen.[20] Moore claimed that at least twenty thousand lingered at Yale during the high-water mark.[21] California merchant James Bell described the scene: "Close above Yale, the river cuts its way through the Cascade Mountains, causing deep foaming chasms, inaccessible either by water, or land, thus have the body of miners been shut off from the Upper Country." Bell further lamented that "there accumulated around Yale, an immense crowd of people. The River at the time was swelled to its greatest hight [sic], caused by the melting of snow on the mountains; The best diggings were all under water, provisions were scarce, consequently high in price. The snow covered Cascade Mountains frowned above, forbidding farther approach."[22]

Bell, like Moore and others, verified that the river above Yale had been as yet imperfectly explored as late as the spring of 1859.[23] The *Victoria Gazette* reported that, for those who waited at Yale for the waters to recede, "their patience [was] aggravated by the extraordinary success of a few more fortunate than themselves in a period of arrival or location of claims."[24] In addition to these hindrances, the *Puget Sound Herald* cautioned that, at diggings immediately above Yale, Natives were deemed "a little troublesome; imposing a tax of a blanket or a shirt on each miner who worked on the ground the Indians claimed."[25] The temptation to risk the rapids above and the unknown reception that might await them by Natives possibly more hostile to their trespasses must have finally become unbearable to the many who forfeited their small savings (made in California) in order to reach the New El Dorado trumpeted by the San Francisco press.[26] The Bellingham Bay editor for Whatcom's *Northern Light* chronicled the apparent futility of the situation: "Above that point, they cannot get on account of the water in the canyon. The whirlpools are frightful. They would swallow a canoe at once. A great many lives had already been lost by the utter recklessness of men. The Indians refusing to go on it, ought to be sufficient caution for white men. But 'Gold!' 'Gold!' is the cry; and they rush heedlessly on to death."[27]

News of the gold discoveries had not reached California until March, and, consequently, as the water rose, a flood tide of emigration began "at the most unpropitious moment ... only to meet with discouragement and disappointment."[28] With all the accessible gold-rush bars on the lower Fraser taken, the newly arrived were confronted with three choices: either return to California, wait for months until the waters receded, or attempt to push on into the upper reaches of the river. For those few who chose the last alternative, Henry De Groot related that "all arrived so utterly impoverished, or completely broken down, as to be unfit to do anything."[29] And yet, along with certain prospectors who climbed the river in early 1858, many goldseekers with less to lose were compelled to advance beyond Fort Yale.[30] In particular were those individuals recently persecuted in the California goldfields – individuals who undoubtedly preferred a universally applied miner's licence as instituted in New Caledonia to the California foreign miner's head tax.[31] For such people, returning south was not an attractive option as xenophobic agitation started in 1849 and, in the early 1850s, drove many "aliens" from Californian mines.

In 1858, J.C. Bryant, a Cornish miner who travelled to British Columbia via the circuitous route of the copper mines of Lake Superior, afterwards Nicaragua, and thence to Grass Valley, California, related a scene from Fort Hope that would not have been out of character had it occurred in the Golden State. Bryant watched as a boat, captained by a white man, approached near the banks of the HBC outpost carrying a large number of Chinese miners. He recounted that "as the boat with the Chinese crew came alongside of the bank, a crowd of Californians lined the top and declared that no Chinese would land there. The white man pleaded that he had been paid to transport these Chinese to Fort Hope ... 'Well, it doesn't matter whether you are paid or not, no Chinese will land at Fort Hope. We'll see who is going to have the say about whether Chinese come here or not. We say they shall not,' said the Californian crowd."[32] The Californians were overruled, however, as HBC chief trader Donald McLean happened to arrive on the scene, quickly enforcing HBC authority and inviting the Chinese to camp within the confines of the fort. Recent scholarship has drawn the conclusion that past conflict over western resources was, in fact, akin to "race wars," and it is likely that, among those who remained on the Fraser after the exodus of Californians returning south, were those non-Anglo-Americans who undoubtedly recalled the ethnic and racial tensions that permeated the Sierra Nevada range.[33]

It was, of course, essentially Euro-Americans from Washington and Oregon territories, some early Californians, in addition to former HBC employees who secured the most profitable claims before the Fraser rose, thus pre-empting gold mining until the fall of the year. That Anglo-American influence was most dominant in the lower Fraser River mines below Yale is made plainly evident by Map 6.1, which illustrates the place names given to major gold-rush bars in this region.[34] To Alfred Waddington's list may be

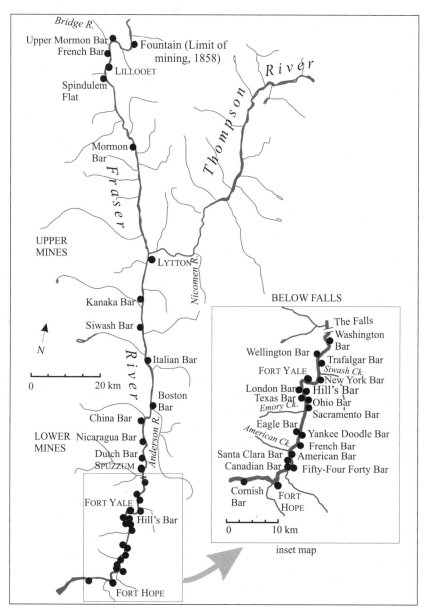

Map 6.1   Gold-rush bar place names reflecting race and ethnicity, Fraser River, 1858. Names of settlements are indicated with capital letters.

added many more that confirm the Californian, but especially British and American, control of this portion of the river. A more complete list of gold-rush bar names includes Cornish, Fifty-Four Forty, Canadian, Santa Clara, Eagle, American, Yankee Doodle, Texas, Sacramento, London, Ohio, Wellington, New York, Trafalgar, and Washington.[35]

Anglo-Americans did not dominate the upper canyon the way they did the lower reaches. Many Californians felt that the combination of high water and high prices, poor trails and poor climate, did make the Fraser River gold rush a complete "humbug." The flood tide of Californians that eventually receded took with it the kind of Anglo-American dominance found in the Lower Mines but not before having forced non-Anglo-Americans out of their space. The extraordinary geography of the Fraser River canyons, unlike the expansive goldfields of California, offered only one choice to disaffected miners – only one direction for travel – and that was to continue up the river. The upper Fraser mines awaited conquest by all those who did not share in the success of the Lower Mines; or, more particularly, those made unwelcome by California mining society, which was centred at Yale. Anxious to escape the discrimination of Fort Yale society, and driven by the commonly held notion that fine placer gold necessarily indicated the existence of an upstream mother lode, many must have felt compelled to break free from the constraints of the lower river into the higher reaches of unexplored terrain. Here, at least, might be offered prospects for gold and a certain degree of spatial autonomy. In contrast to the lack of accommodation afforded by diggings in the Lower Mines, most of the bars above Spuzzum were widely separated, offering alienated miners some peace from ethnic and, indeed, racial, intolerances.[36]

Again, if we focus solely on those place names that reflect ethnic and racial identity, we find evidence of a very different human geography above the dividing line of the Falls.[37] Gold-rush bar place names in this instance are as follows: Dutch Bar, Nicaragua Bar, China Bar, Boston Bar, Italian Bar, Siwash Bar, Kanaka Bar, Mormon Bar, Spindulem Flat, French Bar, and Upper Mormon Bar.[38] The anomalies in this decidedly non-Anglo-American list are obviously Boston Bar and the two Mormon bars. Boston Bar, still a major feature on the map today, was favourably situated across from the mouth of the Anderson River, where it enters the Fraser. It is probable that some of the earliest non-Native miners used A.C. Anderson's old HBC fur brigade trail to this point prior to the swelling of the Fraser in the summer of 1858. The Whatcom Trail from Bellingham (in its second attempt at reaching the Fraser) had connected with such HBC trails, ultimately to places above Yale like the Anderson River.[39] Even so, this name stands in stark contrast to the rest of the list. Mormon Bar and Upper Mormon Bar at the Fountain – the geographical limit of 1858 prospecting[40] – are not so unusual if one remembers that it was in 1857 and 1858 that US federal troops were ordered to invade Salt Lake City. Mormons, not generally liked by the rest of the American population, were persecuted until ultimately driven into the Utah desert.[41] It is reasonable to assume that the cultural milieu of Anglo-American dominance on the lower Fraser would have discriminated against Mormons as though they were, indeed, a race unto themselves.[42] Siwash Bar and Spindulem (Spintlum) Flat (named for a powerful Nlaka'pamux chief), represent the Native population that continued to practice placer mining.[43]

At the same time, Anglo-American culture cannot be viewed as a cohesive and homogeneous whole: Texan, Bostonian, and Ohioan Americans were undoubtedly quite divided. Charles Ferguson, a young Ohioan entering the goldfields of California, recalled how he passed several camps of his fellow countrypeople representing a variety of US regions before joining a group of unknown Ohioans who welcomed him with open arms.[44] Perhaps in this we have an explanation for the separateness of gold-rush bar names like Texas Bar, Ohio Bar, New York Bar, and Boston Bar on the Fraser. Texas had only recently been admitted to the Union, and the American Civil War would shortly divide North and South even further. These tensions must have contributed to the regional pride reflected in gold-rush place names. Still, when compared to non-Americans, there was undoubtedly more that held Americans together, in general, than kept them apart. If nothing else, there existed a consensus with regard to resource development and exploitation.

In Yale mining society, Californian ways had become well rooted. Certainly the combined forces of the Royal Engineer Corps, Royal Navy, Hudson's Bay Company, and colonial British rule ultimately tempered American enthusiasm. Yet the presence of the infamous Ned McGowan and members of the Vigilance Committee of San Francisco, along with Californian merchants, explorers, engineers, saloon-keepers, and newspaper reporters, made the lower Fraser a natural extension of the Californian world – especially with so many claiming that the Lower Mines were inside American territory.[45] With such a secure sense of place established, even in a foreign landscape, the designation of various gold-rush bars with names like "Fifty-Four Forty" were not only jingoistic pronouncements to the non-American mining community (that a Californian culture had arrived on the scene) but also the appropriation of the Fraser River's landscape, perhaps even an assertion of near-sovereign control. Naming legitimated the Californian presence in a British colony in the same way that earlier HBC naming of forts and landmarks authenticated the company's claim to Aboriginal lands.[46]

An examination of early maps produced before and after the 1858 Fraser River gold rush affirms this appropriation of landscape. "Maps are never value-free images," advises J.B. Harley, but "part of the broader family of value-laden images."[47] A.C. Anderson's series of pre-1858 maps is decidedly different from maps produced in San Francisco during 1858 in one

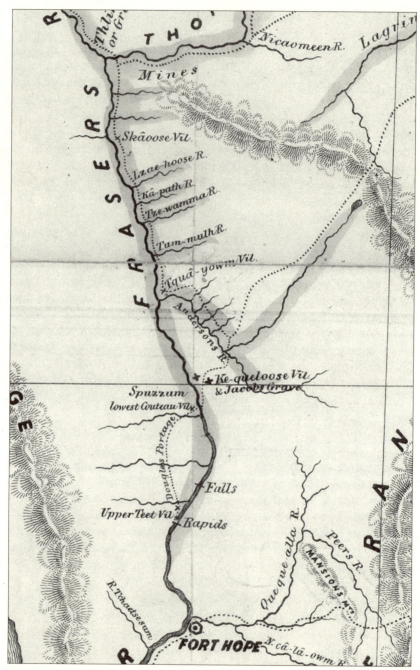

Map 6.2   Detail of A.C. Anderson's fur trade map.
Source: BC Archives, CM-A78.

important regard – Anderson included Native place-naming along the Fraser, while the latter replaced such names with California-style gold camp names.[48] Anderson's explorations of 1846 through 1849 incorporated knowledge of the Thompson and Fraser rivers into a sketch map that clearly identified major Native settlements and appended Native names to these sites and all major rivers flowing into the Fraser (Map 6.2).[49] Many of these names were subsequently retained on an 1858 map produced in San Francisco based on Anderson's earlier work. Instead of the California-style gold-rush bar names that followed, Anderson provided names of a decidedly fur trade nature.

Once again, if we start at Fort Hope and ascend the river to the Fountain, place names function as landmarks of an HBC-controlled world that included the Native as essential in the trade relationship. Consequently, Anderson recorded: "Fort Hope, Rapids, Upper Teet Vil[lage], Douglas Portage, Falls, lowest Couteau Vil[lage], Spuzzum, Ke-quelouse Vil & Jacobs Grave, Anderson R[iver], Tqua-yowm Vil, Tum-mulh R, Tze-wamma R, Kapath R, Tzae-hoose R, Skaoose Vil, Thlikumcheen or Great Forks, Lower Fountain Vil, Bridge R., Upper Fountain Vil[lage]."[50] Anderson's map is considered "unquestionably the most accurate representation of interior British Columbia available" at this time.[51] Yet it detailed no particular gold-rush information from miners working along the Fraser, which is perhaps not surprising if one acknowledges that fur traders and gold miners viewed things quite differently from one another.

By contrast, a sketch map published by the San Francisco *Bulletin* offered a Californian depiction of the goldfields that replaced all Native-HBC landmark names with those that were more inviting to miners (see Map 6.3). The ground was now made familiar to those about to embark on the long sea journey north from San Francisco. A "New El Dorado" was invented out of the "vacant" space of the Fraser corridor and, thus, was brought into "cultural circulation."[52] Arriving at Fort Langley, the Californian would ascend past Fort Hope, Hunter's Bar, Hill's Bar, Fort Yale, Rapids, Sailor's Diggings, Rapids, Mormon Bar, and Grand Falls, assuming the hopeful miner was first able to run the gauntlet of seven separate "Indian Villages" that stood between the mouth of the Fraser and Fort Hope. Native names were removed from the map and, in their place, Native settlements were inscribed, not unlike warning beacons to the wary.[53]

The human geography was about to be changed dramatically by miners who had no understanding of the Native. The effects of placer mining took a considerable toll on the traditional Native landscape. At Hill's Bar, known amongst the Stó:lō as Hemhemetheqw, meaning "good place to make sockeye salmon oil," miners stripped away the ground and overturned many boulders containing pock-marked bowls used for the collection of fish oil.[54] Throughout the Fraser and Thompson corridors, immense amounts of sand,

Map 6.3   Sketch map from the *San Francisco Bulletin* (1858), depicting the goldfields from a California perspective.
Source: BC Archives, CM-A295.

gravel, and other natural debris were washed into the rivers and into age-old fishing and hunting grounds. Places of habitation were scarred by ditches, flumes, and test-holes preparatory to excavating entire hillsides or bench lands.[55]

Californian discourse, in representing Aboriginals as impediments to progress, encouraged a process of colonization that, in effect, not only changed the human geography but also, for Aboriginal peoples, the physical geography of boundary and space. The discourse of naming has been compared to acts of "christening." For example, in *Marvelous Possessions* Stephen Greenblatt argues that, under the authority of Christian imperialism, Christopher Columbus' use of place-naming was akin to christening. Greenblatt maintains that "christening entails the cancellation of the native name – the erasure of the alien, perhaps demonic, identity – and hence a kind of making new; it is at once an exorcism, an appropriation, and a gift. Christening then is the culminating instance of the marvellous speech act: in the wonder of the proper name, the movement from ignorance to knowledge, the taking of possession, the conferral of identity are fused in a moment of pure linguistic formalism."[56] Certainly, the myriad gold-rush bar place names along the Fraser River are evidence of a cancellation of Native names – "the erasure of the alien." And befitting the kind of mass democratic society that California felt it had achieved, acts of possession were now no longer limited to a single mighty explorer but could be proclaimed by all those who "discovered" their own version of a "New World Bar."[57]

These new names were the basis for an invented cultural space that enticed further discovery and the prospect of hidden gold. "For how," as Paul Carter suggests, "without place names, without agreed points of reference, could directions be given, information exchanged, 'here' and 'there' defined? ... they embody the existential necessity the traveller feels to invent a place he can inhabit. Without them, punctuating the monotony, distinguishing this horizon from that, there would be no evidence he had travelled."[58]

Maps are, in fact, a cultural text, and they may well tell more about the social structure of the place of origin than do the actual human and physical landscapes they describe. By 1858, the California goldfields had seen their best years, and with word of a "new" California to the north, expectations ran high. The Fraser River fever compelled many to join the fray, only to be severely disappointed upon arrival. Gold-rush bar place names such as Humbug Bar, Poverty Bar, and perhaps even Pike's Bar are indicative of miners' expectations of a quick and easy wealth that never materialized.[59]

Indeed, it is at times more instructive to see what has been excluded from a map than what has been included. On California-produced representations of British Columbia, we may easily locate bar names of Anglo-American origin, but there is no indication of Nicaragua, China, or Kanaka bars, and virtually no Native presence. J.B. Harley, in viewing the map as a "spatial panopticon" that produces power, wrote that "the map maker merely omits those features of the world that lie outside the purpose of the immediate discourse."[60] In this instance, California-based gold-rush discourse normally referred to non-Americans only when justification was required for the discriminatory practices of white society.

Once the Fraser River rush had subsided, and the remainder of the goldseekers were drawn to the Cariboo goldfields, Californian-style place names were largely dropped from colonial mapping endeavours, or rather, in keeping with a resurgent imperial discourse, they were ignored. A Royal Engineers' map for 1861 only listed Chapman's Bar and Boston Bar; John Arrowsmith's 1862 map of British Columbia contained no gold-rush names; and John Palliser's "A general Map of the route in British North America" marked only Hope, Yale, and Lytton, as befitting a Pacific Colony that now had the institutions of British power more firmly established than had previously been the case.[61] Place names such as Hope and Yale had been bestowed prior to the gold rush by HBC authority, while Lytton honoured the pivotal role played by the British secretary of state for the colonies in 1858.[62]

Not unlike the racial blindness of gold-rush-specific cartographers, officials of Empire preferred to disregard nomenclature of a non-British sort. The mere fact that California-style place-naming could be dropped so quickly from the colonial government's lexicon further illustrates the very transient nature of gold-rush-related human geographies.

By 1870, the Fraser River rush was virtually a forgotten past.[63] The impermanence of gold-rush life meant that communities of miners devoted to the collection of gold dust soon moved on once the river sand bars had been thoroughly depleted through placer mining techniques. Of the first river-bottom bars that were prospected between Fort Hope to the Fountain, Californian historian Hubert Howe Bancroft wrote, "Nearly all of these were wiped out of memory as the inhabitants migrated and the traces of their existence were washed away by the recurring floods of the rivers; so that only a few have found a permanent place in the geography of the country."[64] Yet, though the presence of the goldseeker was ephemeral, the gold-rush bar names that remained had great implications for the human geography of Native settlements in the future.

In 1871, new considerations refocused the colonial government's attention along the Fraser River corridor and rescued many gold-rush bar names from obscurity, ultimately giving them a permanence in the landscape that would perhaps have been inconceivable to earlier British cartographers. Joseph Trutch, as chief commissioner of lands and works, was responsible for gathering information on all surveyed portions of British Columbia. This information was to be included on a new map that came to be considered "a milestone in the historical cartography of B.C."[65] Trutch's map included, between Hope and Lytton alone, American Bar, Emory Bar, Texas

Bar, Yale, Wellington Bar, Spuzzum River, Chapman's Bar, Alexandra Bridge, Big Canon, Anderson River, Boston Bar, Fargo Bar, and Mariner's Bar.[66] Perhaps it was Trutch's eight years of experience as a surveyor and farmer in the United States that gave him an affinity for California-type place names.[67] Of greater significance, though, was the emerging province's need for readily available and identifiable landmarks by which to locate the technical descriptions of the 1870-71 resurvey of Fraser River topography. Gold-rush bar place names would have provided the key for, as Carter maintains, "Naming words were forms of spatial punctuation transforming space into an object of knowledge, something that could be explored and read."[68] The Fraser River had already been defined by the HBC, but it was the gold rush that carved the landscape into a linear series of over a hundred points of reference.

With British Columbia's entry into Confederation, Article 13 of the Terms of Union stipulated that responsibility for Indian affairs would rest with the federal government. Under such a system, Trutch was required to furnish specific information with respect to the location and extent of "Indian Reserves." The act of place-naming under the earlier influences of both the HBC and the gold rush involved instances of de facto near-sovereignty over the landscape, but later colonial power enacted full sovereignty and was aided by existing place names, which explicitly defined the new ordering of life along the river.

When, in the fall of 1858-59, James Douglas attempted to protect Natives along the Fraser River – while also accommodating the advance of gold miners – he established "anticipatory reserves of land for the benefit and support of the Indian races."[69] This was akin to Queen Victoria's paradoxical policy, which promised "to protect the poor natives *and* advance civilization."[70] Lord Carnarvon wrote to Douglas:

> Proofs are unhappily still too frequent of the neglect which Indians experience when the White man obtains possession of their Country and their claims to consideration are forgotten at the moment when equity most demands that the hand of the protector should be extended to help them. In the case of the Indians of Vancouver Island and British Columbia Her Majesty's Government earnestly wish that when the advancing requirements of Colonization press upon Lands occupied by Members of that race measures of liberality and justice may be adopted for compensating them for the surrender of the territory which they have been taught to regard as their own.[71]

Douglas's choice of the word "anticipatory" suggests that future reserves were only to be confirmed in regions where the white mining frontier had already advanced. Indeed, Lytton and Carnarvon warned Douglas that "care s[houl]d be observed in laying out & defining the several reserves, in order to avoid checking at a future day the progress of the white Colonists."[72] In this instance, white colonists can be more aptly referred to as white goldseekers, and these land-development attitudes of the Colonial Office were rooted not so much in the promotion of agricultural settlement as in the fast-paced expansion of the mining frontier. During Douglas' time in office, Indian reserve policy in British Columbia "anticipated" further gold discoveries, which is to say, no reserves were to be marked out and formalized until prospectors had thoroughly scrutinized all the lands of the Mainland colony for valuable mineral deposits. Once an area had been thoroughly explored (and mined, if rich in auriferous deposits), a reserve was subsequently and safely laid out. In the opinion of Douglas, backed by Colonial Office demands not to impede "progress," there was no point in concluding treaties or formally marking out reserves to Native territories before the mining frontier had made a clean sweep of them. To have done so would have run the risk of confirming Native interests to lands that, conceivably, could be overrun by an intractable mining population the following year (which is essentially what had occurred during the 1858 Fraser River War).[73] It is little wonder, then, that with the mining frontier having developed the Lower Mines of the Fraser River in 1858, the first Mainland reserves would be formalized in this region. As goldseekers radiated outwards from the Lower Mines to such places as the Cariboo goldfields to the north or the Rock Creek diggings to the east, Indian reserves were established in these regions, too – after the fact. Though historian Robin Fisher concluded that "the gold miners were the advance guard of the settlement frontier," during Douglas' governorship, the establishment of Indian reserves followed the advancing path of goldseekers, as opposed to agricultural settlers.[74]

Due to the disruptive impact of the gold rush on HBC operations and British sovereignty in the region, the Crown Colony of British Columbia had been established provisionally. Just as responsible government was not conferred on the Mainland in 1858 – due to the unknown and transitory nature of the gold rush – neither was any formal model of land management. Britain had adopted a "wait-and-see" approach, and, in this sense, Douglas, and subsequently Trutch, were not at variance with Colonial Office policy. If treaties or reserves had been confirmed to untested lands, lands in which goldseekers had not yet prospected, colonial authority risked precipitating further Native-white violence by placing potentially rich mining grounds beyond the reach of a well-armed, aggressive mining population that cared little for outside authority. In essence, portions of the traditional Native landscape could have been guaranteed, only to have been subsequently stampeded by miners in the pursuit of gold. As a consequence, Douglas purposely left Native lands in a state of legal uncertainty. When pushed, as in the case of the first Mainland reserves along the Fraser River in 1858, Douglas might order an impromptu reserve to be marked out, so as to keep the peace, but these first confirmations of Natives' lands were never duly recorded.

By comparison, Trutch applied a strict legal definition to all reserves in existence just prior to 1871. He concluded that there was no established system under James Douglas' administration for reserving land, no official gazetting of reserves, and no written instructions on record. Consequently, Trutch determined that "the Indians really have no right to the lands they claim, nor are they of any actual value or utility to them ... they should be confirmed in the possession of such extent of lands only as are sufficient for their probable requirements ... the remainder of the land now shut up in reserves should be thrown open to preemption."[75] Trutch was writing after the time of further smallpox epidemics, which had swept through the Mainland in the early 1860s, leading to a substantial decline in Native populations. Although Trutch enacted a harsh, legalistic (and admittedly racist) approach to Indian lands, it was the earlier nondescript policies of James Douglas, in keeping with Colonial Office edicts, that allowed later colonial administrators, like Trutch, to further marginalize Native claims to the land.

Shortly after being appointed, Trutch demanded an explicit definition of all and future Indian reserves. He declared that "it appears most advisable that it should be at once constituted the definite province of some person or persons, to make a thorough enquiry into this subject throughout the Colony and ascertain as exactly as practicable what lands are claimed by the Indians. What lands have been authoritatively reserved and assured to the various tribes, and to what extent such Reserves can be modified with the concurrence of the Indians."[76] By 1870, John Trutch, the chief commissioner's brother, had resurveyed many of the reserves along the Fraser River. By 1871, when British Columbia joined Confederation (and jurisdiction over Indian affairs in the province passed from Victoria to Ottawa), Joseph Trutch was able to offer the federal government a schedule of seventy-six fully surveyed and legally gazetted reserves, many of which were to be defined by the language of the gold rush.[77]

The chief commissioner's use of gold-rush place names to categorize Indian reserves filled the void called wilderness and left even less room for Aboriginal peoples. The HBC's definition of place had located only the most minimal of landmarks significant for the perpetuation of their trade. Later imperial designs were primarily interested in marking the sites of colonial power and authority. By contrast, the gold rush had labelled stretches of the Fraser River so thoroughly as to suggest that this corridor was fully occupied, and, hence, Natives were confirmed only the barest minimum of land for their essential needs. The erasure of Native sovereignty through the use of California-like place names not only disconnected Natives from the physical geography of the river but also from the very soul of Native culture. As mentioned previously, place names in Native cultures such as the Stó:lō do much more than plot mere points of reference – they give oral history significance by "spatially anchoring" it to a unique and personal geography. The place name, in this instance, offers the memory detailed pictures of the myths, sagas, and community history of centuries. A name will automatically recall a unique point in the land, and, in turn, the land invokes the wisdom of a culture. As in Stó:lō culture, so in Apache culture: geographical features "served the people for centuries as indispensable mnemonic pegs on which to hang the moral teachings of their history."[78] As Raymond Fogelson maintains, "All peoples possess a sense of the past, however strange and exceptional that past may seem from our own literately conditioned perspectives."[79] The consequences of a permanent gold-rush vocabulary have been severely underestimated as they have effectively denied an ancient and sacred worldview.[80]

It is not surprising, perhaps, that a gold rush that had refashioned the human geography of the Fraser River corridor into a series of distinct, ethnically and racially segregated mining enclaves would also compartmentalize Native peoples into a chain of racially defined reserves. Joseph Trutch's reintroduction of gold-rush landmarks naturally intertwined with Indian reserve names as they ascended the Fraser. Surveyor John Trutch used the language of the gold rush when he named the location of "Boston Bar Indian Reserve #5," described Kop-chichen Indian Reserve #6 as "situated on Yankee Flat," and located Shoo-ook Indian Reserve #7 "on Boothroyd's Flat."[81] Ironically, the Fraser River gold rush not only precipitated the institution of the reserve system in Mainland British Columbia but, in certain instances, continued to define many of the limited Indian lands left behind in the wake of the events of 1858-59.

Once British Columbia joined Canada, Joseph Trutch's commemoration of the "cult of first-comers" not only re-embedded these "discoveries" in the geography of the canyon walls and (more permanently) on maps but also, by continuing to legitimate the colonial presence through place names, provided further justification for the curtailment of reserves.[82] Current maps covering a portion of this river feature the ironic, taunting names of "Trafalgar Flat Indian Reserve," "Chapman's Bar Indian Reserve," "China Bar Indian Reserve," "Boston Bar Indian Reserve," "Boothroyd Indian Reserve," and "Cameron Bar Indian Reserve."[83] The mere juxtaposition of gold-rush bar names and Indian reserves is enough to keep alive the memory of the events that led to the appropriation of Native lands, but the incorporation of these signal acts of sovereignty into the very names of the reserves constitutes a continued occupation of the Native landscape by the miners of old (see Appendix B). All other races that had flooded into the canyon to occupy a piece of the river ultimately receded, leaving only a name behind. But the Aboriginal, the final inheritor of a geographical corridor delineated by race, has remained within a matrix of reserves that recalls the segregated landscape of the gold rush of 1858.

Appendix A
List of gold-rush bar names, Fraser River, 1858-59

Below Hope	*Above Spuzzum*
Maria Bar	Chapman's Bar
Hudson Bar	Dutchman's Bar
Blue Nose Bar	Cross Bar
Prospect Bar	Swan's Bar
Cornish or Murderer's Bar	Nicaragua Bar
	China Bar
Above Hope	Boston Bar
Mosquito or Poverty Bar	Tehama Bar
Fifty-Four Forty Bar	Island Bar
Union Bar	Yankee Bar
Canadian Bar	Fargo's Bar
Santa Clara Bar	Mariner's Bar
Posey Bar	Putnam's Bar
Deadwood Bar	Italian Bar
Express Bar	Siwash Bar
American Bar	Kanaka Bar
Puget Sound Bar	Rancheria Bar
French Bar	New Brunswick Bar
Victoria Bar	
Yankee Doodle Bar	*Above Lytton*
Eagle Bar	Mormon Bar
Alfred Bar	Spindulen [Spintlum] Flat
Sacramento Bar	Cameron Bar
Texas Bar	McGoffrey Dry-diggings
Rosey Bar	Horse-Beef Bar
Niagara Bar	Foster's Bar
London Bar	Brady's Bar
Hunter Bar	Rosie Bar
Emory's Bar	Willow Bank Bar
Rocky Bar	
Trinity Bar	*Above Lillooet*
Ohio Bar	Robinson's Bar
Hill's Bar	French Bar (2)
Casey's Bar	Upper Mormon Bar
Fort Yale Bar	
	Limit of 1858
Above Yale	Fountain Bar
New York Bar	
Fletcher's Flat	
New World Bar	
Hole in the Wall Bar	
Trafalgar Bar	
Wellington Bar	

▶

◀ *Appendix A*
List of gold-rush bar names, Fraser River, 1858-59

Above Yale
Pike Bar
Sailor's Bar
Higon or Hiyou Bar
Madison Bar
Savage Flat
Steamboat Bar
Humburg Bar
Surprise Bar
Washington or Bamboo Bar

Note: This list is an approximate ordering of gold-rush bars from below Fort Hope to the Fountain, the northern limit of mining in 1858.
Source: Victoria Gazette (particularly 15 September 1858); BC Gold Commissioner, Yale, "Manual of Record and Land Register, Hope and Yale," GR 252, 12:1, BC Archives; Richard Hicks, Gold Commissioner, *Claims Record Book*, Special Collections, UBC; Alfred Waddington, *Fraser Mines Vindicated: The History of Four Months* (Victoria, 1858); Governor James Douglas, *BC Papers*, No. 26-34; F.W. Howay, *The Early History of the Fraser River Mines* (Victoria, 1926); H.H. Bancroft, *History of British Columbia, 1792-1887* (San Francisco, 1890); and R.C. Mayne, *Sketch of Part of British Columbia* (London: War Office, 1859).

Appendix B
Legacy of the Fraser River gold rush: Remaining gold-rush bar place names

Gold-rush bars	Other features
Hope	
Trafalgar Flat	Trafalgar Flat Indian Reserve
[American Bar]	American Creek
Texas Bar	
Emory Bar	Emory Creek
Albert Flat	Albert Flat Indian Reserve
Hill's Bar	Gordon Creek
Yale	Yale Creek
	Yale Indian Reserve
	Stout Indian Reserve
Sailors Bar	
Wellington Bar	
Chapman's Bar	Chapman's Bar Indian Reserve
Dutchman Bar	
Austin's Flat	Austin's Flat Indian Reserve
China Bar	China Bar Indian Reserve
Boston Bar	Boston Bar Indian Reserve
	Anderson River
	Brunswick Creek
	Boothroyd Indian Reserve
	Siwash Creek
	Niger Creek
Kanaka Bar	
Siska Flat	
Cantilever Bar	

▶

◀ *Appendix B*
Legacy of the Fraser River gold rush: Remaining gold-rush bar place names

Gold rush bars	Other features
Lytton	
Van Winkle Flat	
Spintlum Flat	Spintlum Creek
Cameron Bar	Cameron Indian Reserve
Siwash Bar	
[McGillvray Dry-diggings]	McGillvray Creek
Foster Bar	
Texas Bar (2nd)	Texas Creek
McCartney Flat	Riley Creek
Lillooet	
The Fountain	Fountain Indian Reserve

Source: Surveys and Mapping Branch, Department of Energy, Mines and Resources, 1976-91, Maps 92 H/6, H11, H/13, H/14, I/4, I/5, I/12, and I/13.

Notes

1 "Letter from Fort Yale: Fatal Accident, Serious Trouble Anticipated with the Indians," *Victoria Gazette*, 30 July 1858, p. 2.

2 See "Legacy of the Fraser River gold rush: Remaining gold-rush bar place names," Appendix B.

3 Arthur J. Ray, *Indians in the Fur Trade: Their Role as Hunters, Trappers, and Middlemen in the Lands Southwest of Hudson Bay, 1660-1870* (Toronto and Buffalo: University of Toronto Press, 1991), xi.

4 Paul Carter, *The Road to Botany Bay: An Essay in Spatial History* (London and Boston: Faber and Faber, 1987), xxiii.

5 "Making the World Right through Transformations," plate 1, in *A Stó:lō-Coast Salish Historical Atlas*, ed. Keith Thor Carlson (Vancouver: Douglas and McIntyre, 2001), 7.

6 "Stl'áleqem Sites: Spiritually Potent Places in S'ólh Téméxw," plate 2, Carlson, *Stó:lō-Coast Salish Historical Atlas*, 8.

7 Letter of James Bell reprinted in Willard E. Ireland, "Gold-Rush Days in Victoria, 1858-59," *British Columbia Historical Quarterly* 12, 3 (1948): 240.

8 Robie L. Reid, "Two Narratives of the Fraser Gold-Rush," *British Columbia Historical Quarterly* 5, 3 (1941): 227. Translated from Dr. Carl Friesach, *Ein Ausflug nach Britisch-Columbien im Jahre 1858* (Gratz: Drukerei Leykam-Josepfsthal, 1875).

9 British Columbia, *Papers Relative to the Affairs of British Columbia*, 29, 1 July 1858, 19-20. Douglas noted that the following "nations" that volunteered their labour for the Harrison-Lillooet Road construction were "British subjects, Americans, French, Germans, Danes, Africans, and Chinese." Ibid., 34, 9 August 1858, 27-28.

10 J.S. Holliday, *The World Rushed In: The California Gold Rush Experience* (New York: Simon and Schuster, 1983), 455.

11 Alfred Waddington's letter, *Victoria Gazette*, 15 September 1858.

12 Further work is required in comparing California and British Columbia gold-rush place names as early evidence suggests that similarities found between these two regions could provide a link between emigrant miners in British Columbia and particular regions in California or the wider United States.

13 As quoted in Margaret A. Ormsby, *British Columbia: A History* (Toronto: Macmillan, 1958), 37.

14 For David Thompson's map, which includes the Fraser River, consult BCA, CM/D114.

15 Alexander C. Anderson, *Hand-book and Map of the Gold Region of Frazer's and Thompson's Rivers* (San Francisco: J.J. Le Count, 1858), 7, in British Columbia Archives (BCA).

16 This "age old hostility" between Upper and Lower Natives is also confirmed in T.A. Rickard, "Indian Participation in the Gold Discoveries," *British Columbia Historical Quarterly* 2, 1 (1938): 15.

17 Governor James Douglas confirmed the earlier interest of Washington and Oregon, prior to the rush from California, in Douglas to Labouchere, 8 May 1858 (no. 19), *Correspondence Relative to the Discovery of Gold In Fraser's River District* (London: 1858), 12. Bellingham Bay was to become the main stop-off point for American miners who wanted to evade the British port of Victoria and, more particularly, the miners' licence fee. See R.L. Reid, "Whatcom Trails to the Fraser River Mines in 1858," *Washington Historical Quarterly* 18 (1927): 199-206, 271-76. For first news of this rush, which effectively closed down the Bellingham Bay Coal Company, see "Gold Discovery Confirmed!" *Puget Sound Herald*, Steilacoom, Washington Territory, 26 March 1858.

18 Moore claimed not to have left Yale to go upriver until 17 December 1858. He and his party reached Lytton on 26 January 1859. See James Moore, "The Discovery of Hill's Bar in 1858," *British Columbia Historical Quarterly* 3, 3 (1939): 220.

19 Army desertions in Washington Territory and the anticipated rush from California are noted in the *Puget Sound Herald*, 2 April 1858.

20 F.W. Howay, "To the Fraser River! The Diary and Letters of Cyrus Olin Phillips, 1858-59," *California Historical Society Quarterly* 11, 2 (1932): 156. Phillips also visited Whatcom on Bellingham Bay and noted that three thousand miners were waiting there.

21 Moore, "Discovery of Hill's Bar," 218.

22 Ireland, "Gold-Rush Days in Victoria," 224.

23 Ibid., 245.

24 "Rush to the Upper Fraser," *Victoria Gazette*, 18 September 1858.

25 In particular, this had occurred above Sailor's Diggings. For the approximate location of Sailor's Bar, see Appendix A. For the above quotation, see *Puget Sound Herald*, 4 June 1858.

26 Referred to by discouraged miners as the "Fraser River hysteria" or "Fraser River humbug," many left the Fraser River and returned to California, having become "flat broke." The combination of high water, high prices, poor weather, and poor trails drove many of them away. Only the most determined remained through the fall-winter of 1858-59. See Rodman W. Paul *California Gold: The Beginning of Mining in the Far West* (Lincoln: University of Nebraska Press, 1947), 177-79. See also Rodman W. Paul, *Mining Frontiers of the Far West, 1848-1880* (New York: Holt, Rinehart and Winston, 1963), 38-39. For an early refutation of the humbug thesis, see Alfred Waddington, *The Fraser Mines Vindicated: The History of Four Months* (Victoria: P. de Garro, 1858).

27 *Northern Light*, Whatcom, Bellingham Bay, Washington Territory, 10 July 1858.

28 "Too Early – That's All," *Northern Light*, 31 July 1858.

29 Henry De Groot, *British Columbia; Its Conditions and Prospects, Soil, Climate, and Mineral Resources, Considered* (San Francisco: Alta Californian, 1859),16-17.

30 Douglas had claimed that John K. Ledell had travelled further than anyone else up the Fraser in the early spring of 1858, or so the prospector maintained to his wife. "Narrative of a Miner's Trip to the Head Waters of the Gold Region," *Northern Light*, 16 March 1858. Ledell named Foster's Bar.

31 In 1850, the prohibitive Foreign Miner's Head Tax was twenty dollars a month and, although technically applied to all non-Americans, was in practice levelled primarily against Chinese and Mexicans. See William S. Greever, *Bonanza West: The Story of the Western Mining Rushes, 1848-1900* (Moscow, ID: University of Idaho Press, 1990 [1963]), 71.

32 Story of J.C. Bryant as told in "A Sturdy Prospector," in W.W. Walkem, *Stories of Early British Columbia* (Vancouver: News-Advertiser, 1914), 123.

33 For the above source and a discussion of race relations in the American West, see Sarah Deutsch, "Landscape of Enclaves: Race Relations in the West, 1865-1990," in *Under an Open Sky: Rethinking America's Western Past*, ed. William Cronon, George Miles, and Jay Gitlin (New York and London: W.W. Norton, 1992), 113.

34 See the inset in Map 6.1.

35 See Appendix A for an extensive listing of gold-rush bar place names.

36 As Waddington noted, the Lower Mines comprised only twenty-three kilometres out of the approximate 230 kilometres from south of Hope to the Fountain above Lillooet.

37 See Map 6.1, particularly between Spuzzum and the Fountain.

38 See Appendices A and B. There were two French Bars on the Fraser, one in the Lower Mines, the other in the Upper Mines. Perhaps there is a distinction to be drawn between Continental French and French Canadiens. French Canadiens, formerly employed by the HBC, undoubtedly would have been early arrivals in the Lower Mines. Gudde notes that the adjective "French" was used more than any other ethnic description in Californian place-naming. See Erwin G. Gudde, *California Gold Camps* (Berkeley: University of California Press, 1973).

39 R.L. Reid, "The Whatcom Trails to the Fraser River Mines in 1858," *Washington Historical Quarterly* 18 (1927): 199-206, 271-76.

40 Waddington detailed the extent of mining during the 1858 rush as follows: "All the diggings that have been worked up to this day [1858], have been strictly speaking river diggings and lye between Murderer's [Cornish] Bar, 4 miles below Fort Hope, and the Fountain, 6 miles above the Big Falls, stretching over a total length of 140 miles: and that the three quarters of them have been worked over a distance of 14 miles between Fort Hope and Fort Yale." See Waddington, *Fraser Mines Vindicated*, 7.

41 In the "Mormon War" of 1857-58, President Buchanan sent 2,500 troops, or one-sixth of the entire US army, to suppress a Mormon rebellion. See Richard White, *"It's Your Misfortune and None of My Own": A New History of the American West* (Norman and London: University of Oklahoma Press, 1991), 163-69.

42 Although of European stock, the Mormon practice of polygamy was abhorred. For a discussion of discrimination in mining camps against Mormons and other groups, see Duane A. Smith, "Not All Were Welcome," in *Rocky Mountain Mining Camps: The Urban Frontier*, (Bloomington and London: Indiana University Press, 1967), 29-41.

43 For an examination of Native mining during the Fraser rush, see Daniel P. Marshall, "Rickard Revisited: Native 'Participation' in the Gold Discoveries of British Columbia," *Native Studies Review* 11, 1 (1997): 91-108. Further work is required to establish the multiracial flavour of the gold-rush era. Certainly church archival records may prove to be an invaluable source. A tantalizing example is found in the early Anglican Church records for Lillooet, where the marriage register for 1861 recorded the first formal exchange of vows in this locale between two Latin Americans, one from Chile and the other from San Salvador. See St. Mary's Church Register, Lillooet, 1861-1915, UBC Special Collections.

44 Charles D. Ferguson, *The Experiences of a Forty-Niner* (Cleveland: Williams, 1888).

45 Until formal surveys were finally completed in keeping with the Oregon Boundary Settlement of 1846, many Americans claimed that the Fraser – at just twenty-three kilometres inside the BC border – was actually in American territory.

46 The idea that naming legitimates a colonial presence is developed in Carter, *Road to Botany Bay*, xvi.

47 J.B. Harley, "Maps, Knowledge, and Power," in *The Iconography of Landscape: Essays on the Symbolic Representation, Design and Use of Past Environments*, ed. Denis Cosgrove and Stephen Daniels (Cambridge: Cambridge University Press, 1988), 278.

48 For a vast dictionary-compendium of California place names comparable to those found on the Fraser, see Gudde, *California Gold Camps*.

49 A.C. Anderson's manuscript, entitled "Original Sketch of Exploration between 1846 and 1849, c. 1850," 8000/L10, Map Division, BCA. For a detailed examination of Anderson's work, see Albert L. Farley, *Historical Cartography of British Columbia* (Madison: University of Wisconsin Press, 1961).

50 Alexander C. Anderson, comp., *Routes of Communication with the Gold Region on Frasers River* (San Francisco: J.J. Lecount, 1858), CM/A78 Map Division, BCA. This map also accompanied the guidebook *Hand-Book and Map of the Gold Region*, UBC Special Collections. This guidebook and map would have been used by the majority of miners travelling from California to British Columbia.

51 See Farley, "The Colonial Era, 1849-1871," chap. 5, *Historical Cartography of British Columbia*, 228.

52 "Cultural circulation" is a term coined by Carter, *Road to Botany Bay*, 28. British Columbia was often referred to as the "New El Dorado," and at least one author made this the subject of a book. See Kinahan Cornwallis, *The New El Dorado; Or, British Columbia* (London: Thomas Cautley Newby, 1858), BCA.

53 "Sketch of Frazer River and the New Gold Mines," *Bulletin* (1858), CM/A295: Sh. 1, Map Division, BCA. A similar map is drawn by merchant C.O. Phillips, who established a store on Bridge River in November 1858. Indians are simply located and gold-rush bars are limited to the following: Sea Bird Bar, Murderer's Bar, Texas Bar, Emory's Bar, and Hill's Bar. See Howay, "To the Fraser River!" Waddington's map of 1858 contains neither gold bar names nor Native information; rather, it simply points out where the rich diggings were located. One exception is that "Indian Diggings" are located along the Thompson River. See A. Waddington, *A Correct Map of the Northern Coal & Gold Regions comprehending Frazer River* (San Francisco: P. de Garro, May 1858).

54 Keith Thor Carlson, ed. *You Are Asked To Witness: The Stó:lō in Canada's Pacific Coast History* (Chilliwack, BC: Stó:lō Heritage Trust, 1997), 61.

55 Elder Harold Wells of Union Bar (near Hope) was told by his grandmother how Chinese miners left a permanent scar, a 3.65 metre quarry, on their land, while they were away visiting relatives farther down the Fraser River. Carlson, *You Are Asked to Witness*, 62.

56 Stephen Greenblatt, *Marvelous Possessions: The Wonder of the New World* (Chicago: University of Chicago Press, 1991), 83.

57 Paul Carter states: "New ... is a name that refuses to admit the place was there before it was named." This was typical of the gold-rush mentality that reinvented the Fraser along Californian lines. See Carter, *Road to Botany Bay*, 9.

58 In essence, naming allowed one to mark the present, possess it, and then travel onward, leaving behind beacons for future travel, landmarks for the map, and a space to enter history. See Carter, *The Road to Botany Bay*, 46-47.

59 Gudde suggests that "Pike" was often used by gold diggers from Pike County, Missouri, and later by those unwilling to tell where they were from; finally, it was applied to rough miners or new immigrants. See Gudde, *California Gold Camps*, 265. A more pertinent explanation, perhaps, is that Pike's Peak Rush in Colorado was greatly exaggerated. It occurred in 1858-59, and it is quite possible that news of its bust would have travelled to the Fraser. Those returning from Pike's Peak to California became known as "Pikers," or failed miners. It might be, therefore, that Pike's Bar on the Fraser is suggestive of dashed expectations. See Paul, *California Gold*, 39, and Greever, *Bonanza West*, 158. Yet another explanation is that the bar could have been named after Zebullon Pike, who had invaded Canada during the War of 1812. Of course, Captain H.M. Snyder had commanded the "Pike Guards" during the Fraser River War.

60 J.B. Harley, "Deconstructing the Map," *Cartographica* 26, 2 (1989): 11.

61 Other maps consulted in the post-1858 period include: H.S. Palmer, "Sketch of Route from Fort Hope to Fort Colville" (1859); Royal Engineer map, "British Columbia: New Westminster to Lillooet" (New Westminster, 1861); and John Arrowsmith, "The Provinces of British Columbia & Vancouver Island" (South Kensington, England, 1862). All of these are located in the Map Division, BCA.

62 Fort Hope was apparently named by the HBC to commemorate the hoped-for route located along the Similkameen Trail that was to replace the HBC's Columbia-Okanagan river route in the aftermath of the Oregon Boundary Settlement of 1846. Fort Yale was named for HBC chief trader James Murray Yale, who was stationed at Fort Langley. Lytton was named for Lord Lytton (Henry Bulwer Lytton), the then secretary of state for the colonies, who presided over the creation of the Crown Colony of British Columbia.

63 See William D. Patterson, C.E., "Map of the Cariboo & Omineca Gold Fields and the Routes there to" (1870)m CM/A123m Map Division, BCA. No such place names listed.

64 Hubert Howe Bancroft, "Fraser River Mining and Settlement, 1858-1878" in *History of British Columbia* (San Francisco: History Company, 1890). Bancroft supplies an invaluable list of gold-rush bar names and other landmarks compiled from a variety of sources.

65 J.W. Trutch, "Map of British Columbia," compiled by Lands and Works Office (1871), BCA. For above quote, see Farley, *Historical Cartography of British Columbia*, BCA.

66 Ibid.

67 His time below the 49th parallel is found in Robin Fisher, "Joseph Trutch and Indian Land Policy," *BC Studies* 12 (1971-72): 3-33. Reprinted in J. Friesen and H.K. Ralston, eds. *Historical Essays on British Columbia* (Toronto: Gage, 1980), 257.

68 Carter, *Road to Botany Bay*, 67.

69 Douglas to Lytton, 14 March 1859, British Columbia, *Papers Connected with the Indian Land Question, 1850-1875* (Victoria: Richard Wolfden, Government Printer, 1875), 16-17. See also *Journals of the Colonial Legislatures of the Colonies of Vancouver Island and British Columbia, 1851-1871*, ed. James E. Hendrickson (Victoria: PABC, 1980), 1:25.

70 James Morris, *Pax Britannica: The Climax of an Empire* (Harmondsworth, UK: Penguin, 1980), 123. My emphasis.

71 Carnarvon to Douglas, 11 April 1859, no. 49, Colonial Office 410/1.

72 Douglas to Lytton, 14 March 1859, no. 114, Colonial Office 60/4. The above quotation was taken from Carnarvon's note appended to the despatch in which Lytton approved "the caution recommended by Lord C[arnarvon]." See ibid. The official response to Douglas stated: "Whilst making ample provision under the arrangements proposed for the future sustenance and improvement of the native tribes, you will, I am persuaded, bear in mind the importance of exercising due care in laying out and defining the several reserves, so as to avoid checking at a future day the progress of the white colonists." See Carnarvon to Douglas, 20 May 1859, *Papers Connected with the Indian Land Question*, 18.

73 For a full examination of the Fraser River War of 1858, which pitted First Nations throughout southern British Columbia and eastern Washington against Fraser River-bound miners, see Daniel P. Marshall, "No Parallel: American Settler-Soldiers at War with the Nlaka'pamux of the Canadian West" in *Parallel Destinies: Canadian-American Relations West of the Rockies*, ed. John Findlay and Ken Coates, 31-79 (Seattle: University of Washington Press, 2002).

74 Robin Fisher, *Contact and Conflict: Indian-European Relations in British Columbia, 1774-1890* (Vancouver: UBC Press, 1977), 96.

75 Trutch to Acting Colonial Secretary, New Westminster, 28 August 1867, *Papers Connected with the Indian Land Question*, 41-43.

76 Trutch to Colonial Secretary, 20 September 1865, F942/17, BCA.

77 See "Schedule of all Indian reserves (surveyed) in the Province of British Columbia" in *Papers Connected with the Indian Land Question*, 104-5. Tracings for schedule A-Q, of the seventy-six reserves noted above were located by Heather West, Surveyor-General's Office, BC Department of Forests and Lands, Victoria. Copies of tracings for Mainland reserves have been deposited by the author at UBC Special Collections.

78 Keith H. Basso, "'Stalking with Stories': Names, Places, and Moral Narratives among the Western Apache," *Text, Play and Story: The Construction and Reconstruction of Self and Society*, ed. Stuart Plattner (Washington: Proceedings of the American Ethnological Society, 1984), 44-45.

79 Raymond D. Fogelson, "The Ethnohistory of Events and Nonevents," *Ethnohistory* 36, 2 (1989): 134.

80 In addition, the building of two transcontinental railways on either side of the Fraser River Canyon must have resulted in the levelling of many important stone monoliths that held the ancient history of these First Nations.

81 See John Trutch's 1870 maps, which correspond to the A-Q schedule of reserves compiled for the federal government in 1871. See, particularly, the sheet entitled, "Indian Reserves situated on or near Fraser River in the Lytton District." Copies deposited by the author at UBC Special Collections.

82 The "cult of first-comers" is described by Carter, *Road to Botany Bay*, xviii.

83 Boothroyd Indian Reserve was named for George Washington Boothroyd, who was a member of Major Mortimer Robertson's "Yakima Expedition," the volunteer miners' militia that fought with Native peoples through the Canadian and American Okanagan in its bid to reach the Fraser River goldfields. Ironically, this Indian-fighter's name defines the space of this particular reserve. Similarly, Stout Indian Reserve is named after Edward Stout, both a '49er and a '58er, and participant in the Fraser River War. See "A Pioneer of '58," in Walkem,

Stories of Early British Columbia, 51-62. It should be noted that, during the writing of this chapter, many First Nations have taken steps to officially rename their reserves according to traditional Native usage. At the time of writing, this reassertion of Native sovereignty and control continues.

7
Innovation, Tradition, Colonialism, and Aboriginal Fishing Conflicts in the Lower Fraser Canyon
Keith Thor Carlson

As Arthur Ray's experience and research show, Native rights litigation is a theatre in which identity and affiliation tend to be drawn in stark, often binary, terms: plaintiffs and defendants, Indians and whites, supporters and opponents.[1] The adversarial judicial process itself reinforces and accentuates these distinctions. Experts who testify on behalf of Native communities seldom testify for the Crown, and visa versa. Throughout the litigation process the affiliations and identities of Aboriginal people are generally easy to determine. In most instances, they are the ones sitting across the room from the Crown's council. Likewise, they are also the ones who tend to be identified as opponents of modernity – as agents of praxis against progress, of stasis against innovation. Occasionally, though, colonialism creates a context within which indigenous interests clash with one another, and within which both sides invoke history to justify innovative means to traditional ends.

Although the contemporary fishing conflicts at the Fraser River's mouth capture more headlines – ostensibly because they reflect racial divisions between Native and non-Native interests – an equally heated contest simultaneously emerges each summer 180 kilometres farther upstream in the lower Fraser Canyon, this one featuring competing Aboriginal interests. The tensions involved in this conflict have at least two dimensions: (1) the contest between Aboriginal families regarding rights to fish in particular "back eddies" and (2) the contest between the Yale First Nation and the Stó:lō Nation regarding the latter's right to be involved in Canadian government-sponsored fisheries regulatory regimes – in particular, initiatives under the Aboriginal Fisheries Strategy (AFS) but also the emerging system of salmon allocation associated with the British Columbia Treaty Commission (BCTC) process.[2]

Inevitably, in such disputes the question of tradition is bound up with the problem of authority as the individuals, families, and First Nations involved all cite history and tradition to support and validate their opposing positions. Families claim that particular fishing "spots" belong to them by right of inheritance and that other claimants are interlopers. First Nations claim that their right to regulate and manage the canyon fishery in order to secure benefits for their members derives from ancient tribal protocols; that they are the true keepers of tradition while other claimants are variously dismissed as "invaders" or patsies of a colonial system that marginalizes genuine indigenous law and custom.[3]

Regarded from this perspective, without racial or allodial divisions to serve as markers and guides, traditions become invoked not merely to highlight historical continuities but also, as Mark Salber Phillips astutely notes in *Questions of Tradition*, "to mark the authority that they carry – and even to endorse and sustain it." And if, as Phillips goes on to assert, scholarship in the wake of Eric Hobsbawm and T. Ranger's influential 1983 collection, *The Invention of Tradition*, has tended to engage only the narrow idea of tradition within "the deconstructive framework of pseudo-traditionality,"[4] then few examples will as adequately illustrate the continuing value of "tradition" as a field of intellectual inquiry as colonial-sponsored contests involving competing indigenous versions of history.

Regarding history as the arbitrator of identity and authority is, of course, not an exclusively Aboriginal phenomenon. As Patrick Geary demonstrates in *The Myth of Nations: The Medieval Origins of Europe* (2002), competing assertions over the historical legitimacy of ethnic communities to land and resources lie at the heart of many of the contemporary world's more violent and contentious conflicts.[5] But within the context of Coast Salish culture and history such debates assume an added urgency. Among the Coast Salish living along the lower Fraser River, "knowing one's history" is directly associated with being high status (*smelá:lh*, or "worthy"). Lower-class people (*s'téxem*, or "worthless") are considered to have "lost or forgotten their history."[6] All assertions that a particular claim is "more traditional" than another, therefore, are tantamount to saying that "my historical knowledge is better than yours. I am, therefore, from a higher-status and more worthy family than you." Moreover, in addition to the issue of status, salmon have long been a lucrative commodity within Aboriginal as well as non-Aboriginal markets.

Challenging someone's right to fish in the Fraser Canyon is, therefore, a direct affront to a person's social and economic well-being and, as such, is not easily shrugged off. Over the past fifteen years, indigenous efforts to secure internal and external recognition of Fraser Canyon fishing rights have included resorting to physical intimidation, using the mainstream media, litigation, negotiating interim treaty measures, and working within various Department of Fisheries management regimes. Thus far, none has proven particularly successful in reconciling the competing indigenous claims.

This chapter does not evaluate the specific merits of the contemporary competing claims to the canyon fishery; rather, by examining similar contestations from the late nineteenth and early twentieth centuries, it reveals that, when it comes to preserving Fraser Canyon Aboriginal fishing rights, "traditional" need not be equated with "non-innovative," nor innovation with assimilation. Indeed, occasionally innovative actions were designed to protect and preserve traditional systems and, as such, within restricted circumstances, a degree of innovation was sometimes regarded as being traditional. At question is the motivation and purpose behind the various invocations of tradition. Were they designed to sustain long-standing indigenous regulatory mechanisms or to undermine them? Were they aimed at reviving core aspects of a tradition that had been thrown into disarray by external non-Native forces or to take advantage of new colonial opportunities? Were there competing traditions prior to the disruption caused by colonial intrusion into Aboriginal space? And, if so, how were they mediated? I argue that, in as much as not all traditions are genuinely traditional, neither are they all invented.

The lower Fraser Canyon salmon fishery has been and continues to be of incomparable significance to the Coast Salish people of southwestern British Columbia and northwestern Washington. It was there, at the site that early Hudson's Bay Company officers referred to as "the Falls," just upriver of the present-day town of Yale and between the surging series of rapids that stretch for seven kilometres between "Sailor Bar" and "Lady Franklin Rock," that thousands of Salish people from as far away as Vancouver Island and northern Puget Sound gathered each summer to catch or exchange salmon. The unique geography of the lower canyon made it an ideal salmon catching and processing region, unparalleled on the entire Northwest Coast.[7] Here, numerous craggy rock outcroppings jut into the river, creating swirling "back eddies" – places where migrating salmon pause to rest before making a dash through the surging current to the next such resting place a few metres farther upstream. Historically, a person with a dip net standing on the edge of such an outcropping could easily catch hundreds of sockeye salmon in a single afternoon. Even today, with the salmon runs vastly depleted, a particularly skilled Native fisher, using only a traditional dip net, has been known to catch over three hundred sockeye salmon in just one hour.[8] Farther downstream in the Fraser Valley, where the weaker currents did not force the salmon to hug the river's edge, catching fish was a much more difficult task.

The ease with which salmon were caught in the canyon only partially explains the region's unique appeal. It was there, and only there, and even then only in early July, that sockeye salmon could be reliably "wind dried" without fear of mould, wasps, or flies (and, hence, maggots) contaminating the catch. In the canyon, the summer sun warmed the rocks to such an extent that they continued to provide drying heat throughout the night (thus preventing the formation of dew, which would result in spoilage), and it was at this point, after struggling upriver for 180 kilometres from the sea without eating, that the salmon were guaranteed to have burned sufficient body fat (5 percent to 6 percent) to make wind drying feasible. Even today, a salmon caught at the river's mouth and immediately transported to the Fraser Canyon will not wind dry because its fat content is simply too high.[9] Accordingly, downriver from the canyon, and along the coast itself, smoking was the only reliable technique for preserving salmon prior to the introduction of canning and freezing technology.[10]

As both Wayne Suttles and Leland Donald have independently demonstrated, the seasonal availability of salmon, coupled with the geographic and climatic restrictions on processing, made the resource especially valuable. Putting away sufficient stores of salmon to last through the long, wet winters was essential not only to survival but also to the flourishing of classical west coast culture.[11] Thus, the lower Fraser Canyon constituted what was arguably the most valuable Aboriginal real estate on the Northwest Coast. Prior to the migrations of the nineteenth century, the "owners" of canyon fishing sites tended to live in one of the several adjacent settlements. Ownership, expressed through the regulation of extended family members' access, was the prerogative of men, although the right was sometimes inherited though a mother's line.

The system of property transfer was the potlatch naming ceremony. Through it, genealogically based rights (associated with names) were transferred across generations. Disputes over ownership rights or even access privileges were serious matters and extremely disruptive to the brief window of opportunity the summer fishing season provided. If other families did not recognize a particular family's ownership, violent conflicts could emerge. Even within families, tensions needed to be constantly mitigated. If orderly access to sites was not guaranteed to all recognized kin and in-laws, people could go hungry and, thus, internal fights could break out. To clarify ownership, representatives of the highest-status families from geographically dispersed settlements and tribes were "called to witness" the potlatch ceremony and associated intergenerational property transfers. In this way, a family's collective ownership was reasserted, and its chosen system of management (the naming of someone charged with regulating access)[12] was widely publicized and ostensibly recognized by others.

One of the best documented examples of the role of potlatches in the transfer of Fraser Canyon fishing rights is the circa 1890 potlatch at which Súx̱'yel (also known as Captain Charlie) transferred his name and the associated fishing rights attached to his family's lower Fraser Canyon fishing site at Aselaw to his youngest son, Patrick Charlie.[13] Súx̱'yel was the leader of a prominent and distinguished family living in the Fraser Canyon above Yale. Like his father, who is buried at Aselaw, Súx̱'yel possessed great wealth: he counted the snake, grizzly bear, and loon among his spirit helpers, and on behalf of his family he acted as steward of valuable hereditary lands and canyon fishing sites. Súx̱'yel was a confident man who boldly engaged with non-Native society, ultimately securing an administrative position with the colonial government, although in what capacity is no longer remembered. In his middle age, Súx̱'yel decided to fully avail himself of the opportunities the new colonial order presented by becoming a European-style farmer. Accordingly, he moved to the flats across the river from Fort Yale, but insufficient water stymied his agricultural ambitions. He determined that, in order to be successful, he would have to leave the canyon altogether. After unsuccessfully trying to establish himself at a second site farther downriver near Fort Hope, an elderly relative at Ohamil (downriver from Hope) suggested he try his luck on the fertile meadows surrounding the mouth of Ruby Creek, which had remained vacant since the first great smallpox epidemic. There, near to the remains of the former villages of Spopetes, and just downriver from the settlement of Sxwoxwimelh (where smallpox survivors had simultaneously cremated and interred their less fortunate relatives in their own pithouses), Súx̱'yel built a farm for himself as well as for some of his children and their spouses. Later, as a result of Súx̱'yel's actions, this settlement was surveyed as an Indian reserve and was registered to the Yale band.

Before Súx̱'yel could move, however, the elders of his family insisted that he transfer his hereditary name and Fraser Canyon land holdings to a member of the next generation. Typically, such a transfer was from father to eldest son, but in Súx̱'yel's case the decision to break with protocol appears to have been influenced by the fact that his youngest son, Patrick, possessed special spiritual potential. Patrick had been born with pierced ears and a bleeding head. What is more, his head bled freshly each spring until he reached the age of twelve. This had "scared the old people," who had unsuccessfully hired a shaman to try to unveil the secrets of Patrick's past life and so explain his strange, stigmata-like symptoms. Ultimately, Patrick learned the identity of his past self and the circumstances of his previous death – knowledge that elevated rather than diminished his status. His special condition appears to have influenced his family elders' decision to select him as the one who would remain in the canyon and carry the ancestral names and property after his father moved away.

Preparation for the name-transferring ceremony occupied Súx̱'yel's family for a full year. Taking advantage of the annual influx of people visiting the canyon fishery each summer, Súx̱'yel's family rejected the normal autumn timing for their potlatch and hosted the naming ceremony in June. Guests were invited from as far north as Sliammon, near present-day Powell

River on the Coast, and as far west as Vancouver Island. Hundreds of people were in attendance to witness and validate the transfer. In addition to the dozens of cattle and pigs that were butchered to feed the guests, well over $1,000 in cash and countless blankets and other items were distributed among the witnesses.

Súx̱'yel's family's potlatch, which worked so effectively c. 1890, was among the last to be held in the region. Independent federal and provincial regulatory initiatives, the first aimed at nurturing non-Native commercial development and the second aimed at undermining indigenous cultural traditions, were working to undermine both the Native economy and indigenous governance. The Salmon Fishery Regulations for the Province of British Columbia, 1868, identified the salmon resource as a commodity that needed to be regulated in the interest of the growing non-Native immigrant population, while the 1884 "anti-potlatch" amendment to the Indian Act designated the large property-transfer gatherings a crime.

In order to regulate the fishery for the benefit of non-Native immigrants and the growing industrial fishery associated with the emerging cannery industry, the Salmon Fishery Regulations curtailed the Aboriginal fishery by prohibiting the sale of non-tidal caught salmon, by banning Native in-river fishing technologies like weirs and dip nets, and by defining Aboriginal fishing rights to exclude an economic component (beyond simply meeting the need for subsistence, ceremonial, and social consumption).[14]

The criminalization of the commercial aspect of the Aboriginal in-river fishery left canyon residents with few viable economic opportunities. Certainly, the region's arid, rocky environs were ill suited to the government's preferred Aboriginal occupation/activity of farming. As such, a canyon out-migration, which began at least two generations earlier with the establishment of new economic opportunities associated with the HBC forts at Yale (1846), Hope (1846), and Langley (1827), was reinforced by the imperative of participating in European-style agricultural activities.

The indigenous inhabitants were thus doubly pressured to relocate onto Indian reserves that were being established for Aboriginal agricultural purposes on the fertile valley lands located many kilometres downstream. So successful were the government's efforts that, in contrast to an 1830 HBC census that indicated as many as 2,574 people residing in permanent settlements in the lower Fraser Canyon (and at least 1,592 in 1839),[15] government records show that, by 1878, there were only 276.[16] By 1881, the number had dropped to 143,[17] and in 1914 there was a mere 27.[18] By way of contrast, the downriver communities experienced a corresponding population increase over this same period. Even Lixwetem, the renowned Yale leader, relocated to the agricultural reserve of Seabird Island in the central Fraser Valley. Observing the results of this movement in 1950, the anthropologist Wilson

Duff noted that "in more recent times ... because of movements of population down-river and further intermarriage, the nominal owners [of canyon fishing spots] have come to be as far afield as Musqueam [at the Fraser River's mouth].[19]

If postcontact migration set the stage for debates over the nature and legitimacy of hereditary fishing rights, the process of Indian reserve creation established a context within which innovative means came to be regarded by some indigenous people as the most effective and appropriate way to secure or defend customary ownership and tenure.

The process of reserve creation in the Fraser Canyon began in earnest in 1876, after the British Columbia and Canadian governments appointed A.C. Anderson, Gilbert M. Sproat, and Archibald McKinley to form the Joint Indian Reserve Commission (JIRC) to address Aboriginal concerns over their lands. Fishing was a key feature of the JIRC's mandate. In reviewing the commission's progress in 1878, L. Vankoughnet, the deputy superintendent general of Indian affairs, observed: "In the instructions given by both Governments to the Commissioners, great stress was laid upon the necessity of not disturbing the Indians in their possessions *inter alia* of fishing stations, and [further] on the impolicy [sic] of attempting to make any violent or sudden change in the habits of the Indians engaged among other pursuits, in fishing."[20]

Indeed, in the spirit of avoiding anything that "could interfere with or mitigate against the establishment of friendly relations between the Dominion government and the Indians of British Columbia," the original instructions provided by the minister of the interior, David Laird, to the commissioners emphasized that, though "it appears theoretically desirable as a matter of general policy to diminish the number of small reserves held by any Indian nation, and when circumstances will permit to concentrate them on three or four large reserves, thus making them more accessible to missionaries and school teachers," the commission should nonetheless "avoid anything which might be calculated to alarm or disturb the Indian mind." In particular, the commissioners were directed "not to disturb the Indians in the possession of any villages, fishing stations, fur-trading posts, settlements or clearings, which they may occupy and to which they may be especially attached, and which may be to their interests to retain." Certainly, despite the imperative of eventually "turn[ing the Indians'] attention to agriculture," the minister of the interior was clear that it "would not be politic to attempt to make any violent or sudden change in the habits of the Indians ... now engaged in fishing."[21] Later, the fisheries department confirmed that the traditional Indian fishery was not to be interfered with and gave Commissioner Anderson permission to suspend the application of the British Columbia fishery regulations with respect to Indian fishing should they be determined to be in conflict with Aboriginal fishing practices.[22] In this regard, the federal government was acting in a manner consistent with earlier BC colonial policies, dating to the governorship of James Douglas (i.e., pre-May 1864).[23]

The JIRC, in other words, was guided by the principal that the reserve-creation process should not interfere with, and where possible should facilitate, the broader assimilation process; however, it was not necessarily to be assimilative in and of itself. The only "special objection," according to Laird, that might justify a concession to the principal of non-interference with existing fishing practices arose "where the Indian settlement [was] in objectionable proximity to any city, town, or to a village of White people."[24] In this way, compromised by concerns to placate non-Native settlers while establishing favourable conditions for future religious, educational, and occupational transformation, the JIRC muddled its way towards protecting land for existing indigenous industries and occupations – or what might be thought of as Aboriginal traditions.

By 1878, politics and government fiscal constraint had taken such a toll on the JIRC that Anderson and McKinley abandoned their positions, leaving Sproat alone to address what had come to be known as the "Indian Land Question." Though the commission had visited Aboriginal communities throughout the province and, in doing so, had travelled back and forth through the Fraser Canyon corridor, it had yet to officially meet with the lower Fraser chiefs. In anticipation of that meeting, BC superintendent of Indian affairs I.W. Powell reaffirmed the commission's mandate, adding the following additional justification for respecting Aboriginal fishing rights:

> There is not, of course, the same necessity to set aside extensive grants of agricultural land for Coast Indians; but their rights to fishing stations and hunting grounds should not be interfered with, and they should receive every assurance of perfect freedom from future encroachments of every description.[25]

Thus directed, G.M. Sproat visited "most of the Lower Fraser River Chiefs" to assess their fishing techniques, protocols, and associated reserve land requirements. In other parts of the province, Sproat had found the process of reserve identification and creation relatively straightforward. People living on, or adjacent to, certain lands were considered to have a primary interest in its future, and reserves were created accordingly. In the lower Fraser Canyon, however, Sproat discovered that his assumptions about the direct relationship between proximity of residence and land interest did not necessarily apply. Stopping at the regional hub-town of Yale, he learned that the Aboriginal people who gathered there each summer to fish for salmon were an amalgam of different tribal communities "composed of Upper Frazer [sic] and Lower Frazer [sic] Indians."[26] Puzzled, Sproat set himself the task of ascertaining the indigenous relationship between identity, residency, and land ownership before attempting to assess and assign reserve lands. He faced thorny questions. To which Natives would the reserve be assigned? Which Natives should be able to use the reserves and under what circumstances? What would the reserves' purpose be? In a letter to Prime Minister John A. Macdonald (in his capacity as minister of Indian affairs), written in a rain-soaked camp near the town of Hope on 26 November 1878, Sproat explained that,

> as the Indians on this Lower portion of the river are one people, and though claim to belong to particular villages, move about constantly from one place to another ... I propose before assigning land to any of the tribes to ascertain who *are* Lower Fraser Indians, and to take a view as to the people as a whole.[27]

Approaching his task from this broader perspective, Sproat quickly came to appreciate that the seven-kilometre-long canyon fishery was a unique space, central to the social, political, and economic lives of the region's Aboriginal population. "The settlement [adjacent to Yale] is one of the oldest in the country," he wrote, not only because of its convenient proximity to the HBC fort and associated growing non-Native urban centre but also because of its "having a peculiar value to the Indians from its nearness to the salmon fisheries in the 'canyons' immediately above Yale."[28]

The centrality of the canyon fishery to the broader Aboriginal community meant that the model used to assign reserves in most other parts of the province would not apply on the lower Fraser. Rather than merely taking into account the needs of the local resident population, the canyon fishery reserves needed to accommodate the interests and requirements of Aboriginal people who resided most of the year in settlements many kilometres downstream. Moreover, some of the local Aboriginal people living in the village beside Yale had only recently come to reside there. Their parents or grandparents had lived year round in one of the more than half dozen canyon settlements of the Ts'akua:m tribe, wedged between the rushing Fraser and the steep rock walls of the lower canyon above Yale. In addition to suffering from the economic lure of the HBC forts, these communities had dwindled further in numbers following the disruption caused by the construction of the Cariboo Road in 1862 (a trend further accentuated by the building of the Canadian Pacific Railway in the years leading up to 1885). Thus, although for government administrative purposes Sproat ultimately came to identify specific reserves with particular local settlements, he explicitly stated that such designations were not to imply that people from farther afield who had seasonal access to the canyon fishery could or would be barred from future use. And yet, as is shown below, despite Sproat's intentions, his actions inadvertently contributed to the idea, in both non-Aboriginal and certain Aboriginal people's minds, that the winter settlement was the privileged collective entity, invested with whatever land management rights the increasingly ubiquitous provisions of the Indian Act bequeathed.

Ironically, as Sproat's appreciation of the often indirect relationship between the proximity of Salish residence and indigenous interest in specific properties deepened, the Dominion government was moving forward with a policy of reifying the winter village community as the legitimate administrative unit. The imposition of exclusive band membership lists, the election or appointment of "chiefs," and the creation of a governing apparatus through which all federal funding and communications were channelled were inconsistent with the informal and dispersed expression of social and political governance traditionally operating in the region – a system one insightful anthropologist described as "a social and biological continuum."[29]

For the indigenous people of the lower Fraser River region, connections between kith and kin living in various geographically scattered settlements were often stronger and more meaningful than whatever social or political associations might link unrelated families within a single village. Sproat's concern in establishing reserves, consistent with his instructions, was not to compel Fraser River Aboriginal peoples to think and act in terms of Dominion Indian policy and goals but merely to set aside sufficient and appropriate lands to allow them to regulate their own fishery as they had in the past. However, despite this awareness and intent, he never fully escaped the problems associated with identifying Aboriginal people with particular plots of land.

"Yale Indians," for Sproat, were generally those lower Fraser Natives who congregated seasonally in the vicinity of the non-Native town of Yale. Such designation was, in fact, consistent with the administrative system the federal government established at the time British Columbia joined Confederation. In 1871, the province was divided into "Indian districts," with names typically drawn from centrally located non-Native towns. The "Yale District," in this context, included all of the Fraser River settlements from Popkum (a few kilometres east of the municipality of Chilliwack) upriver as far as the lower canyon. Coincidentally, this grouping parallels the rather enigmatic "upper Stó:lō" Tít "tribal" grouping. According to Wilson Duff, the Tít were distinct from other lower Fraser tribes in one important way: "the only resource areas actually owned were the fishing rocks in the upper canyon; hence, the only tribal boundary which they sharply defined was their upper boundary on the river, adjacent to Lower Thompson fishing

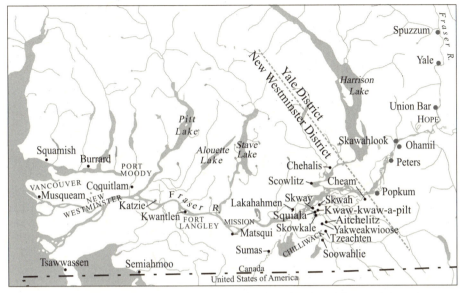

Map 7.1   Locations of lower Fraser River Indian bands and Indian Administration Districts, 1878. Names in capital letters refer to non-Native settlements.
Source: Copyright Keith Thor Carlson, cartography by Jan Jerrier.

grounds ... down river the Tít felt no need to define a lower boundary to their territory. There were no fishing rocks in that area."[30] (See Map 7.1.)

"Yale Indians," therefore, came to be the term of preference for government officials seeking to describe the variously and inconsistently identified "tribes," "nations," and "subgroups" of the lower Fraser living in the Yale administrative district. It also, occasionally, was meant to include all those Aboriginal people from somewhat farther afield who gathered seasonally to fish in the Fraser Canyon near Yale. In such a context, one might expect Sproat's periodic use of the term "Yale Indians Proper" to have referred consistently to a much more narrowly defined collective – likely those Aboriginal people of Xwoxwela:lhp ("willow tree place") immediately adjacent to the non-Native town of Yale. And yet, on the pages of the commissioner's correspondence and Minutes of Decision, the expression remained problematic. It alternatively referred to the residents of Xwoxwela:lhp (by explicitly excluding either the people associated with the "Union Bar Subgroup" located between Yale and Hope or the "Hope Subgroup"), while on still other occasions it included all Native "tribes" downriver as far as, but not including, the settlement of Cheam near Chilliwack. Even "Yale Indians Proper," in other words, was a vaguely defined term that occasionally included a combination of what Sproat sometimes characterized as "subgroups" and even "other tribes."[31] Whatever its use, the term is best considered an enigmatic English gloss that awkwardly linked a convenient administrative boundary with a complex amalgam of indigenous associations and affiliations. It was, in other words, a designation whose meaning was alternatively both traditional and foreign to the local Aboriginal people.

Despite the confusing nomenclature, Sproat clearly appreciated the intricate relationship the region's indigenous peoples had with the Fraser Canyon. On 5 August 1879, he assigned a series of lower canyon reserves to various configurations of the "Yale Indians Proper," all the while making clear that he was simultaneously protecting the entire seven-kilometre stretch of the lower canyon fishery for all Aboriginal people who had, since time immemorial, fished there. He was not restricting the traditional ownership and regulatory protocols of Aboriginal people who did not reside in the canyon year round. This decision is what contemporary lower Fraser Aboriginal fishers refer to as the creation of the "Five Mile Fishery":

> The right of these *and other Indians* who have resorted to the Yale fisheries from time immemorial to have access to, and to encamp upon the banks of the Fraser River for the purpose of carrying on their salmon fisheries in their old way on both sides of the Fraser River for five miles up from Yale is confirmed so far as the undersigned has authority in the matter.[32]

And indeed, Sproat's authority in this instance was significant for, as he later reminded Deputy Superintendent General Vankoughnet, a special Order in Council had given him the "power to make final decisions on the spot within the extensive District of Yale."[33]

In a further attempt to protect the traditional system of geographically dispersed property rights of the lower Fraser Aboriginal peoples, especially as relates to the salmon fishery, Sproat explained that, while demarcating reserves for the "Hope Indians" – another "Yale sub-group," – he considered himself to be protecting "small land areas, referred to as 'fishing reserves' where particular families traditionally fished, or where large numbers of people came to catch and cure fish."[34]

In recognizing the need to clarify that the canyon reserves were designed to facilitate the "old ways" of fishing, Sproat was being sensitive not only to Aboriginal customs but also to the economic role the canyon fishery played in Aboriginal peoples' lives. Appended to his Minutes of Decision were two notes clarifying that subsistence and convenience were not the only factors that made the canyon fishery of vital concern to Aboriginal peoples. The first explained that "Yale is a fishing and also a traveling place of resort of many Indians in addition to the Indians proper of Yale."[35] The second clarified that

The greatest anxiety was shown by all the Indians as to their salmon fisheries above Yale. Not only are the salmon caught there used for the sustenance [sic] of the tribes of the neighborhood; they are a commodity in intertribal traffic over a great extent of the country.[36]

As is so often the case in Canadian history, when one government official actually takes the time to try and understand Aboriginal issues in order to shape policies that are meaningful and intelligible to indigenous peoples, another individual in another branch or level of government representing the interests of a non-Native constituency steps in and disrupts the cart. Despite the Aboriginal fishers' desires, and Sproat's intentions, the fishing sites Sproat identified and reserved near Hope and Yale were not immediately and officially registered. Presumably, Sproat's sudden retirement from the JIRC left the federal and provincial governments scrambling to find a mutually satisfactory replacement. From an administrative point of view, this makes sense, given that Sproat himself acknowledged he was retiring "without having finally adjusted all Yale Indian land matters."[37] In the meantime, however, his files sat collecting dust on a desk in Victoria, and with each passing month more non-Natives availed themselves of the opportunities provided through the provincial land title office to purchase tracts of land in the upper Fraser Valley and lower Fraser Canyon.

To the extent that other officials regarded Sproat's work as in any way encumbering the long-awaited construction of the Canadian Pacific Railway through the Fraser Canyon corridor further undermined Aboriginal claims. Indeed, Sproat himself discovered that some of the lands Aboriginal leaders identified as important to their traditional fishery had already been registered to settlers – in at least one case to an Anglican minister. Sproat therefore proposed a reserve system that, ostensibly, could accommodate non-Native fee-simple ownership as well as hereditary Salish ownership, so long as the intended uses of the two tenures did not work at cross-purposes. Each "owner" needed to constrain their use so as not to interfere with the other owner's rights. In describing this system to Superintendent Laird in Ottawa, Sproat explained that the Aboriginal "right of access to these places is confirmed, but in such a manner as to not inconvenience the [non-Native] owners of the lands in the least, and the Indians are not to occupy these places except for capturing and drying the fish in their accustomed way, and only in their fishing seasons."[38]

This compromise tenure system may have prevailed, at least with regard to small-scale private ownership, had the province not regarded it as a threat to British Columbia's economic and urban development. In 1882, with Sproat's work still unacted upon, the BC government declared that the proposed Indian reserve allotments in the vicinity of Hope could not be recognized because the land had already been "set apart by Colonel Moody [of the Royal Engineers] in 1860 for public purposes in connection with the town site."[39] The province rigidly adhered to this line of reasoning, despite a counter-argument by the federal Department of Indian Affairs, showing that "correspondence preserved with the archives of the province" actually explained that "the land involved was set apart originally by Col. Moody [in 1859] at the request of His Excellency Governor Douglas for the Indians – and not for town site purposes."[40] For the BC chief commissioner of lands and works, such facts were unimportant: "The land referred to is part of the Town of Hope [and] was not open for allotment to the Indians by the Late Reserve Commissioner. I must therefore respectively decline to confirm it as an Indian reservation."[41] It was not until a new provincial chief commissioner of lands and works was appointed seven years later, in 1889, that the province finally agreed to the reserves that Sproat had laid out "for the use of the ... Hope Indians."[42] Oddly, the other reserves farther upstream in the lower canyon were also never registered, despite the fact that the provincial government raised no specific opposition to them.

In 1880, Peter O'Reilly replaced Sproat as the reserve commissioner. By this date, the anti-Aboriginal agenda of the federal fisheries department had been firmly set in step with the non-Native commercial fishing industry. In terms remarkably reminiscent of the provincial chief commissioner of lands and works, the Dominion fisheries commissioner W.F. Whitcher announced in 1883 that his department did "not recognize any unauthorized appropriations of public fishing rights by the Department of Indian Affairs for the Exclusive use of Indians."[43] Indeed, Whitcher articulated a new interpretation of policy, whereby the reservation of fishing stations depended on Department of Fisheries approval.[44] The ongoing interdepartmental rivalries continued throughout the 1880s, the result being that the federal government committed to an in-river Aboriginal fishery while simultaneously acquiescing to the interests of the ocean-based industrial fishery. Faced with government incoherence, Aboriginal peoples were compelled to look for new and innovative ways to protect their increasingly undermined traditional canyon fishery. Internal federal conflicts over jurisdiction might never have risen beyond bureaucratic memoranda exchanges were it not for the actions of various and sometimes competing Native fishery interests. To Salish peoples watching their fishing stations being gobbled up by non-Native private citizens and railroad and highway interests, and seeing the economic component of their fishery being eroded by a government that defined their rights in terms of subsistence or sustenance, the situation was becoming critical. It was the government's 1884 amendment to the Indian Act, which banned the potlatch, however, that most threw the Fraser fishery into a state of crisis. Unlike in most other regions of the province, where Aboriginal villages were situated a great distance from non-Native populations, the lower Fraser reserves were within the province's most-travelled transportation corridor and adjacent to the quickest-growing urban centres. It is no surprise that the first person arrested under the anti-potlatch law was a lower Fraser River Aboriginal man from Chilliwack named Bill Uslick.[45] Government officials hoped that Uslick's conviction and two-month prison sentence would "deter others from following his example."[46] Without large-scale potlatch naming ceremonies families could not effectively communicate (and thereby reassert) their claims to hereditary property, the most important being canyon fishing sites. As a result, old intertribal and intrafamily disputes became accentuated, while other entirely new ones emerged.

In the early summer of 1901, an Aboriginal man known as Peter from "Katz Landing" (just downstream from Hope) contacted Frank Devlin, the regional Indian agent, to ask for assistance in resolving a dispute over a canyon fishing station between his wife and another Indian named Billy Swallsea, who lived in the village of "Ewawass" (just upstream from Hope).[47] Devlin replied affirmatively to Peter and sent an additional letter to Swallsea, inviting him to help "investigate the question of ownership of the rock."[48]

No records of that meeting appear to exist, but, according to John McDonald, who replaced Devlin as Indian agent after the latter's death, Devlin adjudicated the dispute in favour of Billy Swallsea after learning that the latter had been in possession of the rock "for many years."[49] Shortly thereafter, however, in time for the following summer's sockeye salmon run, another Native man from Hope, named Paul Skitt (possibly "Peter of Katz's" wife's brother[50]), with the support of Chief George Ohamil and others, took the unprecedented action of bringing charges of trespass against Billy Swallsea in a court presided over by the justice of the peace in Yale. It was there, on 17 June 1903, as subsequently reported by Chief Joseph Stewart, that, "upon the evidence of eight or nine witnesses," the government magistrate "found, proved and declared ... that the fishing station did not belong to Swallasea and he was a trespasser."[51] Billy Swallsea was subsequently fined $6.25 and ordered to "keep away from the rock."[52]

The decision to involve first the Indian agent and then the justice of the peace clearly indicates (1) that Native society was not split into clear camps of supporters of tradition versus supporters of innovation and (2) that innovative means were not regarded as irreconcilable with traditional ends. Indeed, the prominent leader at Yale, Chief James, had sent a telegram to McDonald a week before the trial asking the Indian agent to attend the court proceedings.[53] Later, Chief James explained that he and other Natives at Yale looked with "great disfavour" upon the decision of the court, his reason being that Billy Swallsea had been in possession of the rock for a long time, "and with the support of the Indian Agent."[54] To this, McDonald's terse reply was simply to inform the chief that Superintendent Vowell had advised that "no further action can be taken"; that Swallsea "must obey the court's decision ... and thereby avoid further trouble and expense to himself." McDonald ended the correspondence instructing the chief to "be good enough to caution Swallsea against any further interference with the said rock."[55]

Billy Swallsea, however, was not easily dissuaded. Some of his confidence no doubt derived from the fact that he carried one of the highest status hereditary names in the region. As the anthropologist Franz Boas learned, Swallsea was the name of the legendary heroic first ancestor of the Ts'akua:m tribe, which, prior to the late nineteenth-century migrations, occupied the string of villages in the prized seven-kilometre stretch of canyon real-estate just upstream from Yale.[56] Within weeks of hearing the bad news from Chief James, Swallsea visited McDonald's New Westminster office and stated that Captain Jemmet, the surveyor who had marked off the Indian reserves following Sproat's visit, had informed all the Natives that "all the land along the river from Yale to No. 2 reserve four and a half miles above Yale ... was an Indian reserve." Swallsea asserted, "Since that time" the Natives "had all believed it to be so."[57] What Swallsea now wanted to know was whether this was true. Was the "five-mile fishery" promised by Sproat actually protected as Indian land, and, if so, was the disputed rock beyond the jurisdiction of the provincial magistrate? McDonald was at a loss and turned to Vowell for guidance. Three days later, McDonald wrote to Billy Swallsea, referring him to an attached tracing of a map Vowell had provided of all registered Indian reserves in the lower Fraser Canyon. The "five-mile fishery" was not included. It was, therefore, "plainly seen" that the rock "did not come under the jurisdiction of the Indian Department."

Rather than discouraging Swallsea, McDonald's letter merely emboldened him. The following month he made an application to purchase fee simple title to one acre of "rocky ground which included the disputed fishing rock."[58] The rock where both his father and grandfather had fished was, apparently, beyond the jurisdiction of both the Department of Indian Affairs and the provincial magistrate for, as Crown land within the federal railway belt, it was open to pre-emption. His own claim, therefore, was doubly threatened, first by the competing indigenous assertions of ownership advanced by Paul Skitt and Peter Katz's wife, as endorsed by the Yale magistrate, and by the looming prospect that the disputed land might be purchased by outside non-Native interests. Indeed, it turns out that the land containing the fishing rock had already passed through the hands of four non-Native owners, and only now, due to a failure on the part of a Mr. Mayes (the most recent title holder) to pay his taxes, was the land available.[59] Thus, seeking to turn the threat of fee simple expropriation to his favour, and in a bold move to circumvent the magistrate's decision, and the Department of Indian Affairs' inertia, Swallsea paid twenty-five dollars to the Dominion Land agent and applied to purchase fee simple title to the land himself.[60]

When word of Swallsea's efforts reached the Indian affairs office, all previous advice was quickly forgotten. Indeed, there was general agreement that such initiative deserved to be supported. Indian Agent R.C. McDonald observed that, since Paul Skitt and the other Aboriginal claimants were apparently aware of Swallsea's actions, it was in the department's best interest to approve Swallsea's application for title. Moreover, supporting Swallsea would "put an end to all disputes as to the ownership," thereby disentangling the federal government from future involvement in similar contests.[61] Pleased with what he perceived to be an indication of progress towards the development of Western-style individualism, Indian Superintendent Vowell concurred with McDonald's recommendation, noting, "We are anxious to meet every reasonable request from an Indian or Indians who are really going to make use of lands."[62] What both officials failed to appreciate was that the fact that Swallsea was availing himself of a different system to acquire title to land did not mean that he was planning to make non-traditional use of the land. The greater irony is that Swallsea's intended traditional use included an economic component, as Sproat had identified. The Western categories of aboriginality, economics, and civilization simply could not be reconciled with indigenous people's reality.

In the end, however, it was not Swallsea's intentions for the site that were to become a problem for Vowell; rather, it was the surprising strength and determination of Paul Skitt and other indigenous people who rejected both Swallsea's claim and his method of achieving it. On 22 December 1903, "Chief Joseph Stewart Indian on behalf of Peter Paul Skitt, Chief George, Ohamil, Chief Tom, Ruby Creek and many others" wrote directly to the minister of Indian affairs expressing their "grievances in regard to [their] fishing station." According to the chiefs, it was the Skitt family, and not Swallsea, whose "ancestors ha[d] inherited the rights of this fishing station unmolested for generations past":

> Indian Swallasea of union Bar for a long time past, since the death of several Indians, viz., Wescoux, Quatash, Jackson and several other Indians of the Hope tribe who formerly inherited this station and enjoyed peaceable possession without any interference from any other Indians ... has brought in a claim for the said fishing station under false pretences and who has caused us so much annoyance, – at times provoked – irritation upon the matter, therefore to shun any possible trouble we beg to lay the matter before you in your Department to sustain our just rights and give us justice to our claims.[63]

What was objectionable, in the eyes of those opposing Swallsea, was not the use of Western newcomer systems of jurisprudence and governance in itself but, rather, the application of such systems to circumvent or challenge traditional protocols and governing mechanisms. The irony, of course, lay in the fact that it was the Canadian government's outlawing of the potlatch governance system, coupled with the threat of further non-Native incursions onto Native lands, that resulted in the need for both Swallsea and his opponents to use Western means to indigenous ends.

Chief Stewart, for his part, argued that the erasure of hereditary systems of ownership and access was threatening on many levels, especially if it was applied piecemeal, without regard for history or the economic well-being of those who depended upon the older indigenous system. Misfortune would befall people, he asserted, if Swallsea's efforts succeeded, for "there are very many Indians concerned in this one fishing and curing station to provide dry salmon for many families with their winter's food."

Those interested in preserving the traditional Aboriginal fishery, regardless of whether they supported Paul Skitt or Billy Swallsea, were willing to use the government's system to supplement indigenous dispute-resolution mechanisms. As Chief Stewart made clear, "There are many other fishing stations for the many other Indians, and they all sing the same[,] that the Government cannot sell nor lease any of those fishing stations which are inherited by the Divine rights of our Indian Fore-fathers, preserved to us as our own inheritance as fishing stations along the canyons of the Fraser River to provide us with dry salmon as food for our maintenance."[64]

Clearly, those regional Native leaders who challenged Swallsea's claim to the fishing spot were not impressed with his innovative attempt to obtain a form of title through non-Native processes. But that did not mean that, when necessary, they were above using non-traditional Western means to protect their own interests. They had come to regard fee simple title as a threat to Aboriginal rights and traditions because it threatened to extinguish hereditary regulations and remove decision-making processes from the hands of indigenous people. Placed in context, the passing of a generation whose ownership rights and access privileges had been broadly understood and accepted had caused chaos in a world where the potlatch naming system of intergenerational property transference was forbidden.

When the secretary of Indian affairs in Ottawa, J.D. McLean, learned of the broad indigenous opposition to Swallsea's land application, he immediately instructed Vowell to re-evaluate his support of the fee simple application. In his first directive on the matter, McLean linked the chiefs' opposition to Swallsea with Sproat's long overlooked "five-mile fishery" reserve allotment, making specific reference to Sproat's 1879 Minutes of Decision.[65]

Either ill informed of the operations of Indian affairs within his jurisdiction or attempting to skirt responsibility for the growing dilemma, the BC superintendent of Indian affairs, A.W. Vowell, responded to McLean by arguing that it had been his understanding that Sproat had only been empowered to reserve lands "informally." The Aboriginal leaders' decision to challenge Swallsea before a justice of the peace, Vowell cynically asserted, demonstrated that they, too, shared this understanding as it was only after this avenue failed that those opposed to Swallsea had claimed that the land had been reserved by Sproat.

Further, in composing his response to McLean, Vowell had in mind the assessment of Dominion land agent, John McKenzie, who had earlier advised him that the "'Rock' question may be more a question of sentimentality than utility."[66] This would explain Vowell's attempt to dismiss the chiefs' description of the fishing sites as being of broad significance and his counter-suggestion that they were in reality important for only a few families. Despite his strong opinions on the subject, however, Vowell closed his letter by stating that he had directed the local Indian agent to visit the site and consult directly with "other Indians at Yale ... as to its vital importance to the band."[67]

Upon examining the situation at Yale, Indian Agent R.C. McDonald reported to Vowell that "[the site] has been used for many years by the Indians as a fishing station in the same way as many similar rocks, on both sides of the river, for three or four miles above Yale." Not understanding the social significance of hereditary links to specific rocks, McDonald naively asserted that "there are plenty of these rocks for all the Indians who wish to use them." The most interesting knowledge McDonald acquired was confirmation that the dispute over the fishing rock was not a recent phenomenon between clear-cut owners and interlopers but, rather, that "some of the Indians state this rock has been in dispute for the past fifty years."[68]

Given the complicated and protracted nature of the dispute, the Indian agent proposed that the most expeditious means of bringing an end to the affair was to simply assign fee simple title to Swallsea. J.D. McLean, however, cited a petition from Chief Tom of Ruby Creek and others opposed to Swallsea as indicating that such action would jeopardize the Dominion government's reputation in the region. While he believed that the rock in question was "of little value or importance," from a non-Native perspective, clearly such was not the case within lower Fraser River Aboriginal society. Accordingly, he asked Vowell to travel to the canyon personally and determine for himself "whether application should be made to the Department of the Interior for this spot to be set apart as an Indian reserve, or such other action which you may think advisable."[69]

Bowing to pressure from above, Vowell directed McDonald not to give permission for Swallsea to acquire title until he had first visited the site.[70] Inclement weather, however, forced Vowell to postpone the journey, and so once again McDonald was ordered to Yale in the superintendent's stead. Apparently the matter was not a priority for either man, and indeed one could be forgiven for thinking the Department of Indian Affairs had been modelled upon Charles Dickens' incompetent "Office of Circumlocution" in *Little Dorrit* for, when McDonald finally arrived in Yale, almost a full year and a half had passed and two salmon-fishing seasons had come and gone. What he discovered was that Swallsea had not sat idly waiting for approval from Indian affairs and that, indeed, all the Natives at Yale were now under the assumption that title had in fact already been granted to Swallsea.[71] No doubt the arrival of government surveyors working on behalf of Swallsea in the summer of 1904 reinforced that impression. And, as far as P.G. Keyes, the secretary of the Dominion Lands Office, was concerned, the only outstanding matter left to resolve before Swallsea was granted full title was clarification of whether his proper name was "William or Billy Swallasea or Swallsea."[72]

In light of these developments, by the time McDonald finally arrived in September 1905, support for Paul Skitt against Swallsea had transformed into general opposition to further fee simple alienations and the resolution that the best means of protecting the traditional system of access and inheritance was to have the government confirm Sproat's work and have the remaining fishing stations designated Indian reserves. Towards this end, "Chief James of Yale, Chief Pierre of Hope, Chief George of Ohamil, Captain Tom of Ruby Creek, and twenty other interested Indians" took McDonald on a tour of the lower canyon and identified for him twenty-five hereditary fishing sites and their current owners/users – twenty of whom (due to recent migrations) were by then living most of the year downriver in the Fraser Valley on Indian reserves that were better suited to agriculture (see Map 7.2). Significantly, McDonald learned that "the relatives of those above mentioned have the privilege of fishing on these rocks." Moreover, the Aboriginal leaders and fishers were still insistent that Vowell himself come to meet with them, and they asked that they be given a week's notice of his arrival so that all could "be on hand."[73]

Alerted to the social complexity of the canyon fishery and no doubt eager to disengage from any further entanglements associated with trying to determine whose claim was stronger than another's, Vowell decided not to issue title to Swallsea – that is to say, he never provided the secretary of Dominion lands with the proper spelling of Billy Swallsea's name. Instead, six months later, armed with authorization from the secretary of Indian affairs in Ottawa to create reserves throughout "the five-mile fishery," Vowell finally journeyed to Yale himself.[74] There, on the evening of 23 April 1906,

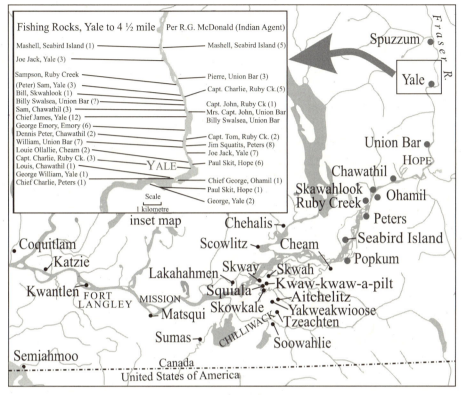

Map 7.2 Valley owners of canyon fishing sites, 1904.
Source: Copyright Keith Thor Carlson, cartography by Jan Perrier.

and in the company of "Chief James and several of the interested Indians," he inspected the numerous fishing sites throughout the canyon. Also accompanying Vowell was a surveyor who immediately translated the chiefs' intentions, as relayed through Vowell, into sketches that would serve as the basis for formal reserve surveys. In the end, Vowell included the majority of the lands Sproat had identified nearly three decades earlier as reserves, including the lands Swallsea had attempted to acquire as fee simple title.[75] A week later, Vowell confidently reported that his "allotments appeared to give the greatest satisfaction to those interested and the old time rights of the different claimants were not disputed."[76] By protecting lands from non-Native outsiders and removing the option of fee simple ownership on the part of Native fishers, Vowell not only disengaged from the internal disputes but also ostensibly re-established the groundwork for indigenous self-governance over the lower canyon salmon fishery – albeit in a political vacuum in which the potlatch was still prohibited.

Even a fully functioning potlatch governance system, however, might have had trouble mitigating, or even anticipating, the confusion and intertribal conflict that ultimately would derive from inconsistencies in the two versions of the official Minutes of Decision that Vowell composed following his visit to the canyon fishery. In the first, penned 26 April 1906, Vowell simply identified the locations of what were to become known as the "Yale reserves." No mention was made as to who fished at any given site.[77] In the second, appended to a letter to Secretary McLean, Vowell attached a short prefatory note explaining that the reserves were "fishing stations" and clarifying with which Indian community each station was associated (i.e., IR 19 "claimed by the Hope Indians," IR 20 "used principally by the Squawtits Indians," IR 21 "used by the Skawahlook and Yale Indians," etc.).[78] It was the earlier, less specific version that eventually found its way into the Order in Council.

At the time, likely nobody worried about the discrepancies. It was clear to all involved that the canyon fishery was used by, and specific rocks were claimed by, Aboriginal fishers from communities all along the upper Fraser Valley. And yet, as decades passed and the reserve communities became increasing reified, what might be thought of as the true spirit and original intent behind Vowell's Minutes of Decision became obscured. Indeed, continuing the process of word economization and the trend towards identifying Native people according to government-created agencies and districts rather than traditional tribal groupings or geographically dispersed extended family clusters, in his preface to the copies of Vowell's Minutes of Decision (which he sent to the secretary of the interior), Secretary of Indian Affairs J.D. McLean explained that it was his "desire" that "the tracks of lands in the Fraser which have been used from time immemorial by the Indians for fishing purposes ... should be set apart for the use of the Yale Indians."[79] Six months later, in his follow-up correspondence, McLean referred to the lands simply as "those which have been used from time immemorial by the Yale Indians for fishing purposes."[80]

Despite the fact that the vast majority of the land was available, action was not immediately forthcoming. The following summer, in a letter to the secretary of Indian affairs, Vowell explained that, because of the high cost of labour, he had deferred the official surveys of the "Yale fisheries reserves."[81] After two further years of inaction, Vowell again wrote to the secretary of Indian affairs, this time reminding McLean that eight reserves remained to be surveyed near Yale.[82] Only then were surveyors dispatched and the "Yale Reserves" number eighteen through twenty-five officially registered.[83]

Over the following decades, various adjustments were made to the registries, the most significant being the transfer of authority over the largest canyon reserve at Kuth-lath from the Yale band to the downriver community of Ohamil. The reserve had originally been identified by Sproat for the "Yale Indians Proper ... and more particularly to the Indian Sche-a-thela, whose people had a settlement there."[84] However, as Chief James of Yale explained in 1917, Sche-a-thela's people had subsequently relocated downstream to Ohamil, and he wanted "the right to the land [at Kuth-lath] to go to the Ohamil Indians."[85] Chief James' role in the transfer of Kuth-lath is especially significant given his assertion before the Royal Commission on Indian Affairs three years earlier: "It is sure that the land surrounding here now is my land; the mountains are mine, and the timber is mine, and the fish is mine."[86] Clearly, Chief James recognized that innovative means were needed to ensure that the broadly dispersed traditional indigenous interests in the Fraser Canyon were protected and properly situated.

In the end, the Indian reserve system of land tenure that was implemented was imperfect. It did not fully meet the expectations of any of the various Aboriginal, federal, or provincial parties. It was, however, workable. That the text associated with the canyon reserves was variously modified so that it did not always specify that the land was intended to protect fishing sites for the broader lower Fraser River Aboriginal community did not immediately become an issue, although clearly it has subsequently. For the Aboriginal leadership, the creation of reserves addressed immediate concerns over further challenges to hereditary rights and customary regulatory systems posed by provincial tenure-granting authorities – be they launched by individual indigenous people or non-Native settlers. While the Canadian Northern Railway ultimately gained rights of way through the reserves on the eastern shore to match those of the Canadian Pacific Railway line on the west, further fee simple alienations ceased.

Billy Swallsea's innovative effort to secure fee simple title to fishing rocks for the purpose of conducting a traditional fishery, and the opposition to this move by Paul Skitt and others, provided a valuable lesson for Aboriginal people up and down the river. In addition to spurring the government to finally create reserves in the canyon, and providing the community with practical courtroom experience, it demonstrated that Canadian jurisprudence was ill equipped to deal with the complexities and nuances of indigenous laws and regulatory mechanisms. Moreover, Swallsea's and Skitt's rejection of one another's efforts to involve non-Native authorities in resolving their dispute reveal that while Stó:lō people were willing to employ innovative means to traditional ends, the conclusions and decisions meted out by these agencies were not necessarily embraced as legitimate by those Stó:lō who held contrary or dissenting views. As a result, in the years following, such disputes were dealt with internally. Indeed, the site contested by Swallsea and Skitt came to be known as a place where community leaders met to discuss pressing concerns and politics.[87] The hereditary claims of both Swallsea and Skit were, apparently, heard and adjudicated there for, in the end, both families maintained adjacent fishing sites within the land Billy Swallsea had tried to purchase. And it was there, during one hot fishing season in the 1930s, that a young man named Alan Gutierrez, to whom

Billy Swallsea had transferred the hereditary name "Swallsea," fell in love with and later married Matilda Jackson, a member of Paul Skit's extended family. The two families, now merged, continue to share the formerly disputed sites to this day.[88]

In 1938, Denis Peters (son of "Peter's of Katz's Landing") led the lower Fraser Aboriginal population in raising funds and erecting a stately granite marker on the edge of the Cariboo Wagon Road just above the fishing rocks formerly disputed by his cousin, Paul Skitt, and Billy Swallsea. It was a memorial designed principally to honour the memory of the ancestors whose remains had been re-interred there after developments associated with the building of Canada's two transcontinental railways disrupted their original resting places. It also represented a bold assertion of shared Stó:lō collective identity and a broad communal title to the canyon fishery itself. Cast in bronze are these words: "Erected by The Stallo Indians – In memory of many hundreds of our forefathers buried here. This is one of six ancient cemeteries within our five mile native fishing grounds which we inherited from our ancestors. R.I.P." Though internal tensions between Stó:lō fishers would continue, the Iyem Memorial signalled a recognition that the principal threat to Aboriginal fishing rights now came from non-Native interests and, implicitly, that internal disputes could and should be handled internally.

Ideally, the federal and provincial authorities of the contemporary era will be quicker than were their predecessors of a century ago to recognize the value of not trying to involve themselves directly in the Aboriginal dispute-resolution process. Should they not, however, it is probably safe to assume that indigenous peoples of the present age will be just as adept at invoking innovative methods to secure traditional rights and customs as were their ancestors.

Acknowledgments

This chapter is a significantly revised version of a technical report I wrote with Sara Eustace in 1996 for the Stó:lō Nation entitled "The True Spirit and Original Intent of the Fraser Canyon Fishing Reserves." I am indebted to Ted Binnema, M.T. Carlson, John Lutz, Sonny McHalsie, Jim Miller, Gordon Mohs, Susan Neylan, Clarence Pennier, Brian Thom, David Schaepe, David Smith, Lissa Wadewitz, and Wendy Wickwire for their helpful and supportive comments on earlier drafts of this chapter. Thanks also to MacKinley Darlington for her help copy-editing; to Jan Perrier, of Perrier Design, for her cartographic and design work on the maps; and to Lissa Wadewitz for assisting in transferring certain RG 10 files from microfilm to digital form.

Notes

1 Arthur J. Ray, "Native History on Trial: Confessions of an Expert Witness," *Canadian Historical Review* 84, 2 (2003): 253-73.

2 At least twice in the past thirteen years the Yale First Nation and the Stó:lō Nation have been in court arguing over jurisdiction to the canyon fishery: *Chief Robert Hope et al.* v. *Lower Fraser Fishing Authority et al.* (1992), Supreme Court of British Columbia, no. C924333; *Yale First Nation* v. *Her Majesty the Queen in Right of Canada et al.* (2000), Supreme Court of British Columbia, no. 746.

3 Within these disputes emotions run high. In 1992, Chief Robert Hope of the Yale band filed an injunction in the Supreme Court of British Columbia against the Lower Fraser Fishing Authority, representing the leaders and communities of the majority of Indian bands along the lower Fraser River and arguing that only the Yale chief had a right to allocate and regulate the canyon Aboriginal fishery. See affidavit of Chief Robert Norman Hope in the Supreme Court of British Columbia, *Chief Robert Hope et al.* v. *The Lower Fraser Fishing Authority and others*, July 1992, no. C92-4333, Vancouver Registry (67/62519/002). Also, affidavit of Lawrence Hope in the Supreme Court of British Columbia, *Chief Robert Hope et al.* v. *The Lower Fraser Fishing Authority and others*, defendants, no. C9204333, Vancouver Registry, 67/62519/002, July 1992, paras. 29-32, and 48. Additionally, see Yale First Nation, "An Approach to the Treatment of Land and Resources Management as Part of the Yale First Nation Treaty," tabled by the Yale First Nation, 24 January 1997, and presented to the Fraser Valley Treaty Advisory Committee 25 March 1997. More recently, Chief Hope has been quoted in local Fraser Valley newspapers as viewing the Stó:lō use of the canyon fishery as an "invasion" of the Yale First Nation's traditional territory ("Yale Territory Defended from Sto:lo Invasion," *Chilliwack Progress*, 7 April 1998), and an article of the same title a few days later in *Chilliwack Progress*, 12 April 1998). Spokespersons for the Stó:lō Nation responded by dismissing the Hopes' interpretation of the historical role of the Yale chief in assigning fishing rights in the Fraser Canyon and argued that the right to regulate access to, and transfer control over, canyon fishing spots had always been held by families and transmitted within families. See, in particular, "Family Feud: Sto:lo Say Fight over Fishing Rights with Yale Band Comes Down to Respect for Traditional Fishing Rights," *Chilliwack Progress*, 17 April 1998).

4 Mark Salber Phillips and Gordon Schochet, eds., *Questions of Tradition* (Toronto: University of Toronto Press, 2004), ix, x.

5 Patrick J. Geary, *The Myth of Nations: The Medieval Origins of Europe* (Princeton and Oxford: Princeton University Press, 2002). See also Eric Hobsbawm and Terence Ranger, eds., *The Invention of Tradition* (Cambridge: Cambridge University Press, 1983).

6 This idea is developed by Wayne Suttles in his 1958 article, "Private Knowledge, Morality, and Social Classes among the Coast Salish," in *Coast Salish Essays*, ed. W. Suttles, 3-25 (Vancouver: Talonbooks, 1989). My own field experience among the Coast Salish confirms Suttles' findings for the more recent era.

7 The one comparable area was the "Dalles" on the lower Columbia River.

8 Personal communication with Bill McHalsie. Using a dip net, Bill caught just over three hundred sockeye in one hour in the summer of 1989.

9 See Keith Thor Carlson, "Expressions of Collective Identity," in *A Stó:lō-Coast Salish Historical Atlas*, ed. Keith Thor Carlson (Vancouver: Douglas and McIntyre, 2001), 26.

10 Perhaps the popularity of smoked salmon among modern consumers has led to the assumption that, traditionally, smoked salmon preserved and stored equally as well as did wind-dried salmon. In fact, according to Aboriginal people, smoked salmon that is not refrigerated runs a significantly higher risk than does wind-dried salmon of spoiling – either due to summer heat or winter dampness. In the past, coastal people prized canyon wind-dried salmon, as is indicated by the thousands of people described in the Fort Langley Journal who travelled to the canyon to acquire it. See Morag McLaughlin, *The Fort Langley Journals* (Vancouver: UBC Press, 1998). In the fall, cooler temperatures rendered wind-drying less reliable, and so the runs of Pink ("Humpies") and Chum ("Dog") salmon were preserved by a combination of wind and smoke as the canyon drying racks were enclosed and smouldering fires lit at their base.

11 See Suttles, *Coast Salish Essays*, esp. "Coping with Abundance: Subsistence on the Northwest Coast" (45-66), and "Productivity and Its Constraints: A Coast Salish Case" (100-36). See also Leland Donald, *Aboriginal Slavery on the Northwest Coast of America* (Berkeley: University of California Press, 1997), esp. 15-32, 103-20.

12 The extended family member charged with regulating kith and kin's access to a fishing site was known as a Sia:teleq (personal communication with Rosaleen George, 1995).

13 The following information about Súx'yel comes from Wilson Duff's Stalo Fieldnotes, book 1, Royal British Columbia Provincial Museum; and from the oral history preserved within

Sux̱'yel's family. In particular, I am indebted to Sonny McHalsie, Sux̱'yel's great-great-grandson, for sharing his knowledge of his ancestor. Elsewhere, I have presented additional information on Súx̱'yel. This is described in greater detail in Keith Thor Carlson and Sonny McHalsie's *I am Stó:lō: Katherine Explores Her Heritage* (Chilliwack: Stó:lō Trust, 1999), 84-92.

14 In 1877, the federal Fisheries Act was applied for the first time to British Columbia. Fisheries Inspector A.C. Anderson was instructed that "where fishing with white men and with modern appliances, the Indians so fishing should be considered as coming in all respects under the general law." See Department of Fisheries, Annual Report, 1877, Canada, *Sessional Papers*, no. 3, 1878, "Report of the Inspector of Fisheries for British Columbia, 1877," cited in Reuben Ware, *Five Issues, Five Battlegrounds: An introduction to the History of Fishing in British Columbia 1850-1930* (Chilliwack, BC: Coqualeetza Education Training Centre, 1983), 18. This regulation first seriously affected Stó:lō fishers in 1881, when Anderson used it to prevent Stó:lō people from catching salmon "above-tide-waters with their own appliances" to sell to industrial canneries in New Westminster. See Department of Fisheries Annual Report, 1881, Canada, *Sessional Papers*, no. 5, 1881, p. 189, cited in Ware, *Five Issues*, 18. In 1894, the Fisheries Act was again amended, this time making it illegal for Aboriginal people to catch fish for anything other than food unless they purchased a commercial fishing permit and licence. See Clause 1, British Columbia Fishing Regulations, Dominion Order-In-Council No. 590, 3 March 1894 (transcribed in Ware, *Five Issues*, app. 5, 125). See also Dianne Newell, *Tangled Webs of History: Indians and the Law in Canada's Pacific Coast Fisheries* (Toronto: University of Toronto Press, 1993), esp. 28-45. See also Douglas Harris, *Fish, Law, and Colonialism: The Legal Capture of Salmon in British Columbia* (Toronto: University of Toronto Press, 2001), esp. chaps. 1 and 3.

15 Reported in Keith Thor Carlson, "The Numbers Game," in Carlson, *Stó:lō-Coast Salish Historical Atlas*, 78, 79.

16 G.M. Sproat, Indian Reserve Commissioner, to Sir John A. Macdonald, Superintendent General of Indian Affairs, 3 December 1878, Land Registry, Department of Indian Affairs, Vancouver Regional Office [hereafter DIA, VRO], Letterbook no. 2, p. 349. See also Canada, DIA, "Indian Census of Yale Tribe, 1878," Library and Archives Canada [hereafter LAC], RG 10, vol. 10012A.

17 Peter O'Reilly to the Honourable G.A. Walkem, 23 May 1881, LAC, RG 10, vol. 3716, file 22195, reel C-10125.

18 Meeting with the Yale band, or tribe, of Indians at Yale, British Columbia, on Thursday, 19 November 1914, Royal Commission on Indian Affairs for the Province of British Columbia, Lytton Agency, Meeting Minutes with Bands and Royal Commission, 1913-15, p. 313.

19 Wilson Duff, *The Upper Stalo Indians of the Fraser Valley, British Columbia* (Victoria: British Columbia Provincial Museum, Anthropology in BC, Memoir no. 1, 1952), 78. August Jim, one of Duff's informants, reported that a hereditary fishing spot on/or near Yale IR 21 was owned by his maternal grandfather, who was from Musqueam.

20 L. Vankoughnet, Deputy Superintendent General of Indian Affairs, to Sir John A. Macdonald, Superintendent General of Indian Affairs, 30 June 1878, LAC, Annual Report, 1878, p. 16. All DIA annual reports are now available online through the LAC website: http://www.collectionscanada.ca/indianaffairs/index-e.html.

21 David Laird, Minister of Interior, to Alexander Caulfield Anderson, 25 August 1876, LAC, RG 10, vol. 3633, file 6425-1.

22 Canada, *Sessional Papers*, no. 5, 1877, "Report of the Inspector of Fisheries for British Columbia for the year 1876," Department of Fisheries, Annual Report, 1877, Canada, *Sessional Papers*, no. 1, 1878, p. 29.

23 For example, in 1859, G.D.F. MacDonald applied to the colonial government for exclusive fishing privileges on the Chilliwack River – one of the lower Fraser's main tributaries. The government denied this request, stating it was "not in his Excellency's power to grant to him or any other person the exclusive right to fishing in the Chillwayhook river." Such action would have infringed upon the local Aboriginal fishery. See Good to Col. Moody, 11 October 1859, British Columbia, Colonial Secretary, Correspondence Outward, *Letterbook 1859-1861*, BC Archives [hereafter BCA], no. 84.

24 David Laird, Minister of Interior, to Alexander Caulfield Anderson, 25 August 1876, LAC, RG 10, vol. 3633, file 6425-1.

25 I.W. Powell, Superintendent of Indian Affairs for British Columbia, LAC, *Annual Report,* 1878, p. 3.

26 Sproat to Superintendent General, 1 May 1878, LAC, RG 10, vol. 3612, file 3756-18, reel C-10106.

27 Sproat to Superintendent General, 26 November 1878, "The Lower Fraser," BCA, GR 1965, file 2 (emphasis in original).

28 Sproat to Superintendent General, 6 December 1878. Letterbook, JIRC, DIA, VRO, pp. 349-50.

29 Wayne Suttles, "'They Recognize No Superior Chief': The Strait of Juan de Fuca in the 1790s," in *Culturas de la Costa Noroeste de América,* ed. José Luis Peset (Madrid: Turner, 1989), 252.

30 Duff, *Upper Stalo Indians,* 19.

31 See discussion in Sproat, 5 August 1879, under heading "Yale Indians Proper," JIRC, DIA, VRO, Minutes of Decision and Sketches, vol. entitled "Books of Interrupted Work by Retirement of Commissioner from Office – Lower Fraser Ri [sic] below Spuzzum," pp. 4-23.

32 Sproat, 5 August 1879, JIRC, DIA, VRO, Minutes of Decision, volume entitled "Work Interrupted by Retirement of Commissioner from Office – Lower Fraser Ri [sic] below Spuzzum," pp. 10, 24. Also found in LAC, RG 10, vol. 3090, file 107-297-3. Additionally, see Canada, *Sessional Papers,* no. 9, 39, Annual Report of the Department of the Interior for the Year Ended 30 June 1875, pp. ixvii-iv.

33 Sproat to L. Vankoughnet, 29 July 1879, Minutes of Decision, Correspondence and Sketches, Letterbook no. 3, JIRC, DIA, VRO, p. 364 (emphasis on original).

34 Sproat, 16 August 1879, Minutes of Decision for Hope Indians, LAC, RG 10, vol. 11028, file SRR-2, reel 3967, 611-28.

35 Sproat, 5 August 1879, Minutes of Decision, volume entitled: "Work Interrupted by Retirement of Commissioner from Office – Lower Fraser Ri [sic] below Spuzzum," JIRC, DIA, VRO, p. 23.

36 Ibid., 24.

37 Sproat, 5 August 1879, Minutes of Decision and Sketches, under heading "Yale Indians Proper," volume entitled "Books of Interrupted Work by Retirement of Commissioner from Office – Lower Fraser Ri [sic] below Spuzzum," JIRC, DIA, VRO, p. 4.

38 Sproat, 16 August 1879, Minutes of Decision for Hope Indians: "The fishing places of these Indians in this neighborhood are as follows: (1) a rock on the left bank of the Fraser below the sawmill on land which is said to be owned by the Rev. A.D. Pringle. (2) a rock on the bank not far from the house of Pierre, the Chief, in the Hope town reserve (3) a rock on the right bank of the Fraser opposite to but about 1/4 mile below Ay-waw-wis [Iwówes] (4) a rock about a mile below Hope on right bank of the Fraser. Their right of access to these places is confirmed, but in such a manner as to not inconvenience the owners of the lands in the least, and the Indians are not to occupy these places except for capturing and drying the fish in their accustomed way, and only in their fishing seasons." LAC, RG 10, vol. 11028, file SRR-2, reel 3967, 611-28. See also a detailed report of 17 July 1879 concerning the Neklakapamuk Indians of the Lytton area, 1879-81, LAC, vol. 11028, file SRR-2, reel T-3967.

39 W.S. Gore, BC Surveyor General, to I.W. Powell, 16 January 1882, BCA, GR 440, vol. 17, p. 5080.

40 I.W. Powell, Ind. Supt., to Chief Commissioner Lands and Works, 11 September 1882, BCA, GR 868, file 40, p. 1201.

41 Robert Beaven, Chief Commissioner Lands and Works, to I.W. Powell, 22 December 1882, BCA, GR 440, vol. 18, p. 394.

42 F.G. Vernon, Chief Commissioner Lands and Works, to P. O'Reilly, 9 May 1889, LAC, RG 10, vol. 11009, p. 145.

43 Fisheries of the Upper Nass Villages, British Columbia, 1881-83, LAC, RG 10, vol. 3766, file 32876, reel C-10135.

44 See W.F. Whitcher, Commissioner of Fisheries, to S.L. Vankoughnet, Deputy of the Superintendent General of Indian Affairs, Ottawa, 9 January 1883, 12 January 1883, 15 January

1883, 26 January 1883; and Vankoughnet to Rt. Hon. Sir John A. Macdonald, 28 July 1884, LAC, RG 10, vol. 3766, file 32876, reel C-10135.

45 Uslicks currently fish at the Iyem site in the lower Fraser Canyon right next to the spot claimed by Paul Skitt's wife and Billy Swallsea (as discussed below). I do not know whether the potlatch at which Uslick was arrested involved the transfer of hereditary fishing rights to a lower Fraser Canyon site, but, in light of subsequent Uslick family use of the site and controversies surrounding this use, it is probable.

46 Devlin to Vowell, 1896, cited in Forest LaViolette, *The Struggle for Survival: Indian Cultures and the Protestant Ethic in British Columbia* (Toronto: University of Toronto Press, 1973), 70.

47 Swallsea is pronounced Swal-see-ah. Frank Devlin, Indian Agent, to Peter Katz Landing, 11 September 1901, transcript in Stó:lō National Archives(SNA).

48 Frank Devlin, Indian Agent, to Billy Swallsea, 11 September 1901, transcript in SNA.

49 R.C. McDonald, Indian Agent, to A.W. Vowell, Indian Superintendent, 22 July 1903, LAC, RG 10, vol. 1459, reel C-14269, p. 318. See also R.C. McDonald, Indian Agent, to A.W. Vowell, Indian Superintendent, 29 April 1904, LAC, RG 10, vol. 3748, file 29858-3, reel C-10131.

50 In the 1980s, Peter Dennis Peters explained that his father, Denis Peters, and Paul Skitt were cousins. Dennis Peters was also the son of the man described by the Indian agent as "Peter of Katz's landing." Peter's wife's name was Louisa (née Skookum, a relative of Gabriel and Louie Skookum), personal communication, Sonny McHalsie.

51 Chief Joseph Stewart, Indian, on behalf of Peter Paul Skitt, Chief George, Ohamil, Chief Tom, Ruby Creek, and many others, to Minister of Indian Affairs, 23 December 1903, LAC, RG 10, vol. 3748, file 29858-3, reel C-10131. Also, John McDonald to A.W. Vowell, 29 April, 1904, LAC, RG 10, vol. 3748, file 29858-3, reel C-10131. According to contemporary oral tradition, Chief Stewart was the secretary of Pierre Ayessick (nephew of "Peter of Katz's Landing") and a leader in the Indian Land Claims movement of the early twentieth century (per Sonny McHalsie).

52 R.C. McDonald, Indian Agent, to A.W. Vowell, Indian Superintendent, 21 (?) July 1903, LAC, RG 10, vol. 1459, reel C-14269, p. 308. See also R.C. McDonald, Indian Agent, to Chief James of Yale, 25 July 1903, LAC, RG 10, vol. 1459, reel C-14269, p. 333.

53 R.C. McDonald, Indian Agent, to A.W. Vowell, Indian Superintendent, 21 (?) July 1903, LAC, RG 10, vol. 1459, p. 308, reel C-14269.

54 R.C. McDonald, Indian Agent, to A.W. Vowell, 20 July 1903, LAC, RG 10, vol. 1459, reel C-14269, p. 332.

55 R.C. McDonald, Indian Agent, to Chief James of Yale, 25 July 1903, LAC, RG 10, vol. 1459, reel C-14269, p. 333.

56 Franz Boas, "Indian Tribes of the Lower Fraser River," *64th Report of the British Association for the Advancement of Science for 1890* (London, 1894), 454.

57 R.C. McDonald, Indian Agent, to A.W. Vowell, Indian Superintendent, 18 August 1903, LAC, RG 10, vol. 1459, reel C-14269, p. 440.

58 John MacKenzie, Agent Dominion Lands, to A.W. Vowell, 28 October 1903, British Columbia – Field Office Correspondence Regarding Reserve Lands, 1903-4, LAC, RG 10, vol. 3748, file 29858-3, reel C-10131.

59 Sproat, 5 August 1879, under heading "Yale Indians Proper," Minutes of Decision and Sketches, volume entitled "Books of Interrupted Work by Retirement of Commissioner from Office [sic] Lower Fraser Ri [sic] below Spuzzum," JIRC, DIA, VRO, p. 3.

60 Also, John McDonald to A.W. Vowell, 29 April 1904, LAC, RG 10, vol. 3748, file 29858-3, reel C-10131.

61 John McDonald, Indian Agent, New Westminster, to Superintendent of Indian Affairs A.W. Vowell, 23 December 1903, LAC, RG 10, vol. 3748, file 29858-3, reel C-10131.

62 Marginal notes by A.W. Vowell on correspondence of John MacKenzie to A.W. Vowell, 28 October 1903, British Columbia – Field Office Correspondence Regarding Reserve Lands, 1903-4, LAC, RG 10, vol. 3748, file 29858-3, reel C-10131.

63 Chief Joseph Stewart, Indian, on behalf of Peter Paul Skitt, Chief George, Ohamil, Chief Tom, Ruby Creek, and many others, to Minister of Indian Affairs, 23 December 1903, LAC, RG 10, vol. 3748, file 29858-3, reel C-10131.

64 Ibid.
65 J.D. McLean, Secretary, Indian Affairs, to A.W. Vowell, 8 January 1904, British Columbia – Field Office Correspondence Regarding Reserve Lands, 1903-4, LAC, RG 10, file 29858-3, vol. 3748, reel C-10131.
66 John McKenzie, Dominion Land Agent, to A.W. Vowell, 16 January 1904, LAC, RG10, vol. 3748, file 29858-3, reel C-10131.
67 Vowell to R.C. McDonald, Indian Agent, New Westminster, 22 January 1904, LAC, RG 10, vol. 1281, 413-15.
68 Letter from R.C. McDonald, Indian Agent, New Westminster, to A.W. Vowell, 29 April 1904, LAC, RG 10, file 29858-3.
69 Letter from McLean, Secretary Indian Affairs, to A.W. Vowell, Indian Superintendent, 18 May 1904, British Columbia – Field Office Correspondence Regarding Reserve Lands, 1903-4, LAC RG 10, vol. 3748, file 29858-3, reel C-10131.
70 Letter from Vowell to McDonald, Indian Agent, New Westminster, 27 May 1904, LAC, RG 10, vol. 1281, 512 reel C-13901.
71 R.C. McDonald, Indian Agent, New Westminster, to A.W. Vowell, 19 October 1905 (second letter of same date), British Columbia – Field Office Correspondence Regarding Reserve Lands, 1905-6, LAC, RG 10, vol. 3749, file 29858-4, reel C-10131.
72 P.G. Keys, Secretary, Dominion lands, to John McKenzie, Dominion Lands Agent, 6 August 1904. See also John McKenzie, Dominion Lands Agent, to A.W. Vowell, 12 August 1904, LAC, RG 10, vol. 3748, file 29858-3, reel C-10131.
73 R.C. McDonald, Indian Agent, New Westminster, to A.W. Vowell, 19 October 1905 (second letter of same date), British Columbia – Field Office Correspondence Regarding Reserve Lands, 1905-6, LAC, RG 10, vol. 3749, file 29858-4, reel C-10131.
74 Secretary of Indian Affairs to A.W. Vowell, 5 December 1905, LAC, RG 10, vol. 3749, file 29858-4, reel C-10131.
75 Vowell to the Secretary, Department of Indian Affairs, 4 May 1906, British Columbia – Field Office Correspondence Regarding Reserve Lands (Plans), 1905-10, LAC, RG 10, vol. 1282, reel C-10132, pp. 339-40.
76 Vowell to Secretary of Indian Affairs, 10 May 1906, British Columbia – Field Office Correspondence Regarding Reserve Lands (Plans), 1905-10, LAC, RG 10, vol. 1282, reel C-10132, pp. 345-47.
77 A.W. Vowell, Minutes of Decision, 26 April 1906, LAC, RG 10, vol. 3750, file 29858-10, reel C-10132.
78 A.W. Vowell, Minutes of Decision (as defined 26 April 1906), 10 May 1906, LAC, RG 10, vol. 3750, file 29858-10, reel C-10132.
79 Secretary of Indian Affairs, J.D. Mclean, to Secretary of the Interior, P.G. Keys, 17 July 1906, LAC, RG 10, vol. 3750, file 29858-10, reel C-10132.
80 McLean to Secretary of the Interior, P.G. Keyes, 7 December, 1906, British Columbia – Field Office Correspondence Regarding Reserve Lands (Plans), 1905-10, LAC, RG 10, vol. 3750, file 29858-10, reel C-10132.
81 Letter from Vowell to the Secretary of the Department of Indian Affairs, 11 June 1907, Indian Reserve Commission – Letterbooks, Series A, 1905-7, LAC, RG 10, vol. 1282, 710, reel C-13902.
82 Letter from Vowell to the Secretary, Department of Indian Affairs, 17 January 1910, Indian Reserve Commission – Letterbooks, Series A, 1907-10, LAC, RG 10, vol. 1283, 466-69, reel C-13902.
83 The Department of Indian Affairs ultimately balked at the cost of surveying and secured the pro bono services of the Canadian Northern Railroad's "Right of Way" surveyor. To this day, IR 17 has never been surveyed because the CNR surveyor assigned the task refused to scale the site's treacherous rocky slopes.
84 Sproat, 5 August 1879, under heading "Yale Indians Proper," Minutes of Decision and Sketches, volume entitled "Books of Interrupted Work by Retirement of Commissioner from Office – Lower Fraser Ri [sic] below Spuzzum," JIRC, DIA, VRO, p. 6.
85 "I Chief James of the Yale Band of Indians on the Province of British Columbia, make oath and say that I as Chief of the Yale Indians was present when Kulthlalth Reserve as allotted

by the Indian Commissioner, the right to the land to go to the Ohamil Indians as this has been their burial ground for years but Yale Indians were to retain the right to take timber from this reserve for their private use owing to the scarcity of timber on their own reserve." Memorandum by Department of Indian Affairs Surveyor, 5 April 1934, containing a copy of affidavit of Chief James of Yale, 7 August 1917, LAC, RG 10, vol. 3747, file 29858. Sche-a-thela's son was Chief George, and his father was Siamya, a prominent man from the settlement of Iyem in the lower Fraser Canyon (personal communication with Sonny McHalsie).

86 Evidence given during the Royal Commission on Indian Affairs for the Province of British Columbia, meeting with the Yale band or Tribe of Indians at Yale, BC, on Thursday, 19 November 1914. Royal Commission on Indian Affairs for the Province of British Columbia, Lytton Agency 1914, evidence transcripts, Victoria, Royal Commission on Indian Affairs, 1914. Copy of transcript located in SNA.

87 Sonny McHalsie, personal communication.

88 As do Chief Stewart's descendents. In 1950, Wilson Duff took a picture of the dry rack at this site. At the time, it was being used by Edmund and Adeline Lorenzetto of Ohamil. Adeline was Pierre's daughter.

8
Meanings of Mobility on the Northwest Coast
Paige Raibmon

Colonial situations are riven with contradiction and irony. Rhetoric and practice pull in opposite directions. Colonizers produce the circumstances that they decry. These so-called "tensions of empire" are characteristic of colonial settings around the world, and the Northwest Coast is no exception.[1] Testament to this can be found in the swirling diversity of meanings that accrued to various manifestations of movement on the late nineteenth-century Northwest Coast. In the decades following British Columbia's entrance into Confederation, Aboriginal mobility became a marker of both colonial oppression and Indigenous resistance.[2] From the perspective of newcomers, the colonial era had ended, but for Aboriginal people it was entering a new and more intense phase.[3] Aboriginal people engaged in new patterns of mobility, sometimes with volition, sometimes under duress. Skip Ray's early and mid-career research emphasizes how, for two centuries, Aboriginal movement and migrations constituted a central characteristic of the fur trade in Rupert's Land.[4] On the Pacific Coast, too, after commerce in furs had ceased being the central point of contact between Native and newcomer, Aboriginal mobility became the vehicle for a range of activities as diverse as the seasonal round, feasting, wage labour, residential schooling, political protest, and flight from violence and the law. Aboriginal migrants and colonial observers attributed very different meanings to such activities. To many colonial observers, the movements of Aboriginal people seemed constant and ubiquitous. Colonial rhetoric cited Aboriginal mobility as justification for the appropriation of Aboriginal land. Missionaries and government officials juxtaposed stereotypes of shiftless, wandering Indians against an idealized image of civilized, sedentary farmers.[5] Such evaluations of Aboriginal mobility were disingenuous on at least two counts. First, they overlooked the fact that colonialism had physically displaced, that is *moved*, Aboriginal people; and second, they ignored the highly mobile lives of the newcomers themselves. For Aboriginal people seasonal mobility was a means to survival and an assertion of inherent rights. Aboriginal people shared some of their understandings of mobility with the McKenna McBride Royal Commission of 1913-16. They reported on forced displacements and expressed a fierce attachment to their territories. Their testimony suggests that they enacted this attachment, at least in part, through movement. The commissioners were ill-prepared to understand these mobile expressions of ownership and title; eighty years later, non-Aboriginal British Columbians have still not done enough to open their minds and ears to meanings of mobility that differ from their expectations. Given its prominence in both Aboriginal lives and colonial imaginations, mobility deserves historical analysis in its own right. In the spirit of initiating such analysis, this chapter offers an introductory commentary on Aboriginal mobility at the turn of the twentieth century.

Long before the arrival of Europeans on the Northwest Coast, Aboriginal people had – through their seasonal mobility – turned the 1,600-kilometre stretch of coastline between Puget Sound and the Gulf of Alaska into a maritime region. Aboriginal people traversed this region in their annual migrations to their fishing, sealing, and berrying grounds: they circulated through winter villages and summer camps to attend important gatherings and feasts, and they transported goods and slaves along trading networks that ran the length of the coast. By the late nineteenth century, international boundaries trifurcated this long-standing region into British Columbia and the American-owned territories of Alaska and Washington to the north and south, respectively. Still other colonial lines appeared that parsed the Indigenous world further still into Indian agencies, reservations (in Washington), and reserves (in British Columbia).

With the proliferation of colonial lines that were supposed to contain human movement, some patterns of Indigenous mobility expanded rather than contracted. From at least the 1850s, Aboriginal people from British Columbia and Alaska (then Russian America) had been travelling to Puget Sound, where they earned cash working in sawmills, in the sex trade, and at a variety of other occupations. In subsequent decades, opportunities for wage labour increased. Aboriginal people continued to travel far beyond the boundaries of their traditional territories to earn money at canneries, logging camps, fishing and sealing stations, hop and berry fields, and even world's fairs. Some crossed the Pacific on sealing expeditions to Japan and Hawaii.[6] The movements of Nuu-chah-nulth from the west coast of Vancouver Island offer just one example. Many Nuu-chah-nulth, who had long hunted fur seals for food, began to work in the commercial pelagic seal hunt that took them on winter journeys from the Pribilof Islands to California.[7] Then, in early summer, Nuu-chah-nulth families fanned out, moving between familial gatherings, hereditary fishing sites, and wage work in Victoria, New Westminster, Steveston, and/or Washington Territory.[8] The diaries of a Tsimshian man, Arthur Wellington Clah, describe a comparable pattern of movement on the north coast.[9]

This expanding circle of movement poses a bit of a paradox. Certainly colonial rhetoric promised the reverse. Lines on the map showed Aboriginal people relegated to an ever-shrinking land base. And colonial rhetoricians equated civilization with idealized images of sedentary yeoman farmers following agrarian lifestyles.[10] Rural landownership was the cornerstone of the resettlement of British Columbia, and colonial land policy attempted to tie settlers to their pre-emptions by requiring continuous residence.[11] Missionaries and government officials, in turn, cited highly visible instances of Aboriginal mobility as evidence of the need for state and church intervention in Aboriginal lives. The deputy superintendent general for Indian affairs captured this sentiment in his annual report for 1898:

> Cultivation of the soil necessitates remaining in one spot, and then exerts an educational influence of a general character. It keeps prominently before the mind the relation of cause and effect, together with the dependence upon a higher power. It teaches moreover the necessity for systematic work at the proper season, for giving attention to detail, and patience in waiting for results. It inculcates furthermore the idea of individual proprietorship, habits of thrift, a due sense of the value of money, and the importance of its investment in useful directions.[12]

Civilized Indians were to be sedentary ones. The Indian agent among the Cowichan, for example, believed that migratory labour encouraged improvidence and that agriculture was preferable to what he termed the "precarious help which may or may not be obtained from outside sources," such as hop field or cannery labour.[13] The Indian agent from the west coast of Vancouver Island agreed, going so far as to express satisfaction when a smallpox outbreak in Victoria induced many Nuu-chah-nulth to refrain from travelling to work in the hop fields and canneries, despite the fact that they would be significantly poorer for the lack of wages. Financially, he admitted, they would be significantly worse off, but morally, he believed them much improved for staying closer to home.[14] Wage-induced mobility was one thing. Such proponents of sedentarist ideology found mobility associated with the gatherings they called "potlatches" still more egregious. The missionary among the Kwakwa̱ka'wakw decried travels that drew people away "for the purpose of receiving blankets," as he put it.[15] He criticized the participants for the opportunity cost of such events: "Have they (say 200 able men among them) earned or produced $2 per day, i.e. 1 cent per man during this stay? I believe not."[16]

Missionaries and government officials opposed Aboriginal mobility for practical as well as ideological reasons. Indian agents had difficultly inspecting their wards; teachers and missionaries had trouble filling schoolrooms and church pews.[17] In order to keep pace with those they sought to administer, some agents and missionaries followed in the migratory wake of their Aboriginal charges.[18] Colonial officials designed residential schools and boarding schools as an antidote for the uncivilized migrations of Aboriginal people. But the practice of removing children from their families in order to send them to school created a new circuit of Aboriginal mobility, one that became the most traumatic and disruptive force in the lives of many Aboriginal families across several generations.[19] This was only one of the ways in which colonial practice engendered the Aboriginal movement that colonial rhetoric condemned.

Pro-agrarian rhetoric aside, colonial authorities enlisted Indian land policy in the cause of supporting the nascent capitalist economy and, in so doing, facilitated expanded patterns of Aboriginal migration. It was no accident that, as Aboriginal people entered the new economy, they overwhelmingly did so not as bosses but as workers. While pre-emption regulations tried to fix settlers to the land, Indian land policy worked in the opposite direction. Government officials in British Columbia implemented a reserve policy that relegated Aboriginal people to ever smaller and less arable pieces of land, with the explicit design of propelling Aboriginal people into the workforce and marketplace.[20] This policy served the interests of immigrants by opening up much of the province to non-Aboriginal pre-emption. Land was available for pre-emption as long as it was not a designated Indian reserve and did not contain "Indian improvements." This latter condition could be overcome if the said improvements had been "abandoned." Differential meanings of mobility produced conflicts over the definition of "abandoned," however, as the colonial discourse of mobility supported the interpretation of seasonal absences as abandonment.

Storekeepers and small businesspeople likewise benefited from the integration of Aboriginal people into the cash economy. Taken together, the cycles of labour and gift-giving were good for business. Labour provided the wages necessary to purchase the large amount of goods to be distributed at feasts. The fall conclusion of the hop season in Puget Sound, for example, was like an early Christmas for storeowners, when thousands of Aboriginal workers from the length of the Pacific coast began to spend their earnings.[21] When it suited their bottom line, businesspeople intervened on behalf of their Aboriginal customers. In 1887, storekeepers in Nanaimo opposed the efforts of the Indian agent to evict an encampment of Lekwiltok and send them home to Cape Mudge.[22] Whether Aboriginal customers bought goods for give-aways or for personal use made little difference to businesspeople who put their money in their cash registers.

Not least, government land policy bequeathed to the resource industry the gift of a large, mobile, and flexible labour force. The highly seasonal, resource-based economy depended upon migrant workers. As one reporter explained when the hops were almost ready to harvest: "The question of questions with the hop growers is, Will enough come? If so, will they arrive in time?"[23] One Washington hop farmer tried to answer this question by offering pickers two dollars "booty" (the equivalent of two days' wages) if they arrived by 1 September as well as by offering Indian agents a commission if they sent their wards to his farm.[24] Such expenses were worth this farmer's while: he had lost over a thousand dollars the previous year because he lacked the workers to begin the harvest on time. Fish canneries faced similar difficulties in securing enough labour at the right time. Canneries sometimes took proactive steps in order to secure enough workers for the coming season by effectively contracting them months in advance. In 1895, they distributed food and goods to families as an advance against their wages for the coming season.[25]

Land policy was only one arm of the colonial law that helped fuel Aboriginal mobility. Many Aboriginal people found that they *had* to move around to find work because on-reserve economic opportunities were frequently denied them. When some Squamish who preferred not to go to work in the city established a gravel business on their reserve, officials quickly shut it down. In the words of Chief Mathias Joseph: "Just like that as if I was stealing my own gravel to make a living."[26] In this and other instances, the need to make a living facilitated inter-reserve and off-reserve mobility among the Squamish.[27] The gravel on the Squamish reserve was only one of many resources to which colonial policies restricted Aboriginal access. Aboriginal people were also forbidden from logging their reserves and selling the timber. This restriction eliminated what might otherwise have been potentially viable and profitable on-reserve businesses for many reserve communities. Aboriginal people throughout the province voiced their frustration about this policy to the McKenna McBride Commission.[28] Understandably, some Aboriginal people came to feel completely hamstrung, as though all options *except* migrant wage labour were futile. In the words of a Cowichan man, John Elliot:

> The white people tell us that we Indians do not till the land, that we are a class of people who will not work. Now, if we were to go to work and grow stuff on our lands, we would not be able to find a proper market for our produce. The white men will not buy from us ... Besides, if we cultivate the land, where are we going to keep our cattle. There is not enough land on the Reserves, and no man with a small piece of land can make a decent living out of it. Then again, if our land is fenced in to keep the cattle off the roads, white people very often come down on fishing expeditions, climb over and break our fences, and, when spoken to, they say we have no right

here. It pays the Indians better to go fishing in the Fraser River, where they can some times make 600 or 700 dollars in a season, then it would to stay at home and try to farm the small pieces of land which they have. The land is altogether too small.[29]

Aboriginal people confronted an accumulation of policies and practices that discouraged farming and restricted on-reserve businesses and resource harvesting. These policies and practices directly contradicted colonial rhetoric, which held that civilization would settle Aboriginal people permanently. But if this made colonial rhetoricians uneasy, it appeased investors, boosters, and industrial capitalists who worried about keeping much-needed seasonal workers close at hand. Non-Aboriginal bosses did not want to see their flexible labour force turn into an independent merchant class.

Employers received an addition to their potential employment rolls when, regardless of policy or the law, settlers took action to displace Aboriginal people directly. As John Elliot continued, "The white people come on our lands and shoot, telling us we have no title to the land. It is hardly likely then that the Indians will go to work and till the land."[30] White squatters in the Nass Valley attempted to drive Nisga'a inhabitants from their land at gunpoint.[31] An Ahousaht man, Joe Didian Sr., faced threats first from a white settler and later from an Indian agent, who, rather than offering him protection, simply warned him that settlers were coming to burn down his house.[32] The Indian agent passed on the same message to Kelsomaht chief Charlie Johnnie's community, where people fled (or, to use the term from the pre-emption legislation, "abandoned") their village of thirteen houses.[33] Johnnie's community was forced to relocate to an unprotected site that was prone to rough and treacherous water. This, in turn, hampered fishing efforts and required community members to make yet more migrations in order to make a living.[34]

In some instances, Aboriginal people relied upon mobility to escape the threat of physical violence; yet, in other instances, mobility increased their vulnerability to violent displacement. Returning from fishing, wage work, or ceremonial events, Aboriginal people might find their houses occupied by white squatters who claimed to have pre-empted their land. In 1912, an Ahousaht man on Vargas Island returned home to find a white man, Mr. Hopkins, occupying his house.[35] Josephus, also an Ahousaht, was likewise displaced from his house and garden by a white settler.[36] Clearing land on the dense rainforest of Vancouver Island's west coast was (and is) no easy feat. From the settlers' perspective, the appeal of pre-emptions that included a standing house and clearing is easy to understand.[37] Aboriginal homeowners had further reason to worry that their houses might be entirely destroyed in their absence, as was the case with several Muchalaht houses along the Gold River sometime in the early twentieth century.[38] The perpetrators of such destruction may have been vandals, squatters, or even settlers in search of accessible firewood. The latter was the case on Haida Gwaii, where immigrants saw, in seasonally vacant homes, the fuel they needed to keep their own houses warm.[39]

Those inclined towards violent displacement were perhaps emboldened by the fact that, in British Columbia, pre-emptors could often precede surveyors by many years.[40] There was plenty of time to entrench and benefit from one's fraudulent claim before anyone finally, if ever, came to restore the legal order. This state of affairs has been aptly termed by one scholar as the "short arm of the law."[41] It meant not only that conflicts were more likely to occur but also that, when they did, the parties involved had little recourse to formal structures. Government officials tended to instruct settlers to resolve disputes on their own, a practice that must have encouraged settler violence even as it opened avenues for the exercise of Aboriginal power (as Carlson's chapter in this collection so aptly demonstrates).[42] Indeed, confrontation was sometimes the only way a settler could get a surveyor out to the pre-emption in question.[43] When Aboriginal victims of the ensuing violence complained to authorities, some Indian agents pleaded impotence in the face of settler aggression.[44] Perhaps settlers felt justified in their actions because the law required them to inhabit their pre-emption continuously or else face losing it.[45] Regardless, once a house was torn down or occupied by a white squatter, it must have been difficult for the Aboriginal owner to regain possession.

Legally, settlers could not pre-empt Indian reserves or improvements unless the land had been "abandoned" by Aboriginal people. But in a colonial world where "abandonment" could be read into seasonal absences or affected through violence, some of the most desirable lands on the west coast seemed up for grabs. Debates dating to the 1860s between Aboriginal and non-Aboriginal people over the definition of "settlement" continued through the turn of the twentieth century.[46] In 1915, for example, the Chilliwack City Council attempted to acquire reserve lands that it claimed had not been continuously occupied in recent years.[47] Members of the Courtney Agricultural Society on Vancouver Island similarly sought access to land that the Cowichan used on a seasonal basis. Speaking for the society, a Mr. Cameron stated that the land in question was

> of no use to the Indians at the present time ... I would just like to say that I think the reason the chief has taken up his residence on that land is because he hears that the Agricultural Society wants it and he is afraid that some one is trying to "jump" the place on him. He has previously lived there only at such times as he came down for fishing.[48]

Cameron missed the mark on at least two counts. First, he judged land used in service of the Aboriginal fishery to be "of no use to the Indians." This is a critical error. Reserves throughout British Columbia were laid out to provide access to the fishery. It was a gross distortion to deny the legitimacy of reserve lands linked to fisheries; such a claim implicitly questioned the status of almost all of British Columbia's coastal reserves.[49] Second, Cameron erred in casting the chief's actions as opportunism. Settlers vying for land had long used this charge against Aboriginal people who took action in response to White encroachment.[50] If, as Cameron suggested, the chief had in fact recently taken up permanent residence on land previously used on a seasonal basis, then his actions seem better understood as a wise strategy to retain land rights threatened by the colonial regime. Repeatedly confronted with powerful non-Aboriginal judgments about land use, occupancy, and ownership, there can be little doubt that many Aboriginal people came to understand the vulnerability of unattended land. They built structures such as houses and fences and buried their dead, marking their ownership of the land in a language that colonizers understood.[51] Colonialism increased the vulnerability of unattended lands, villages, and houses to an extent that must have given many Aboriginal people pause before departing on seasonal journeys. And once one was the victim of settler violence, seasonal wage migration and its attendant vulnerability became even more difficult to avoid. Lost property needed to be replaced, and that required some cash. People pushed off sites to which they had hereditary rights likely travelled to relatives who would agree to share their access. But if the displaced lacked this option, the wage economy might have been their only alternative.

These circumstances may seem explanation enough for why Aboriginal people incorporated migrant wage labour into their pre-existing trajectories of mobility. But if there was plenty of "push" behind much Aboriginal mobility, there was often a fair degree of "pull" too. The "prestige economy" on the Northwest Coast, in which elite status rested on the dual axes of heredity *and* wealth, predisposed coastal peoples to enter the wage economy.[52] As one scholar argues, while the journeys of migrant workers were not without their perils, they were generally quicker and less risky avenues to wealth acquisition than were the three pre-existing options of manufacturing, trading, or raiding.[53] Through their incorporation into the capitalist economy, Aboriginal workers fed their own Indigenous economy of wealth distribution at events known in the colonial world as "potlatches" (but known more properly by Indigenous names among each First Nation).

In addition to facilitating the acquisition of wealth and prestige, labour migrations provided opportune locations for Indigenous gatherings. Labour camps were common settings for visits with extended kin, feasts, and gambling. These were old activities, but in the late nineteenth century they were under new threat. Governments and missionaries attempted to suppress the potlatch in Canada and the United States. By combining Indigenous agendas with capitalist ones, Aboriginal migrants could perpetuate traditional practices while shielding themselves somewhat from the prying eyes of missionaries and Indian agents. This was true at canneries and hop fields alike, where workers incorporated feasts and gambling matches into their journeys.[54] Several times during the season of 1899, for example, Tsimshian Arthur Wellington Clah and his fellow workers at the Rivers Inlet cannery boarded steamers, taking their canoes in tow, and headed off to feasts, weddings, and other social gatherings.[55] Clah subsequently travelled from Rivers Inlet to the Washington hop fields, where one hundred people attended a Coast Salish feast held on the Hayes hop farm.[56] Labour camps likewise drew people together to play slahal and other gambling games.[57] Similar factors drew Aboriginal people to the hop yards north of the border in the Fraser Valley.[58] Gatherings that combined labour with Indigenous priorities were especially significant for Coast Salish elites who relied on intervillage audiences to legitimate their positions of privilege.[59] For the Coast Salish, travel had always been a prerequisite for maintaining high-status intervillage ties. Wage labour added a new variation to the trajectory of that age-old travel.

In some instances, Aboriginal travellers truly combined labour with cultural gatherings; at other times, they used labour merely as a pretense for travel. In early twentieth-century Washington, Indian agents attempted to prevent Aboriginal people from leaving their reservations unless they could produce proof of employment. Chief Squiquoi, or Billy Barlow, did not let this stand in the way of his desire to host a give-away feast in April 1904 on Whidbey Island. He simply distributed "jobs" as gifts and paid guests "wages" for their participation in the mortuary feast, putting them to work preparing the body, cooking, gathering fuel, and drawing water.[60] The roughly four hundred guests who attended likely included relatives from British Columbia, as Barlow was cousin to Charlie Wilson from Kuper Island in the Gulf of Georgia.[61]

In the context of colonial attempts to control Indigenous people, mobility itself became an expression of opinion. Aboriginal people "voted with their feet" for a variety of reasons. Some fled to avoid prosecution by the law. In 1884, for example, a group of Kyuquot confronted the local priest Father Nicolaye after he forcibly confined two pupils who had been absent from school. Some sixty community members entered the priest's house and restrained him while they released the students. By the time the Indian agent reached Kyuquot, the so-called "ringleaders" and many others were conveniently away at the Washington hop fields.[62] In other instances, international flight provided safety for those who fled charges ranging from intoxication to murder.[63] Others fled the Church rather than the state. Squamish chief Simon Baker writes that the late nineteenth and early twentieth centuries were a time when "the church, you might as well say, ran the reserve ... The priests were in control ... Those who didn't want to accept that environment left the community. A lot of them moved to the States."[64] And still others, such as the Tsimshian followers of William Duncan, sought increased political freedom within the Christian faith by migrating from British Columbia to Alaska in 1887 (the subject of Neylan's chapter in this volume). Yet, many such migrants no doubt learned, as did the Tsimshian, that their rights were not necessarily better protected on the other side of the border.[65]

Migratory patterns that arose in the colonial context were not always an easy fit with Indigenous priorities and values. In the mid-1880s, a Nuu-chah-nulth chief struggled to find guests to attend his daughter's puberty feast. When he and his emissaries went to various villages and to the Steveston canneries to deliver the invitations, the Songhees, Saanich, and Cowichan declined his invitation because they were on their way to the hop fields.[66] These refusals were a significant insult.[67] In this instance, the mobility necessitated by the wage economy interfered with the traditional order. This Nuu-chah-nulth chief was not the only one to confront such difficulties. A decade later, Kwakwaka'wakw chiefs noted a different sort of disruption to their way of life when they complained to the Indian agent that women from their communities travelled to Victoria for "illegitimate purposes," implying that the women found work there as prostitutes.[68] Some of these women may well have worked in Victoria's sex trade, but others likely worked at a variety of other pursuits such as cleaning houses or washing clothes. Regardless, these Kwakwaka'wakw men were unhappy about the women's journeys and they sought a way to control them.[69]

Aboriginal mobility in the late nineteenth and early twentieth centuries was the product of a concatenation of individual agency and structural coercion. The complexity of factors that shaped Aboriginal movement was rarely visible to non-Aboriginal observers. Colonial rhetoric about shiftless, wandering, uncivilized Indians was readily available and politically expedient. Few non-Aboriginal people had reason or motivation to look beyond this explanatory framework. The gulf between Aboriginal and non-Aboriginal understandings of mobility was particularly apparent with regard to the all-important land question. Testimony from the McKenna McBride Commission is replete with examples of the inability or unwillingness of non-Aboriginal officials to hear what Aboriginal people were saying. Individual witnesses came from dozens of different First Nations from all corners of the province. Although they did not conspire at the time to present a unified front, read today, their testimony evinces a remarkable commonality of voice.

Again and again, Aboriginal witnesses to the McKeanna McBride Commission articulated notions of land and resource rights that were associated with mobility rather than negated by it. They testified that seasonal or even lengthier absences did nothing to alter their Indigenous title to the land. "How long is it since anyone lived in that house?" asked one of the commissioners. "Every year that man lives there. He lives there every year – he goes there for a part of the year," replied the Ahousaht witness.[70] A Klahoose witness offered a similar answer when asked whether there was "any person living there [on IR 9] all the year round?" "Yes. There are six people living there but they all come over here [to Squirrel Cove] in the winter time."[71] Or, as Captain Jack, a "subchief" of the Mowachaht said, "What we have we want to keep, because we use them all the year round – perhaps not all the year, but sometimes there are families on them and at times the whole tribe frequent the one place."[72] Witnesses repeatedly insisted that they lived on "every" reserve,[73] that they had more than one "home,"[74] and that they had "interest" in more than one reserve.[75] Such replies were as common as they were unintelligible to commissioners who conceived of residency in the singular.

The testimony of Chief Kieteer from Ahousaht typifies the point of view that confused commissioners even as it seemed commonsensical to the witnesses. Kieteer explained: "We stay all round these islands all the time; there are several houses on this side of the island where we stay out there for about two months in the year."[76] To the commissioners' ears this was an inherently contradictory statement: "all the time" did not mean the same thing as "two months in the year." But for Kieteer and other Indigenous witnesses who made similar pleadings, the phrases were not incongruous. Both phrases expressed the permanence of Aboriginal occupation: "two months in the year" meant two months *every* year; "all the time" did not mean every day of the year but every year since time immemorial. Entrenched over countless generations, to the Indigenous witnesses, these patterns of mobility were anything but signs of itinerancy.

Chiefs who spoke to the commission embedded their words within a much longer and deeper chronology than did either commissioners or settlers. As chief Sam from Semihamoo stated: "I got the land from my mother. If I did not have the land I would have nothing to eat or make my living out of. My people lived here all the time and I was raised here, and I think I am going to be here all my life – I would not leave this place at all."[77] Josephus, an Ahousaht displaced by an illegal pre-emption, stressed the ancestral nature of his claim:

Q: How long have those houses been there?
A: It is a long time ago since those houses were built. My forefather's house, my father's house, and my house are all over there ...

Q: Have the Indians been using that place as long as you can remember?
A: Yes, when I first saw the day I saw the houses over there – there were houses there before I was born. All the places where the Indians used to go there used to be houses over there.[78]

Michael Inspring from the Nass Valley, who had been threatened at gunpoint by a pre-emptor, spoke with similar force about Nisga'a ownership rooted in the passage of generations:

And we know that this land belongs to us and that they have put up houses and the houses have rotted away. Some of our people have even died at this place and have graves here and if you want to see the graves we can point them out to you – this is another reason why we know that this land belonged to the Indians from time immemorial.[79]

Chief Harry Peters of the Sam-ah-quam band went into greater detail, sharing the story of his people's original migration, which gave them ownership of their territory. Peters first validated the story with an "oral footnote": "My great grandfather he was the Chief of this country and my father he was Chief after him and he is now close to 100 years old so he knows everything that was going on before." Peters then proceeded to point out what must have seemed obvious to him, namely, the fact that he was not the newcomer in the room: "There is one thing I know – I don't come from any other nation I don't come from China or Japan – I know I was born right here, that is what I know." This statement further validated the story that he went on to recount:

A long time ago during the flood, my father he knew about it and he told me and it was [sic] been told from one generation to the other so that history would never be forgotten. My father he is over 100 years old, he told me, and then we tell the others. There is one high mountain where two canoes were tied up – they were from Pemberton and one of these canoes got loose and was lost – we don't know whether they were drowned or what happened – Just one canoe was saved and after the flood, these people that were saved they went back to Pemberton again and that is where we originated from – that is the reason why I think we ought to own a little of this place. My father he did not tell me whether we would rent this place to the Government or not – that is what my father tells me all the time – I don't say that I own the whole of BC – I only want a little of it.[80]

Essentially, Peters was saying the same thing as the Gitxsan elder on the other end of the twentieth century: "If this is your land, where are your stories?"[81] All of these men spoke of inheritances passed down through clear lines of descent, not through land deeds but through oral narratives. They spoke of inheritances stretching across vast spans of time, and herein lies a clue that can help us hear what the commissioners could not. With ownership so deeply entrenched across generations and through time, changing patterns of mobility were like waves on the surface of a bottomless sea. Constantly shifting, constantly there, waves do nothing to change the nature of the sea itself.

This long sense of history also shored up Indigenous confidence that their presence on the land stretched permanently into the future. When told that a village site with standing houses had been pre-empted by a white settler, Chief Kieteer responded in the manner that one would expect of someone who planned to return: he asked about the condition in which his land would be left once the pre-emptor was gone.

> Is this man that made this application for this land going to go and pull down the houses? Because I don't want the houses to be taken down by this man, and we are not going to pull these houses down. We used to live there a long time ago and our descendants we leave will live there after us, and they will live there all the time and in the future.[82]

Without agreeing to the legitimacy of the pre-emptor's claim, Kieteer understood that the settler might be there for a while. This was the position of a pragmatist, not a defeatist. Even as he admitted the possibility that his land would be occupied, Kieteer thought ahead to the day that his descendants would reclaim and reoccupy their territory. He believed that the settler would eventually leave and that the land would be restored to its rightful possessors.

Kieteer's belief was rooted in historical precedent. Generations earlier his relatives from Nootka Sound had weathered the storm of the Spanish military occupation of their traditional village at Yuquot. In the 1780s, led by Chief Maquinna, they abandoned the village site that they had occupied continuously for thousands of years and moved south to seek refuge in Clayoquot Sound. By 1795, the Spanish had withdrawn, and Maquinna and his community returned home.[83] Kieteer had good reason to believe his people would once again outlast the newcomers.

For many Aboriginal people who spoke before the McKenna McBride Commission, as for Chief Kieteer, it was the white newcomers who seemed transient. As another Nuu-chah-nulth chief, also displaced at the hands of a pre-emptor, said:

> The Indian is not like the whiteman. The whiteman comes around here and buys a piece of land and puts a house on it, and after living in it for 4 or 5 years, he sells it and makes more money than what he paid for it. The Indians don't do that – they want to keep the land where their houses are.[84]

Chief Taku Jack from northwestern British Columbia likewise told the commission:

> This is my own country and I want to keep it. A white man comes to a creek and gets gold out of that creek after a while he leaves it ... but we are not like that – we stay here all the time because the land is ours. It is no good for us to move out of this place because this is our country. We gave the names to the places around here and these old names came from our old forefathers and they are just named the same to this day – I don't think you believe me when I tell you I belong to this place.[85]

Peneleket chief Hulburtson concisely expressed a similar point: "An Indian will stay in one place all the time, and his gets it after him."[86] This was a world in which seasonal movements were entirely consonant with staying "in one place all the time."

These patterns of seasonal mobility and resource use were historically long-standing, but they were not timeless. Among the Nuu-chah-nulth, for example, year-round occupation of major villages was the norm prior to the arrival of European pathogens. Depopulation necessitated the amalgamation of localized, self-contained groups into larger confederacies whose territories could not be exploited from any single location. From the early days of contact, then, mobility marked Indigenous attempts to spread their thinned numbers across the landscape in order to survive.[87] Rather than nullifying ownership, mobility was the idiom through which Aboriginal people exercised their ownership. Wage labour had since altered Indigenous trajectories of movement, but it had not changed the age-old relationship to territory that was affirmed each year when people moved throughout their territory and exercised their hereditary rights.[88]

These expressions of land rights – deeply rooted in time and place – should not be as unfamiliar as they perhaps are. Non-Aboriginal immigrants – from places as far-flung as Ireland and China, for example – often migrated to North America with the intention of securing and retaining title to their ancestral lands at home. Part of the meaning of their mobility lay in attachment to land to which they would not return for decades, land to which they would sometimes return only in death.[89]

Mobility itself was part of life for Aboriginal and non-Aboriginal people alike in turn-of-the-century British Columbia. Most immigrants were recent arrivals. Once in British Columbia, many of them continued to lead highly mobile lives.[90] The trajectories of movement for many of these settlers and workers were not entirely dissimilar from Aboriginal ones. Many "farmers" participated in a mixed economy of subsistence agriculture, commercial agriculture, hunting, gathering, and "off-farm" wage work in the resource and government sectors.[91] White settlers might easily have empathized with the hard-working Cowichan who planted grain in the spring before leaving for work in the canneries, returning home to harvest the crop in the interval before the hop-picking season in Washington drew them away again.[92] The Saltspring Island farmer relied on this mobility no less than did the Cowichan one. Of course, in some instances, they were one and the same person: settlers married Indigenous women and together they led lives in which various meanings of mobility overlapped.[93]

Not only was mobility a necessity for Aboriginal, non-Aboriginal, and mixed families alike, it was also a risk for all concerned. Like Aboriginal migrants who worried about the threat that would-be pre-emptors posed to the security of their land and houses, pre-emptors themselves hoped their claims would not fall prey to "canny land-watchers" while they were away earning much-needed wages at seasonal work.[94] There must have been instances when these similarities bred empathy, particularly when the ties of marriage and family bound Aboriginal and non-Aboriginal people together. But the examples of settlers evicting Aboriginal people from their houses at gunpoint and of pre-empting reserve lands containing clearly visible improvements also remind us of the fact that similarity can just as easily breed contempt.

Common patterns of mobility notwithstanding, a crucial difference separated the experiences of Aboriginal and non-Aboriginal migrants. Immigrant settlers basked in the unearned privilege of free or almost free land granted them by the pre-emption system. The holders of Aboriginal title to that same land had been denied that right since 1865. As one scholar notes of land policy in British Columbia from Douglas' time through the early decades of the twentieth century, "provided that the land was to be used in all good faith, unlimited quantities might be had for practically nothing."[95] Pre-emptors often took many years to pay for their allotments, if indeed they paid for them at all. Many pre-emptors never planned to pay for their pre-emption. Some used their initial pre-emption as a temporary stop while looking for the ideal piece of land. Others "abandoned" their pre-emption only to have it immediately pre-empted again by their children, thus effectively bequeathing the land to their heirs without ever paying for it.[96] And even if settlers did forfeit their pre-emption, they could easily acquire another somewhere else. Or, they could leave altogether and return to their native land.[97] The same could not be said for Aboriginal families who were *in* their native land and whose ties to the land extended back to time immemorial. Denied the possibility of acquiring "free land" within their own homeland, these families went to great lengths – and great distances – to maintain a hold on their traditional territories. It was this fact that so many chiefs attempted to convey to the royal commissioners.

Many immigrants to British Columbia, overlooking their own recent and often ongoing mobility, turned their faces from Aboriginal understandings of the relationship between mobility and land rights. Government officials used evidence of "itinerant Indians" to curtail and deny Aboriginal rights and title. They did so at the same time as the explicit violence of the settler frontier, and the more implicit violence of the capitalist one, propelled Aboriginal people into greater cycles of mobility over which they exercised less and less control. There is no question that mobility was a central component of Aboriginal people's economic and cultural autonomy. Mobility was both a time-worn practice that endured through the colonial encounter and a new strategy for mitigating the colonial threat. But for colonizers, forgetful of their own migratory history, and insistent that the future and not the past was what mattered, Aboriginal mobility was a powerful justification for the resettlement of the West.

The legacy of this colonial past is with us still. It remains difficult for us to hear Aboriginal articulations of mobility and place. In her recent memoir, Helen Piddington, long-time resident of Loughborough Inlet on the central BC coast, takes note of the shell middens that mark the precontact Aboriginal presence in the inlet. She interprets the subsequent absence of year-round Aboriginal residents as evidence of a universal process: "so memories fade, connections to place blur and dissolve."[98] She is not unsympathetic towards Aboriginal people; yet, in her assumption that Aboriginal connections to Loughborough faded away long ago, she unwittingly reiterates the colonial view, one shared by the McKenna McBride commissioners, that recognizable Aboriginal presence and title must come in the form of sedentary, year-round residency. The postcontact Aboriginal presence in Loughborough seems uprooted and migratory to her. As she puts it, "They all seem to have come from somewhere else – not people of this place."[99] Having heard tell of a man known as "Loughborough Bill," the "Chief of Loughborough," she remains uncertain "whether he was part of a group or alone or even from this area," and so she situates him beyond the bounds of her otherwise sensitive history of place. Yet, if we turn to the recollections of Chief Harry Assu from Cape Mudge, we learn that the fact that Bill may not have been a year-round resident of the inlet did not mean that he was not a *permanent* resident, nor did it mean that his proprietary interest was diminished. Loughborough Bill was not part of some distant past – he was a character in Assu's twentieth-century lifetime. As Assu remembers, when people entered the inlet, Loughbourough Bill would paddle out to meet them, calling out, "Who are you? Who is your father?" Only upon receiving a satisfactory answer, that is, upon hearing a name that linked the visitor to the genealogical geography of place, would Bill reply, "Oh, I see ... you can come in!"[100] Aboriginal lives in British Columbia have long been simultaneously mobile and rooted.[101] And for far too long, non-Aboriginal society has seen Aboriginal mobility as an erasure rather than an enactment of attachment and entitlement to place.

Notes

1 See for example, Frederick Cooper and Ann Laura Stoler, eds., *Tensions of Empire: Colonial Cultures in a Bourgeois World* (Berkeley: University of California Press, 1997); Nicholas Thomas, *Colonialism's Culture: Anthropology, Travel, and Government* (Cambridge: Polity Press, 1994); Nicholas B. Dirks, especially *Castes of Mind: Colonialism and the Making of Modern India* (Princeton: Princeton University Press, 2001); Nicholas B. Dirks, *The Hollow Crown: Ethnohistory of an Indian Kingdom* (New York: Cambridge University Press, 1987); Cole Harris, *The Resettlement of British Columbia: Essays on Colonialism and Geographical Change* (Vancouver: UBC Press, 1997); and Brett Christophers, *Positioning the Missionary: John Booth Good and the Confluence of Cultures in Nineteenth-Century British Columbia* (Vancouver: UBC Press, 1998).

2 This is a theme of my own work. See Paige Raibmon, *Authentic Indians: Episodes of Encounter from the Late-Nineteenth-Century Northwest Coast* (Durham and London: Duke University Press, 2005).

3 This can be seen in part through the demographic shifts in the province in these decades. See Hugh Johnston, "Native People, Settlers and Sojourners, 1871-1916," in *The Pacific Province*, ed. Hugh Johnston (Vancouver: Douglas and McIntyre, 1996), 166-67.

4 Arthur J. Ray, *Indians in the Fur Trade: Their Role as Hunters, Trappers, and Middlemen in the Lands Southwest of Hudson Bay, 1660-1870* (Toronto: University of Toronto Press, 1974), esp. 94-116; and Arthur J. Ray, "Bayside Trade, 1720-1780," in *Historical Atlas of Canada*, Vol. 1, *From the Beginning to 1800*, ed. Cole Harris, cart. Geoffrey Matthews (Toronto: University of Toronto Press, 1987), plate 60.

5 For an overview of these images in British Columbia, see Robin Fisher, *Contact and Conflict: Indian-European Relations in British Columbia, 1774-1890*, 2nd ed. (Vancouver: UBC Press, 1992), 73-94.

6 John Lutz, "Work, Sex, and Death on the Great Thoroughfare: Annual Migrations of 'Canadian Indians' to the American Pacific Northwest," in *Parallel Destinies: Canadian-American Relations West of the Rockies*, ed. John M. Findlay and Ken S. Coates (Seattle: University of Washington Press, 2002), 82; John Lutz, "After the Fur Trade: The Aboriginal Labouring Classes of BC, 1849-1890," *Journal of the Canadian Historical Association*, new series 3 (1992): 69-93; Rolf Knight, *Indians at Work: An Informal History of Native Labour in BC, 1858-1930*, rev. ed. (Vancouver: New Star Books, 1996).

7 Earl Maquinna George, *Living on the Edge: Nuu-chah-nulth History from an Ahousaht Chief's Perspective* (Winlaw, BC: Sono Nis Press, 2003), 61-67.

8 Canada, Department of Indian Affairs [hereafter DIA], Annual Report (hereafter AR) 1882, *Sessional Papers* [hereafter *SP*] 1883, no. 5, 57.

9 Robert Galois, "Colonial Encounters: The Worlds of Arthur Wellington Clah, 1855-1881," *BC Studies* 115-16 (1997): 135-46; Arthur Wellington Clah, "Journals," 1877-1909, Library and Archives Canada [hereafter LAC], reels A-1706-1709 and A-1712-1714.

10 Cole Harris, *Making Native Space: Colonialism, Resistance, and Reserves in British Columbia* (Vancouver: UBC Press: 2002), 275-78; Richard White, *Land Use, Environment, and Social Change* (Seattle: University of Washington Press, 1992), 57, 117-18, 158. White rightly notes that this pro-agrarian rhetoric betrayed its promise not only to Aboriginal people but also to poor settlers/colonizers. In both instances, the idealization of the farmer went hand-in-glove with the capitalist production of wealth. See White, *Land Use, Environment, and Social Change*, 141.

11 R.W. Sandwell, "Negotiating Rural: Policy and Practice in the Settlement of Saltspring Island, 1859-1891," in *Beyond the City Limits: Rural History in British Columbia*, ed. R.W. Sandwell, 83-88 (Vancouver: UBC Press, 1999).

12 DIA, AR 1898, *SP* 1899, no. 14, xxi.

13 DIA, AR 1892, *SP* 1893, no. 14, xx.

14 DIA, AR 1892, *SP* 1893, no. 14, 235.

15 A.J. Hall to Church Missionary Society, 13 January 1879, "Original Letters, Correspondence, etc., Incoming 1882-1900," Church Missionary Society, LAC reel A-106. See also *Weekly Colonist* (Victoria), 19 March 1896, LAC, RG 10, file 6244-1, vol. 3628.

16 *Weekly Colonist* (Victoria), 19 March 1896, LAC, RG 10, file 6244-1, vol. 3628.

17 Pidcock, "Diary," 1 June 1888; A.J. Hall to Church Missionary Society, 16 March 1880, "Original Letters, Correspondence, etc., Incoming 1882-1900," Church Missionary Society, LAC, reel A-106, Marie Mauzé, *Les Fils De Wakai: Une Historie des Indiens Lekwiltoq* (Paris: Éditions Recherche sur les Civilisations, 1992), 121; United States (Bureau of Education), "Report by Sheldon Jackson, General Agent of Education for Alaska," in *Annual Report of the Commissioner of Education Made to the Secretary of the Interior for the year 1891-1892 with accompanying papers* (Washington, DC: GPO, 1894), 878; United States (Bureau of Education), "Report by Sheldon Jackson, General Agent of Education for Alaska," in *Annual Report of the Commissioner of Education Made to the Secretary of the Interior for the year 1902 with accompanying papers* (Washington, DC: GPO, 1903), 1232-33; United States (Bureau of Education), "Education Report for Alaska," in *Annual Report of the Commissioner of Education Made to the Secretary of the Interior for the year 1907 with accompanying papers* (Washington, DC: GPO, 1908), 394; 9 June 1911, Annual report of Cassia Patton and Jeannette H. Wright, Teachers, Sitka, to W.T. Lopp, US Bureau of Education, Seattle, School Files – Sitka, General Correspondence 1908-35, Record of the Bureau of Indian Affairs, Alaska Division, RG 75, US National Archives, Alaska State Historical Library, AR-37, microfilm roll 23; July 1908, Annual Report of Dorothy Doyle, Teacher, School Files, "Haines 1908-1935," Record of the Bureau of Indian Affairs, Alaska Division, RG 75, US National Archives, Alaska State Historical Library, AR-37, microfilm roll 8.

18 DIA, AR 1885, *SP* 1886, no. 4, 84; Tate Family Papers, 25-26 October 1897, 6 July 1898, 4 September 1898, 20 September 1898, 18 September 1899, 18 September 1901, 23 September 1901, 20 August 1902, 20 July 1904, 24 September 1905, 23 July 1905, 11 September 1905, 18 July 1906, 28 July 1907, 1 August 1907, 4 August 1907, 2 August 1908, 22 July 1909, 2 September 1909, 10 August 1911, 4 September 1911, 17 July-13 September 1913, 4 July 1914, 26 July 1914, 26 July 1914, 18 July 1915, 10 September 1915, 9 September 1916, 6 August 1917, 11 October 1917, 28 September 1919, 26-30 September 1920, 24 July 1921, 15 September 1921, 22 September 1922, British Columbia Archives [hereafter BCA].

19 John Lutz, "Seasonal Rounds in an Industrial World," and Jody R. Woods, "St. Mary's Roman Catholic Boarding School," in *A Stó:lō-Coast Salish Historical Atlas*, ed. Keith Carlson, 62-69 (Vancouver: Douglas and McIntyre: 2001), plates 22 and 23.

20 Harris, *Making Native Space*, 87-90, 274, 278.

21 Michael A. Tomlan, *Tinged with Gold: Hop Culture in the United States* (Athens: University of Georgia Press, 1992), 6; J.A. Costello, *The Siwash: Their Life, Legends and Tales, Puget Sound and Pacific Northwest* (Seattle: The Calvert Company, 1895), 165; "History of Snohomish County," Hops Vertical File, White River Historical Society, Auburn, Washington.

22 W.H. Lomas to I.W. Powell, 30 December 1887, Cowichan Agency Letterbook, 1887-89, LAC, RG 10, vol. 1354.

23 "Hop Fields of Puyallup and White River," *The West Shore*, 10, 11 (1884): 345. On the scarcity of labourers in the hop industry, see also John Muir, *Steep Trails*, ed. William Frederic Badè (Boston: Houghton Mifflin, 1918), 257; "Sumner – Five Years Ago," *Puyallup Valley Tribune*, 16 September 1905, 2.

24 William Lane to W.H. Lomas, 26 July 1891, Cowichan Agency Incoming Correspondence 1890-91, LAC, RG 10, vol. 1337; William Lane to W.H. Lomas, 16 July 1891, Cowichan Agency Incoming Correspondence 1890-91, LAC RG 10, vol. 1337.

25 DIA, AR 1895, *SP* 1896, no. 14, 153.

26 Royal Commission on Indian Affairs for the Province of British Columbia (McKenna McBride Commission), New Westminster Agency (pt. 1, 1913), 42.

27 Ibid., 28-29.

28 See, for example, ibid., New Westminster Agency, 16, 292, 321, 311; West Coast Agency, 39, 63, 75, 51, 83, 86; Nass Agency, 56ff; and Cowichan Agency, 12, 145-46, 255, 271, 308.

29 Ibid., Cowichan Agency, 46.

30 Ibid.

31 Ibid., Nass Agency, 176-77.

32 Ibid., West Coast Agency, 112.

33 Ibid., 97-98.

34 Ibid. Such displacements were not limited to the coast but occurred in the interior too. See Harris, *Making Native Space*, 140-41.

35 Royal Commission on Indian Affairs, West Coast Agency, 107-8, 116-17.

36 Ibid., 116-17.

37 On the difficulty of clearing land, see, for example, Sandwell, "Negotiating Rural," 96; Richard Mackie, "Cougars, Colonists, and the Rural Settlement of Vancouver Island," in Sandwell, *Beyond the City Limits*, 133; and White, *Land Use, Environment, and Social Change*, 56.

38 Royal Commission on Indian Affairs, West Coast Agency, 159-60, 161, 162. For another example, see New Westminster Agency, 122-23.

39 Ibid., Queen Charlotte Agency, 43.

40 Bruce Stadfeld, "Manifestations of Power: Native Resistance to the Resettlement of British Columbia," in Sandwell, *Beyond the City Limits*, 37.

41 Ibid., 34.

42 Ibid., 43.

43 Ibid., 38.

44 Royal Commission on Indian Affairs, West Coast Agency, 97-98, 112.

45 Robert E. Cail, *Land, Man, and the Law: The Disposal of Crown Lands in British Columbia, 1871-1913* (Vancouver: UBC Press, 1974), 15; Sandwell, "Negotiating Rural," 85-88.

46 Stadfeld, "Manifestations of Power," 35.

47 Royal Commission on Indian Affairs, New Westminster Agency, 225-26, 236.

48 Ibid., Cowichan Agency, 93-94. See also New Westminster Agency, 31-32

49 Douglas Harris, "Land, Fish, and Law: The Legal Geography of Indian Reserves and Native Fisheries in British Columbia, 1850-1927" (PhD diss., York University, 2005).

50 Stadfeld, "Manifestations of Power," 35-36.

51 Ibid., 39-43.

52 Lutz, "Work, Sex, and Death," 84.

53 Ibid., 85.

54 Raibmon, *Authentic Indians*, 103-9.

55 Clah, "Journals," 24 June, 30 June, 29 July, and 11 August 1899, LAC, reel no. A-1707.

56 Ibid., 1 October 1899, reel no. A-1707.

57 Susan Lord Currier, "Some Aspects of Washington Hop Fields," *Overland Monthly*, 2nd series, 32 (1898): 544; Clah, "Journals," 9 and 16 September 1891, LAC, reel no. A-1713; Currier, "Some Aspects of Washington Hop Fields," 544; Clah, "Journals," 9 and 16 September 1891, LAC, reel no. A-1713.

58 Clah, "Journals," 1 October 1899, LAC, reel no. A-1707. See also Carlson, *A Stó:lō-Coast Salish Historical Atlas*, 70.

59 Wayne Suttles, *Coast Salish Essays* (Vancouver: Talonbooks, 1987), 209-30; Carlson, *A Stó:lō-Coast Salish Historical Atlas*, 24-29, 32-33.

60 Van Olinda, "The Last Potlatch," Pamphlets – Indians of North America – Oregon and Washington, Special Collections, University of Washington.

61 R.J. Roberts, "Farm Diaries," 10 December 1886, BCA. Wilson was related to Barlow through his mother, who was from Whidbey Island. See ibid., 1882.

62 DIA, AR 1884, *SP* 1885, no. 3, 100.

63 Myron Eells, *Ten Years of Missionary Work Among the Indians at Skokomish, Washington Territory, 1874-1884* (Boston: Congregational Sunday-School and Publishing Society, 1886), 100; DIA, AR 1884, *SP* 1885, no. 3, 98; DIA, AR 1884, *SP* 1885, no. 3.

64   Simon Baker, *Khot-La-Cha: The Autobiography of Chief Simon Baker*, comp., ed. Verna J. Kirkness (Vancouver: Douglas and McIntyre, 1994), 8, 9.
65   "More injustice to Alaskans," *The Alaskan*, 28 April 1893, 3; John G. Brady to Elizabeth Brady, 2 November 1903, box 1, fol. 13, John G. Brady Papers, Beinecke Rare Book and Manuscript Library, Yale University; Alfred B. Atkinson and Fredrick Ridley to Sheldon Jackson, 5 December 1904, Sheldon Jackson Correspondence, Sheldon Jackson School Library, Sitka; "Status of Natives in Alaska" (ms), John G. Brady Papers, box 11, fol. 36, Beinecke Rare Book and Manuscript Library, Yale University; Mark Hamilton to John Brady, n.d. (1901?), box 2, fol. 36, John G. Brady Papers, Beinecke Rare Book and Manuscript Library, Yale University.
66   Edward Sapir and Morris Swadesh, *Nootka Texts: Tales and Ethnological Narratives* (New York: AMS Press, 1978), 149, 151.
67   Ibid., 230.
68   Indians to R.H. Pidcock, 8 March 1895, LAC, RG 10, vol. 1648; R.H. Pidcock to A.W. Vowell, 20 March 1895, LAC, RG 10, vol. 1648; R.H. Pidcock to A.W. Vowell, 24 April 1895, LAC, RG 10, vol. 1648. The request for legislation was the second notice sent to Indian Superintendent Vowell in less than a month that discussed the declining influence of hereditary chiefs among the Kwakwa̱ka'wakw. Unknown to A.W. Vowell, 25 February 1895, LAC, RG 10, vol. 1648C.
69   See Jean Barman, "Taming Aboriginal Sexuality: Gender, Power, and Race in British Columbia, 1850-1900," *BC Studies* 115-16 (1997): 237-66.
70   Royal Commission on Indian Affairs for the Province of British Columbia (McKenna McBride Commission), West Coast Agency, 117.
71   Ibid., New Westminster Agency, 207.
72   Ibid., West Coast Agency, 158.
73   Ibid., 29.
74   Ibid., Cowichan Agency (pt. 3), 53.
75   Ibid., New Westminster Agency (pt. 2), 457; 330-31, 336-37, 337-38, 457; (pt. 1), 31, 32.
76   Ibid., West Coast Agency, 110-11.
77   Ibid., New Westminster Agency, 76.
78   Ibid., West Coast Agency, 116-17
79   Ibid., Nass Agency, 176-77.
80   Ibid., New Westminster Agency (pt. 2), 370-71.
81   J. Edward Chamberlain, *If This Is Your Land, Where Are Your Stories? Finding Common Ground* (Toronto: Vintage Canada, 2004), 1.
82   Royal Commission on Indian Affairs, West Coast Agency, 111.
83   Alan D. McMillan, *Since the Time of the Transformers: The Ancient Heritage of the Nuu-chah-nulth, Ditidaht, and Makah* (Vancouver: UBC Press, 1999), 187.
84   Royal Commission on Indian Affairs, West Coast Agency, 107.
85   Ibid., Stikine Agency, 21.
86   Ibid., Cowichan Agency, 144.
87   McMillan, *Since the Time of the Transformers*, 196, 197, 212, 213.
88   Raibmon, *Authentic Indians*, 109-10.
89   See, for example, Denise Chong, *The Concubine's Children: Portrait of a Family Divided* (Toronto: Viking, 1994); and Richard White, *Remembering Ahanagran: A History of Stories* (New York: Hill and Wang, 1998).
90   Johnston, "Native People, Settlers and Sojourners," 165-204; Sandwell, "Negotiating Rural," 91; Mackie, "Cougars," 133; Harris, *Making Native Space*, 285.
91   Sandwell, "Negotiating Rural," 90-91.
92   DIA, AR 1890, *SP* 1891, no. 18, 105.
93   Jean Barman, *Maria Mahoi of the Islands* (Vancouver: New Star Books, 2004).
94   Sandwell, "Negotiating Rural," 88.
95   Cail, *Land, Man, and the Law*, xiii.
96   Sandwell, "Negotiating Rural," 91-95, 98-100.
97   Johnston, "Native People, Settlers and Sojourners," 165.

98 Helen Piddington, *The Inlet: Memoir of Modern Pioneer* (Madeira Park: Harbour, 2001), 21.

99 Piddington, *The Inlet*, 21.

100 Harry Assu with Joy Inglis, *Assu of Cape Mudge: Recollections of a Coastal Indian Chief* (Vancouver: UBC Press, 1989), 18.

101 For a sampling of how migration and identity have been configured over time among the Stó:lō, see Keith Thor Carlson, "Expressions of Collective Identity," in Carlson, *A Stó:lō-Coast Salish Historical Atlas*, plate 8, pp. 24-33.

9

"Choose Your Flag": Perspectives on the Tsimshian Migration from Metlakatla, British Columbia, to New Metlakatla, Alaska, 1887

Susan Neylan

I have a vivid memory of the first time I read Arthur J. Ray's *Indians in the Fur Trade,* and faint pencil marginalia remain to this day in my copy attesting to these impressions.[1] I was especially struck with his emphasis on the degree of Aboriginal movement and migration that participation in trade with Europeans precipitated. This was not mere displacement by Europeans but, rather, migrations to serve Aboriginal needs with regard to commerce or in response to the shifts in the balance of power wrought by Native groups vying for dominance and monopoly control of trade with the newcomers. I saw the same patterns in my own study of Northwest Coast groups under Protestant missionization, begun under Ray's supervision when I was a doctoral student at the University of British Columbia.[2] On British Columbia's north Pacific coast, villages moved locations in the wake of sustained contact with Europeans. They created new mission communities and Native Christian identities. These were neither completely voluntary migrations nor entirely forced removals. One of the most spectacular examples occurred in the summer of 1887, when around 800 of the approximately 950 members of the Tsimshian First Nation left their mission village of Metlakatla, British Columbia (see Map 10.1 on p. 221), in their traditional homeland and migrated over a hundred kilometres to Annette Island, Alaska, where they founded New Metlakatla.[3] In 1891, New Metlakatla became the first and only American federal reservation in Alaska. This chapter seeks to examine the history of the two Metlakatlas in the 1880s and to analyze the discourses about the Tsimshian relocation, which highlight the event in diverse and sometimes contradictory ways.

With a wealth of source material, ranging from newspapers, governmental correspondence, petitions from the Tsimshian, missionary letters, royal commissions, and other publications at the time, the public discussion provides ample perspectives for consideration, many far removed from reality. American newspapers celebrated the Tsimshian decision to flee from persecution by Church and State. Many Alaskans allegedly welcomed them into their fold, particularly for the good example these "Christian Indians" might have on other Native peoples in the territory. The vast majority of American perspectives based their interpretations entirely upon a pro-Duncan book published by Henry S. Wellcome the same year as the migration.[4] Accepting Wellcome's interpretation, American newspapers almost universally cast William Duncan as the heroic Moses in this exodus, both instigator and leader of the migration. Evoking the American founding myth, the Tsimshian became pilgrims seeking a promised land or citizens of a country that freed them from the political constraints of monarchy and empire.

In contrast, Canadian newspaper editorials railed against the loss of the Tsimshian, framing the action as supreme disloyalty and blaming Duncan for misleading them. Annual reports produced by the Canadian Department of Indian Affairs (DIA) harkened back to the "troublesome Metlakatlans" who had prompted a royal commission inquiry in 1884 and another in 1887. In the 1880s, the government had laid out reserves on the north coast without treaty or other such secession of land title, and it blamed the missionaries for the vocal and often physical resistance it encountered from First Nations in the region.

Native people needed no prodding on this account. Unlike many Aboriginal peoples, who were divided artificially by borders drawn across their territories by outsiders, the Tsimshian people to this day live on both sides of a border they chose to cross. While the non-Native discussion often casts the Tsimshian in a passive role as Duncan's "followers," certainly with regard to the issue of land and access to resources, they had their own agendas. The Tsimshian who left their ancestral homelands did so for complex and rational reasons that had little to do with the will or whims of "whites." Tsimshian discourses, while more difficult to find in the written record than white discourses, speak to a desire for autonomy and an awareness of the colonial forces that assaulted them in nineteenth-century British Columbia.

One cannot study any aspect of missionization of Native peoples in British Columbia, or even perhaps in all of western Canada, without some reference to William Duncan's utopian mission near the mouth of the Skeena River. Duncan was likely one of British Columbia's best known and most controversial missionaries to First Nations. From Yorkshire, England, Duncan was an evangelical lay preacher, appointed by the Church Missionary Society (CMS) to open the first formal mission on the north coast of British Columbia in 1857. After commencing operations at the Hudson's Bay Company trading post, Fort Simpson, he soon saw the need to isolate Native Christians from the negative influences of British presence as well as from their own "traditional" culture. Thus, a first migration of various Tsimshian villagers occurred in 1862, when Duncan moved about fifty Native converts from the fort to an old Tsimshian site known as Metlakatla (meaning "saltwater channel passage" or "where the wind dies down") near what is today Prince Rupert Harbour. By the 1870s, Metlakatla was the centre of the Anglican North Pacific Mission, populated by nearly a thousand Tsimshian Christians and other First Nations from the region.

Metlakatla was designed to promote Victorian "progress" and the merits of European civilization. It had a reading room and museum, mission houses, a jail, a boarding school, and a guest house for visitors to Duncan's "utopia." Victorian-style homes, workshops, gardens, and a seawall collectively attempted to convert Tsimshian space as well as souls. Metlakatla was also created to be economically self-sustaining, and Duncan established a number of commercial enterprises to this end (e.g., sawmill, soap factory, furniture factory, blacksmith shop, trading post, salmon cannery). Many of these operated as community-owned cooperatives with Native shareholders. The economic aspect of the mission and the perceived self-sufficiency of the community had a measurable impact on the Tsimshians' decision to move to Alaska.

But, of course, Metlakatla was a religious mission too. The Native-built church, St. Paul's, was reputedly the largest west of Chicago and north of San Francisco and was capable of seating over a thousand people.[5] The first Christian village of Metlakatla lasted from 1862 until 1887. Using Metlakatla as a model of practice and as a physical base from which to launch new missionary endeavours and regular itinerant circuits, Anglican missions and church personnel spread from there, yet constantly relied upon it as a point of reference. After 1878, it became the Episcopal see of the Diocese of Caledonia.

Conflict with Church policy and Church personnel (particularly the new bishop of Caledonia) led to William Duncan's dismissal from the CMS in 1881. Rather than turn over the reins, Duncan split from the Anglican Church entirely and established a non-denominational independent Native Church – "The Christian Church of Metlakahtla" – which most Metlakatla Christians joined. They also took an oath in the form of the "Metlakathla Mission Declaration of Resident," which stated that they accepted an evangelical form of Christianity based exclusively upon biblical teachings, that they chose "to be governed by the laws of the Queen of England" and to "submit to the by-laws imposed by the Native Council of the settlement."[6] Six years later, this schism proved critical as the members of the independent church were the ones to abandon the location for a new home in Alaska.

In March 1887, Tsimshian men from Metlakatla – David Leask, John Tait, Edward Benson, Adam Gordon, and Fred Ridley – accompanied by English lay missionary Dr. J.D. Bluett-Duncan, headed north into American territory in search of a suitable location for the new community.[7] They found it on the northwest site of Annette Island, over one hundred kilometres north of their original mission, at an old Tlingit winter village site known as *T'ak'waan*, or *Ta'gwaan*, which had been only recently abandoned. [8] Most of the town followed on 7 August 1887, the day chosen as the official date of the founding of a "New Metlakatla."

Over the years, Duncan kept a number of scrapbooks pertaining to his mission work, with an obvious majority of newspaper clippings originating from friends, colleagues, and mission supporters. Among them was a scrapbook containing roughly 450 separate articles related to the Tsimshian migration to Alaska, representing some three hundred different newspaper and journal sources from the United States, Canada, Great Britain, and elsewhere in Europe. [9] While a problematic source in many respects because of Duncan's own involvement in the migration and the kinds of articles he might have chosen to include or not include, this material does, nonetheless, provide intriguing evidence regarding how the 1887 move and the issues behind it was portrayed to a public far removed from Tsimshian territory. Supplementing this collection are the many clippings files of newspaper accounts of the move included in the DIA's papers among the voluminous correspondence the event precipitated between officials at various levels of government. [10]

Examining the general perspectives on the migration to Alaska in American and Canadian newspapers reveals interesting differences in how each country reflected upon the meaning of the move. In the mid-1880s, Duncan visited a number of American cities (Boston, Philadelphia, Washington) on lecture-junkets in an attempt to drum up support for his plan to approach the American government for a grant of land. [11] He met with an enthusiastic response in several places and even managed to meet with President Grover Cleveland and his staff. [12] American newspapers also obliged in covering his speeches and rallied additional support through a public fundraising campaign. Letters, accompanied by cheques, were sent to papers that had run articles lamenting the plight of the "poor Metlakatlans."

Dating predominantly from 1887 to 1888, well over half the newspaper articles in Duncan's scrapbook mention Wellcome's *The Story of Metlakahtla* by name or review the book explicitly (257 articles). The significance of this for the American press should not be underestimated as an overwhelming number of pieces followed Wellcome's pro-Duncan interpretation of events. Indeed, only a few even identified the book as an opinion piece. These frequent references illustrate how the wealthy entrepreneur, Henry S. Wellcome, had become a key player in publicizing the move from Old Metlakatla among American audiences. [13] By the 1880s, Wellcome had met Duncan in person and quickly became a staunch supporter of missionary efforts sympathetic towards the plight of Metlakatla. In 1887, he self-published *The Story of Metlakahtla*. An unabashedly pro-Duncan account of the rift between Duncan, the Church Missionary Society, and the Anglican Church in British

Columbia, all proceeds of the book went towards funding the migration to
Alaska. Monica Leigh Pastor, who has written about the changing visual
representations of the two Metlakatlas, notes that Wellcome's book exemplified the "shift in the targeted audience from CMS donors to American
legislators, philanthropists, and tourists."[14] Hence, the events of 1887 as they
were reported in the American press were inextricably connected to Wellcome's book, and writers quoted freely from its pages, as though it were a
purely objective account of events. "It is not a sensational romance," declared the Brooklyn *Times*, "but the true account of a drama now enacting."[15]

Moreover, and not surprisingly, over a quarter of the newspaper articles
follow Wellcome's reading of events by referring to state persecution (125
articles) and Church tyranny (123 articles, with 57 references linking Church
and State) as central motivators for the Tsimshian migration. The purpose
seems to have been to arouse sympathy and to promote financial support
in a way that echoed American national myths, which would appeal to
American readers. While not denying a certain irony, the *Newburyport Herald*
(Massachusetts) could still criticize Canadian Indian policy: "It is a curious
story that the United States, which have served so many Indian tribes in the
same way these have been served by the Canadians should furnish an asy-
lum for these people exiled from their lands."[16] "Americans saw in the book,"
historian Peter Murray summarizes rather succinctly, "a chance to twist the
British lion's tail."[17]

What US newspapers reported was "a story of oppression sure to win the
sympathy of American readers for it bears on its face every evidence of
truth."[18] Phrases like "tyrannical oppression," "gross and malicious persecution of church and state" (a phrase taken directly from Wellcome's book),
"ecclesiastical despotism and the avarice of men surrounding the settlement" appeared frequently in explanations of the Tsimshian's exasperation.[19]
Facing "ecclesiastical fanaticism ... and down-right robbery," Metlakatlans
had "abandoned all hope of getting justice in Canada and have petitioned
our government for land in Alaska"; hence, they fled "out from under the
iron heel of Briton."[20] Headlines such as "Robbed of their Lands a Prosper-
ous Indian Community Evicted under Canadian Laws" were common, and
newspapers called for "Aid for the Oppressed" in the hope that the
Metlakatlans would "soon find themselves sheltered beneath the American
flag and free from the persecution of an arrogant church."[21] After all, "they
ask only to prove themselves worthy of American citizenship" and receive
"the protection of Uncle Sam's smile."[22]

The "protection" they sought in Alaska, many writers assured their readers,
was security of land tenure as much as religious freedom: "They want to be
where religion is free, where they can secure the ownership of the product of
their hands and brains."[23] Clearly, one of the most popular images used to

evoke this migration as a flight from persecution was the American flag, as evidenced in this none too subtle analogy with revolutionary independence:

> Mr. William Duncan, of Metlakahtla fame, started last week for Alaska to select a village site for the Metlakahtla Indians, who are now seeking the protection of the United States from cruel Church and State persecution in Canada. On his way out, Mr. Duncan stopped off an hour in Philadelphia to receive from American friends, as a present to his people, an American flag 12 by 18 feet in size for the village pole. The presentation was made in Independence Hall, the Stars and Stripes being spread upon the table upon which the Declaration of Independence was signed.[24]

Writers assured American audiences that the Metlakatlans were metaphorically "seeking refuge under the American flag," while literally raising American flags in Metlakatla, among them perhaps that same one gifted to Duncan in Independence Hall, so intimately connected to a new nationalism.[25] Upon arriving in Alaska, Metlakatlans "rallied round the flag" during the reception by Commissioner Dawson of the US Bureau of Education, while the Tsimshian "clustered about the flag-staff and sang several hymns in the native vernacular."[26] A Tsimshian chief, Daniel Ne-ash-kum-ack-kem (grandfather of the berry-eater), addressed the government official: "We are told ... that there are no slaves under the flag of England. For a long time our hearts relied upon this as truth ... We now find it is not so."[27]

Other common images in American press coverage included historical groups who had endured similar persecution, such as pilgrims and Acadians, the former having yet another evocative association with US history and nation building. Like the Puritans fleeing religious persecution in Europe, the Tsimshian were willing to give up their ancestral homes to obtain freedom of faith.[28] The latter image of Acadians, directly linking the Tsimshian to the French residents of Nova Scotia, at first glance appears to be simply another jibe at the British – an overt reference to the removal of a people who had a language, culture, and religion different from that of the British colonial authority. However, it may be further evidence of the pervasive influence of Wellcome's book as *The Story of Metlakahtla* was "dedicated to the cause of justice, truth, and humanity" and was accompanied by a quotation from Longfellow's poem about the Acadian expulsion, "Evangeline."[29]

By late autumn 1887, the move itself was being extensively covered by the press in a way that harkened back to the founding of the American colonies. A number of marine vessels were engaged or volunteered to assist in the transport of people and their belongings during the potentially dangerous crossing. The Methodist mission ship *Glad Tidings* had even been involved in towing canoes over a hundred kilometres northward in open waters, with sometimes as many as fifty boats behind it, and it went back and forth several times.[30] Moving day was a grand affair: brass bands played "Yankee Doodle, Hail Columbia, and other patriotic American" tunes, flags were raised, and special songs were composed to invite the people to make the move.[31] Tsimshian chief George Usher travelled back to the original site to call on the people to relocate. In the Tsimshian manner, he reputedly sang in *Sm'algyax* (Coast Tsimshian language) while in his canoe offshore:

> The great chief has come.
> He has gone to our new home.
> Now he sends me to you.
> He bids you come, one and all.
> We shall be slaves no longer.
> The land of freedom has accepted us.
> The flag of the "Boston men" is hoisted
> At the site of a new Metlakahtla.
> It will protect us and our freedom.
> We can worship God in peace.
> We can secure the happiness of our children.
> They will be the freemen of a great nation.
> Come, therefore, one and all.
> Gather your little ones around you.
> Push the canoes from the beach.
> Good wind will fill our sails;
> We will hasten to the land of freedom.[32]

The song expresses themes of emancipation in the "land of freedom," symbolized by the flag of the "Boston men" (the Aboriginal term for Americans, dating from the eighteenth-century maritime fur trade) and references to the United States as their new home. It also contains obvious biblical imagery, which depicts the migration itself as the exodus of God's chosen people to a promised land. Yet, not everyone heeded the song's calling. A hundred or so Metlakatlans opted to stay behind, hence kin and community were now divided by an international border. For descendants today, this division may be the most important part of the story.

Newspapers also often focused on the missionaries who worked among the Tsimshian. Duncan is mentioned in nearly all of the articles and is almost universally represented as having a leading and positive role in events. A full quarter of the clippings paint Duncan as the heroic saviour of the Tsimshian people (112 articles). A mere handful of newspapers (fourteen articles) portray him as the villain of the story, and these overwhelmingly appeared in Canadian papers. In contrast, in about a quarter of all the pieces (109 articles), the Anglican bishop at Metlakatla, Reverend William Ridley, was singled out as a failed missionary among the Tsimshian and was blamed for their decision to leave British Columbia. Descriptions of his role in the affair often represented him in a very unflattering light: "Being a poor imitation or sham Bishop, a creature of mere uniform, his attempt to suspend a real missionary, although only a layman, proved futile."[33]

As historians such as Jean (Usher) Friesen have explored in considerable detail, Duncan was an avid evangelical and was much influenced by the policies of his sponsor organization, the internationally active CMS under the guidance of its honourary secretary Henry Venn.[34] But he was also a man possessed of a strong-willed personality who craved control. When the new bishop for the Anglican Diocese of Caledonia, the Reverend William Ridley, arrived in 1879, a struggle over authority at the mission ensued. Duncan's autocratic style of leadership frequently brought him into conflict with other missionaries and church officials. However, by far his greatest conflict was with Ridley. The clashes between these two individuals had profound effects on Metlakatla and upon the climate of mission work in the area, and the Tsimshian were directly drawn into the antagonism.

Both contemporary accounts from the nineteenth century and many historical interpretations thereafter frame the decision to move from Metlakatla to Alaska within the Duncan-Ridley dispute, making the whole affair linked to what non-Natives wanted. Ridley had been appointed to ensure that the Anglican- and CMS-sponsored missions adhered to current Church of England practices and customs. The bishop reported "an unexpected absence of Christian instruction and privileges in the settlement," including one of the central sacraments of the Church – communion.[35] Duncan disagreed, claiming the use of wine and bread representing the blood and body of Christ would be misunderstood by the recently converted Tsimshian, who might associate it with former pre-Christian practices.[36] Duncan himself refused to accept ordination by the Church and strongly disagreed over matters of formalized ritual during church services.

Hence, by the early 1880s, Duncan broke with both the CMS and the Anglican Church. Much of the newspaper coverage centred on the divisiveness that ensued within the community at Metlakatla. The CMS was dubbed a "heartless corporation," and American writers, perhaps with a dose of sarcasm, quipped: "This is a terrible arraignment of the foremost Foreign Missionary Society in the world, and a dark stain on the 'Christian' government now celebrating the Jubilee of its 'Christian' Queen."[37] The "devil of sectism," "this episcopal or high church absurdity" began when "a church functionary [i.e., Ridley] in London practically drove these converts out of British territory because they would not accept certain forms and dogmas of his church."[38] Rather than "submit to the tyranny of the bishop and his associates," the Metlakatlans were thus "driven from their settlement ... by the mistaken interference of the British Church" headed by a "bigoted bishop."[39]

Yet, as much as it was an issue of religious freedom or personality conflict, the migration of the Metlakatlans in the newspaper discourse was heavily connected to land issues (122 articles). Well over a third of all articles emphasized the "civilized" nature of the Tsimshian (182 articles), who were considered to be especially threatened by the lack of political autonomy and land title. Indeed, the appropriation of Native lands and resources without the extinguishment of Aboriginal title coincided with this turmoil over Christian expression and religious authority.[40]

Land issues were undisputedly a regional concern, apart from their local manifestations at Metlakatla. In the 1880s, the Canadian government laid out reserves for Native peoples on the north coast of the province, through the Indian Reserve Commission. Led by Peter O'Reilly, it visited Tsimshian territory for the first time for this purpose in 1881, when few Tsimshian were actually at home. Facing an immediate and negative response from even those Tsimshian present, O'Reilly returned six additional times in the 1880s and 1890s (in 1882, 1888, 1889, 1891, 1893, and 1896) to revise or reassess the system.[41]

One of the earliest strategies of resistance to this unsatisfactory appropriation of lands by the Crown involved the tack taken by the Metlakatlans, although it was by no means unique to them. They actively removed any survey markers and equipment they could find from their communities and physically drove out the surveyors.[42] They wrote letters and sent representatives to speak directly with DIA officials in Victoria and Ottawa. The Tsimshian eloquently defended their land claims and their freedom from non-Native interference, sometimes by appealing to ostensibly shared Christian values. In 1883, one Tsimshian man reasoned with the government representative that Tsimshian lands were protected under God's law. After carefully eliciting an admission from the government agent that Canadian society was governed according to Christian principles and laws, he argued that Christians should not take land from other Christians.[43] Yet, Tsimshian dissatisfaction remained unaddressed. They lobbied the Canadian federal government in Ottawa, saying that they felt that the provincial government was unresponsive, and then they lobbied the governor general and other representatives of the British Crown in both Canada and England. This land issue found a religious expression in Metlakatla at a place known as Mission Point.

The existence of two churches in Metlakatla – the non-denominational Christian Church of Metlakatla (or Duncan's group, the majority of villagers) and the Anglican Church proper (or the bishop's group) – did little for community harmony; a Christian "love-thy-neighbour" relationship it was not. The schism in the village rapidly developed into a confrontational and occasionally violent conflict. The CMS claimed two acres of the Metlakatla reserve known as Mission Point as "church property." Most Metlakatlans disagreed and argued that the land had always been theirs. In fact, they succeeded in having the community revoke its permission for the Anglicans to even use the land. The pro-Duncan Tsimshian dismantled and then rebuilt the village store a few yards away because it had stood on Mission Point; they also tore down the schoolhouse and prevented the Anglicans from using the big church.

As early as 1882, the bishop, said to have adopted a belligerent stance, announced that a "riot" had broken out and called for the assistance of a gunboat. "Can we give greater proof of the unfitness of Bishop Ridley for the post he was sent to occupy," asked a writer for a US paper, *The Friend,* "than to state that on two if not three occasions, when afraid his flock should proceed to violence in resistance to his authority, he sent for a man-of-war to keep them in check?"[44] The American press had a field day with these kinds of rumours, using them to belittle the Anglican bishop. Ridley "proved to be a firebrand in the community. He punched one or two natives, and went about with a gun as if afraid for his life. He insisted on being called 'My Lord,' and the people, not liking any of this, rebelled when he sought to pre-empt a part of their land for church uses."[45]

The provincial government attempted to defuse the situation by convening an inquiry and sending in Indian agents.[46] Their efforts were all to no avail. The agents were promptly rejected, and the government was forced to try again to calm the situation with a formal investigation and royal commission in 1884. The report, filed by Commissioners Alex E.B. Davie, Henry M. Ball, and A.C. Elliott, emphasized the reluctance of both provincial and federal governments to acknowledge Aboriginal title to land or resources. In 1885, they concluded that land issues (both the recognition of Tsimshian title to all the land and, specifically, to Mission Point were denied), the break with the CMS, and the authority of the village council were the principal causes of the "disquietude."[47]

Both inside and outside British Columbia, Canadian perspectives expressed in the popular press seemed profoundly reactionary. Many Canadians indicated confusion after reading American accounts of land issues, although they agreed with American writers that the religious dispute was the root cause of the Tsimshian exodus. In general, the events of 1887 were viewed as the result of the personality dispute between Ridley and Duncan; Aboriginal protests over the only recently imposed Indian Act and reserve system were ignored. Israel Wood Powell, the superintendent of Indian affairs in British Columbia, frequently wrote to Canadian, and sometimes even American, papers to contribute his interpretation of the events of 1887:

> The charges of ill treatment and injustice to the Indians in question have not the least foundation in fact, and the pretense of raising money from the American people to liberate them from so-called oppression and tyranny is a false one ... No subjects of Her Majesty ... enjoy greater liberty and

protection ... It is a matter of great regret that a number of them have been induced to exile themselves and sacrifice their rights under such flagrant misguidance [i.e., from William Duncan].[48]

Reports that, prior to their departure, the Alaska-bound Metlakatlans removed whatever public and personal property they could from their old village in British Columbia – including the gutting and burning of St. Paul's church (and they may or may not have set other buildings on fire) – spawned curious stories about "the attempt of the Indian tribe recently forced out of British Columbia to steal their church and transport it to Alaska."[49] The Toronto *Mail* quipped, "The Indians must be hard-pressed for a place to worship in when they will steal one."[50] The DIA was alerted that, among the damage, was the symbolically rich "destruction of a large Canadian flag which was presented to the village by this Department, and which was torn and trampled on by the Indians."[51]

The decision regarding Mission Point also did not resolve the issue in the majority of the Metlakatlans' minds. Among the correspondence between DIA officials on the matter are copies of telegrams announcing requisitioned gunboats and a police force late in 1886 with orders to "eject Duncan's Indians from the mission grounds."[52] Indeed, there was another reason for the government to be concerned with the exodus of the Tsimshian to Alaska. DIA officials were well aware of the connection between the migration to Alaska and Aboriginal dissatisfaction over unresolved land claims. On several occasions, other First Nations from the region issued threats that they, too, would leave British Columbia if their concerns over land and resources continued to go unaddressed by the government. In the wake of another inquiry on the north coast in 1887, commissioners Clement Cornwall and J.B. Planta were told by one Port Simpson representative who was unhappy with the reserve system and the imposition of the Indian Act: "We have only one way left after our patient waiting, and that is to follow our brethren into Alaska."[53] To Canadians, after the Metlakatlan migration it was clear that British Columbia had lost an industrious and thriving community. Government representatives visiting the original Metlakatla less than a year after the migration lamented that all that remained was a "shadow of Old Metlakatla," abandoned except for a mere hundred residents, "dreary in the extreme."[54]

DIA officials making their annual reports to the government of Canada laid the blame squarely upon Duncan's shoulders, again denying the Tsimshian activism in this matter. It was "his guiding hand" behind the "hostile attitude assumed by his followers, and in the many rebellious acts against law and order" that "have disturbed and agitated both settlers and Indians in that section of the country."[55] Surveyors operating in the region certainly blamed missionaries for growing Tsimshian demands for recognition of their land title. "I am clearly of the opinion that Mr. Duncan of Metlakahtla," wrote government surveyor Samuel Parker Tuck, "is largely and perhaps wholly responsible for their present position and the unfriendly action on their part. It is he, I feel confidently, who tells them they will be protected under English laws in preventing a survey of the Reserve and that they owe no allegiance to Canada and its laws."[56]

The disloyalty theme also reverberated in the insistence that the migration decision, once made, was a final one. In 1888, DIA officials proposed a prohibition against Tsimshian returning to Old Metlakatla in order to keep them from "enjoying any of the privileges which they previously enjoyed in connection with lands or waters within British territory, unless they shall return to and take up their permanent residence upon the Reserve at Metlakahtla by the first of May next."[57] This reiterates the government's denial of any pre-existing Aboriginal title or rights within the region.

The larger context of Aboriginal/non-Aboriginal relations in western Canada must have had some bearing on the federal and provincial governments' positions. In the 1880s, plains First Nations were in crisis and were extremely dissatisfied with Canada's lack of commitment to the treaties it had just signed with them in the preceding decade. The Métis resistance that erupted in Saskatchewan in 1885 precipitated the then largest mobilization of troops in Canada's history. The spectre of similar unrest in British Columbia informed the governments' responses in the North Coast region.[58]

British perspectives on the controversy at Metlakatla and the move to Alaska were mixed. Duncan's lobbying in London, England, in 1886 had garnered the attention of the Aborigines Protection Society (APS), which expressed concern that the Tsimshian may not have received the same treatment afforded other Aboriginal peoples within Canada. In a letter to Canada's high commissioner, the APS remarked upon the "departure from the system which in other parts of the Dominion has made the Indians loyal and contented subjects of the Crown" through settled land claims and treaty rights. "We are informed that although the Aborigines of British Columbia are not a conquered race their rights in the soil are virtually ignored and that the local Government claim to exercise supreme control over all the lands of the province."[59] Moreover, the APS chastised the Canadian government for not taking action to address Aboriginal concerns over land issues resulting from the Reserve Commission. Other English writers concurred. An article in the magazine, *The British Friend,* raged against the injustice regarding land title: "The very land of this inhospitable country – land occupied by their ancestors for centuries before Columbus discovered America – was claimed from them – land as certainly theirs by moral right as that of any acres inherited by any of us in England."[60]

In response, both DIA authorities and the Committee of the Privy Council of Canada reassured the APS that surveying the region was vital to the protection of Aboriginal rights: "It is to be regretted that either Mr. Duncan or any one else should endeavour to induce the Indians to contend for the exclusive ownership of the soil of British Columbia. That Claim has never been recognized by the provincial authorities and it is quite certain that it will be resisted by both the Government and the Legislature of the Province."[61]

The British-based CMS, however, seemed to side with the provincial and federal governments' opinion rather than with those of Duncan and the majority of Metlakatlans. In response to the 1884 royal commission and the turmoil over Mission Point, in 1886, the CMS intervened with its own inquiry, reporting that Duncan's stubborn attitude precluded any sort of peaceful resolution at the mission.[62] It concluded that, with the Canadian federal government "as prompt dispenser of justice, as settler of their disputes, and preserver of the peace, insuring [sic] to all the Indians, freedom of trade and freedom of religious views and worship, there will be a very fair hope of their rapid advancement in social and spiritual life, and the present difficulties will pass away."[63]

While both the APS and the CMS felt obliged to keep up a correspondence with Canadian authorities in order to clarify matters, the United States felt no compunction to report to the Canadian DIA to solicit its opinion, being secure in the impression that Duncan and Wellcome had provided an accurate account of events.[64] Much of the Canadian response in the popular press attempted to challenge the misinformation in the United States that seemed to inform the opinions of government officials and ordinary citizens alike. The *Ottawa Citizen* declared that "there seems to have been a frightful amount of misrepresentation resorted to induce the Indians of Metlakahtla to remove to Alaska" and that often what had appeared in American papers was "without a particle of truth."[65] Compelled to retell the narrative without criticism of Canadian "Indian" policy, the *Montreal Witness* explained that the Tsimshian would surely return "home":

> There is a certain pathos about Metlakahtla, a village ... in ruins ... And all this is because the missionary, Mr. Duncan, who could so well bring the Indians to a higher life, could not himself tread the highest path of complete self-sacrifice, did not restrain the people from violence against his Bishop and the Church, fell himself into schism, and exiled nearly all of his people from their native land ... His people come down from Alaska to get work, although too proud to confess they are one by one binding fresh interests on Skeena and Naas Rivers, even a few are returning quietly to Metlakahtla.[66]

"The trouble is entirely of religious origin," said writers in the *Toronto Mail*, "the Indians have been the victims of an unfortunate quarrel over a religious matter."[67]

Victims or not, the attempted recreation of the Tsimshian village outside of their traditional homelands and under a new colonial/territorial regime was not an easy one for the Tsimshian. And the migration was not necessarily one that involved a unified community. If we can get at any sort of Tsimshian perspective through the public record, separate from Duncan, Ridley, or the DIA, it seems that the Tsimshian connected the move to Alaska to a loss of power over their everyday affairs and to the land issue, both of which had become acute concerns for First Nations throughout the region by the 1880s. To many Tsimshian and their neighbours, this was nothing short of outright theft. As one Metlakatlan resident told a visiting official:

> White people carry two pockets in the trousers in which they keep their money ... the two rivers Skeena and Nass are our two pockets where we obtain our food ... white men are now putting their hands into our two pockets and robbing us and we hope you will plead for us among the white chiefs.[68]

Most nineteenth-century sources place the ultimate decision in the missionary Duncan's hands. Yet, while Duncan clearly had enormous influence over his flock, the decision to leave a homeland the Tsimshian had inhabited since time immemorial could not have been one simply "imposed" on them. I agree entirely with historian Brian Hosmer's assessment: "This is an important point, for as much as Duncan sought to disconnect his charges from their former lives, the Metlakatlans retained a sense of identity as Natives."[69] Rather than exclusively viewing the motivations for migration as being solely in the hands of non-Native missionaries, one can certainly argue that the same quality that made Duncan unwilling to share leadership of the village with other mission officials also brought him into conflict with older Tsimshian power structures. While the majority of the community did make the move to Alaska, some – just over a hundred – stayed behind. A split between a significant minority of hereditary chiefs and their families reveals Duncan's ultimate failure either to create a unified Christian community or to integrate Tsimshian social roles. Still another group of Old Metlakatlans went south instead of north. A group of Southern Tsimshian, or Gitk'a'ata ("People of the Cane"), Christians had converted and moved to live at Metlakatla until Duncan's departure in 1887. Many chose not to follow Duncan to Alaska and returned to their traditional homeland, where they founded Hartley Bay as a Christian settlement.[70]

Again, this speaks to Tsimshian decisions and priorities and argues against seeing missionary agendas as the sole factor behind the move.

Tsimshian discussions of the meaning and motivation behind the 1887 migration entered the public written record well before that date through testimonies published with commission reports and through reproductions of their letters and petitions in newspapers.[71] While matters for the Tsimshian seem to have developed to a crisis point that precipitated the migration to Alaska (e.g., in 1886 the arrest of eight Metlakatlans for destroying property and obstructing survey work for laying out reserves), tensions had been building since the early 1880s. Indeed, there had been a long protest "against our land being given away to any white people without our consent."[72] Metlakatlans had rejected the authority of both the Anglican Church and the Canadian government (by disallowing surveyors, Indian agents, or any implementation of the federal Indian Act with respect to governance or land).

As one writer to the editor reminded the readers of the *New York Tribune*, "It occurs to me that a thousand or more civilized Indians might be allowed to form their own opinion."[73] Indeed, whether attributed to specific Tsimshian chiefs or simply to "the people of Metlakathla," one of the most common authors voicing Tsimshian opinion throughout the 1880s was Duncan's right-hand man David Leask. Leask had been born to a Tsimshian woman and Orkneyman who worked for the HBC. Certainly one of Duncan's protégés in both Metlakatlas, Leask was a school teacher, a father, a bookkeeper at the Metlakatla store, an elder in the church, and the secretary for the village council. It was in his capacity as council secretary that his words most frequently entered the historical documentary record, and donations from American sympathizers were often sent directly to him. In reply to comments made by Powell that reserve lands provide "exclusive use" rights for Aboriginal communities, Leask wrote back unequivocally claiming an Aboriginal right to the lands:

> We own these lands and are still occupying them and we are using them more than our forefathers did. If the Government has already claimed our lands, we ask you again, does the Queen's law allow the property of the weak and poor to be taken by the stronger party? We were not told by our forefathers that they had sold their land to the Government and therefore we cannot surrender it.[74]

Of note is Leask's reference to a lack of oral evidence that might have substantiated non-Native claims of land ownership and his reference to the protection Aboriginal peoples should have been afforded under the "Queen's law." In another letter sent to Powell a week later, Leask confirms that the religious dispute did have a bearing on community disunity, and he suggests that it was only those who stayed behind who were the real pawns of missionary agendas: "We do not blame our brethren who separated from us [by not joining Duncan's independent church] for being the main source of the trouble but rather the Agents of the Church Missionary Society, who have drawn them away from us and made them do what they are doing."[75] However, the government's attempt not only to steal Aboriginal lands but also to impose the Indian Act would, as Leask so eloquently put it, "be like trying to put a small pair of shoes on feet too large for them. It would only cramp our feet and prevent us from walking as far as we did without such regulations."[76]

In the late 1950s, William Leask (New Metlakatlan and son of David Leask) recalled Duncan's actions and the sequence of events prior to the migration. Leask had been a young boy when he had accompanied the original party of Tsimshian who had been sent to scout out a new location for the community on Annette Island.[77] His recollections echo those same concerns expressed by his father over three-quarters of a century earlier:

> He went down to Victoria to ... to settle up about this land, this dispute about the land, and some troubles. And from there the government won't ... give what Father Duncan wants, and so he goes right on down to Washington, American side, and from Washington he came back. But he arrived in Alaska – New Metlakatla, Alaska – on the 7th of August and he came from Washington with the Superintendent of Education. This was an American, ya, and he was the man that gave the flag to be hoisted up right on the beach at New Metlakatla.[78]

But of course, the process involved more than simply choosing a new flag to raise on the village's beach. Tsimshian Rod Davis remembers making the move to New Metlakatla as a child. It was not simply the freedom and land that attracted them: they also felt that, in British Columbia, their access to resources was being endangered through the recent laying out of reserves, the lack of treaties, and an ever-expanding non-Aboriginal-owned commercial fishery within their traditional territory:

> When we landed in Metlakatla, Alaska, now, at that time it was a nice beautiful day. How well I remember that day; it was bright and sunny, and there was a lot of fish. We camped at one of the creeks on Saturday night just back of Metlakatla now, and we spent that Sunday there ... at the mouth of the Puzzahin [?] Creek, and in those days that creek was just loaded with salmon, pink salmon. There must have been millions of them in that creek. How well I remember.[79]

In a 1959 radio show on Metlakatla, CBC interviewer John Must gave the first word to Tsimshian (an Old Metlakatla resident) Peter Ryan. When asked why the Tsimshian moved to Alaska, Ryan made it clear that religious matters and/or personality disputes were secondary to land issues pertaining to territory marked by the ancestors' continuous use of resources on land and water:

> I don't know who planned it, that they should lay out land for Metlakatla people. They – Duncan – gave orders to his people to stop the surveyors to lay out land for. They had an idea that the whole, all around Rupert, between Simpson and halfway to Skeena river, that it belong to them. And it did belong to them, all in the summer when they go to fix their salmons. They had several camps on the Skeena.[80]

Similarly, Rod Davis discusses the significance of land rights and the migration for the Tsimshian people as a struggle that Aboriginal people still wage:

> Every chance I get ... when I get over there on the Canadian side ... my friends over there at Port Simpson, Hartley Bay, Kitkatla, they ask me ... they brought up this question when I'm over there, and I always encourage them to demand their right before the white people came in here. We're not given a break at all. That's one of the reasons why we left Old Metlakatla, just because we were deprived of our right mostly ... I know it's something deeper than that too, but it's the land argument that I'm talking about. We're not treated right. In this country, we're not treated right.[81]

It is ironic that, in order to protest the appropriation of their traditional homelands, the Tsimshian had to abandon them, move to another country, and relocate within another Aboriginal group's (Tlingit) territory. Over the first winter at New Metlakatla, Alaska, in 1887-88, totem poles marked the landscape at the Tlingit winter village of *T'ak'waan,* decaying but still standing alongside the newly erected Tsimshian cabins and tents.

Taking the events of the entire decade together, strife in Metlakatla in the 1880s led to the desire to reinvigorate the community, just as Duncan had sought to do in 1862, when his first fifty converts made the move to create Metlakatla. As Jean (Usher) Friesen puts it, "internal disintegration of the Metlakatla system thus gave a strong impetus to a new utopian movement in which a renewed idealism could recapture that which had been lost at old Metlakatla."[82] A case in point is the ambiguous information derived from anthropologist Viola Garfield's interview with Tsimshian Herbert Murchison in the 1930s. The loyalty to the missionary's work is apparent in Murchison's insistence that Duncan had won the hearts of the people primarily through his religious message: when "Duncan paid attention to business – people drifted," he informed Garfield.[83] Murchison also described the divisive effect of the Ridley-Duncan dispute on his community at Old Metlakatla. In regard to the actual decision to move in 1887, he pointed to Duncan's deception and the importance that the Tsimshian be seen as "civilized" Christians: "People really moved to New M[etlakatla] because Duncan misinterpreted. Surveyors working at Prince Rupert. Are coming here to survey this town and put you on the Indian reserve. Reserve is a disgrace, fenced out from civilizations. They went out and stopped the surveyor and made them mad."[84]

Like the other Tsimshian sources previously mentioned, Murchison also highlighted Native concerns for securing an adequate land base in the new territory for future generations. Here, Duncan was a mere spectator on the sidelines:

Robert Hewson ... [w]aited to buy land in Alaska so gov. would not try to boss them. Raised $1,300 to buy 1,000 acres of land. Hewson and Broth. sent to Victoria to see Duncan. He went to Wash. D.C. Squatters rights to land. Given to Annette Isl. You understand our need before [?] later times – mineral 'n other things will want to be taken. That's the reason we don't want grant. Money papers of whites will take away the land. $40,000 raised in Wash. D.C. by Christians for him. [85]

The lure of material benefit was tied to the story of the move to New Metlakatla. Murchison told Garfield that Duncan made specific promises to the migrants: "Everyone who moves from here from Old M to New M will receive a bucket full of silver dollars. so people packed up. Tore down sawmill and ... brot [sic] store goods over 300 or so went back when they found Duncan did not intend to give them the dollars."[86] Historian Brian Hosmer's reading of Tsimshian identity in the 1880s links it to economic change, which equated political independence and cultural survival with material security.[87] Attacks on Duncan, Hosmer argues, were interpreted by the Tsimshian as "threats to their hopes for the future. When this happened they mobilized and articulated a Native-centered ideology that went far beyond the loyalty to their white leader." This was an ideology that meshed with Aboriginal concerns over rights to land and resources throughout the region.[88]

Today, the two Metlakatlas remain fragments of the divided community they had once been. In 1932, some members of the two villages reconciled on religious matters. After Duncan's death, a number of New Metlakatlans returned to the Anglican Church by joining its American counterpart in the region, St. Elizabeth Episcopal Church of Ketchikan. Representatives of the congregation of St. Elizabeth visited Old Metlakatla in the winter of 1932 and presented the community with a series of resolutions, offers of friendship, and reconciliation: "This Committee wishes to express its sincere sorrow and contrition for this long-standing separation and misunderstanding in the tribe and its willingness, yea, eagerness to do all in its power to terminate this un-Christian situation as soon as possible."[89] The visitors were reportedly well received, and the gesture was welcomed by the Anglican congregation of St. Paul's Church at Old Metlakatla.

However, in terms of the Aboriginal concerns over land and resources, neither community has triumphed. Canadian Citizenship, in 1960, did not resolve their territorial claims or demands for the recognition of their autonomy. The Tsimshian of British Columbia have no land treaties, although their neighbours, the Nisga'a, signed the twentieth century's sole Aboriginal claims settlement in British Columbia. The Tsimshian in Alaska, the only indigenous inhabitants in the state to reside on a federal Indian reservation (which had been created by an Act of Congress on 30 March 1891 and was expanded by presidential decree to include surrounding waters in 1916), annually celebrate their "Founders' Day" on 7 August. Government officials continue to recognize their "tradition of independence, perseverance, and hospitality," and the pioneering spirit of (New) Metlakatla, "one of the state's oldest established communities."[90] Yet, in 1971, the Alaskan Tsimshian opted out of the Alaska Native Claims Settlement Act, which terminated Aboriginal land claims and hunting and fishing rights in the state but created 44 million acres of "Indian Country," which, in principle at least, was to be managed by Alaska Natives. Ironically, their contemporary self-designator – *Ta'gwaan* (*T'ak'waan, Tugwan*), the Tlingit name for the village that had existed on the land before the Tsimshian resettlement – reminds them that they did not relocate to empty land but, rather, to a place with a prior Aboriginal presence.

Whether represented as pilgrims searching for religious freedom and/or revolutionaries finding solace under a new flag (as American newspapers would have it) or as missionary-led dupes responding to a church schism and personality conflict (as many Canadian newspapers argued), historians should be wary of how these perspectives belie Native interpretations. Land and resource rights, along with struggles for political and cultural autonomy, remain central issues for the Tsimshian regardless of "the flag they chose" in 1887.

Acknowledgments

Earlier versions of this chapter were presented at the Western Historical Association Conference, Colorado Springs, Colorado, October 2002, and at the Native-Newcomer Relations Conference, Saskatoon, Saskatchewan, May 2003. Thanks go to my research assistant Melinda Nosal-Buzak for help with the hundreds of newspaper clippings and manuscript sources in Duncan's Papers and RG 10. "Choose Your Flag" is taken from an 1887 newspaper editorial in the *Victoria Times*, n.d., as quoted in Peter Murray, *The Devil and Mr. Duncan: A History of the Two Metlakatlas* (Victoria: Sono Nis Press, 1985), 196.

Notes

1 Arthur J. Ray, *Indians in the Fur Trade: Their Role as Hunters, Trappers, and Middlemen in the Lands Southwest of Hudson Bay, 1660-1870* (Toronto: University of Toronto Press, 1974).

2 Susan Neylan, "'The Heavens are Changing': Nineteenth-Century Protestant Missionization on the North Pacific Coast" (PhD diss., University of British Columbia, 1999).

3 Contemporary nineteenth-century sources like newspapers or Wellcome's book stated the number of individuals who moved to Alaska in August 1887 as 823. However, the list held by the Anglican Church identifies approximately 716 names. See newspaper clippings files, William Duncan Papers, University of British Columbia Library, AW1 R2597, reel 14 (M-2328), files 12840-12981; Anglican Church of Canada, "List of People who moved to New Metlakatla, Alaska, 1887," Anglican Archives of the Diocese of Caledonia, Prince Rupert, BC, 96-03. John Arctander assured his readers that "quite 823 of the 948 constituting the population of the village left that Fall for New Metlakahtla." See John W. Arctander, *The Apostle of Alaska: The Story of William Duncan of Metlakahtla* (Toronto: Fleming H. Revell Co., 1909), 295. Regardless of the exact number, there was some back-and-forth movement for several years following the initial migration.

4 Henry S. Wellcome, *The Story of Metlakahtla* (New York: Saxon and Co., 1887).

5 William Henry Collison, *In the Wake of the War Canoe*, ed. Charles Lillard (Victoria: Sono Nis Press, 1981 [1915]), 8 (see also the illustration of the church between pages 98 and 99).

6 I.W. Powell, Indian Superintendent, Annual Report, dated 31 October 1883, *Sessional Papers 4: Department of Indian Affairs Annual Reports, 1883* (Victoria: Queen's Printer, 1884), 106.

7 Arctander, *Apostle of Alaska*, 290. J.D. Bluett-Duncan is no relation of William Duncan.

8 Thanks to Ken Campbell for clarification and current spellings: *T'ak'waan* for BC Tsimshian, *Ta'gwaan* for Alaskan Tsimshian, and *Tugwan* or *Taquan* as anglicized versions of the name.

9 William Duncan Papers, UBC Library, AW1 R2547, reel 14 (LAC M-2328), newspaper clippings files, pp. 12840-12981.

10 Department of Indian Affairs Papers, LAC, RG 10, vol. 3606, file 2959, pt. 1-4.

11 C.L. Higham, *Noble, Wretched, and Redeemable: Protestant Missionaries to the Indians in Canada and the United States, 1820-1900* (Calgary/Albuquerque: University of Calgary Press/University of New Mexico Press, 2000), 144, 149-50, 200.

12 His positive reception included several missionary bodies (e.g., the Board of Indian Commissioners), and he was well received at the annual meetings of the Conference of Missionary Boards and Indian Rights Associations. Wellcome, *Story of Metlakatla,* app. Also reproduced in Phylis Bowman, *Metlakahtla: The Holy City* (Chilliwack: Sunrise Printing, 1983), 86-93.

13 American-born Wellcome was trained as a pharmacist and became a leading entrepreneur in the expanding field of pharmaceuticals in the late nineteenth century. His London-based business (with his partner, Silas Burroughs) specialized in compressed medicine tablets. Wellcome soon became a wealthy man and was the recipient of numerous honours over the course of his lifetime, including a knighthood in 1932. However, medicine was not his only calling. Wellcome had been raised in a deeply religious environment, the son of a minister, and his interest in religion combined with a passion for collecting (while specializing in books and artefacts relating to medicine, he also had a fascination with the Northwest Coast of North America). Biographical information on Wellcome from "History about the Burroughs-Wellcome Fund," http://www.bwfund.org/about_us/history.html; "Sir Henry Wellcome," Egypt Centre, University of Wales, Swansea, http://www.swan.ac.uk/egypt/infosheet/Wellcome.htm; and the Wellcome Trust, Wellcome Library for the History and Understanding of Medicine, http://archives.wellcome.ac.uk.

14 Monica Leigh Pastor, "Imaging the Metlakatlas: Shifting Representations of a Northwest Coast Mission Community" (MA thesis, University of British Columbia, 1999), 36.

15 *Brooklyn Times*, 25 June 1887.

16 *Newburyport Herald* (Massachusetts), 14 January 1888.

17 Peter Murray, *The Devil and Mr. Duncan: A History of the Two Metlakatlas* (Victoria: Sono Nis Press, 1985), 196.

18 *Philadelphia Times,* 21 June 1887.

19 *St. Louis Southwestern Methodist,* 25 June 1887; *Ann Arbor Courier,* 29 June 1887; and *Dayton Christian World,* 30 June 1887, quoting phrases from Wellcome's book; and *Brooklyn Daily Eagle,* 17 January 1887.

20 *Boston Watchman,* 8 September 1887; *New York Standard,* 16 July 1887; and *Mankato Register,* 30 June 1887.

21 *New York Herald,* 14 January 1887; *New York World,* 30 June 1887; and *Albany Argus,* 19 June 1887.

22 *Rural New Yorker,* n.d. (1887); *New York Daily Tribune,* 23 December 1886.

23 *Rochester Express,* 20 June 1887.

24 "A Flag for the Indians," *New York Times,* 16 June 1887; *Philadelphia Press,* 16 June 1887, reprinted in "The Story of Metlakahtla," in *Oil, Paint, and Drug Reporter* (New York), 26 June 1887.

25 *Mankato Daily Free Press,* evening ed., 20 June 1887.

26 *Washington Post,* 26 September 1887.

27 Ibid., also quoted in the *Oregonian* (Portland), 28 August 1887.

28 This is also an observation made by Monica Pastor, who analyzed the images presented in Wellcome's book in similar terms, "to arouse empathy and identification with an American audience." Pastor, "Imaging the Metlakatlas," 43-44.

29 Wellcome, *Story of Metlakahtla,* xii.

30 Entries for 26 August-20 September 1887, Logbook of the *Glad Tidings,* in Robert Clyde Scott Papers, BCA, Add. Mss. 1299, box 2. It might be interesting to speculate about the Methodist motivation in these actions. Was this merely an act of Christian charity, manifesting a genuine desire to aid the relations of those whom the Methodists also missionized? Reverend Thomas Crosby, Duncan's key rival for so many years in the area, recorded in his memoirs that the move was on account of "serious trouble with the officials of his Church and with the government." See Thomas Crosby, *Up and Down the North Pacific Coast by Canoe and Mission Ship* (Toronto: Missionary Society of the Methodist Church and the Young Peoples Forward Movement, 1914), 359. On the one hand, the decimation of the Anglicans' largest mission on the north coast was undoubtedly advantageous for other denominations like the Methodists, and it certainly gave a boost to the morale of missionaries who had struggled in the competition for souls, which had characterized the work in the region for decades. On the other hand, the tangential Methodist participation in the Metlakatla migration may point to solidarity among missionaries in the region who viewed the recent imposition of the Indian Act and the reserve system not only as an intrusion into their domains but also as an affront to Aboriginal land and resource rights, which they supported. It is worth noting that missionaries were banned from reserve commissions in the 1880s by the government for what it regarded as "interference."

31 *Worcester Daily Spy* (Mass.), 3 December 1887.

32 Arctander, *Apostle of Alaska,* 293. Also quoted in Bowman, *Metlakahtla,* 137.

33 *New York Age,* 22 October 1887.

34 Jean Usher (Friesen), *William Duncan of Metlakatla: A Victorian Missionary in British Columbia,* Publications in History no. 5 (Ottawa: National Museum of Man, 1974).

35 Eugene Stock, *The History of the Church Missionary Society* (London: Church Missionary Society, 1899), 3:251.

36 Most historians suggest that Duncan believed the Tsimshian would relate the sacrament to rituals related to the *Xgyedmhalaayt,* or Human-Eating Dancers Society. *Xgyedmhalaayt* is widely translated as the Cannibal Dancers, which is incorrect. The biting and eating of human flesh that characterized their performances was done by non-human spirits who used humans as vessels (i.e., the human vessels were not the eaters and never digested human flesh).

37 The *Oregonian* (Portland), 12 February 1888; and *New York Philanthropist,* 14 July 1887.

38 *Chicago Christian Cynosure,* 23 June 1887; *Detroit Herald,* 23 June 1887; and *San Francisco Argonaut,* 16 July 1887.

39 *New York World,* 15 December 1887; *San Francisco Call,* 9 January 1888. "Bigoted bishop" was a favourite phrase in the American press, one that again echoed Wellcome. For example,

see: *Rochester Morning Herald,* 13 June 1887; *Chicago Tribune,* 12 June 1887; and *Portland Transcript* (Maine), 20 June 1887.

40 Robin Fisher, *Contact and Conflict: Indian and European Relations in British Columbia, 1774-1890* (Vancouver: UBC Press, 1992 [1977]), 205.

41 For a discussion of O'Reilly's work, see Kenneth Brealey, "Travels from Point Ellice: Peter O'Reilly and the Indian Reserve System in British Columbia," *BC Studies* 115/16 (1997/98): 180-236.

42 This was by no means a unique action. First Nations of British Columbia actively opposed encroachments on their lands in a myriad of ways. For an overview of Native land claims in British Columbia and First Nations resistance, see Paul Tennant, *Aboriginal People and Politics: The Indian Land Question in British Columbia, 1849-1989* (Vancouver: UBC Press, 1990); and Cole Harris, *Making Native Space: Colonialism, Resistance, and Reserves in British Columbia* (Vancouver: UBC Press, 2002).

43 "Testimony of Arthur Wellington Clah," Report of the Meeting of Port Simpson Indians with Indian Agent J.W. MacKay, 8 December 1883, LAC, RG 10, vol. 3818, file 57837, p. 2.

44 *The Friend,* 2 January 1888.

45 Baltimore *Commercial Advertiser,* 30 November 1887.

46 It sent Agent Elliot, then Agent J.W. MacKay, to no avail (Indian agents were rejected outright not only by Metlakatlans but also by their Tsimshian neighbours at Port Simpson/Lax Kw'alaams). Indeed, no Indian agent was appointed to the region again until 1887, when Charles Todd assumed control over the new North West Coast Agency and was posted at Old Metlakatla.

47 British Columbia, *Metlakatlah Inquiry 1884: Report of the Commissioners together with Evidence* (Victoria: Richard Wolfenden, Government Printer, 1885), 133.

48 I.W. Powell, Superintendent of Indian Affairs for British Columbia, "The Metlakathlans," (in response to American newspaper reports, particularly those published in the Philadelphia *Ledger* throughout November 1887), *Victoria Daily Times,* 16 December 1887.

49 *San Francisco Chronicle,* 22 October 1887; another example can be found in the *Chicago Times,* 11 November 1887.

50 *Toronto Mail,* 28 October 1887.

51 L. Vankoughnet, Superintendent General of Indian Affairs, "Memorandum to the Deputy Minister, 11 July 1890," typescript (14 April 1910), LAC, RG 10, vol. 3606, file 2959, pt. 3.

52 J.W. Powell, Telegram to Sir John A. Macdonald, 22 October 1886, LAC, RG 10, vol. 3606, file 2959, pt. 2.

53 Clement Cornwall and J.B. Planta, Commissioners, Special Appendix no. 2, Annual Report of the Department of Indian Affairs, *Sessional Papers,* no. 15 (Ottawa: Maclean, Roger and Co., 1888), civ.

54 Clement J. Cornwall and J.B. Planta, *Report of the 1887 Commission Appointed to Enquire into the Condition of the Indians of the North-West Coast* (Victoria: Richard Wolfenden, Government Printer, 1888), 3. Also reproduced in Canada, Annual Report of the Department of Indian Affairs, *Sessional Papers* (Ottawa: Maclean, Rogers, and Co., 1888), special appendix no. 2, p. xcviii.

55 I.W. Powell, Annual Report for the Department of Indian Affairs, 26 November 1887, *Sessional Papers* (Ottawa: Maclean, Rogers, and Co., 1888), 133-35.

56 S.P. Tuck, Letter to I.W. Powell, Superintendent of Indian Affairs in BC, 6 September 1886, LAC, RG 10, vol. 3606, file 2959, pt. 2.

57 W. White, Superintendent General of Indian Affairs, Letter to Privy Council of Canada, 5 January 1888, LAC, RG 10, vol. 3606, file 2959, pt. 2.

58 In the 1884 Metlakatlah Inquiry, several times the commissioners reiterated their fears that land claims in the region were far from settled: "[G]enerally ... the Naas Indians and the Skeena Indians have been moved to take the stand they have regarding lands, by reason of the example set by Metlakahtlah; and while expressing this opinion, the Commissioners do not forget Lord Dufferin's utterances, and the communication of them to the Indians. Disaffection has also extended to the Queen Charlotte Islands." See British Columbia, *Metlakatlah Inquiry 1884,* 135. The mention of "Lord Dufferin's utterances" refers to a speech made by Frederick Temple Blackwood, the first marquis of Dufferin, the then governor

general of Canada, who, in 1876, visited British Columbia and (among other places) Tsimshian territory, where he called for the recognition of Aboriginal rights in the province.

59 R. Fowler and F.W. Chesson of the Aborigines Protection Society, Letter to Sir Charles Tupper, High Commissioner of Canada, 22 July 1886, LAC, RG 10, vol. 3606, file 2959, pt. 2, no. 31970.

60 *The British Friend* 45, 12 (1 December 1887).

61 John J. McGee, Clerk of the Committee of the Privy Council, Letter to Sir John A. Macdonald, Superintendent General of Indian Affairs in Canada, 10 November 1886, LAC, RG 10, vol. 3606, file 2959, pt. 2. This letter reported to the prime minister (and also to the high commissioner in London) the substance of the discussion from the preceding summer between the high commissioner for Canada in London, Sir Charles Tupper, and the APS. The direct correspondence from Tupper to the APS could not be located.

62 Church Missionary Society, with General Touch and Rev. W. R. Blackett, *Report of the Deputation to Metlakatla* (London: n.p., 1886).

63 G. Mitchinson, Major General and Lay Secretary of the CMS, letter to Sir John A. Macdonald, 19 August 1886, LAC, RG 10, vol. 3606, file 2959, pt. 2.

64 The correspondence between DIA officials in Canada alludes to the lack of consultation with the Americans while Duncan was lobbying for a land grant. See, for example, L. Vankoughnet, Deputy Superintendent General of Indian Affairs, to Sir John A. Macdonald, Superintendent General of Indian Affairs in Canada, 11 March 1887, LAC, RG 10, vol. 3606, file 2959, pt. 3.

65 *Ottawa Citizen*, 26 November 1887.

66 *Montreal Daily Witness*, 11 September 1888.

67 *Toronto Mail*, 22 September and 15 November 1887.

68 Samuel Pelham, "Speeches by the Indians to Admiral Prevost," 22 January 1878, Letterbook no. 2, William Duncan Papers, reel M-2321, file 8883, pp. 171-79. As quoted in Brian C. Hosmer, "'White Men Are Putting Their Hands into Our Pockets': Metlakatla and the Struggle for Resource Rights in British Columbia, 1862-1887," *Alaska History* 8, 2 (1993): 193.

69 Hosmer, "White Men," 16.

70 Kenneth Campbell, "Hartley Bay, British Columbia: A History" in *The Tsimshian: Images of the Past; Views for the Present*, ed. Margaret Seguin (Anderson), 3-10 (Vancouver: UBC Press, 1993).

71 It is worth noting that these very issues were frequently discussed by First Nations and that, in referring here to the "public written record," I mean in addition to what was preserved in the public oral record kept by the Tsimshian themselves.

72 "Women of Metlakatlah" (Sarah Neashumachkem, Lucy Spencer, Barbarre Lachteethsl, and 264 others), Letter to the Commissioners Alex Davie, Henry Ball, and A.C. Elliott, *Metlakatlah Inquiry, 1884*, app., lxxxii.

73 *New York Tribune*, 28 January 1888.

74 David Leask, Secretary of Metlakatla Village Council, to I.W. Powell, Superintendent for Indian Affairs in BC, 24 November 1883, LAC, RG 10, vol. 3606, file 2959, pt. 4.

75 David Leask, Secretary of Metlakatla Village Council, Letter to I.W. Powell, Superintendent for Indian Affairs in BC, 30 November 1883, LAC, RG 10, vol. 3606, file 2959, pt. 4.

76 David Leask, Secretary of Metlakatla Village Council, Letter to J.W. McKay, Indian Agent, 30 November 1883, LAC, RG 10, vol. 3606, file 2959, pt. 4.

77 Bowman, *Metlakahtla*, 137.

78 William Leask (Tsimshian), interviewed by John Must for "The Story of Metlakatla." Recorded in 1959, Prince Rupert City and Regional Archives, Tape no. 170/CD 65.

79 Rod Davis, oral interview with Mrs. Robert Tomlinson, n.d. (1959?), BCA, tape 1238, track 1.

80 Peter Ryan (Tsimshian), interviewed by John Must for "The Story of Metlakatla," recorded in 1959, Prince Rupert City and Regional Archives, tape no. 170/CD 65.

81 Rod Davis and Mrs. Robert Tomlinson, oral interview, n.d. (1959?), BCA, tape 1238, track 1.

82 Usher, *William Duncan*, 135.

83 Viola Garfield, Interview with Herbert Murchison, 27 June 1932, Viola Garfield Papers, Special Collections, University of Washington Library, Field-notebooks, accession no. 2027-

72-25, box 7, fol. 11, vol. 3, p. 178. While Garfield's notebooks are comprehensive with regard to her recording of interviews, they are not necessarily accurate representations of the interviewees. These were not always verbatim accounts, and undoubtedly the information recorded was filtered through Garfield or her interpreter, William Beynon, who frequently worked with her.

84 Ibid., 182-83.

85 Ibid., 183-84.

86 Ibid., 184.

87 Brian C. Hosmer, *American Indians in the Marketplace: Persistence and Innovation among the Menominees and Metlakatlans, 1870-1920* (Lawrence: University Press of Kansas, 1999), 180.

88 Hosmer, "White Men," 16.

89 "The Great Reconciliation Takes Place at Metlakatla," *North British Columbia News* 88 (April 1932): 111.

90 State of Alaska, executive proclamation declaring Founder's Day in Metlakatla, by Governor Tony Knowles, 5 August 2002. The brief historical sketch included in this proclamation completely excludes the twenty-five-year history of the community in British Columbia and makes no mention of prior Tlingit occupancy at Metlakatla's new site.

10

Gitxsan Law and Settler Disorder: The Skeena "Uprising" of 1888

R.M. Galois

One of the characteristics of Skip Ray's long and distinguished career has been his willingness to make his academic expertise available to the needs of First Nations, particularly in the realm of litigation. Such excursions, in turn, have helped to shape both his and wider academic research agendas. I became aware of this during the early 1980s, when collaborating with Skip on research about the history of the fur trade in the Cordillera – research that would be published in the *Historical Atlas of Canada*.[1] Skip was also engaged in research on behalf of the Gitxsan/Carrier Tribal Council, as it was then known, concerning their claim to Aboriginal title over their traditional territories. To my good fortune, Skip also recommended that the Tribal Council ask me to undertake some research for the intended court case, now known as *Delgamuukw* v. *Regina*. One of the questions raised by the litigation in *Delgamuukw* involved the nature of Gitxsan and Wet'suwet'en resistance to the entry of Europeans and Euro-Canadians into their territories. This applied research led me to examine, and now to re-examine, the Skeena "Uprising" of 1888.

Prior to 1860, the Gitxsan people of the upper Skeena region were linked to the Euro-Canadian economy primarily through the operations of the fur trade (see Map 10.1). Well-established posts at Fort Simpson, Fort Kilmaurs, Fort Connolly, and Fort St. James were integrated into indigenous trading systems that carried European goods to the Gitxsan in exchange for furs of various kinds. This system was gradually undercut in the 1860s as the influences of gold rushes in southern British Columbia filtered northward. The rush to Omineca (1870-71), although modest in scale, brought prospectors, miners, and traders to the upper Skeena region. Hazelton, the first non-Native settlement in Gitxsan territory, was established as a service and transshipment centre for those travelling to the mines via the Skeena River. Over the next fifteen years, with a transport system still reliant upon muscle power for most of the journey, settler economy and society impinged in a rather

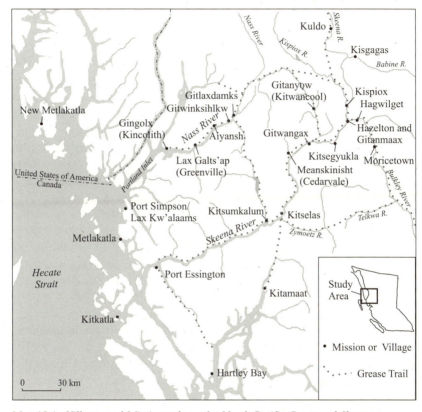

Map 10.1   Villages and Missions along the North Pacific Coast and Skeena and Nass River watersheds, ca 1880s.

Source: Prepared by Ted Binnema.

uneven manner on the Gitxsan and their neighbours, the Wet'suwet'en. Nonetheless, from a settler perspective, the pattern was clear: the upper Skeena was one more area to be incorporated as a hinterland within the ambit of an expanding imperial system, its resources to be commodified and exported. Successful integration would require the extension of legal/administrative structures, both provincial and federal, to facilitate and legitimate the process.

For the Gitxsan, who continued to make up the overwhelming majority of the population in the region until the early twentieth century, the intrusions of settler society into their homeland brought new and challenging problems. Their responses were shaped by what may be termed their system of laws, here viewed as the principles and rules (including sanctions) that established the basis for their "social order, and ... the peaceful resolution of conflict."[2] This pattern was most clearly manifested in a series of confrontations that culminated in the "uprising" of 1888. An incident at Kitsegyukla in 1872, involving the "accidental" destruction of the Gitxsan village by travelling miners, was eventually resolved in terms that closely conformed to traditional Gitxsan procedures: following an initial denial of access to other members of the "white tribe," compensation was paid by the lieutenant-governor in a feast-like situation at Metlakatla.[3] In 1874, when miners used Gitxsan territory as a route to the Cassiar mining region, "exactions" were made "for the privilege of passing through their Country" – suggesting Gitxsan ideas about territory and trespass.[4] Then, in 1884, after a flurry of mining activity at Lorne Creek, within Gitxsan territory, a merchant at Hazelton was killed for violating the Gitxsan customary law of *xsiisxw*. A.C. Youmans had refused to pay compensation for the death of one of his Gitxsan employees during a canoe trip along the Skeena.[5] The potent concoction of interracial tensions revealed by these events continued to ferment in the ensuing years. In 1888, they produced what has come to be known, rather inappropriately, as the Skeena "Uprising."[6]

I begin with an outline of the principal events of the Skeena Uprising, derived primarily from contemporaneous documentary sources. This outline is reconsidered in the light of information contained in Gitxsan narratives collected by Marius Barbeau and William Beynon in the 1920s. The narratives provide significant new information and illuminate Gitxsan perceptions of the events. With this fuller version in place, it is possible to broach the more complex question of interpretation. This requires inserting the events of 1888 into their wider historical context. The Skeena Uprising becomes one moment, albeit an important one, that reveals the growing tensions between Natives and settler society as they competed for access to land and resources. The discussion concludes with a consideration of the more immediate consequences of the events of 1888.

The Documentary Version

The Skeena Uprising emerged from the growing complexity of the contact process on the upper Skeena, but its immediate trigger was an internal conflict that erupted among the Gitxsan of the Kitwancool Valley early in 1888. In March, the Reverend A.E. Green, a Methodist missionary stationed in the Nass Valley, informed Provincial Secretary John Robson of the events that led Kamalmuk to kill Neatsqua. Green's information came from W.H. Pierce, a fellow missionary resident at Kitsegyukla, who stated that a few weeks earlier a dispute had arisen about who should "fill the seat" of a deceased blind chief.

> The murdered man [Neatsqua] wanted the seat himself. "Kit-wan-cool Jim" [Kamalmuk] wanted to put his son in it, and many hard words passed

between them. Some time after this, the son of Jim died of the fever [measles] so common this winter among the Indians and then a younger child of Jim's died. And Jim now blamed "Neatsqu" for bewitching his children and causing their deaths because of the dispute over the seat.[7]

Thus Kamalmuk had exercised one of the traditional sanctions permitted by Gitxsan customary law. But, still following Gitxsan customs, he also attempted to prevent further bloodshed by seeking a settlement with the "friends of Neatsqua" at Kitsegyukla. Kamalmuk sent forty blankets and a copper as "payment for the life." However, the offer was refused, leaving the feud unresolved and prompting Kamalmuk to return to Gitanyow to fortify his house.[8] Shortly thereafter, when visited by Pierce, Kamalmuk expressed regret over the death of Neatsqua but added that "he wished Mr. Pierce to tell the government and the officers, that, if they come after him, he would give them his work (meaning he would kill them)."[9]

By this time the friends and relations of Neatsqua were "much excited" and contemplating revenge. Pierce was attempting to prevent such actions when a singular development took place: the head chiefs at Kitsegyukla remembered a "paper" given them by a "Government officer on board a Man-of-War" in 1872. The paper stated that the people of Kitsegyukla had promised "never again to take the law into their own hands and that the Government promised to help them if any Indians of other tribes should kill any of them. They decided to keep their promises and to lay the matter before the Government for adjustment."[10] The chiefs now wished to test their "alliance" with the "government" and informed Pierce accordingly.

Information about these events on the upper Skeena reached the provincial government from a variety of other sources. S.Y. Wootton, a stipendiary magistrate, and Constable W.B. Anderson, both stationed at Port Simpson, sent separate letters to the attorney general early in April. However, they provided little new information other than indicating their own inability to cooperate on an appropriate course of action. Wootton also reported that two white residents of the upper Skeena would soon be in Victoria to provide the attorney general with first-hand information. These were C.W.D. Clifford, the Hudson's Bay Company (HBC) clerk at Hazelton, and B.W. Washburn, an independent trader on the upper Skeena.[11]

The provincial government, however, had already decided how to respond to the situation. On 31 March, Constable Anderson was ordered to proceed to Gitanyow, make an arrest, and return to Port Simpson with the prisoner and witnesses. In this task, Anderson was to be accompanied by Indian Agent Charles Todd and as many "specials" as he deemed necessary.[12] For various reasons – lack of suitable "specials," problems over the availability of Todd, and the reluctance of Anderson – it was not until 8 May that Todd and a party of five special constables, with Washburn in charge, "started up the Skeena River."[13] By this time, news of a second incident among the Gitxsan had reached the coast. At Kisgagas, a woman had been stabbed to death and, in response, the murderer's brother had been shot by the woman's relatives. Washburn's party of specials, armed with arrest warrants, was expected to resolve this matter also.

The five specials reached Hazelton on 23 May, having stopped at Kitsegyukla en route.[14] At the latter village, Todd, before parting company with the specials and returning to the coast, had sent an oral and written message to Kamalmuk, then reported to be "in the mountains near the Nass." This measure achieved its objective, and, by the middle of June, Kamalmuk was at Gitwangax, in the house of Legenetta, a Gitanyow chief. He had Todd's letter and, according to his wife, intended to surrender. News of Kamalmuk's presence soon reached Hazelton, and three of the specials – Holmes, Parker, and Green – were dispatched to carry out the arrest. Their first attempt to persuade Kamalmuk to surrender ended in failure. During the second attempt, for which Hiskamla was hired to assist, Kamalmuk ran from Legenetta's house, only to be fatally shot by Constable Green. News of these events was carried rapidly to Hazelton, but it was not until three days later, on 19 June, that Washburn and the remaining special, Constable Loring, reached Gitwangax.[15] Loring remembered the village being awash with excitement. People armed with

> guns, axes and hatchets lined up along the shore shouting and waving us off from landing. After some parlaying, a landing was made, and, having laid down our rifles, the Indians did likewise. Having the corpses of Kitwancool Jim unwrapped from a whole bolt of white cotton, I made notes of the wounds inflicted, and convincing the people that Constable Green would be held responsible for the deed, they became much pacified.[16]

After arranging for the burial, Washburn and Loring returned to Hazelton, arriving the next day.[17]

A week later, on 27 June, Washburn reported the death of Kamalmuk and some of its consequences to the attorney general. In addition to the "excitement" at Gitwangax, he noted that the Natives at Gitanmaax showed "a defying, insulting and saucy demeanor." Amidst rumours that the Gitanyow were seeking revenge, a chief at Gitanmaax warned Washburn that it would be better for him "to move out of this village, so it would not be a scene of bloodshed. The friends of the dead murderer are swearing to exterminate all belonging to the opposite party and expecting to hear of more murders every day."[18] Washburn added that the HBC building at Hazelton was being fortified and recommended that the government, without delay, send "15 or 20 good men with a good and determined leader."[19]

In the interim, Washburn appears to have followed the precedent set by Thomas Hankin in dealing with the fire at Kitsegyukla in 1872. He informed the attorney general that he had promised the Gitanmaax that "a high government chief was to arrive as soon as the stage of water would permit and to wait and lay their grievances before the same."[20] For their part, the relatives of Kamalmuk issued their claim for *xsiisxw*, or compensation: "$1,000 and a man in place of the man killed ... and the gun that had done the killing as a momento."[21]

A petition from non-Native residents of Hazelton, seven in all, confirmed the general disposition of Natives and non-Natives in the area. It mentioned the "hostile and threatening attitude" of the Gitxsan and expressed the fear that settlers "lives and property" were in great and "immediate danger."[22] In spite of these apprehended dangers, Mr. Borland, a packer, after some debate at Kitsegyukla, was permitted to carry the petition down to Metlakatla and on to Victoria, where he had "several interviews" with the executive council.[23]

The information provided by these sources – Borland, Washburn and the petition – prompted the government into renewed action.[24] Superintendent Roycraft, of the provincial police, who had visited the upper Skeena in 1884 in connection with the murder of A.C. Youmans, was summoned to Victoria from Nanaimo.[25] Shortly thereafter negotiations were initiated with representatives of the federal government (Superintendent for Indian Affairs in British Columbia I.W. Powell) and the naval authorities at Esquimalt. These negotiations, concerning the appropriateness of, and responsibility for, particular responses, produced the Skeena River "Expedition."[26] Consisting of eighty-four men and officers of "C" Battery (the local militia), Superintendent Roycraft, and twelve provincial constables, the "Expedition" departed from Esquimalt on board HMS *Caroline* on 16 July. As events unfolded, the militia, under Colonel Holmes, proceeded no further than a camp established near Port Essington at the mouth of the Skeena. Only the force of provincial constables under Roycraft ascended the river, reaching Hazelton on 1 August.[27]

At Hazelton, Roycraft encountered another "official" participant in the complex of events unfolding on the upper Skeena. This was Captain Napoleon Fitzstubbs, recently appointed gold commissioner and stipendiary magistrate for the Skeena District.[28] After some delay at Metlakatla, Fitzstubbs had obtained passage on a freight canoe, arriving at Hazelton on 23 July.[29] His journey had not been without incident. At Gitwangax, he was "practically stopped" until grievances were aired. He was "addressed by several of the elder men, who complained that the whites had interfered with the operation of their own laws and had taken the life of one of their own race, that life being by the payment of a stipulated sum, no longer forfeit."[30] This report by Fitzstubbs is of particular interest as it contradicts part of the information provided by the Reverend A.E. Green. Fitzstubbs indicates that a settlement had been reached between Kamalmuk and Neatsqua's relatives; the traditional Gitxsan mechanism for settling disputes had been put into effect.

However, both Fitzstubbs and Roycraft saw the operation of Gitxsan law as the equivalent of "lawlessness." They were concerned with inculcating respect for Canadian "law and order" on the upper Skeena.[31] To this end, they initiated a series of measures designed to demonstrate both the workings of the judicial process and the coercive powers of settler society. These steps were accompanied by recourse to the classic colonial tactics of divide and rule, while seeking to incorporate the indigenous leadership.

The preliminary hearing of Constable Green was part of this pattern. Held at Hazelton under Roycraft and Fitzstubbs, it resulted in Green being transported south, to stand trial at Nanaimo.[32] This demonstration of "impartial" justice was supplemented by displays of military prowess. The police squad performed "drill and target practice," which, Roycraft believed, "surprised the Indians very much especially the long distance shooting."[33] Fitzstubbs, in contrast, sought to incorporate the Native leadership into the hierarchy of authority articulated by settler society. He proposed that the chiefs in each of the villages should act as special constables, a suggestion that Roycraft had no hesitation in endorsing. Fitzstubbs also hoped to meet the chiefs separately, thereby confining "each tribe to the consideration of such matters as affect it as a tribe and thus separate them as much as possible and prevent their making common cause."[34]

The outcome, however, was a public meeting, held at Hazelton on 8 August, with ten Gitxsan and three Wet'suwet'en chiefs, along with Roycraft and Fitzstubbs, in attendance.[35] The chiefs, from five villages (Gitanmaax, Kispiox, Kitsegyukla, Gitwangax, and Hagwilget), provided a "very attentive audience" for speeches by the two officials and responded with statements on their own account.[36] Roycraft was satisfied with this exchange of views and the general state of affairs in the upper Skeena. Thus, the following day, accompanied by most of the specials, he began the return journey to Victoria. On arrival, he provided the attorney general with an assessment of the impact of the expedition. There could be "no doubt," Roycraft believed, that it would have a "salutary effect" on the Native population and that there would be no further trouble between Natives and settlers. "They seem," he concluded, "now perfectly to understand our power" and have "promised to keep the law and their chiefs will bring all offenders to justice."[37]

However, this optimistic appraisal was not shared by all of the settlers of the Hazelton area. CMS missionary John Field, for example, while noting the "wholesome effect" of the expedition, pointed out that most of the Natives were absent when the expedition arrived, and he feared the situation could change when they returned from fishing, berry picking, and hunting.[38] Fitzstubbs held similar views but situated them in the political context of settler society. He questioned the wisdom of withdrawing all government representatives, lest it be interpreted as "a practical transferring of the country to the rule of the Indians who in their wildest moments, never dreamed of such a consummation." Moreover, after the expenditure of so much money, such a step would furnish "the political enemies of the Government ... with ammunition for an attack."[39] Hence Fitzstubbs requested that two of the special constables remain in the area. This interim solution, accepted by Roycraft, endured until the establishment of the Babine Indian Agency in 1889.

The Barbeau/Beynon Narratives

In the course of fieldwork undertaken among the Gitxsan during the early 1920s, C.M. Barbeau collected a number of narratives about the events of 1888.[40] These sources make possible a discussion of Gitxsan perceptions of the uprising. I focus upon seven components of the narratives: the events leading to the murder of Neatsqua, the murder of Neatsqua, responses to the murder of Neatsqua, the origin of the "Skeena Expedition," the flight and return of Kamalmuk, the death of Kamalmuk, and reactions to the death of Kamalmuk.

The Gitxsan narratives confirm the rather sparse outline provided by the Reverend Green of the events that culminated in the shooting of Neatsqua by Kamalmuk. Their quarrel grew out of conflicting claims to inherit the name of Hanamuk, and came to a head during a feast, apparently held at Gitwangax.[41] Kamalmuk, in claiming the name for his son Gamuxon, took the initiative by arriving early and seating Gamuxon in the place reserved for the holder of the name Hanamuk. On his arrival, Neatsqua was both angered and shamed by this initiative. As a shaman, his response was to threaten Gamuxon: "you'll not sit in that place very long ... [meaning that] the boy would die after a while." At the conclusion of this feast, the action moved to Gitanyow where a second feast was held. It was on this occasion that Neatsqua's threat took on the mantle of reality with the death of Gamuxon.[42]

As many of the narratives make clear, this death was one of many that occurred during the winter of 1887-88, the result of a measles epidemic that swept through the Gitxsan villages. Nonetheless, Kamalmuk's wife, Gisaxitutkibu, insisted that the witchcraft of Neatsqua was responsible for the death of her sons.[43] This assertion was significant for it required the application of the traditional Gitxsan response: "It was a life for a life."[44] In other words, to atone for the death of his son, Kamalmuk should kill Neatsqua. Initially, it would seem, Kamalmuk was reluctant to take such a step, perhaps because he had "adopted many of the habits of the white man." Before long, however, Kamalmuk accepted his wife's view and set out from Kitsegyukla to exercise the traditional sanction.[45]

The narratives contain a good deal of information on where, when, and how Kamalmuk shot Neatsqua. Such details, though, are not essential for the present discussion; only the basic facts are required. The murder took place between Gitwangax and Gitanyow, as Neatsqua was returning from the latter village to his home in Kitsegyukla. News of the shooting soon reached Neatsqua's relatives in Gitanyow, who retrieved the body for burial. At this stage, there was some danger that the situation might escalate into a "big war."[46] However, before there were any further serious incidents, a complex series of negotiations were brought to a peaceful conclusion.[47] The crucial stage in this process involved the men of Neatsqua's household travelling to Gitanyow to demand the payment of "Ksisux [*xsiisxw*], blood or money." As described by Charles Mark, Kamalmuk and his family responded in the following manner:

> When the murderer came out [from his house], he was dressed in a grizzly's skin and in his mouth he bit a copper hazetsu [shield?] and he came down on all fours like a grizzly bear. This meant he was going to pay. And they brought out and behind him ... the most valuable thing they had, blankets, coats and guns and moosehides. Then after the payment was made, it was all over. There was peace among themselves.

This settlement was confirmed by a feast at Kitsegyukla, attended by the "whole village" and all of Kamalmuk's family. Here, Wiget performed the necessary ceremonial acts to conclude the pact: "He danced the peace dance and ... blew white down on the visitors and no one could fight after that. The white down meant peace." Thus the conflict, much as reported by Fitzstubbs, was resolved in accordance with Gitxsan law – and without further violence or injury.[48]

There is some uncertainty in the Gitxsan narratives about the reasons for the subsequent involvement of the provincial police. Several accounts offer no explanation at all, simply noting the arrival of the police on the scene. Others indicate that "Mr. Washburn," a trader at Kitsegyukla, played some kind of role in the process. Like a number of other independent traders in the region, Washburn had taken a Gitxsan wife: in his case, a niece of Neatsqua. Presumably, he used this relationship as a means of interceding in the drama of 1888.[49] After approaching Guxsan, a Kitsegyukla chief, and examining the "paper" of 1872, Washburn advised Neatsqua's family to return the compensation they had received from Kamalmuk: in other words, to reject the traditional settlement. Washburn then departed for Victoria, taking Neatsqua's blood-stained clothes as evidence, to report the murder. He returned to the upper Skeena in charge of the "posse" of policemen seeking Kamalmuk.[50]

When Washburn and the detachment of police arrived on the scene, Kamalmuk, of course, had disappeared. Some informants attribute this to a "flight" from the police; others point to the breakdown of the compensation procedures; still others imply that Kamalmuk was following the normal annual round of activities. There may be an element of truth in all these explanations, but there is general agreement that Kamalmuk spent the spring months in territory to the north of Gitanyow.[51] Here, no doubt, Kamalmuk could have remained safe and secure from police pursuit – as the later example of Simon Gunanoot would demonstrate. Instead, by July, Kamalmuk came down to Gitwangax.[52] He had been drawn back to the Skeena primarily as a result of a letter from the magistrate "Mr. Beach" (presumably a reference to Indian Agent Todd). The letter was delivered by Kamalmuk's wife, and its impact may have benefited from the fact that "Beach" and Kamalmuk "had met before at the Stickeen." In substance, the letter offered some reassurances to Kamalmuk: it stated that the matter would be settled in the courts but that "the government's law will not hang" him.[53]

The Gitxsan narratives provide considerable information about the circumstances surrounding the shooting of Kamalmuk. Although there are variations between informants and disagreements over details, taken as a whole, the narratives reflect the preceding documentary reconstruction. Equally important, the narratives provide supplementary information about the question of Gitxsan participation. They confirm the role of Hiskamla in providing the police with information and assistance in their second attempt to arrest Kamalmuk.[54] Yet there were divisions within Gitxsan society regarding the propriety of aiding the police. The antagonistic position was expressed very clearly by Lelt, who had also been approached by the police to help in capturing Kamalmuk.[55] Lelt explained the reasons for his refusal: "I was asked not to go with the [police] party by my own house, as I was to give a yexk [*yukw*, i.e., a feast] in the near future and I would be taunted with the fact that I used money which I got from this source in my yexk." Clearly, as a man of high status, Lelt was sensitive to arguments based on traditional values and the potential loss of respect.[56]

Like the documentary sources, the Gitxsan narratives recount that, immediately before he was shot, Kamalmuk had evaded the police at Legenetta's house in Gitwangax. According to some descriptions, he was armed at the time and even, by one account, fired two shots during the chase.[57] Nonetheless, there is considerable agreement that Kamalmuk was not trying to escape from the police: he had stopped, and in two versions he was sitting down when he was shot from behind.[58] Semedik gives these apparently discordant accounts some coherence by placing Kamalmuk's actions within Gitxsan cultural norms: "The reason why he [Kamalmuk] had taken to flight was that he had so much pride that he could not simply think of surrendering without a little struggle." Kamalmuk's pride stemmed from his high status within Gitxsan society. He was, according to Semedik, practically the head chief at Gitanyow and "in a few years would have succeeded to the head chieftainship."[59] Charles Mark, in an effort to bridge the cultural gap between Euro-Canadians and Gitxsan, stated that had Kamalmuk been "white," he would have been "called a gentleman."[60]

The immediate response of the Gitxsan to the shooting of Kamalmuk was constrained by the fact that relatively few people, mostly women, were present ar Gitwangax. Even so, there was undoubted anger and hostility. Semedik, having found the police weapons unattended, stated that he would have liked to shoot the constables but "did not know how to fire the gun."[61] According to Lagaxnitz, the police were ordered from the village and the anger of the people was exacerbated by the rough manner in which the corpse was handled by the police – a lack of respect that added insult to injury.[62]

Other narratives, apparently picking up the story at a slightly later stage, confirm that the cadaver became the focus of some attention. When Constable Loring reached Gitwangax, after the death of Kamalmuk, he examined the corpse and was surprised by the tattoos on the chest. "This was a chief," Loring is reported to have said, "it [is] too bad he died the death he has died."[63] Moreover, Constable Loring is remembered as having issued a significant promise at this juncture. Mrs. Lagaxnitz stated that the shooting of Kamalmuk caused

> great excitement and the blame was placed on the government against the government. A letter has been sent by the government saying it would compensate the bereaved family of the death of Gamxl [Kamalmuk]. They think this letter is still in the possession of this man who keeps the clothes. But the Government did not fulfill the promise. It was through Mr. Loring. He was a constable at that time.

Viewed in isolation, this account is rather perplexing. How, for example, could a letter from the government have reached Gitwangax at this time? But if the statement is placed in context – alongside the statement by Loring and the demand for compensation by Kamalmuk's relatives – the meaning becomes clearer.

In order to defuse the situation at Gitwangax, Loring probably assured the Natives that Constable Green would be tried and punished according to the laws of settler society. He may have added, as Thomas Hankin had done at Kitsegyukla in 1872, that the government would consider some kind of a payment as recompense. This, it may be noted, is the interpretation put forward by Barbeau. Moreover, there is evidence that an offer of compensation was made, by Fitzstubbs, later in the year.[64] Be this as it may, the narratives are very clear that the bitterness engendered by the shooting of Kamalmuk lasted well beyond 1888.

Contexts

The events of 1888, for Natives and non-Natives alike, were both dramatic and memorable. However, to grasp their full significance, it is necessary to move beyond the narratives and to examine the broader temporal and spatial contexts. The Skeena Uprising was not an isolated event but, rather, the culmination of a process initiated by the Omineca gold rush nearly two decades earlier. The conflicts of 1872, 1874, and 1884 had illustrated, but hardly resolved, the uncertainties and ambiguities of the contact process in the upper Skeena. Writing after the death of Kamalmuk, the Reverend Field observed that, for "several years," there had been "a very bitter feeling between the two races and this most recent misfortune has rekindled the smouldering embers."[65] Neither unprecedented nor a repetition of previous episodes, the "uprising" points towards a new stage in the contact process in the upper Skeena. Moreover, the novel scope and scale of government responses were informed by a perception of considerable Native discontent that extended, spatially and temporally, beyond the confines of the upper Skeena in 1888.

Captain Fitzstubbs, on arriving at Hazelton in July 1888, noted the widespread disaffection among the Natives and thought the "general bearing" of those he had met was "one of hostility."[66] Three days later, after some reflection, Fitzstubbs elaborated upon what he took to be the underlying reasons for this state of affairs. The first item, and the one that played the most immediate role in triggering the events of 1888, was the measles epidemic of the previous winter. This had killed some 240 Gitxsan, and it lay at the root of much of the ill feeling towards settlers. They professed "to believe that the whites had designedly brought it amongst them."[67]

This interpretation was shared by Margaret Hankin, a mixed-blood woman who was better informed about Native views than were other residents of Hazelton. She stated that the Gitxsan believed the whites, out of spite, had "put the measles into the sugar and sold [it] to them." This, no doubt, was a reference to the actions of Clifford, the HBC clerk at Hazelton. It also explained why the Natives "had such a bad feeling" the previous winter; however, there had been a softening of views when they heard that white children had also died.[68]

The second item listed by Fitzstubbs as contributing to the "turbulence of the Indians" was more nebulous but can best be described as expressions of Gitxsan autonomy. Three factors, in Fitzstubbs' opinion, had led to this regrettable situation. First, for years their "misconduct [had] ... received no check whatever," with the result that they believed "themselves invincible to none but themselves." Second, a growing familiarity with the few non-Natives in the area had tended to reduce, if not destroy, "the respect and fear in which our race was once held by them." Hence, the third reason: the Gitxsan were "intensely disgusted that the law should assert itself in their country with the chance of a check put upon their rapacity and extortion."[69] These perceptions were shared by the Reverend Field. The previous year, he had reported that there was "practically no law here." Thus, the Gitxsan "laugh at the idea of being ruled by outsiders, and the government does not make the faintest show of asserting its rights."[70]

An integral part of any claim to autonomy, although viewed separately by Fitzstubbs, was the question of the ownership of land and resources. This was not a new issue on the upper Skeena. The influx of miners to Lorne Creek in 1884 and the events surrounding the death of A.C. Youmans had raised the topic in a direct fashion.[71] Although mining activity soon diminished, the underlying problem remained, and a variety of other factors conspired to keep the issue current. Fitzstubbs, like C.W.D. Clifford before him, chose to blame missionaries in general, and Robert Tomlinson in particular, for this unfortunate state of affairs. Tomlinson, it was said, had inculcated the idea that "the whites intend to deprive them ... [the Natives] of their land."[72]

Thus future settlement of the upper Skeena – which Fitzstubbs antici-pated primarily in the "rich grazing country" of the Bulkley Valley, Wet'su-wet'en territory – would have to overcome Native claims to the region. Under existing circumstances, Fitstubbs stated, "The consent of the Indians would be necessary to peaceable occupation, which will not be given until they are disabused of the correctness of the belief, almost an instinct in respect of their possessory rights in the land: and this I think may require force."[73] Fitzstubbs pointed to the experiences of Turner-Turner and James, who vis-ited the upper Skeena on a hunting tour in the winter of 1886-87, as an example of the problems that non-Natives could encounter. The Gitxsan and Wet'suwet'en, Fitzstubbs added, were "most jealous of strangers, whom they suspect of being surveyors and hold [them] in utmost detestation."[74]

The reference to Turner-Turner and James is of particular interest since the former, in 1888, published an account of his visit to the upper Skeena.[75] Turner-Turner was not a sympathetic observer of the Gitxsan, but his ac-count bears examination for two reasons: first, he spent eight months on the upper Skeena at an important period in the development of Native/non-Native relations; second, as a big-game hunter, he encountered the Gitxsan in a different manner than did most non-Native visitors to the region – his activities brought him into direct contact with Gitxsan laws governing access to land and resources. A specific example will serve to illustrate the flavour of Turner-Turner's experience.

Armed with the assumption that game was an open-access resource and that he could go wherever and do whatever he wished, Turner arrived at Gitanmaax in September 1886. Over the next several months his every attempt at hunting was sabotaged and frustrated by the Gitxsan. Finally, on the advice of Clifford, the HBC clerk, Turner hired "Kishpyox Jim" to conduct him to a hunting ground, located beyond Kisgagas in the Atnah, or Skeena, mountains, "where grizzly bears abounded." Turner-Turner's explanation for this step is noteworthy: Kispiox Jim had "two wives, one of whom belonged to the village of Gishgegars [Kisgagas], which gave him hunting rights there."[76] But Kispiox Jim's right of access to this hunting territory was not unconditional, and events at Kisgegas further illustrate the operation of Gitxsan laws on this topic.[77] When the party reached the Babine River opposite Kisgagas, Turner-Turner learned that many of the residents "were opposed to ... [his] hunting, even in the spot where they dared not venture themselves." Kispiox Jim, though, was prepared for this difficulty. He "had brought several little presents of plain cakes composed of flour and water, with which rare luxuries ... he won over the chief and most important of the tribe."[78] In other words, Turner, through the actions of Kispiox Jim, had conformed with Gitxsan rules in securing access to hunting territory. Here, as in many of his other encounters with Gitxsan customary law, Turner-Turner had been denied the deference he considered his civilized due. Unable, or unwilling, to recognize the operation of customary law, he registered Gitxsan actions as manifestations of an absence of law.

Two other factors, not noted by Fitzstubbs, contributed to discontent on the upper Skeena: the death of Haatq and the actions of the HBC. Late in 1887, while serving his sentence for murdering A.C. Youmans, Haatq died in New Westminster Gaol. According to John Field, consequent Gitxsan discontent focused on Youmans' widow. She was "fined" – probably a payment of compensation – and harassed to the point where she withdrew to Victoria for several months.[79] Of broader impact were measures taken by the HBC to reorganize its transportation system from Hazelton to Babine Lake. Because of the "exorbitant rate" charged by the Native packers over the Babine trail, the HBC decided to employ the firm of Veith and Borland, of 150 Mile House, to do the job. Native reaction to this assault on their "privileges" was prompt. In the winter of 1887-88, they informed the HBC clerk at Hazelton that "they would not allow the Hudson's Bay Company or anyone else to have a pack train on the portage" to Babine Lake and that they would "kill any animal" brought there for that purpose. These threats were not carried out, but they undoubtedly contributed to the impression that the Gitxsan and Wet'suwet'en were "generally quarrelsome and very troublesome to settlers and others."[80]

Some settlers thought that the Natives were more than simply troublesome. The Reverend Field reported, early in 1888, that the HBC clerk's "life was really in danger," and rumours were circulating that the "people were to have risen and massacred all the whites in the country." At one time things looked so bad that plans were made for the non-Native residents of Hazelton to abandon their houses and "take refuge in the HBC store."[81] Another version of these events, recorded by Fitzstubbs later in the year, added that a meeting to discuss the possibility of killing all of the whites in the Hazelton area had been held in the house of the Gitanmaax chief (presumably Geddumcaldoe). Unlike Field, however, Fitzstubbs did not take the threat seriously. Noting the lack of unanimity, he concluded that, as "they were so easily turned from their professed purpose, one can scarcely suppose they were very serious about it."[82]

Whatever the reality of this threat, the disruption caused by the changes in the transportation system was no passing issue. The animosity that the HBC provoked by the introduction of the pack train was still evident as late as 1893.[83] Moreover, prices and the general treatment Natives received at the HBC post at Hazelton also aroused discontent. One Gitanmaax man complained to Roycraft and Fitzstubbs that if "we want a higher price for our skins than they care to give us they strike us, and why blame us for retaliation?" When Natives did retaliate, non-Natives took up "pen and paper" and wrote to the government "to send up armed men to punish us wicked savages."[84]

Native assertions of ownership of lands and resources in the 1880s were not restricted to the Gitxsan. Indeed, there is reason to believe that the Gitxsan, in dealing with the influx of Euro-Canadians, learned from the experiences of their coastal neighbours, the Tsimshian and the Nisga'a.[85] On the Coast, William Duncan's dispute with the ecclesiastical authorities had become inextricably intertwined with the "land question" and the establishment of a system of reserves. The most obvious result of these developments was the departure of Duncan and several hundred Tsimshian followers to Alaska in 1887 – a powerful statement about the level of Native discontent with conditions in British Columbia. Opposition to the reserve system and the elaboration of a clear expression to Aboriginal title over land and resources were equally pertinent.

The evolution of this opposition during the 1880s was a complex process that two royal commissions, the Metlakatlah Inquiry of 1884 and the Commission on the Condition of Indians of the North-West Coast in 1887, endeavoured to describe and contain. The latter, for example, noted that the people of Greenville, the upper Nass, and Port Simpson all held "pronounced views on the question" of Aboriginal title; furthermore, they "professed to speak for the Upper Skeena people." Some of the former demanded that a "treaty be made," but the Royal Commission did not deal with such issues.[86] These developments prompted the Reverend Green to observe, at the end of 1887, that the past year had been "a most trying one" as the unrest "over the

'Indian Land Question' and the exodus of the people of Metlakatla to Alaska have kept the Indians in a constant state of excitement."[87]

The establishment of Indian reserves on the northern coast, initiated in 1882, aroused a good deal of antagonism that was soon communicated to the "up-country tribes." Responses among coastal peoples extended to the use of force. At two locations, Metlakatla in 1885 and Gitlaxdamks (upper Nass) in 1886, surveyors were physically prevented from carrying out their work. The antagonism of the Gitxsan towards the entry of surveyors into their territory should be understood in the light of these earlier incidents.[88]

The extension of two other aspects of the administrative system of settler society to the northern coast also contributed to the pattern of discontent. The first Indian agent for the North West Coast Indian Agency was rejected in 1884, and, as late as 1887, a Port Simpson spokesperson stated: "We do not want reserves at all. We do not want the Indian Act. We do not want an Indian Agent."[89] Moreover, the establishment of the industrial salmon fishery brought the beginnings of a system of regulation that was seen as a threat to Native access to a fundamental resource.[90]

These developments among the Tsimshian and the Nisga'a contributed to the shaping of Gitxsan attitudes and responses to settlers. The links between the peoples were long-standing. More immediately, the conflicts at Metlakatla, including opposition to governments and surveys, were transferred directly to the CMS station at Gitwangax by some of Duncan's and Tomlinson's Gitxsan adherents. In short, the events on the Coast contributed to an atmosphere of hostility that encompassed portions of the Interior.[91]

Non-Native perceptions of these developments contributed to the way that events unfolded in 1888. The Royal Commission, which visited the north coast late in 1887, may have helped to dissolve some of the tension, but it did nothing to resolve the underlying issues. Native discontent was the result of a complex of interrelated causes, but it was rooted in a growing awareness of the consequences of the expanding non-Native presence. This realization occurred earlier in the northern coastal region than it did in the Interior, but it was well developed on the upper Skeena by 1888. For settler society, the manifestation of discontent on such a regional scale was the cause of some alarm; the display of force, in such circumstances, was a standard response.

Consequences

The Skeena Uprising concluded, as already noted, to the evident satisfaction of Superintendent Roycraft. He informed the attorney general that the Natives of the upper Skeena had learned a lesson and were suitably impressed by the power of settler society. This view was shared by Fitzstubbs, who congratulated the government on the impact of the "Expedition." The Natives, "even to the remotest interior," he thought, had learned that "the few scattered whites" in such distant parts of the province were "neither forgotten, nor uncared for." Furthermore, exaggerated stories were circulating about "the vast numbers and power and appliances of the military encamped at the mouth of the Skeena."[92] Such proximate assessments were both one-sided, paying scant attention to Native views, and, in due course, overtaken by events. The legacy of 1888 proved to be more complex and ambiguous.

Following the departure of Roycraft and the expedition from Hazelton, Fitzstubbs, as stipendiary magistrate, was responsible for the exercise of governmental authority. His suggestion that chiefs, where possible, should be "special constables" had met with the approval of Roycraft, who promised to have a "number of police badges made ... for distribution ... to the Indian constables."[93] In spite of this auspicious beginning, the plan soon encountered difficulties. Within the year, Fitzstubbs informed the attorney general that the Native Methodist teachers had slighted "the authority of the law" and "ridiculed the idea of assumption of police duties by the chiefs." As a result, except at Kitsegyukla, the chiefs had "shrunk from their acceptance with aversion, though they were at first emulous of them."[94]

But on this question, much more than missionary opposition was involved. This became apparent during Fitzstubbs' visit to Kispiox. On arriving opposite the village, he was faced with the refusal of the Kispiox to ferry him across the river. Fitzstubbs, however, proved equal to this challenge. Near the crossing, there was

> an excellent piece of cover where waiting until a canoe came over for an old couple, on her landing I ran down and got in to the chagrin of those in the village who were shouting to the men not to ferry us over. However, he had to take me over, leaving interpreter and packs behind.[95]

This was a blow for the ingenuity, if not the majesty, of "settler" law and its representative.

In accordance with the manner of his arrival, Fitzstubbs' reception at Kispiox was less than enthusiastic: "not an Indian" would acknowledge Fitzstubbs' "salutation." Undeterred, Fitzstubbs eventually obtained access to a house in which he conducted "a long interview with the chiefs." The outcome, he thought, was an agreement that the chiefs would "keep order amongst their people and be sworn and wear a badge." A meeting was then arranged, to embrace the whole village, at which the ceremonial investiture of the chiefs would be the highlight. At first all went well. After addressing the populace, Fitzstubbs was on the point of swearing in the chiefs, when "a young Indian stood up and ... said he had no wish that his chief should give countenance and aid to the government, they were a people of themselves, had their laws and would acknowledge none other."

Similar views were repeated by six other speakers, so that when Fitzstubbs called "on the constables to stand up and be sworn in, they tremblingly [?] declined, backed down in fact before intimidation." In response, Fitzstubbs berated the chiefs but to no effect. He consoled himself by announcing that "the Government would find policemen on all occasions requiring them, that the law would reach offenders no matter how the Kispayooks or any others were affected towards it." Thereon Fitzstubbs bowed and took himself, and what remained of his dignity, back to Hazelton.[96]

This turn of events prompted Fitzstubbs to seek the aid of the Reverend A.G. Morice in dealing with the Wet'suwet'en. Even this move produced mixed results: "Nicaul accepted," Fitzstubbs noted, "but Nerseberse and Simoigetlcamp distinctly refused to accept the Crown with its implied duties." This setback, like many others, was laid at the feet of "Methodist agents." The identification of a non-Native "culprit" is revealing in itself, but the problem was, in part, a product of Fitzstubbs' misunderstanding of the nature of the chiefs' authority.[97] On this topic, the remarks by Geddum-caldoe to Constable Brown during the Cassiar Trail incidents of 1874 are worth recalling as they indicate some of the limitations upon his power as a chief.

> Although I am recognized as the Chief, I have not the power enough even to make the people come here to listen to your message. I expressed a wish to have all that were at home here. It is of no use for me to make a good speech to send to the Governor, for as soon as you are gone, the people would do as they like and I will be held responsible.[98]

If the tactic of appointing Native constables was less than a complete success, an alternative solution to the problem of "Indian" administration on the upper Skeena was soon found. The Babine Indian Agency was established by the Department of Indian Affairs in 1889, and R.E. Loring, one of the special constables who ascended the Skeena in 1888, was appointed the resident Indian agent.[99] There can be little doubt that this development met with the approval of the provincial government. Indeed, it may be argued that the provincial government reacted so forcibly in 1888 in order to achieve some such result.[100] When reviewing these events, the provincial Executive Council claimed that, since Confederation, the federal government had done little with respect to the Native peoples of the Skeena River: "Not a step has been taken to show any of the Indians referred to that there is over them a paternal Government to whom their interests have been intrusted and who are desirous of fostering amongst them a spirit of friendliness and goodwill, by attending to their interests, wants and cares."[101]

The establishment of the Babine Agency provided an answer to such criticism. A distinct and separate "Indian" administration in the area had the advantage of creating a channel for Native complaints and discontent that was directed towards, and funded by, Ottawa, not Victoria. Moreover, an Indian agent on the spot might be expected to deflect and deflate problems before they became political issues.[102] In the event of failure, the agent could shoulder the responsibility.

From the perspective of "settler society" then, the events of 1888 were of considerable importance. They focused attention on the problem, manifested in various expressions of discontent, of Native autonomy in the upper Skeena region. The solutions developed, if not entirely satisfactory, were acceptable – at least in the short term. Yet this interpretation is one-sided and must be tempered by an attempt to determine the Native view. Even with the availability of considerable documentation, it is by no means easy to ascertain how the Gitxsan viewed the events of 1888. Nonetheless, it is reasonable to assume that, as with the burning of Kitsegyukla in 1872, traditional culture provided the basic framework of understanding. From this perspective, two particular features of the Skeena Uprising stand out as worthy of further discussion: the death of Kamalmuk and its consequences and the meeting held at Gitanmaax on 8 August.

Kamalmuk was by no means the first person whose death the Gitxsan saw as the result of settler actions and, hence, the responsibility of the non-Native "tribe." As in earlier cases, notably the murder of A.C. Youmans, a negotiated settlement involving the payment of compensation was the appropriate response. Moreover, there is reason to believe that, in Gitxsan eyes, Constable Loring's actions conformed with the preliminary stages of this process. After examining Kamalmuk's body at Gitwangax, Loring promised – in writing, according to Mrs. Lagaxnitz – that the courts would provide appropriate redress. Loring may well have intended to do no more than provide assurance that due process of Canadian law would be followed. For Kamalmuk's relatives, however, redress implied compensation according to the precepts of Gitxsan law. Charles Mark believed that the entire affair "would have blown over and the shame of his [Kamalmuk's] death washed away had the government offered some payment, no matter how small." Instead, the resentment persisted. This situation was confirmed by Barbeau in the 1920s, when he observed that "no white man to the present can set foot on the tribal domains of the Gitanyow natives."[103]

Ironically, although Constable Green was acquitted at his trial at Nanaimo, and no compensation was forthcoming from that direction, a payment may have been made to Kamalmuk's widow. Fitzstubbs, in a letter to the attorney general, reported that, with respect "to a donation to the widow of Kit-wan-cool Jim, it would be a graceful act and indeed one of humanity ... By all means give her some thing, $100.00."[104] But a payment to Kamalmuk's wife, even if it took place, would not have satisfied his family, as defined by the rules of matrilineal descent, in Gitanyow. Indeed, it may well have added insult to injury.

In considering the persistence of resentment at Gitanyow, the lack of representation from the village at the meeting of 8 August at Gitanmaax is also significant. Fitzstubbs and Roycraft had convened the meeting, in part, to defuse the hostility of the Gitxsan after the shooting of Kamalmuk. The meeting on board HMS *Scout* in 1872 may have served as a precedent, but the Gitanmaax meeting had far fewer of the characteristics of a traditional feast. It was, however, a formal and public occasion, with speeches made by representatives of "settler" authorities and five of the Gitxsan and Wet'suwet'en villages. Furthermore, as I describe shortly, some kind of understanding, if not agreement, between the two sides seems to have emerged. Even so, the absence of the injured party, Kamalmuk's family from Gitanyow, would have left them unimpressed by such a development.

To those in attendance, Fitzstubbs stated that his objective was to inform them "why we have been sent here, of our duties and yours, and to inform you of the terms on which for the future we are to live."[105] The "terms" Fitzstubbs had in mind involved, essentially, the application of "British law not the Indian law." Thus disputes between Natives, for example, should be submitted to "the law for enquiry and adjustment." Nonetheless, the chiefs were called upon to play a crucial role in this system. "You may not settle your own quarrels," Fitzstubbs warned, but each chief should be "the promoter and preserver of good order within his own tribe, and it is his duty, on all occasions where his Indians are doing wrongly to apply to the Magistrate appointed ... who will do what the law directs." Each chief, in other words, would "be held responsible for the behaviour of his people."[106]

The responses of the chiefs to these demands, as translated by Margaret Hankin, can only be described as polite and accommodating. For example, Geddumcaldoe, the leading chief at Gitanmaax, stated:

> Great chiefs and Fellow chiefs ... Before we disperse I trust we will all have learned a good lesson. We have gone through a great excitement this last summer and we feel that you have acted very friendly in coming up and explaining to us the danger we incur by acting as we have done. We are like so many children, and we need some one to control us. We are thankful for your kind words: they have kindled a light that will shine brightly far and near. I acknowledge my incapability as Chief, but in the future I shall act better.[107]

Roycraft interpreted this, and other similar speeches, as indicating acceptance of "settler" demands by the Gitxsan and Wet'suwet'en. On returning to Victoria, he informed the attorney general that the Natives had "promised to keep the law" and that their chiefs would "bring all offenders to justice."[108]

It is unlikely that Gitxsan and Wet'suwet'en perceptions of this meeting, and its implications, were quite so straightforward. Attended by thirteen chiefs, at a busy season of the year, it was clearly an important public occasion. Moreover, one of the chiefs indicated the steps that would be taken to circulate reports of what had transpired. "Soon," Guxsan of Kitsegyukla informed his audience, "we will have a great feast in our village and we will tell our young men all the good and kind words you have said to us."[109]

The role of the chiefs, both at the meeting and in implementing any promises, was crucial, as Fitzstubbs recognized. Yet the insistence that the chiefs were representatives – or intermediaries – for their people was little more than a restatement of their traditional role in novel circumstances. Thus Geddumcaldoe was reported to have posted a notice on his house stating that "any white man having any grievance against an Indian was to come to the chief and he would preserve the peace."[110] However, as noted earlier, Fitzstubbs' attempt to appoint chiefs as special constables was a failure. This may have been the result, in part, of missionary opposition and advice, as Fitzstubbs clearly believed. But there was also a lack of congruence between the role of chief and special constable. The power of the chief, as Geddumcaldoe indicated in 1874, did not extend to the forms of coercion inherent in the position of constable. If so, the Gitxsan view of any promises made at Gitanmaax were more constrained than the officials appreciated.[111]

On the other hand, there was clearly a range of Gitxsan responses. Some, well before the Gitanmaax meeting, were prepared to accept a white official as an arbiter of some intra-Native disputes. The gold commissioner at Lorne Creek, A. Graham, complained in 1885 that Natives "from various tribes" had many "trivial grievances among themselves which they bring to the Government 'Judge' to settle."[112] Such approaches were adaptations to a changing environment, but they did not mean, as Fitzstubbs hoped, an abandonment of customary laws. As Guxsan indicated, there would be a "feast," in which the new situation would be discussed.

Conclusion

For the Gitxsan, and to a lesser extent the Wet'suwet'en, the dramatic events of the "uprising" posed, in a new and acute form, a fundamental problem: how to respond to the growing incursions of settler society. The history of direct contact stretched back at least sixty years, but the pace of interaction had quickened since the Omineca gold rush. A sequence of incidents, between 1872 and 1884, arose out of the operation of Gitxsan laws and their application to members of settler society. These incidents did not occur randomly across Gitxsan territory but reflected, and were responses to, the shifting geography of settler incursions into the upper Skeena region. Official responses to these incidents were ad hoc in nature. The "uprising" of 1888 brought this phase of the contact process to a conclusion.

Unlike earlier incidents, the uprising grew out of settler intervention in an internal Gitxsan dispute – a conflict over the inheritance of a name and its associated socio-political status. Thus, in a contradictory fashion, the show of force manifested in the Skeena River Expedition, and the official reports it generated, were testimony to the operation of Gitxsan laws, however poorly comprehended. On the other hand, officials sought to undermine the legitimacy of the indigenous system and Gitxsan assertions of autonomy in general.

The novel scale of the official response must be seen in the context of the widespread pattern of Native discontent that developed in British Columbia in the 1880s, encompassing the Gitxsan, their coastal neighbours the Tsimshian and the Nisga'a, and, to a lesser extent, the Wet'suwet'en. In other words, the "Skeena Uprising" was a regional incident, and the Skeena River Expedition was designed to impress the peoples of the lower as well as the upper Skeena.[113]

The uprising also played out in the context of enduring federal-provincial tensions over jurisdiction and expenditures. The result was the incorporation of the upper Skeena into the federal "Indian" administrative system. The Babine Indian Agency, with its resident agent, was an administrative structure intended to prevent, or resolve, subsequent difficulties with the Gitxsan "on the spot." As such, it was a manifestation of a beneficent paternalism – one that also acted as a vehicle for securing access to the land and resources of this distant hinterland. For settler society, this represented the extension of law and order into a void of lawlessness, at federal expense; in time, Gitxsan laws would be rendered invisible – a situation that the *Delgamuukw* case, a century later, sought to rectify.

Notes
The following abbreviations are used in the notes:
BAL   Babine Agency Letterbooks
BCA   British Columbia Archives
BCSP   British Columbia *Sessional Papers*
B/F   Barbeau/Beynon, Northwest Coast Files, CMC
BS   Black Series, DIA Files
CMC   Canadian Museum of Civilization
CMS   Church Missionary Society
DIAAR   Department of Indian Affairs, Annual Reports
DSGIA   Deputy Superintendent General, Indian Affairs
LAC   Library and Archives Canada
SGIA   Superintendent General, Indian Affairs
UBCL   University of British Columbia Library
VDC   *Victoria Daily Colonist*

1 Robert Galois and Arthur J. Ray, "The Fur Trade on the Cordillera, to 1857," in *Historical Atlas of Canada*, vol. 2, *The Land Transformed, 1800-1891*, ed. R. Louis Gentilcore (Toronto: University of Toronto Press, 1984), plate 19.

2 Gisday Wa and Delgam Uukw, *The Spirit in the Land* (Gabriola, BC: Reflections, c. 1992), 35-36. This outlines Gitxsan laws and relates them to more familiar views. Daly provides a detailed discussion of many aspects of Gitxsan culture, including legal issues such as the system of ownership and transmission of land and resources. See Richard Daly, *Our Box Was Full: An Ethnography for the* Delgamuukw *Plaintiffs* (Vancouver: UBC Press, 2005).

3 R.M. Galois, "The Burning of Kitsegukla, 1872" *BC Studies* 94 (1992): 59-81. Lieutenant-Governor Trutch described the payments to the Kitsegyukla chiefs as a matter of "grace," reflecting both paternalism of colonialism and his desire to avoid legal precedents.

4 The comments are taken from LAC, RG 10, BS, vol. 3617, file 4573, Powell to SGIA, 15 April 1875. For an outline of these events, see R. Galois, "History of the Upper Skeena Region, 1850 to 1927," *Native Studies Review* 9, 2 (1993-94): 113-83. Daly, *Our Box Was Full*, 258-63, outlines Gitxsan ideas on trespass.

5 "Xsiixsw" is defined in Neil Sterritt, Susan Marsden, Robert Galois, Peter R. Grant, and Richard Overstall, *Tribal Boundaries in the Nass Watershed* (Vancouver: UBC Press, 1998), 294, as a system of compensation "in which one house relinquishes wealth, names, crests, or territory to repay a crime committed by its members against those of another house. Compensation for the accidental death of an individual might involve a gift of material wealth." See also Daly, *Our Box Was Full*, 268-70.

6 These events have been described and analyzed in a number of different works, published and unpublished, scholarly and popular. See Cecil Clark, *Tales of the British Columbia Provincial Police* (Sydney, BC: Gray's Publishing, 1971); Barry Gough, *Gunboat Frontier: British Maritime Authority and Northwest Coast Indians, 1846-1890* (Vancouver: UBC Press, 1984), 205-9; and I.V.B. Johnson, "The Skeena Uprising, 1888," Canadian Museum of Civilization, Ethnology Division, Box 259, file 22 (copy at the Office of Gitxsan Chiefs, Mss 79-F 51). By far the most interesting description of the "uprising" was produced by C.M. Barbeau in *The Downfall of Temlaham* (Edmonton: Hurtig, 1973 [1928]). It grew out of Barbeau's anthropological fieldwork in the upper Skeena region, undertaken between 1920 and 1924, and straddles the scholarly and popular fields. *The Downfall of Temlaham*, or at least the section on Kamalmuk, is based upon oral testimony, both Native and non-Native, collected during these field sojourns. Barbeau's version blends information from a variety of different sources, without identifying the particular contributions of specific informants. His objectives, it would appear, were literary rather than academic. Fortunately, the Barbeau/Beynon Files make it possible to examine the sources that Barbeau used.

7 BCA, GR 677, file 711, Green to Robson, 14 March 1888. Pierce was a mixed-blood Tsimshian who had been ordained in 1887. See W.H Pierce, *From Potlatch to Pulpit, Being the Autobiography of Rev. William Henry Pierce* (Vancouver: Vancouver Bindery, 1933).

8 Gitanyow is the Gitxsan name for the village in the Kitwancool Valley; the anglicization is also used for the village in some sources – hence "Kitwancool" Jim.

9 BCA, GR 677, no. 711, Green to Robson, 14 March 1888. Thus he would not surrender, as Haatq had done in 1884, following the murder of Youmans.

10 Ibid. This was part of the resolution of the incident of 1872, see Galois, "The Burning of Kitsegukla."

11 BCA, GR 677, nos. 291 and 346, Anderson to Attorney General, 5 April 1888, and Wootton to Attorney General, 3 April 1888.

12 BCA, GR 677, no. F 709, Deputy Attorney General to Anderson, 31 March 1888. Todd had only recently been appointed to the Northwest Coast Agency.

13 See, for example, BCA, GR 677, nos. 295, 296, 299, 333, 346, 348, 399, F 716, F 792, F 803, F 805, F 806, and F 808. The party of special constables was recruited in Victoria and departed on a steamer for Port Essington on 27 April.

14 Unless otherwise stated, information on the killing of Kamalmuk is taken from the report of the trial of Constable Green, published in the *Nanaimo Free Press* (7 November 1888), and the official report of I.W. Powell, Supt. of Indian Affairs in British Columbia, LAC, RG 10, BS, vol. 3802, file 49774, Powell to DSGIA, 14 July 1888.

15 The delay in reaching Kitwanga was caused, in part, by the difficulties Washburn experienced in hiring a canoe. News of the shooting appears to have reached Hazelton on Saturday, 16 June; it was not until Monday that a canoe was obtained, and then only by purchase. See BCA, GR 677, no. 487, Washburn to Attorney General, 27 June 1888. Unfortunately, the first page of this report is missing; hence, there is some uncertainty about when the news reached Hazelton.

16 *Victoria Daily Times*, 18 July, 1923. This account was recorded at a time when Loring had retired from the position of Indian agent for the Babine Agency – a post he had occupied from 1889 to 1921.

17 Green, Holmans, and Parker had left Kitwanga, by trail, for Hazelton before the arrival of Washburn and Loring. The specials were reunited on 20 June, when Washburn and Loring, also having travelled overland, reached Hazelton.

18 BCA, GR 677, no. 487, Washburn to Attorney General, 27 June 1888.

19 Washburn decided to forego pursuit of the Kisgegas murderers. After the conclusion of the "uprising," however, one of the murderers, Pacht, was arrested at Kispiox early in December 1888. Fitzstubbs, then serving as stipendiary magistrate at Hazelton, reported on the arrest and provided a synopsis of the preceding events (LAC, RG 10, BAL, vol. 1584, Fitzstubbs to Attorney General, 5 January 1889).

20 BCA, GR 677, no. 487, Washburn to Attorney General, 27 June 1888.

21 Ibid.

22 BCA, GR 677, no. 491, Field et al. to Attorney General, 1 July 1888.

23 On Borland's journey, see, UBCL, CMS, vol. 124, no. 61, Field to Fenn, 16 July 1888; BCA, GR 677, no. 490, Wootton to Attorney General, 5 July 1888; BCA, GR 1198, Minutes of the Executive Council Relative to the Indian Troubles on the Skeena River, pp. 9-10. The last mentioned source indicates that Borland was allowed to leave the area, "on the distinct promise ... that the canoe in which he proceeded, should not be used for the purpose of bringing back policemen, the Indians stating that it was only because he was a stranger to the locality and had nothing to do with the troubles then existing that he would be allowed to proceed down the river."

24 Letters also were received from Fitzstubbs and Wootton, both dated 5 July and written from Nass Harbour and Metlakatla, respectively. They added little, however, to the picture provided by the aforementioned sources (BCA, GR 677, nos. 489 and 490). Borland reached Victoria on 11 July (VDC, 12 July 1888).

25 BCA, GR 677, no. 536, Roycraft to Attorney General, 12 July 1888.

26 The points at issue between the federal and provincial governments were both jurisdictional and financial. The provincial government also wanted Powell to accompany any force that was sent to the upper Skeena. This was an offer that Powell declined to accept. The detailed course of the exchanges between the various parties to these negotiations can be traced in GR 677. Subsequently, in an attempt to obtain reimbursement from the federal government, the province claimed that the costs of the Skeena Expedition amounted to $5,441.08 for sending "C" Battery and $2,645.58 for sending the party of constables (see, BCSP 1888, Papers Relating to the Mission of the Honourable Mr. Robson to Ottawa, in October 1888, p. 161).

27 VDC, 15 July 1888; BCA GR 677, nos. 592-99, 664, and G207-24; LAC, RG 2, vol. 532, no. 1490G (a), Holmes to Middleton, 29 August 1888. The *Colonist* sent a "war correspondent" with the expedition.

28 Fitzstubbs was appointed to his position on 23 May 1888. His predecessor, A. Graham, had departed from Lorne Creek towards the end of August 1887, leaving "all government property" with W.H. Dempster at Aberdeen (*BC Gazette*, 25 May 1888, p. 250; BCA, GR 526, vol. 28, no. 661, Graham to Provincial Secretary, 8 September 1887). Apart from the visit by Indian Agent Todd and the specials under Constable Anderson in May 1888, there was no "official" presence on the upper Skeena between the end of August 1887 and July 1888.

29 BCA, GR 677, nos. 489, 661, and 625, Fitzstubbs to Attorney General, 5 and 24 July 1888; Wootton to Attorney General, 7 July 1888. Fitzstubbs' difficulties were the result of the Natives being fully occupied at the canneries: the departure of Duncan and the people of

Metlakatla in 1887 contributed to a shortage of Aboriginal labour on the Coast during the 1888 canning season.

30 BCA, GR 677, no. 661, Fitzstubbs to Attorney General, 24 July 1888.

31 At Kitsegyukla, while on his way to Hazelton, Fitzstubbs had encountered what appeared to be further repercussions of the Kamalmuk-Neatsqua feud. The village was "almost deserted, the people having left for the woods in a state of terror at the double homicide of a few days before" (BCA, GR 677, no. 661, Fitzstubbs to Attorney General, 24 July). Tobush, a local shaman, had killed Neeseyequet, the father-in-law of Kamalmuk. The reasons for this murder are not clear in the documentary sources, but Tobush, in turn, had been shot by Morlcken, a chief of the tribe and brother of Neeseyequet (BCA, GR 429, box 2, file 1, Inquest of Tobush, Kitsequecla Indian). Morlcken was arrested by Washburn on 10 July (BCA, GR 677, no. 626, Washburn to Attorney General, 16 July 1888). At the ensuing inquest into the death of Tobush, a verdict of "justifiable homicide" was returned and Morlcken was released (BCA, GR 429, no. 666, Roycraft to Attorney General, 14 August 1888). These events, no doubt, added to the tension among the sparse non-Native population of the region.

32 The trial was held in November and resulted in an acquittal (*Nanaimo Free Press*, 7 November 1888).

33 BCA, GR 429, no. 666, Roycraft to Attorney General, 14 August 1888.

34 BCA, GR 677, no. 661, Fitzstubbs to Attorney General, 24 July 1888.

35 LAC, RG 10, BS, vol. 3802, file 49774, Nelson to Secretary of State, 18 October 1888. The report was made by David Chalmers, with Margaret Hankin as translator. The chiefs identified were Guthumuldoe (Geddumcaldoe) and Spawr of Gitanmaax; Wassamlaha of Kispiox; Leechol and two sons of Kitassemnop of Hagwilgate; Morelahan, Koockezun (Guxsan), and Arra of Kitsegyukla; and, Cawgh, Liggenthala, Lululth, and Niscouglah of Gitwangax. The report of the meeting, with minor variations, had been published two months earlier. An account: VDC, 16 August 1888.

36 Hagwilget was a Wet'suwet'en village at the north end of the Bulkley Canyon; the other villages were Gitxsan settlements located on the Skeena River.

37 BCA, GR 429, no. 666, Roycraft to Attorney General, 14 August 1888.

38 BCA, GR 677, no. 665, Field to Roycraft, 6 August 1888, and Washburn to Roycraft, 7 August 1888.

39 BCA, GR 677, no. 665, Fitzstubbs to Roycraft, 6 August 1888.

40 These Gitxsan narratives, supplemented with accounts from white informants, were blended into a single "fictional" narrative by Barbeau and published under the title of *The Downfall of Temlaham* in 1928.

41 The most detailed account of these events is provided by Jim Lagaxnitz and Sinclair. They identify Kitwanga as the site of the initial feast (CMC, B/F/201.7, pp. 1 and 4). Other accounts, apparently conflating the sequence, locate both the feast at which the conflict began and the subsequent death of Kamalmuk's son, Gamuxon, at Kitwancool (CMC, Guxsan, B/F/89.7; Mrs. J. Lagaxnitz, B/F/201.6).

42 CMC, Lagaxnitz and Sinclair, B/F/201.7, pp. 1-4.

43 A second son, Kumas, also died during the epidemic (CMC, Guxsan, B/F/89.7, pp. 1-2). In a number of the narratives Kamalmuk's wife is identified as Hanamuk, indicating that she had inherited the name previously claimed for her son. During Barbeau's visits she lived at Andimaul and had acquired an English name, Fanny Johnson (Semedik, B/F/89.4, p. 1 and Mark, B/F/89.9, p. 7). For further details on the measles epidemic, see LAC, RG 10, BS, vol. 3818, file 57837, Letter from the Methodist Missionary Society, Statement by W.H. Pierce, 32.

44 CMC, Charles Mark and Mrs. Cox, B/F/89.9. See also, Semedik, B/F/201.3, p. 1 and Lelt, B/F/89.2, p. 1. It was this same Gitxsan law that had culminated in the murder of A.C. Youmans in 1884.

45 CMC, Mrs. Lagaxnitz, B/F/201.6, p. 5. According to the narrative of Semedik (B/F/89.4, p. 1), the maternal relatives of Neatsqua did pay an "indemnity" to Kamalmuk for the death of his son. But this was done only after Neatsqua had been shot and without the usual accompanying ceremony.

46 Kamalmuk had been born at Gitanyow but, in 1888, lived in Kitsegyukla with his wife and family. Kitsegyukla was also the home village of Neatsqua, but, as the narratives show, he had relatives in Gitanyow. This reference to a big war is found in Semedik (CMC, B/F/201.3, p. 4), following a statement that his wife, a cousin of Kamalmuk, had nearly become a victim of the feud.

47 The various stages in the negotiations, with residents of Kitwanga acting as intermediaries, are described by Lagaxnitz (CMC, B/F/201.7, pp. 10-11).

48 A similar, but less detailed, account was provided by Guxsan (CMC, B/F/89.7, p. 3).

49 This was the opinion of Lelt (CMC, B/F/89.2, p. 5). Mrs. Lagaxnitz (B/F/201.6), in a slightly different version, states that the relatives of Neatsqua "reported the matter to the police." Given that Washburn was related by marriage, these statements are not necessarily incompatible. The background information on Washburn can be confirmed, in part, from documentary sources. Reverend Field, when passing Kitsegyukla in 1886, "saw a whiteman called Washburn. He has been a miner, is now keeping a store on his own a/c at his village" (UBCL, CMS, vol. 124, no. 63, Field to Fenn, 20 May 1886). Moreover Walter Washburn, a mixed-blood boy from Kitsegyukla, was reported to be attending the Port Simpson Industrial School in 1893. The boy was aged twelve and a half years, which suggests that his father reached the area by 1879 or 1880 (Vancouver School of Theology Archives, Port Simpson District, Minutes 1893, p. 32).

50 CMC, Mark, B/F/89.9, p. 4; Isaac Tens, B/F/68.7, p. 6; and Guxsan, B/F/89.7, p. 4. Wiget, in an ambiguous section, claims that he reminded the people of Kitsegyukla of the 1872 agreement. The results of his action are not stated, but the implication is clear enough: "The fathers on the men of war [in 1872] told us that we must not kill each other, but we must bring all our troubles to them and they would judge them."

51 All but one of the narratives that identify a destination for Kamalmuk during this period refer to the Nass River. The exception, Semedik (CMC, B/F/201.3, p. 5), refers to Tsetsaut country, which is a difference more in the form of identification than in substance. For maps of Gitanyow territory see Sterritt et al., *Tribal Boundaries*. The locations on the Nass are described variously.

52 CMC, Semedik, B/F/201.3, p. 5. Simon Gunanoot, after being suspected of murdering two non-Native men at Hazelton in 1906, lived on the land until 1919. He then surrendered to the police and was acquitted at trial (Sterritt et al., *Tribal Boundaries*, 229-30).

53 Lagaxnitz (CMC, B/F/201.7, p. 14). A similar version of this message is contained in Mark (B/F/89.9, p. 4), with the exception that Loring is identified as the author. Lelt (B/F/89.2, p. 3) indicates that a second letter was sent, via 'axg t, but by this time Kamalmuk had returned to Gitanyow, on his way to surrender. The reference to Stickeen refers to Gitxsan involvement in the Cassiar gold rush of the 1870s.

54 See, for example, Anna Campbell (CMC, B/F/68.2, p. 3) and Lagaxnitz (B/F/201.7, pp. 17-18).

55 According to Lelt (CMC, B/F/89.2, p. 2), the terms offered for his assistance involved his family moving to Hazelton where they would "receive compensation and I was to receive $50.00 for my trip to Gitwintkul [Gitanyow]. If I was to deliver the message to Jim [Kamalmuk], I was to receive $100.00."

56 CMC, Lelt, B/F/89.2, p. 3.

57 CMC, Lagaxnitz (B/F/201.17, p. 19), Wiget (B/F/68.7, p. 3), Charles Mark (B/F/89.9, p. 5), and Anna Campbell (B/F/68.2, p. 4). All state that Kamalmuk was armed. Anna Campbell adds that he fired twice.

58 CMC, Charles Mark (B/F/89.9, p. 5) and Simon Gunanoot (B/F/90.1, p. 3) state that he had stopped; Lelt (B/F/89.2, p. 4) and Semedik (B/F/89.4, p. 2) state that he had stopped and was shot from behind; Anna Campbell (B/F/68.2, p. 3), Lagaxnitz (B/F/201.17, p. 19), and Wiget (B/F/68.7, p. 3) state that he was shot from behind; Mrs. Lagaxnitz (B/F/201.6, p. 3) and Dan Guxsan (B/F/89.7, p. 4) state that he was sitting; Isaac Tens (B/F/89.8, p. 9) states that he was standing by a fence. George Derrick (B/F/89.3, p. 2) provides no details and, curiously, states that Loring shot Kamalmuk.

59 CMC, B/F/89.4:, pp. 2-3.

60 CMC, Mark (B/F/89.9, p. 6). Barbeau, *Downfall of Temlaham*, 141, employed this construction of Kamalmuk's behaviour.

61 CMC, Semedik, B/F/201.3, p. 6. The sex of Semedik is unclear from the transcript of Barbeau's notes. In the section cited here, the third-person feminine is used. Elsewhere, the informant refers to his wife (cf. B/F/201.3, pp. 6 & 4). Presumably, the former is an error in the transcription.

62 CMC, B/F/201.7, p. 20. The criticisms included a reported threat to behead the corpse.

63 CMC, Mark, B/F/89.9, p. 6.

64 Barbeau, *Downfall of Temlaham*, 154-55. On the offer of compensation, see BCA, GR 677, no. 943, Fitzstubbs to Attorney General, 30 September 1888.

65 UBCL, CMS, vol. 124, no. 50, Field Report to CMS, 30 June 1888.

66 BCA, GR 677, no. 661, Fitzstubbs to Attorney General, 24 July 1888.

67 BCA, GR 677, no. 663, Fitzstubbs to Attorney General, 27 July 1888.

68 BCA, GR 677, no. 665, M. Hankin to Roycraft, 7 August 1888. A more detailed version of the measles story was provided to Barbeau by Constance Cox, Margaret Hankin's daughter (CMC, B/F/89.5, p. 1). Margaret McCauly, who was later described as a half-breed, married Thomas Hankin at Fort Rupert in 1871 (VDC, 5 July 1871; UBCL, CMS, A 125, no. 725, Field to Baring-Gould, 30 July 1900). Following the death of Thomas Hankin in 1885, she traded on her own account before remarrying. Her second husband was R.E. Loring, who, after his service as one of the special constables sent to the area in 1888, became the first resident Indian agent at Hazelton.

69 BCA, GR 677, no. 663, Fitzstubbs to Attorney General, 27 July 1888.

70 UBCL, CMS, A 124, no. 508, Field, Report to CMS, 25 May 1887. Such comments are not very different in tone and substance from those made in connection with the Cassiar Trail incidents of 1874. See, for example, the letter by Hazelnut in VDC, 18 October 1874.

71 See, for example, the petition from the Chiefs of Gitwangax, 10 October 1884, in Return to an Order, BCSP, 1885, 284-85. The original, written by Tomlinson, is found in BCA, GR 526, box 25, 628/84.

72 BCA, GR 677, no. 663, Fitzstubbs to Attorney General, 27 July 1888. Settler distaste for Duncan and Tomlinson was widespread at this time; in 1887, DSGIA Vankhougnet had recommended that action be taken against them under the Indian Act. Macdonald, however, preferred procrastination (LAC, RG 10, BS, vol. 3670, file 10777, Vankhougnet to Macdonald, 4 April 1887).

73 BCA, GR 677, no. 663, Fitzstubbs to Attorney General, 27 July 1888.

74 BCA, GR 667, no. 663, Fitzstubbs to Attorney General, 17 July 1888.

75 Turner-Turner, J., *Three Years Hunting and Trapping in America and the Great Northwest* (London: Maclure and Co., 1888).

76 Ibid., 101.

77 For a discussion of Gitxsan law governing access to territory and resources, see Daly, *Our Box Was Full*, chap. 7.

78 Turner-Turner, *Three Years Hunting and Trapping*, 102.

79 UBCL, CMS, vol. 124, no. 21, Field to Fenn, January 1888.

80 Information on these developments reached the government through its own channels and through the HBC hierarchy (BCA, GR 677, no. 347, Clifford to Wootton, 6 April 1888, no. 309, T.R. Smith to Provincial Secretary, 27 April 1888; GR 526, box 28, no. 149, A. Graham to Provincial Secretary, 11 February 1888). The quotations are taken from the letters written by Clifford and Smith.

81 UBCL, CMS, vol. 124, no. 21, Field to Fenn, January 1888.

82 BCA, GR 677, no. 663, Fitzstubbs to Attorney General, 27 July 1888.

83 LAC, RG 10, BAL, vol. 1585, Loring to Vowell, 31 July 1894.

84 LAC, RG 10, BS, vol. 3802, file 49774, Nelson to Secretary of State, 18 October 1888; VDC, 16 August 1888. This complaint was directed at HBC clerk C.W.D. Clifford. On Clifford's attitudes towards Natives during the "rush" to Lorne Creek, see British Columbia, *Metlakatla Inquiry, 1884*, vi-vii.

85 Allan Graham, the first gold commissioner at Lorne Creek, provided a fascinating glimpse of the link between Duncan and Tomlinson, at Metlakatla, and the Gitxsan. A number of Gitwangax people had been educated at Metlakatla and considered themselves to be "Duncanites." Moreover, two of Tomlinson's Native teachers had travelled up the Skeena

in the summer of 1885, "with letters to all the villages ... that the Government wanted to take their lands and give to whitemen." It was Graham's opinion that the majority of the Gitxsan were opposed to such missionary endeavours, preferring to rely on the "government to protect them." There were undoubtedly differences of opinion among the Gitxsan about the most effective means of dealing with white encroachments (BCA, GR 526, box 28, no. 149, Graham to Provincial Secretary, 11 February 1886). There were, of course, a variety of more traditional links between the Gitxsan and Wet'suwet'en, on the one hand, and the Tsimshian and the Nisga'a, on the other. These links extended back to the precontact period. See R.C. Harris and G. Matthews, *Historical Atlas of Canada*, Volume 1, *From the Beginning to 1800* (Toronto: University of Toronto Press, 1987), plate 13.

86 British Columbia, *Metlakatlah Inquiry, 1884*. "Papers Relating to the Commission appointed to enquire into the state and condition of the Indians of the North-West Coast of British Columbia," *British Columbia Sessional Papers*, 1888, 422. The Tsimshian had been pointing to the absence of treaties since at least 1881. See, for example, LAC, RG 10, BS, vol. 3605, file 2806, Petition to Indian Reserve Commissioner, Port Simpson, 5 October 1881.

87 Letter written 1 November 1887, cited in D. Raunet, *Without Surrender, Without Consent: A History of the Nishga Land Claims* (Vancouver: Douglas and McIntyre, 1984), 93-94.

88 The travails of surveyor S.P. Tuck in attempting to survey reserves in the vicinity of Kaien Island in 1886 are reported in a series of letters to the Indian reserve commissioner (LAC, RG 10, vol. 11008).

89 J.W. McKay was appointed to the newly established North West Coast Agency in 1884, but he occupied the post only briefly, "owing to the troubles and disturbed condition of matters at Metlakatla." It was not until 1887 that a permanent replacement was found: A.C. Elliott, a provincial stipendiary magistrate, served as an interim agent after the withdrawal of McKay, but nothing is known of his actions (DIAAR 1884, lvii, 120). J.C. Hughes was appointed as Indian agent in June 1886, but nothing more has been found out about him; he was replaced the following year by Charles Todd (RG 10, vol. 11190, file 2, 139). The information on Port Simpson is found in LAC, RG 10, BS, vol. 3699, file 16682.

90 James A. McDonald, "Trying to Make a Life: The Historical Political Economy of Kitsumkalum" (PhD diss., University of British Columbia, 1985), 153. The first resident fishery guardian for the Skeena River was appointed in 1885. According to McDonald, there were, at this time, "numerous restrictions upon the resource and tensions ... [were] growing between the [Coast] Tsimshian and immigrant populations."

91 On the events at Gitwangax in 1886, see LAC, RG 10, BS, vol. 3670, file 10777, Stephenson to Powell, 9 December 1886. For O'Reilly's perception of the links in relation to opposition to reserves, see LAC, RG 10, vol. 1277, 438ff, O'Reilly to SGIA, 20 October 1891.

92 BCA, GR 677, no. 943, Fitzstubbs to Attorney General, 30 September 1888.

93 BCA, GR 677, no. 661, Fitzstubbs to Attorney General, 24 July 1888 and no. 666, Roycraft to Attorney General, 14 August 1888.

94 LAC, RG 10, BAL, vol. 1584, Fitzstubbs to Attorney General, 23 April 1889.

95 LAC, RG 10, BAL, vol. 1584, Fitzstubbs to Attorney General, 5 January 1889.

96 Ibid. Fitzstubbs, in fact, did succeed in obtaining one policeman from Kispiox. This was Big Louis, apparently not a chief, in whose house Fitzstubbs had conducted his initial interview with the chiefs of Kispiox.

97 LAC, RG 10, BAL, vol. 1584, Fitzstubbs to Morice, 7 August 1889. Morice was an Oblate missionary stationed at Ft St. James. In a previous letter, Fitzstubbs had mentioned only one chief at Hagwilgate, although in enthusiastic terms. The unnamed chief had "promised his active co-operation in reducing the Indians of his tribe to subordination and observance of the law. If he is as good as his word, I augur much good from it, as being powerful and determined, he is respected and sometimes feared by the other chiefs, and his example will be salutary" (BCA, GR 677, no. 663, Fitzstubbs to Attorney General, 27 July, 1888). The Methodists had established a mission at Hagwilgate, intruding into "Oblate territory."

98 BCA, GR 526, box 11, file 688, Brown to Provincial Secretary, 8 September 1874.

99 Loring's appointment was approved by Order in Council, 11 July 1889, appropriation having been passed in the previous session of Parliament. He occupied the post for the next

thirty years, retiring on 31 December 1920 (LAC, RG 2, series 1, vol. 425, no. 1688; see also BCA, GR 677, no. 665, Loring to Roycraft, 8 August 1888). For biographical details on Loring, see, LAC, MG 29/C/21, Loring to R.E. Gosnell, 5 September 1896.

100 The federal government initially argued that the "uprising" was a matter of provincial jurisdiction (BCA, GR 677, no. 586, Vankhougnet to Powell, 16 July 1888; Powell to Davie, 15 [?] July 1888). General Middleton, for one, doubted the legitimacy of the way in which the "expedition" was constituted by three members of the provincial cabinet acting as justices of the peace (LAC, RG 2, vol 532, no. 1490G [a], Middleton memo, 7 September 1888).

101 BCA, GR 1198, Minutes of the Executive Council, October 1888, pp. 23-4.

102 That the government of British Columbia was sensitive to political criticism is revealed by the removal of a section of a letter, from Harold Sheldon, as published in the Return to an Order of 1885. An Anglican clergyman serving the white population at the mouth of the Skeena, Sheldon wrote to the premier about the situation in that area. The offending portion of the letter reads: "It is a perfect scandal to the government to allow such a state of lawlessness. If they have any respect for human life, which it really seems as though they had not, they will send a man of war with full powers to quell any uprising or refusal to obey the magistrate's decisions. So far, a Man of War has simply been held up to ribaldry by the Indians, and as for one white constable, it was an act of lunacy to send him up" (BCA, GR 526, box 25, no. 558, Sheldon to Premier, 23 September 1884).

103 CMC, B/F/89.9, Charles Mark; Barbeau, *Downfall of Temlaham*, 162. An outline of protest activity by the Gitanyow people, through to 1929, is found in Galois, "History of the Upper Skeena Region"; and Sterritt et al., *Tribal Boundaries*.

104 BCA, GR 677, no. 943, Fitzstubbs to Attorney General, 30 September 1888.

105 LAC, RG 10, BS, vol. 3802, file 49774, Nelson to Secretary of State, 18 October 1888; VDC, 16 August 1888. See note 35.

106 Ibid.

107 Ibid.

108 BCA, GR 677, no. 666, Roycraft to Attorney General, 14 August 1888.

109 LAC, RG 10, BS, vol. 3802, file 49774, Nelson to Secretary of State, 18 October 1888; VDC, 16 August 1888.

110 VDC, 16 August 1888.

111 For a discussion of the role of chiefs, see Gisday Wa and Delgam Uukw, *Spirit in the Land*, 31-34.

112 BCA, GR 526, box 27, no. 325, Graham to Provincial Secretary, 29 June 1885.

113 This was certainly the opinion of Colonel Holmes of C Battery, LAC, RG 2, vol. 532, no. 1490G (a), Holmes to Middleton, 29 August 1888.

11
Arthur J. Ray and the Empirical Opportunity
Cole Harris

Although Arthur J. Ray – Skip Ray – and I have known each other for more than forty years, I come to his writing as outsider as much as insider. We met when he was an undergraduate and I a graduate student in the geography department at the University of Wisconsin, and our careers have been intertwined ever since. I worked with Skip on plates for the *Historical Atlas of Canada,* and since 1981 we have been at the same university (in different departments). We have taught a graduate course together and have examined each other's students. We both consider ourselves historical geographers. But my interest in European settler societies overseas and his in the fur trade have led us in different intellectual directions. Only recently, as I have written on the effects of settler colonialism on Native peoples and, in so doing, have considered the dispossessions and repossessions of land that underlie some of the court cases in which Skip has been an expert witness, have the trajectories of our research and writing converged somewhat. It is in this sense that we are insider and outsider to each other, and it is from this vantage point that I have particularly enjoyed considering his ample scholarly achievement.

I have vivid memories of the geography department at Wisconsin in which we both found our scholarly legs. The sixties there were heady years for fledgling historical geographers. Andrew Clark presided magnificently, the field was full of promise, and jobs were at hand. Clark's research seminars, their style derived from Carl Sauer's legendary seminars at Berkeley, were exciting affairs. Each year the seminar had a particular theme within which students identified research topics, which the seminar then discussed, and wrote research papers, which, paper by paper, were also discussed. All students were expected to participate in each seminar. The tone was not always polite. Slash and burn often seemed the appropriate agricultural analogy; Clark himself could be acerbic. Beyond the research seminar was the thesis and, for all of us, Clark's close scrutiny. A chapter sent to him was returned almost immediately with pages of his yellow foolscap commentary. He had the rare ability to subject a manuscript to a massive critique while convincing its author that the critique was in proportion to the study's essential merit. The system was rigorous, and it worked. It drew the best from many able students.

Clark was interested in the environments, settlements, and societies created by the migration of Europeans overseas. His seminars and most of the theses he directed (mine included) were on this track. Skip was more original in two basic respects. He shifted his ground away from Europeans and towards the prior, Native inhabitants of the land, and he did this not so much by looking at a particular Native people as by looking at a particular territory, the parkland belt in the northern Canadian prairie between the grasslands to the south and the boreal forest to the north. In effect, he set out to write on the changing economic geography of this territory. In so doing, he was led to study the ways in which precontact Native populations and economies had interacted with the parklands and adjacent spaces, and then the evolution of these patterns as European influences entered the region. In the parkland, these influences came from fur traders. Moreover, because the parkland was deep in the continental interior and, except for high-value, low-bulk goods like furs, was far beyond the reach of the European economy, the fur trade remained a dominating influence there for more than two hundred years. Skip's originality had given him a remarkable opportunity to explore processes of geographical change in which both Natives and Europeans participated, and to assess the effects of the interaction of Native economies with European commercial capital over a considerable reach of time.

Skip came to this work in the late 1960s, when a quantitative and often highly theoretical study of spatial relations was in high geographical fashion. Positivism was still a dominating paradigm, and few considered that knowledge was essentially relative, contextual, and power-laden. Historical geographers rebelled against only part of this agenda. Most of us thought that theory conceived as a prelude to the elucidation of spatial laws was a wild goose chase, but we were attracted to the prospect of a careful, rigorous, and, as far as possible, quantitative empiricism. Clark himself, his background partly actuarial, was particularly comfortable with censuses and numbers. As a group, we were uneasy with theory, especially as presented by the geographical theory of the day, and comfortable with data. Such empiricism was entirely compatible with the human/environment tradition of cultural-historical geography that had emanated from Berkeley and, in Skip's case, with the cultural ecology of Julian Steward and Fredrik Barth, both of whose writings he engaged at Wisconsin. Skip came to the parkland, in short, with a deep interest in human-environmental relationships, a suspicion of untested theoretical claims, and an enthusiastic commitment to careful, empirical research. All of this was inflected by an interest in live-lihoods – in economies – that derived partly from Clark's brand of historical geography, partly from Steward's cultural ecology, and partly from his own predilections.

When Skip began this work, the Hudson's Bay Company had just made microfilm copies of its vast record holdings available in the National Ar-chives of Canada in Ottawa. Before his thesis was finished, the records them-selves were transferred to the Provincial Archives of Manitoba in Winnipeg. He had taken on the parkland at the right time. A huge documentary record was suddenly available, which almost no one had used, and he was among a group of scholars who pounced on this opportunity. Eventually, having soaked himself in this archive, he knew it as well as anyone. Some of its documents – the instructions emanating from London, the traders' reports in return, the correspondence between traders and with London – were relatively easy to use, others (especially the account books) were much more obscure. When he had figured out the accounting system, the data by which a company office in London kept most accurate track of its dispersed North American operations were at his disposal. Moreover, they could be made to yield information about the influence of the trade on Native peoples – in-formation that company directors in London had not sought. In sum, for an empirically minded, quantitatively inclined young scholar, the Hudson's Bay Company Archives were a bonanza. They underlay his thesis, which became his first and perhaps most important book, *Indians in the Fur Trade* (1974),[1] and he has drawn on them in all his subsequent fur trade scholarship.

What has ensued is a life of focused scholarship. Skip is, primarily, a stu-dent of the fur trade. Eventually, there were two other books centred on the trade – *"Give Us Good Measure"* (with Donald B. Freeman, 1978) and *The Canadian Fur Trade in the Industrial Age* (1990) – as well as a good dozen articles, all of them important.[2] When he turned elsewhere, the connec-tions with the fur trade remained apparent. His illustrated history of Native Canada, *I Have Lived Here since the World Began* (1996), deals substantially, as it must, with the fur trade.[3] His book with Frank Tough and Jim Miller, *Bounty and Benevolence: A History of Saskatchewan Treaties* (2000), considers arrangements that were essentially forced on Native peoples as the fur trade economy collapsed.[4] Even his current work on the role of academics in court cases and hearings involving Aboriginal lands stems largely from his own appearances in court as an expert witness steeped in the Hudson's Bay Com-pany Archives and the fur trade.

Throughout this work, the premises on which it was launched have sur-vived essentially intact. Skip has always remained skeptical of theory that has not been empirically supported. In the face of such theory, his response time and again is to go to the archives with as open a mind as possible. Complex issues should not be prejudged; they should be investigated. Such investigation should be as quantitative as possible. Precise data, secured by careful investigation, are essential. With them, useful generalization is feasible, even a measure of theory, inductively derived. But he is no postcolonial theorist – no Foucault or Derrida lurks in the air. His work is a consistent example of a research methodology that is much less hegemonic than it was when his career began; as such, it is particularly appreciated in some quarters and particularly ignored in others. Rather than pronouncing, a priori, on the strengths or weaknesses of his ways, it may be more useful to test his methodology by delving into the archive of Skip's own writing to ascertain, as far as I can, what he has achieved. I do so in most of what follows.

The place to start is with *Indians in the Fur Trade*, the book that established his scholarly reputation and provided the framework for virtually all his subsequent research and writing on the fur trade. It is not a simple work. Centred on the parklands and the two ecological regions – the northern forest and the plains – that abutted them, it explores the changing Native relationship with these lands in response to pressures introduced by the fur trade and, to a lesser extent, by disease. As such, it deals with Native economies as they existed before the fur trade and as they were modified by it, with population displacements, with environmental changes and their effects, with the conduct of trade under competitive and monopoly conditions, with company policies and Native responses to them, and with issues of dependency. There are maps and graphs of a type that the fur trade literature had not seen before, and throughout there is an emphasis on Native agency. The focus is shifted from the bayside posts to the interior, and from white to Native traders. The latter are shown to be shrewd defenders of their own interests, and these interests are shown to have varied greatly in different circumstances. There was never *a* Native response to the fur trade. Yet there was a gradual loss of control as, sooner or later, Native groups lost the means of their own support. By 1870, the peoples of the northern woodlands were virtually Hudson's Bay Company (HBC) employees dependent on the company for food and supplies, while plains and parkland peoples, their bison almost gone, turned to sedentary agriculture and to treaties in which they relinquished almost all their land in return for small reserves and annuities.

The parklands were at the interface of plains people, who moved there in winter to hunt bison, and of northern woodland people, who also depended on winter bison hunts. In the spring the plains people moved out onto the plains and the woodland people into the forest – a pattern of seasonal migration and overlapping economies that brought different ecologies and the people dependent on them in touch with each other. This gave these people a considerable ecological flexibility while facilitating, Skip argued, their adaptation to changing economic circumstances. By the late seventeenth century, the Western Cree were well established in the woodland, and the Assiniboine were moving west to occupy much of the parkland/plains interface. Both were well placed to become principal participants in the fur trade, partly because they were still skilled canoe men (whereas the introduction of the horse was undermining this ability among many plains peoples) and partly because they were relatively close to the sources of European goods. For others, farther away, the fine calculation of canoe carrying capacity (for provisions as well as trade goods), travel time, and date of winter freeze-up inclined them to rely on middlemen, and the Cree and Assiniboine were in a position to monopolize this carrying trade. Increasingly, they did. Some of them became full-time traders who bargained for furs with Native suppliers and with French or English traders for European goods.

How, then, and what, did they trade? Skip pictures a somewhat hybrid trade not easily described by any one model. Native ceremonialism, particularly gift-giving, was always important – trade would not take place without it – though he suggests that, over time, gift-giving lost the political meaning it may initially have had and became one of the transaction costs of trade. HBC traders invented a currency that Native people could understand – the made beaver – and valued all goods accordingly. A gun or a fox skin was worth so much in made beaver. All skins were assigned a fixed value in made beaver (the comparative standard), as were European goods (the official standard), and both were well below European market values. The trader's standard (the prices traders actually charged and paid) was different again, always to the company's advantage. This difference was the overplus, and traders were judged by their ability to achieve it. Native traders were also sensitive to price, and they bargained closely. Over time, they tended to trade their lighter, more valuable furs to the French, taking high value-low bulk goods in return, and to trade heavier furs for more bulky goods such as kettles and firearms with the English. As competition intensified, consumable luxury goods became more important; the French relied on brandy and the English on Brazilian tobacco. Overall, however – and this, Skip suggests, is the major difference between this trade and the classic model of market economies – the trade had to adjust to the inelasticity of the Native demand for European goods. If the price of furs rose, Native traders brought in fewer furs. Demand inelasticity was related partly to the carrying capacity of canoes, partly to mobile lifestyles in which goods quickly became impediments, and partly to cultures that assigned no status value to material acquisition.

The role of the Cree and Assiniboine as middlemen in the fur trade was abruptly undermined after 1770 as competition between Hudson Bay- and

Montreal-based traders led to a proliferation of posts in Cree and Assiniboine territory and to efforts to bypass these middlemen by moving beyond them. By the 1780s, Montreal traders had established posts in the Mackenzie watershed and, after 1805, across the continental divide in what is now northern British Columbia. With the proliferation of posts, local Native trappers and European traders were able to deal directly with each other, and, with the northwestward expansion of posts, the long-distance carrying trade also bypassed Cree and Assiniboine middlemen. They had become redundant. Competition between traders from Hudson Bay and Montreal was more directly joined. It increased the scale of gift-giving and, as traders fixed on Native "captains" and showered them with gifts, may have begun to make wealth a prerequisite for chieftainship. It deluged the western interior with tobacco and alcohol, addictive consumables that lubricated trade when the demand for durable goods was satisfied. It drained the woodland and parkland of beaver, marten, and other furbearers, and much of the eastern woodland of game animals as well. The latter remained abundant in the parkland and on the plains, and as the demand for provisions – country produce – grew with the proliferation of posts, many Cree and Assiniboine, now that they were excluded from the middleman carrying trade in furs, became suppliers of provisions (dried meat, grease, and pemmican) derived largely from bison. Many of them moved southward, increasingly focused on the plains and on bison and, in so doing, became less dependent on European goods. On the other hand, remaining woodland groups, living close to trading posts and reliant on European goods to compensate for diminishing local resources, were increasingly dependent on the fur trade at a time when fur-bearing animals were disappearing. For many woodland bands, the situation became desperate. Underlying all of this were the effects of epidemics, principally of smallpox in 1781, which, according to the trader-surveyor David Thompson, killed a half to three-fifths of the Native people of the northern plains, parkland, and woodland. Apparently the Assiniboine population rebounded quickly, the Western Cree much more slowly.

With the merger of the Hudson's Bay Company and the North West Company in 1821, monopoly conditions returned to the trade, and the new North American governor of the amalgamated company, George Simpson, set out to rationalize the trade and place it on a secure long-term footing. To this end, he closed the costly trade route to Montreal, greatly reduced the number of trading posts, and released perhaps two-thirds of the employees of the former companies. He instructed traders to reduce gift-giving, restrict credit to trustworthy individuals, and curtail trade in alcohol. He thought that lower-quality trade goods would serve. In an effort to rebuild beaver populations, he banned steel traps and ordered traders to reject skins taken in the summer. He closed some posts with the hope that local animal populations would rebound, and he tried to encourage trade in animals at the peak of their population cycles while restricting trade in others. In 1826, he introduced a quota system limiting the number of pelts the company was prepared to trade, and, to better regulate the trade and manage the resource, he even proposed to settle Native families permanently in defined areas.

Skip shows how difficult it was, even in monopoly conditions, to enforce these measures, and that it was impossible where competition prevailed, as it soon did again throughout the southern margins of HBC territory. Company traders themselves were often loathe to comply, knowing that if they enforced the regulations trade would shift to another post. In Native societies there was no coercive overall administration to enforce such regulation, which, moreover, did not accord with Native understandings of conservation, territoriality, and trespass. Conservation measures were most effective where Native bands were least mobile, as they were where, for want of alternatives, they relied on local resources such as hare and fish. They were least successful on the plains, partly because the company, dependent on provisions from the region, hesitated to enforce its regulations there, partly because of growing competition from American hunters and traders. Throughout these years, bison were becoming scarcer and were found ever farther south and west. The Assiniboine now depended almost entirely on them and moved out onto the plains, abandoning the parkland. Cree occupied the territory they vacated: all the central parkland and much of the northern plains. Ojibwa, originally woodland people from north and east of Lake Superior, had moved into southern Manitoba. The Métis, a newly self-conscious people of mixed Native-European ancestry, lived at Red River and competed with the Assiniboine in the bison hunt and the provisioning trade.

By 1870, the bison were almost gone, and the economies that depended on them were in ruins. The age-old seasonal economic interplay of woodland, parkland, and plains no longer worked. Although its Native population was considerably lower than two hundred years before, the woodland no longer sustained them, and many moved to Red River, there to take up a little farming and find, if they could, seasonal wage work. On the plains, the situation was, if anything, even more desperate. Specialized bison-hunting economies had emerged, but the bison were largely gone, and the skills to live in the woodland, were game to be found there, had been lost. There were no alternative employments. It was in these circumstances that the peoples of the woodland, parkland, and plains faced the dealings with the new Dominion of Canada that led to the numbered treaties, reserves, and the paternalistic management envisaged by the Indian Act.

Such, in outline, is the ground Skip covered in *Indians in the Fur Trade*. He painted a rich picture, and in 1974 most of it was new. The book is a Canadian classic. Essentially, perhaps, it shifted studies of the fur trade towards Native people and the environment and, in so doing, created a framework that recontextualized the trade while exposing many understudied questions. Over the next twenty years, Skip himself would take on some of the analyses that his own work had anticipated.

He had been somewhat ambivalent about whether the fur trade could be explained by European market theory and had entered, but hardly mined out, the account books. E.E. Rich, Oxford-based imperial historian of the fur trade, had argued that the fur trade was dominated by Native conceptions of trade and that Native motives for trading were largely political.[5] Native societies sought allies. In Rich's analysis, gift-giving was one of the Native introductions to the trade, and he suggested that the traders used the overplus to underwrite its costs. Similarly, while Skip was working on *Indians and the Fur Trade*, an impressive young economic historian at the University of Toronto, Abraham Rotstein, was analyzing the fur trade to explore Karl Polanyi's concept of non-market trade.[6] At stake, for Rotstein, were basic issues about culture and economy that extended well beyond the fur trade itself. *Indians and the Fur Trade* had only touched on these matters. It had allowed the possibilities that Native trade was politically motivated and that the overplus was collected against the costs of gift-giving. It had suggested that no one model could explain the fur trade but had not elaborated the argument. There was room for a more probing analysis. And so, in his first major subsequent work, *"Give Us Good Measure"* (1978, with D.B. Freeman), and in several articles published in the late 1970s and early 1980s, Skip drew statistical data from the account books to shed more light on the mechanics of and motivation for trade. As he put it, "By using statistical data ... we hope to avoid the pitfalls inherent in viewing the trade through preconceived interpretations or theories and to provide a new viewpoint on clouded aspects and contentious issues."

In so doing, Skip moved away from the land and its peoples and towards an analysis of trade per se. He provided a more comprehensive description of the HBC accounting system, the principal means by which a limited liability commercial company directed from one side of the Atlantic kept track of its operations on the other, and dozens of graphs and tables about commodities and prices. These data buttress several robust conclusions. In the western interior, and contra Rich, Native participation in the fur trade was not politically motivated. Assiniboine and Cree middlemen, the principal traders with the English at the Bay, turned readily to the French when it was to their economic advantage. They often traded with both. They never sought military alliances with European traders (unlike the Huron-Algonquian relationship with the French along the lower St. Lawrence in the early seventeenth century), although they would not trade with enemies and gift-giving did establish a favourable political climate for trade. Nor was the overplus a means to fund gift-giving; rather, it contributed to the HBC's overall profit, which, derived from the large differential between the price of goods in Europe and at the trading posts, then supplemented by the overplus (a profit on a profit), was substantial. Even during the years of sharpest competition with the French, the HBC paid its shareholders an average annual dividend of more than 8 percent. It hesitated to establish posts inland because its bayside trade was profitable and inland transportation costs were high.

At the same time, Native middlemen, usually the intermediaries between hunters and trappers on one side and European traders on the other, were also sharp dealers. They inspected trade goods closely: they were particularly inclined to reject iron goods with minor flaws, having experienced breakage in cold weather of tools they could not repair. They played English and French traders off against each other, often telling the one about the superior quality of goods that could be obtained from the other. They were good comparative shoppers, while departing in significant ways from European concepts of supply and demand. They expected to market all their furs at one price and would not trade otherwise. When, at the end of the seventeenth century, the European market for coat beaver collapsed, they continued to arrive at the posts. Traders had to take their furs.

On the other hand, if the price of their furs rose, Native traders would bring fewer the following year, a reflection of the inelasticity of demand for European durable goods in Native societies that did not value material wealth. So Skip argued, though not entirely convincingly. He shows that Native traders responded to competitive pressures, expecting and receiving, for example, more gifts from French and English traders when the two competed most vigorously. And, as Native middlemen acquired status by redistributing wealth, as the Native demand for European goods increased with growing dependence on them, as European posts proliferated in the interior (thereby reducing travel time and making more trade goods available to Native consumers), and as many Natives became addicted to alcohol or tobacco, there is ground to question the duration of Native demand inelasticity. Skip's case is open for debate, but it will be hard to budge him from his essential propositions: that Native people were shrewd, economically sensitive traders – far more so than Rich and Rotstein allowed – and that "this trading system is impossible to label neatly as 'gift trade,' or 'administered trade,' or 'market trade,' since it embodies elements of all these forms."

Important as these observations are, Skip is at his best when his analysis is close to the ground, as it is in perhaps his best single article, "Periodic Shortages, Native Welfare, and the Hudson's Bay Company."[7] In it he shows more explicitly than in any of his previous work how, and to what effect, the fur trade altered Native livelihoods.

His argument in this important article is that precontact Native economies sought to minimize risk, and did so partly by moving seasonally through varied ecologies to exploit a wide range of resources, and partly by cooperation and sharing within systems of generalized reciprocity. Sharing, rather than wealth hoarding, incurred reciprocal obligations that could be drawn on in times of need. As the fur trade broke into this world, it increased the risk of resource shortages while reducing the capacity of Native societies to deal with the problem. Native people came to specialize in fur trade-related activities and to depend on external sources of food. Their growing commercial specialization on particular resources depleted these resources at a time when their growing dependence on the European goods obtained by trade in ever more scarce resources made them less willing to share. As their dependence on European goods increased, they were caught. They had to specialize to obtain the goods, yet specialization damaged ecologies and undermined the risk-reducing strategies of precontact livelihoods. Nor, in this new situation, had local societies any institutional means to manage access to scarcer resources. They tended to live in increasingly bounded territories and to depend on fluctuating populations of small animals or on relief from the HBC.

Sooner or later, the principal effect of the fur trade was to replace Native ecological strategies with an entirely different strategy dependent on fixed settlement, specialization, storage, and long-distance shipments at precise times along defined routes. It was in the HBC's interest to bind Native people, their principal source of labour, to this system as closely as possible. When local food stocks were low, Native people had to spend more time searching for food and had less time, therefore, for trapping; often it was to the company's advantage to supply them with flour, even well below cost. Native dependence on the company increased its capacity to manipulate them in its own interest, which was to keep them in the woodlands as trappers and cheap seasonal labourers. It had several means to do so: the distribution of relief and gratuities, summer wage work made available to reliable hunters and trappers (those who paid their debts), and the extension of credit, much or all of which might eventually be discounted. Skip's point is that the credit/barter economy calculated in made beaver was less a reflection of the inability of Native people to operate in a monetized economy – even less, of their essential conservatism – than of the interest of the HBC in a system that maintained high prices, paid low seasonal wages, and secured a cheap supply of labour. Governor Simpson's conservation schemes were part of this same effort to rationalize the peoples and ecologies of much of the northern interior of the continent in the interests of commercial capital.

But the long hold of commercial capital on the western interior was weakening in the late nineteenth century as changes in transportation repositioned the region, opening it to settlers and to industrial capital. While pointing towards them, *Indians in the Fur Trade* barely touched on these matters. They became the focus of the last phase of Skip's writing on the fur trade: a book entitled *The Canadian Fur Trade in the Industrial Age* (1990) and another (with Jim Miller and Frank Tough) entitled *Bounty and Benevolence: A History of Saskatchewan Treaties* (2000).

Much of the former is a sound, methodologically conservative business history concerned with prices, changing fashions and marketing strategies, management practices, and institutional reorganization. As such, it provides an integrated account, not previously available, of the Canadian fur trade between Confederation and the end of the Second World War. To the extent that it emphasizes the mechanics of trade, it is an approximate counterpart of Skip's treatment of the late seventeenth century and early mid-eighteenth century in *"Give Us Good Measure."* Beyond the trade per se were its social and environmental relations, which he also explores. Telegraph, railway, steamboat, and, eventually, bush plane were breaking down distance and bringing outside trappers as well as competitive traders with up-to-date market information. The HBC's monopoly, long challenged in the south, was now collapsing in the north as well. Heightened competition produced effects that had been seen before: increased environmental degradation and pressure on the HBC to abandon the responsibilities it had assumed for Native welfare and the reproduction of its labour force.

A new breed of bottom-line business managers, the Canadian Committee in Winnipeg, sought to manage a trade they knew little about on sound business principles suitable to any efficient modern concern. The London Committee considered it, rather, a business like no other that depended on experienced judgment and entailed a responsibility for Native people – company paternalism advocated from afar and practised by experienced traders. The traders themselves, knowing that successful trade required a surviving Native population, provided a form of welfare. They extended credit and lived with uncollected debt. In limited ways, they looked after the sick and elderly, and distributed food and leather in times of dearth. Moreover, they had lived close to Native people for years, and many of them had Native wives; their space, in a sense, was hybrid. Knowing none of this, the managers in Winnipeg sought to rationalize a trade that, by combining profit-seeking with enlightened self-interest and, often, deep-felt humanitarian concern, had enabled Native people to survive in the bush after the economies and ecological relationships that once had sustained them were destroyed.

But the old order of the fur trade, dominated by the HBC, was going not only because of heightened competition and bottom-line business managers. Government regulation in the form of fish and game laws, nature preserves and parks, registered trap lines, and the like – a new, state-centered governmentality – was spreading north. Environmental management was becoming a government rather than a company responsibility, as was welfare.

Officially, the government had acquired this responsibility in 1869, when it purchased Rupert's Land; but, in practice, the transition was essentially complete only shortly after the Second World War. Given his argument that the old system of barter and credit was a means by which the HBC secured furs and cheap labour while maintaining dependent, poverty-stricken Native people in the north, Skip is surprisingly nostalgic about what had been lost. The government, he suggests, was not well positioned to provide welfare. Its officials knew far less about particular Native circumstances than had fur traders whose experience was no longer in play. An economic relationship had been replaced by a bureaucratic one.

On the plains and in the parkland, as *Bounty and Benevolence* demonstrates, these issues came to a head in the late 1860s and early 1870s with the sale of Rupert's Land to the Dominion of Canada and with the first of the numbered treaties. In 1863, a group of investors principally interested in colonization and railways bought the HBC, and it was they who, in 1869, sold Rupert's Land to Canada for £300,000 plus 50,000 acres near the forts and one-twentieth of the land in the fertile belt. Canada assumed the responsibility for treaty-making. On both sides of the treaty negotiations, treaties apparently offered advantages. For the Canadian government and recent settlers in the West, they were an inexpensive, blood-free way of securing and opening up land for non-Native settlement. For Native peoples, they provided some prospect of escape from a desperate situation. Their precontact economies had gone long since, and now, for want of buffalo, the provisioning trade with the HBC had also failed. They faced starvation. Small annuities, guaranteed by a treaty, offered a measure of welfare, and secured reserve land offered the prospect of some agriculture. After more than two hundred years, the fur trade economy, and the reciprocal relationships between Natives and non-Natives that were embedded in it, had collapsed into this.

Such is the dominant axis of Skip's writing and thought about the fur trade. It remained his central preoccupation for some twenty-five years, but he is not working on it now, nor has he been for most of the last decade and more. He has become increasingly involved as an expert witness in court cases bearing on Native land and resource use, and, out of this experience, has become a student of such witnesses and of the relationship between their political/legal involvements and their academic positions. Moreover, provoked, he says, by a government attorney's narrow understanding of Native culture, he has written a text on the Native history of Canada.

His text, *I Have Lived Here since the World Began*, emphasizes the variety of Native cultures and responses to European influences, the active (and often controlling) participation of Native peoples in contact processes (particularly in new economic opportunities), and the continuity and intensity of their long struggle to maintain their identities and hold on to some of their land as they confronted the array of powers embedded in settler colonialism. It begins with archaeological and Native accounts of the first peopling of North America, and it ends with *Delgamuukw* v. *Regina* [1997], a hugely influential trial, in which Skip himself was an expert witness, over Aboriginal title in British Columbia. Its emphasis is economic, and, as the environmental and spatial analysis is much weaker than in *Indians in the Fur Trade*, Skip is probably right to describe it as a history (rather than a historical geography) of Native involvement with new economies. It is a measure of how much he has accomplished that a good part of this ranging book draws on his own previous work. That work is not extended here, but it is gathered and contextualized in a panoramic account of changing Native circumstances and livelihoods.

Because his work on the relationships of academics to the courts in cases over Native land is in full spate, most of it is not yet published.[8] It involves research in four countries – Canada, the United States, Australia, and New Zealand – and much the same empirical rigour that Skip has always brought to his work. As previously, he has gone into the archives with as open a mind as possible but also, in this case, with much personal experience with the courts and with the often bruising ways in which experts and their evidence are treated there. He is immersed in this research; its first written products evince an excitement matched by the best of his fur trade scholarship.

He is finding that the relationship of expert witness to the courts is anything but that of a provider of facts. In the first place, different national framings of Native land issues affect the "facts" courts seeks to establish. For example, Australian courts, influenced by the British anthropologist A.R. Radcliffe-Brown's arguments that the historical past would always be conjectural and that attention should be directed, rather, to the surviving structural features of Aboriginal societies, have tended to seek information from anthropologists about contemporary Aboriginal land uses. Courts in New Zealand, working in the long shadow of the Treaty of Waitangi (1840) and seeking to understand its terms and intent, have relied much more on historians. But the shaping of academic evidence goes much farther than this. Until recently, the Australian courts were dominated by Radcliffe-Brown's model of Aboriginal society composed of an exogamous local patrilineal group and a "horde," a group of local residential land users living in a defined and bounded estate – a model that apparently captures little of the complexity of Aboriginal land tenures.

In California in the 1950s, arguments before the Indian Claims Commission pitted the anthropologist Alfred Kroeber and his emphasis (derived from Boas) on historical particularism and super-organic cultures against some of his former students, most notably Julian Steward, who sought to establish a comparative cultural ecology linked to the hypothesis of cultural evolution. At issue in California was the question whether Native groups – "tribelets" Kroeber called them – owned and used their whole territory and whether these territories, combined, constituted virtually the whole of California; or whether, within a given territory, they depended on a core area and made little or no use of the rest. At stake was the amount of compensation the government would be required to pay. A team of expert witnesses dominated by Kroeber argued the former case for the Council of Californian Indians, while Steward was part of the team that argued the latter case for the government. Skip shows both that the nature of evidence presented depended on these different theoretical backgrounds and that the inherently combative nature of the hearing process intensified theoretical positions. Steward wrote his most important theoretical contributions to cultural ecology while acting as an expert witness for the government on Native land cases. His ideas about cultural cores (areas of intensive land use), about cultural evolution, and about primitive societies that lacked notions of ownership and did not, therefore, have systems of land tenure, all contributed to the government's case. Indeed, they seem to have been partly created by it. These arguments, Skip shows, surfaced again in *Delgamuukw*.

What emerges, then, is a description of a process in which, even in the positivist bastions of court proceedings and quasi-judicial hearings, facts and theories were so imbricated that it becomes impossible to pull them clearly apart. Long before Derrida, Foucault, and others made it fashionable to say so, some of the protagonists in these affairs knew this full well. Writing in 1955, Julian Steward had this to say:

> In a scientific and literal sense, virtually no evidence presented in these cases can properly be called "primary evidence," "first-hand knowledge," or an "eye witness account" ... In using this secondary, or predigested evidence, both from the Indian informant and the historical source, the anthropologist redigests it according to his own point of view. He himself becomes "evidence" in that his testimony is based to an incalculable extent upon his theory (explicit or implicit), his experiences among the people, his travels over the territory, his reading of the historic documents and his broader knowledge of primitive people.[9]

Not many years after he wrote this, a young Skip Ray read Steward's cultural ecology at Wisconsin and took some of his ideas into the archives, there beginning a process that would lead him far into the fur trade in western Canada, to the courts, and, eventually, to a rereading of Julian Steward.

Such are the main lines and conclusions of Skip's academic writing over the last thirty years. It remains to take brief stock of them. To this end, I would make only three observations.

The first is that he has enormously extended the range and depth of fur trade scholarship. He has shifted its emphasis towards Native people, ecological relationships, and the details of exchange relationships. He has provided an array of grounded ideas backed by rich bodies of evidence. In an introduction to a re-edition of Harold Innis' classic, *The Fur Trade in Canada,* he pointed out that Innis remains important because he raised basic questions about the trade, questions that still focus debate. Skip himself has gone further. He has addressed Innis' questions, posed others, and presented far more convincing evidence than Innis ever did. His work now bestrides fur trade scholarship, and most of his conclusions have become the scholarly consensus. There are still arguments, of course, but his conclusions, grounded as they are, are not easily dislodged. Moreover, they have been put to work, not so much, as with Innis, in conceptualizations of Canada and theories of development and communications, as in the courts in defence of Native rights. Informed and apparently fearless, Skip is a powerful presence in court and has contributed substantially to several important decisions favouring Native peoples. Given the long dominance of the fur trade in much of Canada and the importance, for all aspects of Canadian life, of working out a more just accommodation with Native peoples, both his fur trade scholarship and its applied manifestations in the courts are huge contributions.

The second is that his writing is most compelling when it deals with the changing ecological and spatial circumstances of Native peoples. He writes well on many topics, but, as he has always insisted, he is essentially a historical geographer. Those years at Wisconsin are in him, and when he writes within his pedigree, as it were, his work moves to another register. Some of this type of work is now being done by environmental historians, and I doubt that many of them have read Skip's work closely. They should. The fur trade enframed ecological relationships in much of Canada over many years – relationships Skip understands as well as anyone. *Indians in the Fur Trade* and his article on "periodic shortages" are basic texts in the human ecology of western Canada.

Finally, Skip's work, bedded as it is in an empirical tradition, is now turning up evidence that supports central tenets of contemporary cultural and postcolonial theory. Skip has never been attracted to such theory, nor has he ever intended to contribute to it, a skepticism that, if anything, enhances the power of his current work. But he is moving into a world in which facts lose their autonomy and in which, as Foucault would have said, they are better understood as power-knowledge effects of particular discourses. If this is so, then what are the implications for understanding Skip's own work? Out of what discourse(s) has he written, and with what biases? These are not, now, easy questions to answer. Time may simplify them. In the meantime, and as I reflect on Skip's writing and its context, I am struck by certain similarities between his work and other studies that came out of historical geography at Wisconsin. Andy Clark showed that the Acadians were not a docile peasantry but active traders in pursuit of any chance. I showed that an effete and cumbrous feudalism had not settled over New France and that, in limited economic circumstances to be sure, the habitants along the lower St. Lawrence were largely untrammeled in pursuit of their interests. Skip showed that Native people were canny traders within societies that, at least initially, attached no status to wealth accumulation. Could it be that all of us constructed approximately the same people? It is an uncomfortable thought, but historical geographers can hardly exclude themselves from Julian Steward's observations about anthropologists. Skip knows that, and also that honest scholarship controls its biases – but not those that are implicit and invisible. Although it is too early to assess Skip's work in this regard, it is clear that, when that assessment comes, it will consider a sizeable body of careful, thoughtful scholarship, with which, in some large measure, all subsequent work on its topics has been in an extended conversation.

Notes

1 Arthur J. Ray, *Indians in the Fur Trade: Their Role as Hunters, Trappers, and Middlemen in the Lands Southwest of Hudson Bay, 1660-1870* (Toronto: University of Toronto Press, 1974).
2 Arthur J. Ray and Donald B. Freeman. *"Give Us Good Measure": An Economic Analysis of Relations Between the Indians and the Hudson's Bay Company before 1763* (Toronto: University of Toronto Press, 1978); Arthur J. Ray, *The Canadian Fur Trade in the Industrial Age* (Toronto: University of Toronto Press, 1990).
3 Arthur J. Ray, *I Have Lived Here since the World Began: An Illustrated History of Canada's Native Peoples* (Toronto: Lester Publishing, 1996).
4 Arthur J. Ray, Jim Miller, and Frank J. Tough, *Bounty and Benevolence: A History of Saskatchewan Treaties* (Montreal and Kingston: McGill-Queen's University Press, 2000).
5 E.E. Rich, "Trade Habits and Economic Motivation among the Indians of North America," *Canadian Journal of Economics and Political Science* 26 (1960): 35-53.
6 Abraham Rotstein, "Trade and Politics: An Institutional Approach," *Western Canadian Journal of Anthropology* 3 (1972): 1-28.
7 Arthur J. Ray, "Periodic Shortages, Native Welfare, and the Hudson's Bay Company, 1673-1930," in *The Subarctic Fur Trade: Native Social and Economic Adaptations*, ed. Shepard Krech III, 1-20 (Vancouver: UBC Press, 1984).
8 But see the early reports on this research in Arthur J. Ray, "Aboriginal Title and Treaty Rights Research: A Comparative Look at Australia, Canada, New Zealand and the United Statues," *New Zealand Journal of History* 37 (2003): 5-21; and Arthur J. Ray, "Native History on Trial: Confessions of an Expert Witness," *Canadian Historical Review* 84 (2003): 253-73.
9 Cited in Ray, "Native History on Trial," 256.

Contributors

Ted Binnema is an associate professor of history at the University of Northern British Columbia. A revised version of his dissertation, which was co-supervised by Arthur J. Ray, was published as *Common and Contested Ground: A Human and Environmental History of the Northwestern Plains* in 2001. Binnema also co-edited, with Gerhard Ens and Roderick C. Macleod, *From Rupert's Land to Canada* (2001).

Jennifer S.H. Brown is Canada Research Chair in Aboriginal Peoples in an Urban and Regional Context at the University of Winnipeg. She completed her PhD in anthropology at the University of Chicago shortly after Skip Ray completed his at the University of Wisconsin. Author of *Strangers in Blood: Fur Trade Company Families in Indian Country* (1980) and numerous other publications in Algonquin and Métis History, she has edited or co-edited several works, including *Reading Beyond Words* (1996 and 2003) and Louis Bird, *Telling Our Stories: Omushkego Legends and Histories from Hudson Bay* (2005).

Keith Thor Carlson is an associate professor of history at the University of Saskatchewan. He completed his PhD at UBC in 2003 under Skip Ray's supervision. Carlson has published *"Call Me Hank": A Sto:lō Man's Reflections on Logging, Living, and Growing Old* (2006), *A Sto:lō-Coast Salish Historical Atlas* (2001), and *The Twisted Road to Freedom: America's Granting of Independence to the Philippines* (1995). He has also appeared as an expert witness in several court cases dealing with Aboriginal rights.

Jody Decker is associate professor of geography and environmental studies at Wilfrid Laurier University. After working for twenty years in emergency and intensive care nursing, she completed her PhD in geography in 1989. She has published numerous articles on medical and health issues, including historical articles on Aboriginal health, including the history of infectious diseases in Native communities. Skip Ray was the external examiner for her doctoral dissertation.

R.M. Galois is adjunct professor in the department of Geography at the University of British Columbia. Following his involvement in the *Delgamuukw* case, he has undertaken historical research for a variety of First Nations in British Columbia. He is the author of *Kwakwaka'wakw Settlements, 1775-1920: A Geographical Analysis and Gazetteer* (1994); *A Voyage to the North West Side of America: The Journals of James Colnett, 1786-89* (2004); and co-author of *Tribal Boundaries in the Nass Watershed*.

The career of **R. Cole Harris** intersected with that of Skip Ray for many years. He earned his PhD in geography from the University of Wisconsin in 1964 and taught in the geography departments at the University of Toronto (1964-71) and the University of British Columbia (1971-2001), where he is now professor emeritus. He has published widely on social and cultural change in settler societies, the strategies and tactics of settler colonialism, and the patterns of early Canada. He is the editor of volume 1 of the *Historical Atlas of Canada* and the author of books on early French Canada and on British Columbia as well as numerous articles on explanation in historical geography, social change in immigrant societies, the geographical pattern of early Canada, and the nature of Canadian identity. His most recent book manuscript, currently under review, is "The Reluctant Land: Society, Space, and Environment in Early Canada, 1500-1870." Professor Harris is Fellow of the Royal Society of Canada and Officer of the Order of Canada.

Victor P. Lytwyn was drawn into research in Aboriginal history and geography by Wayne Moodie, a friend and colleague of Skip Ray. As a graduate student of Moodie's at the University of Manitoba, Lytwyn collaborated with Skip Ray on a number of atlas plates depicting Aboriginal people and the fur trade in the northwestern interior of Canada. Skip Ray then served as the external examiner on Lytwyn's PhD committee. They subsequently provided expert evidence together in the *Powley* case. Lytwyn's books include *Muskekowuck Athinuwick: Original People of the Great Swampy Land* (2002).

Daniel Marshall completed his PhD at UBC with Skip Ray as one of his committee members. He currently lectures in the history of Native-Newcomer relations at the University of Victoria. Marshall is the principal of Pacific Reach Consulting, a firm specializing in Aboriginal rights and title cases, and has worked closely with several Vancouver Island First Nations groups in this capacity. He is the author of *Those Who Fell from the Sky: A History of the Cowichan People* (1999), and he has published articles in *BC Studies* (2002), *Histoire sociale/Social History* (1998), and *Native Studies Review* (1996).

J.R. Miller is Canada Research Chair in Native-Newcomer Relations in the Department of History at the University of Saskatchewan. He is the author of several books, including *Skyscrapers Hide the Heavens: A History of Indian-White Relations* *in Canada* (originally published in 1989 but now in its third edition) and *Shingwauk's Vision: A History of Native Residential Schools* (1996). He is co-author, with Arthur J. Ray and Frank Tough, of *Bounty and Benevolence: A History of Saskatchewan Treaties* (2000). Professor Miller is Fellow of the Royal Society of Canada.

Susan Neylan is an associate professor of history at Wilfrid Laurier University. Skip Ray was her supervisor at UBC until her graduation in 1999. Her first book, based on her doctoral dissertation, appeared in 2003 and is entitled *The Heavens Are Changing: Nineteenth-Century Protestant Missions and Tsimshian Christianity*. Specializing in the history of Aboriginal-Christian relations, she has published a number of articles related to this topic in *BC Studies* (2006-7), *Histoire sociale/ Social History* (2003), and the *Journal of the Canadian Historical Association* (2000).

An associate professor of history and a colleague of Skip Ray at the University of British Columbia, **Paige Raibmon** was once his BA honours student. Raibmon completed her PhD at Duke University in 2000. She is the author of *Authentic Indians: Episodes of Encounter from the Late Nineteenth-Century Northwest Coast* (2006), and of articles in, among other places, *BC Studies* (2003) and the *Canadian Historical Review* (2000).

Index

Printed and bound in Canada by Friesens

Set in Stone by Artegraphica Design Co. Ltd.

Copy editor: Joanne Richardson

Proofreader: Megan Brand

Indexer: Annette Lorek